PREFACE.

In submitting to the public the Militia and Yeomanry Cavalry Army List, the Editor has to observe, that no exertions have been wanting on his part to render the Work worthy of the Services it represents. He has to return his most sincere thanks to many Noblemen and Commanding Officers for the valuable assistance and information tendered to him.

Considerable difficulty has been experienced in obtaining the returns of some Regiments, and should an occasional one be wanting in full information, the officers more immediately concerned, and not the Editor, are to blame for the absence of *esprit de corps* exhibited by them in any Regimental page of this Army List, which is blank in the Services and other particulars requested to be furnished by the Commandants or Adjutants.

In the next Edition of this work, those defects will be doubtlessly removed, and any errors which may have crept into the present volume, be corrected and amended. The Editor solicits Officers to forward to him without delay alterations or corrections intended for future Editions.

London : *April,* 1850.

TABLE OF CONTENTS.

INTRODUCTION.   Page

   HISTORY of the Organization of the Militia of the United Kingdom .... v to xviii

   Abstract of the Militia Acts for Amending the Laws relating to the Militia in England .... xix to xxvi

   YEOMANRY CAVALRY Organization, Services, and Discipline... xvii to xxx

   Abstract of Government Regulations for Yeomanry .... xxx to xxxv

YEOMANRY CAVALRY.

   Index to Regiments, arranged Alphabetically according to County or Local Designation.. xxxvii

   Regiments and Corps of Yeomanry Cavalry........................... 1 to 44

   Index to Officers' Names .... 168 to 172

MILITIA.

   Index to Regiments, alphabetically arranged xxxvii

   Regiments of Militia .... 45 to 167

   Index to Officers' Names .... 173 to 186

No. I.   PUBLISHED HALF-YEARLY.

APRIL, 1850.      PRICE 10s. 6d.

THE ROYAL MILITIA

AND

YEOMANRY CAVALRY ARMY LIST:

CONTAINING THE
NAMES AND SENIORITY OF EVERY REGIMENTAL AND STAFF
OFFICER IN THE MILITIA AND YEOMANRY CAVALRY,

DESIGNATING
WHETHER LORDS OR DEPUTY LIEUTENANTS OF COUNTIES, MEMBERS
OF PARLIAMENT, OR JUSTICES OF THE PEACE;

EXHIBITING
THE SERVICES OF SUCH OFFICERS AS HAVE HELD COMMISSIONS
IN THE REGULAR ARMY;

DETAILING
THE COUNTRY SEATS, PARKS, AND DOMAINS OF THE LANDED GENTRY
SERVING IN THOSE CORPS.

THE REGIMENTS OF MILITIA,
ARRANGED ACCORDING TO SENIORITY OF NUMBER;

REGIMENTS AND CORPS OF YEOMANRY CAVALRY,
AS HEAVY AND LIGHT DRAGOONS, HUSSARS, AND LANCERS.

A COPIOUS ALPHABETICAL INDEX OF REGIMENTS
ACCORDING TO COUNTY DESIGNATION;
AS ALSO, THE NAMES OF EVERY OFFICER ALPHABETICALLY ARRANGED, WITH REFERENCE
TO THE REGIMENTAL PAGE IN THE MILITIA AND YEOMANRY CAVALRY ARMY LIST.

A HISTORY OF THE SERVICES, ORGANIZATION, AND EQUIPMENT OF THE
REGIMENTS OF MILITIA AND YEOMANRY CAVALRY:

TOGETHER WITH
AN ABSTRACT OF THE MILITIA ACTS; AND YEOMANRY CAVALRY REGULATIONS.

Arranged and Compiled from Official Documents
CORRECTED TO DATE OF PUBLICATION.

BY

ARTHUR SLEIGH, ESQ.,
LATE LIEUTENANT HER MAJESTY'S 77TH REGIMENT; CORNET UXBRIDGE YEOMANRY CAVALRY.

LONDON:
BRITISH ARMY DESPATCH PRESS,
50, BEDFORD STREET, STRAND.
1850.

HISTORY AND ORGANIZATION

OF

THE MILITIA

OF THE

UNITED KINGDOM OF GREAT BRITAIN AND IRELAND.

SECTION I.

A HISTORY OF THE MILITIA OF ENGLAND, EMBRACING A PERIOD FROM THE HEPTARCHY, A.D. 430, TO THE YEAR 1816.

The Heptarchy and Feudalage.—871, Alfred.—The *Fryd*, or General Armament of the People.—1101, The Assize of Arms.—Acts 1 Ed. III., 5 Henry IV.—Commissioners of Array.—1558, The Impressment Act.—Charles I.; the Right to command the Militia.—13 Charles II.—1757, A Bill to reconstruct the Militia.—1762, Ditto.—1802, Militia Laws of England and Scotland assimilated.—Act 49 George III.; ditto for Ireland.—First Formation of a Standing Army, 1660.—The Train Bands of London.—Disembodiment of the Militia, 1816.

THE HEPTARCHY.—THE MILITIA of England was organized long prior to the establishment or equipment of a Regular Army. Before the Norman Conquest the feudalage originating with our Saxon ancestors, compelled the owners of land, generally grants for military service, to give a quota to the service of their prince. A failure of military aid from the vassal was followed by confiscation of his land; for the tenure purchased "by watch and ward," in the field and fortress, was only retained so long as the sword was ready to defend the soil. The possession of land was not in all cases a hereditary gift, it was generally held only as long as life and limb were serviceable to a feudal chief. An oath of fidelity was demanded of the vassal, and the great feature therein was a sworn allegiance to the baron, whose lands were held in temporary trust. While, in consideration of a ready obedience to the will of the superior, the latter granted protection to the former, and espoused the cause of his followers with the whole force at his disposal. Thus the feudal lord and vassal serf relied upon mutual good faith and military service for a perpetuity of their respective hereditaments. The lord, in his turn, was the subject of the Crown, and lands granted to a chief were held on conditions similar to the acres held by the serf. The earliest record of the feudalage is coeval with the establishment of the *Heptarchy*, A.D. 430, which divided England into the seven distinct Saxon kingdoms, as follows:—1. Kent, comprehending the modern counties of Kent, Middlesex, and Essex; 2. Kingdom of the

South Saxons, comprehending Sussex, Surrey, and the New Forest; 3. Wessex, including Hants, Dorset, Wilts, Berks, and the Isle of Wight; 4. The East Angles, comprehending Cambridge, Suffolk, and Norfolk; 5. Essex, which was dismembered from the kingdom of Kent, and included part of Hertfordshire; 6. Mercia, comprehending the Midland counties, from the Severn to the boundaries of the two last-named kingdoms; and 7. Northumberland, the most extensive of all, and comprehending the whole of the Northern counties.

For a period of nearly 400 years, the various principalities waged war upon each other; chiefs and vassals arraying themselves beneath their respective banners. This period, while it was disastrous to the commonwealth of the Saxons, yet gave a tone and chivalry to the people. The various kingdoms, each in their turn, shone conspicuous for valour, and the fortunes of a predatory warfare vacillated from Kent to Northumberland. In 827, Egbert, King of Wessex, successfully carried his arms to the extreme limits of the Heptarchy, and subduing the seven kingdoms of the Heptarchy, made them bow in fealty to the first Saxon King of England. In Egbert's reign the first formation of feudal lords and vassal soldiers into a body for the defence of the kingdom against the inroads of the Danes took place, and the short period of his successors, Ethelwolf, Ethelbald, Ethelbert, and Ethelred, was one series of engagement with Danish invaders.

IN 871, ALFRED succeeded to the throne, and at once organized the whole male force of the kingdom into a defensive Army, or Militia—from *Miles*, a soldier—a constitutional force, which, to the present day, bear on their colours and appointments King Alfred's crown, their peculiar badge. The first Militia Army of England routed the Danes, and King Alfred, in 879, destroyed the last remnant of their predatory inroads. Thus we perceive the Yeomen of "Merrie Englande," who fought and won at Cressy, and Poictiers, &c., were raised and brought into the field under Alfred's law. Essentially they were the same as the modern Militia, for, as in the reigns of our Edwards, the owner of lands was obliged to bring to the wars, at the King's command, a certain number of men, in proportion to his acres; so, in the reign of the Georges, every parish was called upon to furnish its quota to the Militia, according to its population. In the earlier periods, as we have shown, they were led and commanded by their feudal lords.

Previous to Alfred's reign the feudal system was known as the *Fyrd*, which meant a general armament of the people. Sir Francis Palgrave writes:—

"From the earliest period to which our documents can reach, we find the Fyrd appearing as a general armament of the people, comprehending every rank, though under different obligations and penalties. If the *Sithcund-man*, being a landholder, remained at home, he forfeited all his land; sixty shillings was his fine, whilst thirty shillings was the *Fyrdwite* of the churl, and to the last it continued a levy of all the population of the country."

The first outline of the present system of the fines and penalties inflicted for the non-performance of Militia service is here laid down. That Alfred but improved the *Fyrd*, and efficiently organized that body into our Militia, is authenticated by the opinion of Sir William Blackstone and other great authorities.

NORMAN CONQUEST.—At the period of the Norman conquest, the Fyrd, or Militia, of the Saxons, was still retained. In the reign of Richard I., 1101, the Militia, in the celebrated "assize of arms," was perfectly organized, and the law then was "that all free men are appointed to have arms in their possession, according to a scale of ranks, which consists, first, of the holders of a knight's fee; secondly, of the possessors of chattels or rent to the extent of sixteen marks; thirdly, of the holders of similar property to the value of ten marks; and lastly, of all other burgesses and freemen. The Fyrd, with its periodical exhibitions of arms, was recognised as late as the year 1285, when, by the statute of Winchester (13 Ed. I.) the scale of arms assigned to the respective ranks was revised. The part of the Act which enforces the keeping of arms was adjusted to the progress of the art of war of 1558, and finally abolished in 1604.

EDWARD III.—Various enactments have from time to time borne upon the system of the Militia. By a statute, 1 Ed. III., c. 5, "The King wills, that no man from henceforth shall be charged to arm himself, otherwise than he was wont in the times of his progenitors Kings of England; and that no man be compelled to go out of his shire but where necessity requireth, and sudden coming of strange enemies into the realm; and that it shall be done as hath been used in times past for the defence of the realm."

HENRY IV.—In the fifth year of the reign of King Henry IV. an enactment was made curtailing the powers vested in the "Commissioners of Array," whose office was synonymous with our present Lords and Deputy-Lieutenants of counties. It provides for, 1. Preparation in case of foreign invasion; 2. Empowers the Commissioners to raise and drill "all men-at-arms;" 3. To cause all able-bodied men "to arm themselves according to their substance;" 4. To amerce those unable to bear arms in a similarly adjusted ratio; 5. To require the services of persons so armed on the sea-shore, or wherever danger may be imminent, or the Crown require their services.

ELIZABETH.—In 1558 an Act was passed, granting power to impress men to the service of the State. During the Long Parliament another Act was passed granting to the Commissioners of Array "*temporary*" power to "impress as many men as the King and both Houses of Parliament might appoint." It was further enacted that the subject ought not to be compelled to "go beyond his county." The Act further forms a confirmation of the provisions on this latter head, enacted in the reign of Edward III., above referred to.

CHARLES I.—In Charles I.'s reign a dispute arose between the King and his Parliament as to who had "the right to command the Militia." While some were of opinion that the Crown had the right to command all armies, others thought that the Houses of Lords and Commons should give their consent, prior to any order issuing from the Throne. It was finally arranged that the King should place the Militia in the hands of Commissioners chosen by Parliament.

CHARLES II.—After the Restoration, in the reign of Charles II., two Acts were passed, 13 Charles II., c. 6, and 13 & 14 Charles II., c. 37, which finally settled the supreme power in the command of our armies. It was wisely enacted: "The sole supreme government, command, and disposition of the Militia, and of all forces by sea and land, and of all forts and places of strength is, and by the laws of

England ever was, the undoubted right of his Majesty and his Royal predecessors." Lords-Lieutenants and Deputy-Lieutenants were charged with a commission to raise in their respective counties, soldiers for the Cavalry and Infantry, "according to a fixed scale of property." A slight alteration in the system thus laid down took place in the years 1699, 1714, and 1743.

GEORGE II., III.—In 1757 a Bill to reconstruct the Militia was passed. In 1762 further improvements took place, and in 1802 the Militia laws of England and Scotland were assimilated, and by an Act, 49 Geo. III., c. 120, the same was rendered in force in Ireland.

FIRST FORMATION OF A STANDING ARMY.—1660. Up to this period there was no force known in the kingdom but the Militia; and the origin of a Standing Army was coeval with the commencement of the reign of Charles II. We find at the Restoration the Revolutionary Army of the three kingdoms amounted to more than 60,000 men, but in time this dangerous force was successfully disbanded, regiment after regiment, without exciting mutiny, or any public expression of discontent. The first formation of a Regular Army now commenced. For this purpose, Guards were established for the protection of the Royal person, formed partly out of the best-affected troops of the Protector, and partly by the creation of new regiments. In this way commenced the Standing Military Force of the Kingdom. To General Monk's regiment, raised ten years previously at Coldstream, were added, in 1660, two more regiments, forming the Coldstream Foot Guards. In 1661, the Life Guards were raised, composed and treated like the Guardes du Corps of the French, being formed principally of gentlemen of fortune, who themselves, or their fathers, had fought in the Civil wars. In the same year the Blues were embodied, and called the Oxford Blues, from their first Commander, Aubrey, Earl of Oxford. To these were added the 1st Royal Scots, brought over from France at the Restoration; the 2d, or Queen's, raised in 1661; the 3d, or Old Buffs, from their accoutrements being composed of buffalo leather, embodied in 1665; the Scotch Fusiliers, raised in 1678, and so called from carrying the Fusil, invented in France in 1630; and the 4th, or King's Own, raised in 1680. These formed at first a Force of about 5,000 men, but in the latter part of the next reign this force was augmented to 30,000. We must not omit to state that "Charles II. was of opinion that if their father, at the beginning of the Civil War, had possessed a small *Regular* Force, he might easily have beat the Parliamentarians." Up to the period of the formation of the Standing Army in 1660, we can only refer to each victory achieved by the prowess of our arms, as a tribute to the discipline and courage of the English Militia. From this period, however, the conquests and achievements of our nation, have ostensibly bestowed the laurels of victory to the Regular Army, though the material, as will be shown, of that force, was, in the first instance, chiefly obtained from our Regiments of Militia, who volunteered largely to the Line. On the other hand, to the Militia must all praise be conceded, for the noble stand that force has oftentimes taken in the preservation of our institutions, when threatened by intestine turmoil and civil war. As a constitutional force at home, the preservation of the Constitution has been efficiently carried out by the Militia. Nor has that force ever been backward in granting large subsidies, in men and treasure, to the Armies of their Sovereign.

THE TRAIN BANDS OF THE METROPOLIS.—London, as the chief city in the kingdom, has stood forth conspicuous for the liberality with which she has bestowed men and arms upon many occasions. In the seventeenth century, the powers exercised by the Lord-Lieutenants of Counties, were then entrusted in London to a Committee of citizens, called the Court of Lieutenancy, which has the peculiar power of granting commissions. The London Train Bands bore a conspicuous part at the Siege of Gloucester. "In truth," says Macaulay, "it is no exaggeration to say, that but for the hostility of the City Charles the First would never have been vanquished, and that without the help of the City, Charles the Second could scarcely have been restored."

We further find, on referring to history, that the City has ever been eminent for public spirit and courage, and that not only have the Lord Mayors, as heads of the Corporation, exercised a supreme, and, indeed, active command, both civil and military, from the first existence of the office, but the same Corporation have, on every occasion heretofore, been prominent in contributing to the public safety and national welfare, by various grants of ships, money, men, &c., for the protection of the kingdom at all periods against foreign and domestic foes. In the prosperity and glory of the kingdom they have ever taken a conspicuous part, by marching men, not only to all parts of England, Scotland, and Ireland, but also to France and Germany;— they have even befriended the French and Dutch with troops, raised and armed. On one amongst numerous occasions, they assisted Queen Elizabeth at the trying juncture of the "invincible Spanish Armada," with no less a body than 10,000 men; and moreover, the City supplied 38 of the largest-sized ships for their conveyance. In the reign of Edward the First, A.D. 1318, the City of London provided and furnished 200 men to march against the Scots, being five times the number at that time raised by any other city. In the reign of Edward the Third, A.D. 1354, the citizens of London presented to his Majesty 25 men-at-arms and 500 archers, and sent them to serve in the Army then in France. In 1360, the City assisted in fitting out a fleet of 160 sail, having 14,000 men on board, for the purpose of serving in France. In the reign of Henry the Eighth, A.D. 1545, in August, the City raised, and completely equipped, a regiment of 1,000 men to serve in France. In the reign of Queen Elizabeth, A.D. 1585, the City sent a considerable body of troops to assist the Dutch against the Spanish. In 1589, the City supplied and equipped 1,000 men to assist in placing Henry of Navarre on the throne of France. In 1596, the Lord Mayor twice raised 1,000 able-bodied men, completely armed, in less than twelve hours, to march to the relief of the French in Calais, besieged by the Spaniards.

The old Train-Bands, when complete, were originally of the following strength :—

The Blue Regiment, containing 8 companies	..	1,411	men
The Yellow do. „ 8 „	..	1,526	„
The Green do. „ 8 „	..	1,566	„
The Orange do. „ 8 „	..	1,741	„
The White do. „ 8 „	..	2,088	„
The Red do. „ 8 „	..	1,630	„
	Total	9,962	

The history of the Train-Bands is only so far applicable to our purpose, forasmuch as their organization was more or less similar to that of local Militia, and by Acts of 34 Geo. III., c. 81, and 35 Geo. III., c. 27, the old Trained-Bands of the City of London were regulated and formed into six Regiments of Militia, the services of which were limited to twelve miles from the city. By Act 36 Geo. III., c. 92, the six Regiments were reduced to two Regiments of 600 men each; and again by Act of 1 Geo. IV., c. 100, the two Regiments were reduced to one Regiment only, and the services extended to any part of Great Britain. The whole are now embodied in the 106th, or Royal London Regiment of Militia.

1757 TO 1816.—From 1757, the Militia of the United Kingdom has been embodied and disembodied at various periods. The whole of the Regiments of Militia have not been disembodied at the same time, but certain local Militias have been embodied and disembodied from the period named to 1816, when the whole Militia force of the United Kingdom was reduced.

SECTION II.

Summary of the General Orders issued from the Horse Guards from 1793 to 1816 with reference to the Militia.—Services of the Regiments of Militia and Volunteering to the Line during the War.—Votes of Thanks from the Houses of Lords and Commons, 1802 and 1814.—War Office Circular, 1 Dec., 1845. —Ditto Home Office.—Militias of Scotland and Ireland.

THE GENERAL ORDERS issued from the Horse Guards from time to time have contained various provisions for the equipment and discipline of the Militia. In 1793, the officers of Militia were ordered to provide themselves with camp-equipage. 1793: General Order granting certain allowance of baggage and forage-money to officers of Militia at the following rate :—A Colonel, baggage and forage-money, 35*l*. per annum ; Lieut.-Colonel, 30*l*. ; Major, 25*l*. ; Captain, 20*l*. Forage allowance for officers' horses, when encamped: —A Colonel, 9 horses ; Lieut.-Colonel, 7 ; Major, 5 ; Captain, 3 ; Capt.-Lieut., 2. A Circular, dated War Office, Sept. 18, 1793, respecting pay :—Pay for Sergeant-Major and Quartermaster-Sergeant, 1*s*. 6*d*. ; Sergeant, 1*s*. ; Corporal and Drummer, 8*d*. ; Private, 8*d*. Total of a Private's pay and pecuniary allowances :— Pay, 9*l*. 2*s*. 6*d*. per annum ; bread, 2*l*. 5*s*. 7½*d*. ; for necessaries, 1*l*. 5*s*. 4½*d*. Total, 12*l*. 13*s*. 6*d*. 1795. Several men of the Oxford Regiment of Militia were tried by Court Martial for mutiny, and found guilty. Two were executed, one received 1,500 lashes, one 1,000 lashes, one 500 lashes ! A general order was issued this year permitting the men of the Militia to assist the farmers to thresh the corn ; as also several orders regulating the price of bread, meat, and necessaries. 1796. A general order was issued ordering the Militia, while embodied, to be subjected to the Articles of War, Courts-Martial, &c., same as in the Regular Forces. General order :—The names of officers and Corps of Militia published by War Office authority. General order :—" No resignation will be accepted at this critical time." 1797. A general order for returns to be made of the accommodations and prices of provisions at the various quarters for the use of the Militia, to be sent to the War Office, together with a description of the roads, bridges, ferries, &c. 1797. General order :— The Militia to be increased by a Supplementary Battalion to 1,000 rank and file. General order relative to the baggage and marches of the Army, a very important order, showing how an enemy should be attacked, and prevented from invading the country, &c. 1798, Feb. General order :—A Supplementary Militia to be embodied and added to the Regiments of Militia. General order, April, 1798 :—The Supplementary Militiamen are to have the option of enlisting into the Line, the officers to use their influence with the men to induce them to enter the Line ; they are to receive for so doing seven guineas bounty. The men to serve during the war, and six months after the conclusion of a general peace, and not to be liable to serve out of Europe. Several general orders between April and October, respecting the embodiment of the Supplementary Militias with the Militia Regiments, augmentations and distribution of the officers, &c. 1807. At a General Court-Martial, one more sentenced to receive 500 lashes for being absent from June, 1806, to April, 1807. 1809. General order :—The men of the local Militias not to be tampered with to enlist into the Line. In one Regiment, this year, 2,800 lashes were inflicted; no other punishment awarded but corporeal punishment. 1810. General order :—Men of those Militia Regiments that have not completed their quota of volunteers to the Regular Army, are at liberty to enlist into the 1st Royals, or any other Regiment they may desire. 1811, July 9. General order empowering Lieutenants or Deputy-Lieutenants of counties, Colonels, &c., of Militia, to raise volunteers by beat of drum for the Militia Regiments of their respective counties. 1812. General order, Horse Guards, March 25, states,—That on no pretence whatever is a *Regimental* Court-Martial to award more than 300 lashes. 1813. General order :—Officers, non-commissioned officers, and privates, allowed to volunteer into the Regiments of the Line, for the purpose of prosecuting the war. With every 100 men, a Captain, Lieutenant, and Ensign will be transferred from the Militia into the Line. Volunteers to the Line will receive a bounty of sixteen guineas for unlimited service, and twelve for a limited period.

SERVICES OF REGIMENTS OF MILITIA, AND VOLUNTEERING TO THE LINE DURING THE WAR.

During the above years, large numbers of men volunteered into the Line from the Militia. Amongst other Regiments conspicuous for their gallant devotedness, we find the 6th, or Royal Cheshire Regiment, sent to the Line up to 1813, 1,598 men. The 17th, or Royal Westmoreland Regiment, very largely volunteered into the Line, and formed part of the 3d Provincial Battalion of Militia, commanded by Sir Watkyn Wynn, Bart., which landed at Bordeaux, and formed part of the Division of the Duke of Wellington's Army, commanded by Sir Stapleton Cotton and Lord Combermere. The 21st, or West York Regiment, gave 1,800 men to the Line during the War. The 25th, or South Devon Regiment, served in Ireland with great distinction during the Rebellion; as also the 26th, or Leicester Regiment. The 28th, or Royal Pembrokeshire Regiment : this Regiment volunteered to go with General Moore, and be employed in Spain and Portugal; to be attached to the 43d Regiment. The 31st, or Royal Brecon Regiment, served in Ireland during the Rebellion. The 34th, or East Suffolk Regiment, volunteered during the War 1,119 men to the Line, the greater part of whom joined the 43d Light Infantry ; 83 more men volunteered for service in the Peninsula, in the 2d Provisional Battalion of Militia; making a total of 1,202 men to the Line, " by more than twice its establishment, which was 521 men." The 35th, or Royal Bucks King's Own Regiment, volunteered in 1798, with the Marquis of Buckingham, to serve in Ireland, during the Rebellion ; this Regiment is said to be the first English Regiment of Militia that landed in Ireland ; in 1799, the Regiment volunteered 400 men to the Line, including serjeants, corporals, and privates, with the regulated proportion of officers, all of whom joined the 4th, or King's Own Regiment ; the Regiment afterwards furnished yearly, principally to the 14th Foot, its full quota of men during the War; in 1808, the Regiment volunteered to serve in Spain; the 1st Provisional Battalion of Militia, which landed at Bordeaux, was formed chiefly of men of the Royal Bucks King's Own Regiment, who were commanded by the Duke of Buckingham and Chandos. The 36th, or Warwickshire Regiment, served in Ireland during the Rebellion. The 42d, or Dorset Regiment, served in Ireland during the Rebellion. 48 officers, with their quota of non-commissioned officers and men, volunteered to the Line during the War. The 46th, or Royal Denbighshire Regiment, in 1813, volunteered into the 3d Provisional Battalion of Militia, and served with the Duke of Wellington's Army in the south of France.

The 48th, or Northamptonshire Regiment, was of great service during the Lord George Gordon Riots. The 58th, or Royal West Middlesex Regiment, volunteered for service in France, in 1814. The 61st, or Royal Anglesea Regiment, volunteered in a body for foreign service in 1813. The 62d, or Derby Regiment, a part of the officers, non-commissioned officers, and privates, served in France in the 3d Provisional Battalion of Militia in 1814. The 64th, or Royal Cardigan Rifles, opposed the landing of the French at Fishguard, 22d Feb., 1797. The 85th, or Royal Longford Regiment, engaged the French troops at Castlebar, Aug. 27, 1798; the Light Company served throughout the whole of the Rebellion of that year. The 87th, or south Cork Regiment, highly distinguished itself at the Battle of Vinegar Hill, June 21, 1798, which ended in the total dispersion of the insurgent force. The 89th, or Aberdeenshire Regiment, furnished during the War 647 volunteers to Regiments of the Line. The 92d, or Wicklow Regiment, served during the Irish Rebellion, and on June 24, 1798, retook the town of Castlecomer from the rebels; on the 26th of the same month, the Regiment attacked 4,000 rebels near Kilcomney Hill, killed nearly 1,000, and took 14 pieces of cannon, with a large quantity of stores. The 95th, or Londonderry Regiment, served during the Irish Rebellion, and was engaged with the rebels at Gorey, Arklow, New Ross, Folk's Mill, Blackmore Hill, and Vinegar Hill; towards the close of the year, the entire Regiment volunteered for foreign service. The 98th, or King's County Regiment, distinguished itself during the Irish Rebellion, and fought at Vinegar Hill; afterwards a wing of the Regiment successfully defended the town of Newtown Barry. The 100th, or Royal Dublin City Regiment, served at the Battle of Vinegar Hill, and in the Irish Rebellion. The 102d, or Prince of Wales Donegal Regiment, served in the Irish Rebellion, engaged the rebels at Three Rocks, County Wexford, May, 1798; at New Ross, June 5, and at Vinegar Hill: the Regiment was also engaged at Enniscorthy; two Sergeants were presented with commissions in the Line for their bravery at Ross. The 103d, or Limerick City Regiment, greatly distinguished itself in successfully opposing the entry of the French Troops on the 5th Sept., 1798, into Sligo; the Regiment lost 27 killed, and 40 wounded: the Colonel, one Captain, and one Lieutenant wounded; one Lieutenant, one Ensign killed. The French and rebels about double that number of casualties. This Regiment has also had the distinguished honour of seeing an officer in the Corps become afterwards one of the first Generals in the British Army, for Lord Gough commenced his military career as an Ensign in the Limerick City Regiment of Militia. The 106th, or Royal London Regiment, performed very valuable service in the suppression of the Riots, 1780. The 115th, or Royal Ayrshire Regiment, unanimously volunteered in August, 1808, to serve with the regular Army in Spain; during the period this Regiment was embodied, it gave 11 officers, and 694 men, as volunteers to the Line. The 128th, or Waterford Regiment, served in Ireland with great gallantry during the Rebellion of 1798, and gave several hundred men as volunteers to the Line.

To sum up the eminent services of the Militia, we use the words of a writer in a Military Journal :*—

" And for their deeds and conduct in modern times, our fathers have told us how, during the Gordon Riots, in 1780, when they who should have protected the State and Commonwealth, hesitated and looked coolly on, the Surrey Militia cleared with the bayonet the city and bridges, and rolling back the flood of anarchy and rebellion, saved the metropolis of the Empire from pillage and fire.

" Still later, the County Regiments did good service in Ireland; and during the Peninsular War, they not only performed garrison duty, but sent such a constant supply of *trained* recruits to our gallant Army abroad, as enabled the Great Duke to achieve his matchless victories. To this last fact the late Lord Munster has borne testimony, by recording, that, at Talavera, an immense proportion of the Army had been so recently drafted from the Militia, that they still wore the uniform and knapsacks of their various county regiments.

"Many can recollect the Stafford (King George's favourites), the Lancaster, the East Middlesex (whose proud boast it was, that they, of all the regiments, always had most men on parade, and fewest in hospital), the West Middlesex, the York; but why particularize, where all did their duty, all were efficient, English, Scotch, and Irish, as proved by the Duke of York's order to them before they were disbanded."

VOTES OF THANKS.—For the Services of the MILITIA during the Continental War, the HOUSE OF LORDS met on the 6th of April, 1802, and passed the following Vote of Thanks:—

" MILITIA.—*Resolved, Nemine Dissentiente,* That the Thanks of this House be given to the officers of the several Corps of Militia, which have been embodied in Great Britain and Ireland during the course of the War, for the seasonable and meritorious Services they have rendered to their King and Country.

" *Resolved, Nemine Dissentiente,* That this House doth highly approve of, and acknowledge the Services of the Non-commissioned Officers and Men of the several Corps of Militia, which have been embodied in Great Britain and Ireland during the course of the War; and that the same be communicated to them by the Commanding Officers of the several Corps, who are desired to thank them for their meritorious conduct.

" *Ordered,* That the Lord Chancellor do signify the said Resolutions, by letter, to the Colonel or Commanding Officer of each respective Corps."

In 1814, a similar Vote of Thanks to the Militia was adopted by the House of Lords, *Nemine Dissentiente.*

* "The British Army Despatch and West End Courier."

The HOUSE OF COMMONS, on the 6th April, 1802, passed a Vote of Thanks to the Militia, for "the seasonable and meritorious Service rendered to their King and Country." On the 6th July, the Commons passed another Vote of Thanks to the Militia, "embodied in Great Britain and Ireland during the War," for their Services.

1831 TO 1845.—Since 1831 the Militia has remained completely disembodied. In 1845 the Government partially conceded to the desire expressed by the country for the re-embodiment of the Militia, and instructions were issued from the Home Office, at Whitehall, and from the War Office, addressed to the Lords-Lieutenants of Counties and the Colonels of Regiments of Militia, suggesting the Staffs of the respective Regiments to be perfected at once; Adjutants appointed to vacancies; vacant commissions to be filled up without delay; and effective Sergeants selected to drill the men. The official letters will be found below; but further than an acknowledgment of the reception of the same, no steps have been taken by the Government since 1845, to carry out the provisions of the letters dated 1st and 9th December of that year.

"(GREAT BRITAIN.)
"[CIRCULAR, No. 954.]
"*War Office*, 1 *December*, 1845.

" Her Majesty having been graciously pleased to signify her commands that the Permanent Staff of the several Regiments, Battalions, or Corps of the Militia of Great Britain shall be completed to the numbers limited by the Act of the 5th and 6th William IV., cap. 37, I have the honour to acquaint you that the Establishment of the Staff of the Regiment under your command should be completed as soon as practicable, so as to consist of the numbers specified in the margin.

" A communication will be addressed to you respecting the Adjutant by the Lord-Lieutenant of the County.

" As it appears that there are several vacancies in the rank of Sergeant, and it being highly essential that these vacancies should be filled by active and efficient Non-commissioned Officers whose former Services in the Regular Army have rendered them particularly qualified for the duty of drilling Recruits in the modern and improved principle of Military Instructions, I have caused to be prepared a list of Non-commissioned Officers (pensioners of Chelsea Hospital) whose efficiency and excellent character combine to render them eligible to supply the existing vacancies, and I beg leave to state that upon the expression of your wish to avail yourself of the facility offered by this arrangement, I shall be enabled to recommend to you from among the Pensioners residing in your district the number of Sergeants requisite to complete the Staff.

" Adverting to the recent inspection of the Staff of your Regiment, I have to observe that although the Inspecting Officers have reported that several of the Sergeants are unfit for the performance of duties in the event of the Militia being embodied for active Service, yet that they are not wholly incapacitated from the performance of local duties incidental to the ballot, enrolment, as well as the exercise of the Militia, and would be able to afford valuable information on the first training. Upon these grounds it is not deemed expedient at present to discharge all such Sergeants, and replace them by others, but as there may be some, who, from their great age, long service and infirmities, are no longer competent to the performance of any duties whatever, it would be very desirable that those Sergeants should be discharged, and recommended to the Commissioners of Chelsea Hospital for the grant of a pension, but before any definitive measures are adopted upon that point, I should be glad to receive a statement upon the inclosed form, showing the names and services in all ranks, of the Sergeants whom you may desire to select for discharge upon this occasion, preparatory to the adoption of ulterior measures respecting them.

" I have the honour to be,
" Your most obedient, humble Servant,
" SIDNEY HERBERT.

" *Colonel of the*   *Regiment of Militia.*"

"(CIRCULAR.)
" *Whitehall, Dec.* 9, 1845.

"MY LORD,—I have the honour to inform your Lordship, that her Majesty has been graciously pleased to signify her commands, that the Permanent Staff of the several Regiments, Battalions, or Corps of the Militia of Great Britain should be completed to the numbers prescribed by the Act of the 5th and 6th Will. IV., cap. 37.

"A communication has already been addressed by the Secretary at War to the Colonels of Regiments of Militia respecting the Sergeant-Majors and Sergeants, with the view to the supplying of any vacancies that may at present exist, as well as for discharging such of the Sergeants as have been found by the recent inspections to be totally unfit for the performance of any duty whatever; and also conveying to them a suggestion for the prospective discharge of those who, although they have been reported unfit for duty when the Militia shall be in an embodied state, are nevertheless competent to the performance of local duties connected with the ballot, enrolment, and training of that force.

"I have also to acquaint your Lordship that her Majesty deems it expedient that the Adjutancy of the ——— Regiment of Militia, which has been kept in a state of abeyance under the provisions of the statute referred to, should be filled up as soon as practicable; and in regard to the selection of an officer to supply such vacancy, I am desirous of impressing upon your Lordship the importance of selecting an active and efficient officer from her Majesty's regular Forces. In the event of your Lordship not being prepared to recommend a fit and proper officer to succeed to that commission, I shall be ready, in concert with the Commander-in-Chief, to furnish your Lordship with the names of several officers possessing the requisite qualifications. I beg to add, that the regulations contained in the inclosed copy of the circular letter which was addressed to the Lords-Lieutenant of counties on the 30th of January, 1830, respecting the appointment of such officers, will be strictly adhered to. It being also of considerable importance that the full establishment of officers in the several Regiments of Militia should be completed to the extent prescribed by law, I beg leave to call your Lordship's attention to this subject, and to suggest that, in the event of there being any vacancies (that of Paymaster excepted) in the Regiment of Militia in your county, such vacancies should be filled up before the spring of the ensuing year.

"I have the honour to be, My Lord,
 "Your Lordship's very obedient Servant,
"*Her Majesty's Lieutenant of* "Jas. Graham."
 the County of ——."

The established Militia Force of England and Wales is about 41,000 rank and file; Scotland, 7,600.

Militia of Ireland.—The Militia of Ireland, when embodied, consists of six Regiments, mustering ten companies each, viz., Donegal, Galway, Londonderry, Tipperary, Tyrone, Wexford; Louth nine companies; fifteen Regiments with eight companies each, viz., Antrim, Armagh, North Cork, South Cork, City Cork, City Dublin, Kerry, Kilkenny, King's County, Meath, Monaghan, Limerick County, Roscommon, Waterford, Wicklow; fourteen Regiments with six companies each, viz., Cavan, Clare, Carlow, North Down, South Down, Co. Dublin, Fermanagh, Kildare, Leitrim, Limerick City, Longford, Queen's Co., Sligo, Westmeath; and two, Mayo South and Mayo North, seven companies each.

Of the origin and organization of the Irish Militia we learn,—
"In Ireland the predatory army of gallowglasses, which, even in times of comparative tranquillity, it was found necessary to keep constantly armed for the preservation or the enlargement of the pale, was supported, to a small extent, by supplies from England; but it chiefly depended on exactions from the Anglo-Irish, made by a dexterous application of the many fines and petty tributes originally exigible by the native chiefs. To these the English added the formidable exactions of coign and livery, which embracing free quarters, and all that is generally taken under the sanction of that licence, were the frequent subject of bitter complaint, though not much heeded by a Government which expected that the conquest would at least support itself. In 1715, on occasion of the rebellion in Scotland, an Act was passed by the Irish Parliament (2 Geo. I., c. 9) for raising a Militia to consist of Protestants. Roman Catholics were subject to double rates; and all serviceable horses belonging to them might be seized and made use of, provided that within ten days the sum of 5*l*. (deducting the expense of seizure and keeping) was tendered to the owner of each as full payment. After several partial alterations, the Militia Laws were consolidated by the Irish Parliament in 1793 (33 Geo. III., c. 22) and 1795 (35 Geo. III., c. 8), and accommodated to those of England in 1809."*

Militia of Scotland.—"In Scotland there seems never to have been, except in burghs, a national force for the defence of the citizens, like the Fyrd of the Saxons. The earliest acts of Parliament, however, enforce Practice in the bow, of which the efficiency had been so dearly learned in the English wars; whilst periodical 'wapenshawings' are directed to be held, in which each individual should be armed upon a scale vaguely proportioned to his property. In time of war or rebellion proclamations were issued, charging all

---

* See Irish State Papers, published by authority of Government, vol. ii. p. 477, &c.

sheriffs and magistrates of burghs, to direct the attendants of the respective wapenshawings to join the king's host; and the criminal records contain many prosecutions for 'abiding from' the various 'raids,' which are generally settled by composition with the Lord Treasurer. During the civil wars of the seventeenth century, the army which had been brought into existence by the enthusiasm of the Covenanters, was supported by levies and assessments apportioned by district Committees of War appointed by Parliament, whose duties and powers were modelled on those of the Commissioners of Array in England. In 1662 (1 Car. II., 3, 27), the Parliament made offer of 20,000 foot and 2,000 horse to be at his Majesty's sole disposal, and to be marched to any part of Scotland, England, or Ireland. This body constituted a regular standing army, the organization of which underwent some alterations in the years 1669, 1672, 1693, and 1695. From this last period no legislative improvements were made in the Militia of Scotland until the year 1797, when the system established in England was partially extended to that part of the empire, though not without considerable local disturbance."

In concluding our history of the organization and equipment of the Militia, we cannot do better than quote the observations of the journalist referred to in page xiv :—

"The modern law enjoins that, down to the rank of subaltern, Militia Officers shall possess a landed qualification, half such property to be in the county to which the Regiment belongs; the power to appoint officers to command the Militia is one of the constitutional prerogatives of the Crown. Thus has the original system never been lost sight of. Such was their origin, and such is their constitution; and thus has their use and value been proved by the test of more than a thousand years, though altered and amended as the system has been to adapt it to the advancing state of society.

"With the Parliament it rests to restore the Militia to their former state of usefulness, and numbering, as they do, in the Upper House nearly fifty peers, and in the Lower House about thirty members, who bear Militia Commissions, is it too much to hope that another session will not be allowed to pass without the law being so far re-modelled as to raise the Militia from its present *expensive* state of neglect to its rightful position in the Service ?

"What they once were they might become again. Prudence, justice, and true economy, call loudly for such a measure: many hundred thousands are annually voted for a skeleton Militia and Enrolled Pensioners. The same money, judiciously applied, would give to England a reserve force of Militia worthy of her high place amongst the nations; and that such may yet be done is the hope of every sincere patriot."

SECTION III.

ABSTRACT OF THE MILITIA ACTS,

FOR AMENDING THE LAWS RELATING TO THE MILITIA IN ENGLAND.

[42 GEORGII III., cap. 90, to 2 & 3 VICTORIÆ, cap. 59.]

(CLAUSE 2.)

EMPOWERS his Majesty George III., his heirs and successors, to appoint Lieutenants of Counties, who shall call out the Militia yearly, and appoint deputies, and also officers, whose names and ranks shall be certified to his Majesty, but to such as he disapproves commissions shall not be granted. Officers in the Militia rank with the officers of the Regular Army as youngest of their rank.

6. Declares the qualifications of the officers of the Militia, that every person to be appointed a Deputy-Lieutenant shall be possessed of an estate, of the yearly value of 200*l*., or heir-apparent of the yearly value of 400*l*.; every Colonel shall be possessed of an estate of the yearly value of 1,000*l*., or heir-apparent to one of 2,000*l*. per annum; Lieutenant-Colonel to have an estate of 600*l*. per annum; a Major when an estate of 400*l*. per annum; a Captain when an estate of 200*l*. per annum; a Lieutenant to have an estate of 50*l*. per annum, or personal property to the value of 1,000*l*.; an Ensign to have an estate of 20*l*. per annum, or personal property to the value of 400*l*.

9. Declares, that in all cities and towns which are counties within themselves, the chief Magistrate shall appoint the Deputy-Lieutenant and other officers of the Militia.

10. Declares leases for lives, of 300*l*. per annum, to be deemed equal to a qualification hereinbefore required of 100*l*. per annum, and so proportionately.

11. Declares, that estates granted for twenty years, of an annual value equal to the value of estates required for qualifications, shall be deemed sufficient.

12. Declares, that no Deputy-Lieutenant or other officer shall be appointed till his qualification be delivered to the Clerk of the Peace, who shall transmit a copy to the County Lieutenant.

13. Declares, that the Clerk of the Peace shall enter qualifications upon a roll, and shall insert in the "London Gazette" the dates of commissions, &c., and that all officers shall take the oath within six months of their appointment.

14. Declares, that any person who shall execute any of the powers specified to be executed by Deputy-Lieutenants, Colonels, or Majors, not being qualified, shall forfeit 200*l*.; Captains, not being qualified, 100*l*.; but Peers, or their heirs, may act, though not possessed of qualifications.

19. Declares the number of men to be enlisted in the county of

County	Number	County	Number
Bedford	317	Middlesex	3038
Berks	561	Monmouth	280
Bucks	599	Norfolk and Norwich	1209
Cambridge	481	Northampton	724
Chester	885	Somerset	1556
Cornwall	647	Southampton	850
Cumberland	615	Stafford and Lichfield	1133
Derby	939	Suffolk	1042
Devon and Exeter	1512	Surrey	1336
Dorset and Poole	411	Sussex	803
Durham	492	Warwick and Coventry	853
Essex	1244	Westmoreland	243
Northumberland and New-castle-upon-Tyne and Berwick-upon-Tweed	649	Worcester	616
		Wilts	917
Nottingham	564	West Riding of York and the Town and City of York	2429
Oxford	603		
Rutland	83	North Riding of York, East do., and Kingston-upon-Hull	1475
Salop	991		
Gloucester and Bristol	1163		
Hereford	523	Anglesea	128
Hertford	481	Cardigan	244
Kent and Canterbury	1296	Carnarvon	128
Lancaster	2439	Flint	201
Leicester	643	Merioneth	111
Lincoln	1368	Brecknock	204
Carmarthen	405	Pembroke and Haverford-west	241
Denbigh	344		
Glamorgan	403	Radnor	140
Montgomery	279		

26. Declares, that housekeepers shall, within fourteen days after the notice has been left, return a true statement of the Christian and surname of every man resident in his dwelling-house, between the ages of eighteen and forty-five, and shall sign and deliver the same notice under a penalty of 5l.

27. Declares, that in any case where a notice shall be served upon a Quaker, being a householder, such Quaker shall, within seven days after, produce a certificate to the constable, signed by two respectable Quakers, acknowledging him to belong to their persuasion, and in such case the constable shall make the return of the persons liable to serve in such house.

28. Declares, that constables shall make out yearly lists of the names of all men, between the ages of forty-five, who shall reside in their respective districts, distinguishing such as labour under any infirmity likely to incapacitate them from serving as Militia-men, and which of them claim to be exempt, and on what grounds, and shall affix the same on the church-door on one Sunday before the meeting of Deputy-Lieutenants.

29. Declares, that persons aggrieved may appeal to the Sub-division Meetings, and the determination thereat to be final.

31. Declares, that any person who shall endeavour to prevail on

any constable to make a false return shall forfeit 50*l.*; and if any person shall refuse to tell his Christian and surname, or shall give a false one of any person residing in his or her house, they shall forfeit and pay the sum of 10*l.*

32. Declares, that Deputy-Lieutenants may issue orders for attendance of constables, &c.; and if any shall neglect, to appear, or to return lists, or shall be guilty of any fraud, partiality, or neglect, he shall be liable to a penalty not exceeding 20*l.*, nor less than 2*l.*, or may be committed to gaol for one month.

33. Declares, that two Justices may appoint Deputies to Quakers for carrying this Act into execution.

35. Declares, that this Act shall extend to all extra-parochial places added to parishes; and where no constables or overseers in such place are appointed, the officers of the parish may act; and that all rates made for any parish, and extra-parochial place jointly, to be distinctly made for the purposes of this Act, and shall be levied as the poor-rates.

36. Declares, that the Clerks of all Sub-division Meetings shall, within fourteen days after every Sub-division Meeting, transmit to the Clerk of the General Meeting copies of such rolls as shall be signed at such Sub-division Meeting, or in default of so doing shall forfeit and pay the sum of 20*l.*

37. Declares, that any Clerk to General Meetings who shall neglect to transmit to the Privy Council correct lists of the men liable to serve in the Militia, within one month of the returns of such being made to the General Meeting, shall forfeit and pay for every such offence the sum of 100*l.*

38. Declares, that the Privy Council shall, every ten years, fix the quota of men to serve for each place, as near as may be, by the proportion that the number of men, fit and liable to serve in each place, shall bear to the whole number of men required by this Act to be raised, and shall send notice of the number required to the County Lieutenants, and publish the same in the "London Gazette."

39. Declares, that where the number fixed shall be greater than the former quota, the General Meeting shall appoint what number shall be chosen for each division; and where the number shall be less, shall dismiss the excess by ballot, proportionally out of each division; but men so dismissed are liable to serve, and their names shall be entered in a list, out of which vacancies shall be filled up, by ballot, to serve for the remainder of the time for which they were engaged.

41. Declares, the Deputy-Lieutenants shall, at their second Sub-division Meeting, appoint the number of men to serve for each parish, and within three weeks shall cause the men to assemble and be chosen by ballot, and that all who are chosen shall then and there take the oath required by this Act, to well and truly serve in the Militia for five years. Provided always, that any person shall be allowed to procure a substitute, who, if approved of, shall be enrolled, but such substitute must not have more than one child.

42. Declares, that volunteers may be raised by the inhabitants of any parish, and a rate established for paying them, but the bounties to such volunteers are not to exceed 6*l.* each; and that persons who, by themselves or by substitute, have served in the Militia, are exempt from the payment of such rate.

d

43. Declares, that no Peer, or commissioned officer, or officer on half-pay, nor private soldier or sailor in H. M. S., nor any resident member of the Universities, nor any clergyman, nor any constable, articled clerk, apprentice, nor person employed in any of Her Majesty's dockyards, nor any poor man who has more than one child born in wedlock, shall be liable to serve, but no person who has served only as substitute shall be exempt.

45. Declares, that all persons chosen (except Quakers), and not appearing, shall forfeit 10*l.*, and at the expiration of five years, be again liable to serve, and in default of paying the fine, shall be compelled to serve, and shall be subject to the same punishments for absconding and deserting as he would have been subject to in case he had appeared and been duly sworn in and enrolled as a Militia-man.

47. Declares, that persons chosen shall serve though they remove, and those having more than one residence shall serve where their names were first inserted in the list.

48. Declares, persons to serve in the Militia of the county in which the parish church is situate.

49. Declares, that persons fraudulently bound apprentice, to avoid serving in the Militia, shall be liable to serve, and the master shall forfeit 10*l.*

50. Declares, that two Deputy-Lieutenants may provide substitutes for Quakers, and may levy the expenses by distress, and if he shall not have sufficient goods to realize 10*l.*, he may be committed to gaol for three months, unless he shall sooner pay the fine.

51. Declares, Justices may order payment of costs incurred by levying distress on Quakers who refuse to serve, and that no person shall be deemed a Quaker unless he shall produce a certificate of his being of that persuasion.

52. Declares, no man to be enrolled until examined and approved by a Surgeon, who shall be paid not more than 10*s.* for his daily attendance.

53. Declares, that two Deputy-Lieutenants may discharge persons chosen by ballot who are unfit for service.

55. Declares, that whenever any Militia-man becomes unfit for service, he may be discharged by the commanding officer and two Deputy-Lieutenants.

56. Declares, that whenever any vacancy shall occur, by death or otherwise, in the Militia, they shall be filled up by ballot.

61. Declares, the enrolment of servants shall not vacate their contracts with their masters unless the Militia shall be embodied; and if any dispute arise, touching wages under 20*l.*, a Justice may settle it, and may grant a warrant for levying the money by distress if not paid.

62. Declares, that any person who shall receive money to serve as a substitute, and shall not appear to have been sworn, shall return the bounty, in addition to a penalty not exceeding 2*l.*, or less than 1*l.*, and in default of so doing shall be committed to the House of Correction for fourteen days.

63. Declares, two Deputy-Lieutenants or a Justice may order the money agreed to be given to a substitute, or volunteer, to be paid him on enrolment, where the Militia is not embodied, and where it is, one-half, and the other to the Clerk of the Sub-division, to be remitted to

ABSTRACT OF THE MILITIA ACTS. xxiii

the Paymaster, to be paid to the man on joining and being approved of; and if he shall not join or be approved of, the money shall be paid to the person provided in lieu of him.

64. Declares, enlistment of a Militia-man into the standing Army to be void; and any man so offering to enlist, denying that he is a Militia-man, or offering to serve in any other Regiment of Militia, shall be imprisoned for a term not exceeding six months; and any person so enlisting Militia-men to forfeit 20*l.*; and any soldier offering to serve as a substitute in the Militia shall forfeit 10*l.*, or in default be committed to gaol for any time not exceeding three months.

65. Declares, that if any person shall give any orders to any Sergeant, or other persons serving in the Militia, to beat up for volunteers to serve in the Militia, the person who gave such orders shall, upon proof thereof before a Justice of the Peace, forfeit and pay 20*l.*; and if such Sergeant or other person shall refuse to declare upon oath from whom he received orders, he shall be committed to the House of Correction for three months.

66. Declares, that the penalties for refusing to serve shall be applied to the procuring of substitutes, and the surplus to form part of the Regimental-book.

68. Declares, that the Militia shall be formed into Companies, which shall not consist of more than 120 men, nor less than 60, that to each Company there shall be 1 Captain, 1 Lieutenant, and 1 Ensign; 12 Companies to form a Regiment, every Regiment to have 1 Colonel, 1 Lieutenant-Colonel, and 2 Majors.

78. Declares, that to every Corps, of not less than two Companies of 60 men each, a Surgeon shall be appointed, who shall receive 10*s.* per day for his attendance, during the time the Militia is disembodied, and the usual pay of Surgeons of Infantry, when the Militia is embodied.

83. Declares, that when not in actual service, there shall be 1 Sergeant and 1 Corporal to every 30 men, and when the Militia shall be drawn out into actual service, an addition shall be made, so that there shall be 1 Sergeant and 1 Corporal to every 20 private men; and the daily pay of Sergeants, 1*s.* 6*d.* per day, Corporals, 1*s.* 2*d.*, and Drummers, 1*s.* per day; Sergeant-Majors, and Drum-Majors may be appointed, but no publican shall serve as a Sergeant.

86. Declares, that Sergeants of Chelsea Hospital, and out-pensioners, may receive their allowances therefrom, together with their pay in the Militia; and Sergeants who have served twenty years in the Militia, may receive the Chelsea Pension.

87. Declares, that the Militia shall be called out, once every year, for the purpose of being trained and exercised, for the space of twenty-one days.

89. Declares, that during the time of exercise, the Mutiny Act and Articles of War shall be in force, with respect to such Militia, but that punishment shall not extend to life or limb.

90. Declares, that notices of the times and places for the exercise of the Militia-men, shall be affixed on the Church doors, and that the Constables, and other officers shall give notice in writing to the several Militia-men, who shall be called out by leaving the said notice at their usual place of abode.

92. Declares, that the pay of every Militia-man shall commence on

the day of his joining his Regiment to exercise, but to such as are prevented by sickness from joining, on production of a certificate to that effect, the Commanding-officer may direct an allowance to be made for his support.

93. Declares, that if any Militia-man shall fall sick upon the march, he may be relieved by warrant of a Justice, and the expenses shall be reimbursed by the County treasurer.

94. Declares, Magistrates may billet the Militia when called out to annual exercise, in inns, livery-stables, ale-houses, &c.; and when not embodied, may order lodgings, &c., and for the Non-commissioned Officers and Drummers.

95. Declares, that when the Militia is called out to be trained and exercised, any Justice of the Peace may grant warrants for the impressing carriages for the Militia on its march.

96. Declares, Militia-men, when called out for exercise, may be put under stoppages for providing them with linen and other necessaries, such stoppages not to exceed 4*d.* per day.

99. Declares, that every Militia-man not labouring under any infirmity incapacitating him, who shall not appear at the time and place appointed for his being exercised, or shall desert from the Militia, shall be liable to a penalty of 20*l.*, or to be imprisoned for six months.

100. Declares, that every Militia-man who shall desert, shall when taken be compelled to serve.

101. Declares, that all muskets are to be marked, and if any men sell, pawn, or lose their arms, &c., or neglect to return them in good order, they shall forfeit not exceeding 3*l.*, or be committed to gaol for three months.

102. Declares, that if any person shall knowingly buy or receive any Militia arms, clothing, or accoutrements, the person so offending shall forfeit 10*l.*, or be imprisoned six months, and be publicly or privately whipped, at the discretion of the Justice.

103. Declares, that when the Militia is embodied, the Adjutants, Sergeants, Corporals, Drummer, or other Petty Officer, may be tried by Court-martial for desertion, while the Regiment was embodied, and not taken.

104. Declares, that no sentence of a Court-martial is to be enforced, until approved of by the Commandant.

108. Declares, that all deserters shall be tried by Court-martial.

109. Declares, that every person who shall cause a deserter to be apprehended, shall receive from the Commanding-officer a reward of 1*l.*

110. Declares, that any person who shall harbour or conceal a deserter, shall forfeit for every such offence 5*l.*

111. Declares, that His Majesty may order the Militia to be embodied, and in case of invasion or rebellion, may order them to be led by their respective officers, into any part of Great Britain, and so embodied, they shall be subject to the Mutiny Act, and Articles of War.

112. Declares, that not on any account shall the Militia be ordered or carried out of Great Britain.

116. Declares, that if any Militia-men shall not march in pursuance of order, they shall be deemed deserters, and persons harbouring them, shall forfeit 100*l.*

117. Declares, that Militia-men shall be entitled to the same pay as other Regiments of Infantry, and if maimed or wounded, to be entitled to the benefit of Chelsea Hospital.

118. Declares, that the pay of the officers and men who shall not join on the day appointed, unless prevented by necessity, shall commence only from the day of joining.

119. Declares, that the pay of men enrolled after the Militia is called out, shall commence from the time of joining.

121. Declares, that when the Militia is called out, every Militia-man shall be paid the sum of one Guinea, to be laid out to their advantage.

122. Declares, that any person who may be chosen by ballot to serve in Militia, or who shall provide a substitute, shall be entitled to receive from the parish officers a sum not exceeding 3*l*.

125 and 126. Declares, that in case the term of service shall be prolonged beyond the term of five years, the Receiver-General shall pay to each man the sum of one Guinea, and also to substitutes, or volunteers whose term shall be prolonged, and a like bounty at the end of every three years they shall continue to serve beyond the five years.

127. Declares, that if any Militia-man shall desert, or not join, he may by Court-martial be adjudged to further service in the Militia, or to service in the other Forces; and in the latter case, the Secretary-at-War may order him to be entered as a private soldier, and conveyed to the Head-Quarters of any Regiment, or for recruits of Regiments on foreign stations.

131. Declares, that all Militia-men not appearing when called upon, shall be deemed deserters, shall forfeit 10*l*., and be liable to be embodied.

136. Declares, that any person enrolled and not chosen, not having a child under fourteen years of age, and not being more than thirty-five years old, may be accepted as a volunteer.

137. Declares, that all men attending at the ballot, and not being chosen, shall receive 1*s*. per day for their attendance.

142. Declares, that while any part of the Militia shall continue embodied, His Majesty may order any part not embodied, to be drawn out to be trained and exercised.

145. Declares, that when the Militia is embodied, the officers and men shall be subject to the same orders only as before being drawn out.

146. Declares, that in case of invasion or rebellion, His Majesty may order by proclamation, the Militia to be increased one-half.

156. Declares, that in Sussex and Kent, the Churchwardens and Overseers shall make returns of men liable to serve, and to have the same powers as Constables in other places.

158. Declares, that where the number of men required in any county shall not be raised within a limited period, 10*l*. shall be paid for each man deficient, for which the Justices in session shall make an assessment.

173. Declares, that any Militia-man being a voter going to an election, shall not be punishable for absence.

175. Declares, that any person having served in the Militia when drawn out into actual service, being a married man, may set up and exercise any trade, in any town or place in Great Britain (excepting

Oxford and Cambridge), without molestation from any person whatsoever, under the same regulations as any mariner or soldier in His Majesty's service can do ; and no such Militia-man shall be liable to be removed out of any such town or place, unless he become chargeable to the parish.

176. Declares, that all penalties above 20*l*. shall be recovered by action of debt, bill, plaint, or information in any of His Majesty's Courts of Record at Westminster, or the Courts of Great Session in the Principality of Wales, or the Courts of the Counties Palatine of Chester, Lancaster, and Durham, and that all fines and penalties which do not exceed 20*l*., shall, upon proof upon oath of the offence before a Justice of the Peace, be levied by distress upon the goods of the offender, or in default, shall be committed to the County Gaol, for any time not exceeding three months.

178. Declares, that all proceedings for the recovery of penalties under this Act shall be commenced within six months after the offence was committed.

SUMMARY.

By the above Act, it will be seen that no person is exempt between the ages of eighteen and forty-five, on account of having a family, unless he has two children, and can prove he is not worth 100*l*.

A few of the wives of the Militia-men are permitted to accompany the Regiment, but they must support themselves, neither are they entitled to demand relief from the parish, on account of their husbands being drawn.

Persons who labour under an infirmity, and cannot pay for a substitute, will undergo an examination by a Surgeon, and be excused.

Railway Special Constables are not exempt, the law not considering them as Peace-officers.

Militia-clubs are legal and efficient agents for procuring substitutes. The raising of the money for the drawn members is perfectly practicable, on the scale generally laid down.

The Act allows of two processes for forming the Militia ; one by enrolment, and the other by ballot.

Men eligible to serve in the Militia are classified ; and if the total number of the first class (or first and second together) are found sufficient to give the whole quota required for the county, the ballot may be dispensed with. The first class comprises all men under thirty years of age, and having no child living. In the second class, all men above thirty, and having no child. In the third, all men having no child under fourteen ; and in the fifth, all other men under forty-five years of age.

Solicitors are not themselves exempt, although their articled clerks are.

It is worthy of remark, that by clause 122, any person who is not worth 500*l*. is entitled to receive half what he may pay for a substitute (provided it does not exceed 3*l*.), from the parish officers.

SECTION IV.

YEOMANRY CAVALRY:

ORGANIZATION, SERVICES, AND DISCIPLINE.

THE Yeomanry Cavalry rank next in efficiency to the Line. The organization is so perfect, that in Civil disturbances, the value of this branch of the service cannot be too highly estimated. The privates, yeomen in their counties, are selected from an unexceptionable class of agriculturists, and having an influence in their respective localities, their value as soldiers cannot be questioned. Acquainted with every feature of the country, as aids to the regular Cavalry their knowledge would be all-important; while from the creditable acquaintance with their duties, in service, as a body, they would act with discipline and effect. The local influence possessed by the officers of Yeomanry Cavalry, is also great, as those Corps are generally commanded by noblemen and gentlemen, of large fortune and estates, from whence, chiefly, the privates are selected. In almost every Regiment, there is a mixture of officers from the Regular Army; a most wise and politic measure, reflecting no less credit upon the judgment of the respective Commandants, than acceptable to military men, experienced in the duties of their profession. The Adjutants of Yeomanry Cavalry are invariably selected from the Line.

Since the first formation of Yeomanry Cavalry in Great Britain, their services have been frequently called for, in aid of the Civil Power, and the important nature of those duties has been fully testified by the many marked expressions of royal favour, and the votes of thanks passed by Parliament *nemine dissentiente.* In many parts of the country, there is no other military force, but Yeomanry Cavalry, and upon those Corps the counties rely in periods of disaffection. The Ayrshire Regiment has for fifty-six years given protection to Ayrshire. The 2d Royal Bucks performed efficient service in the Otmoor Riots, in 1830; and in 1848, the Regiment, commanded by the Duke of Buckingham and Chandos, relieved the 1st Life Guards at Windsor, and performed Garrison duty. The Earl of Chester's Regiment has been frequently called out in aid of the Civil Power; as also the Denbighshire Regiment, in 1831, first raised in 1794. The Derby, North Devon, Dorset, and West Essex Regiments, have frequently rendered efficient aid to the Civil Power. The Lymington squadron of Yeomanry Cavalry was formed in 1831, in consequence of the lawless conduct of the labourers in the vicinity of the New Forest, who assembled to the amount of 2000 men, and upwards, and levied contributions under threat of violence on the residences of several Noblemen and Gentlemen in the years 1830 and 1831, for which offences many were tried and capitally convicted. Since the formation of this Yeomanry, no outrages whatever have occurred, and the lawless population about the New Forest has been kept in tolerable order and quiet. The Castlemartin Regiment was called out at Fishguard, in the county of Pembroke, in 1797, where the French troops had landed 1400 strong, and were compelled to surrender; in 1817, at Fishguard, to suppress Corn Riots, which they accomplished; in 1839, at Tavernspite, county of Carmarthen, to suppress Turnpike-gate Riots, which they accomplished; in 1843, at St. Clear's, county of Carmarthen, to suppress Turnpike-gate Riots. Out twenty-six days on duty on the breaking out of the Rebecca Riots; from the 26th June, 1843, to the 18th November, same year, distributed over the counties of Carmarthen, Cardigan and Pembroke, in the suppression of the Rebecca Riots, being 171 days in aid of the Civil Power in that year. The Staffordshire Regiment, for its efficient services in aid of the Civil Power, on many occasions, has received the thanks of the Crown; in the Riots in 1842, the Regiment was on duty for six weeks. The Suffolk Borderers have also been called out frequently in aid of the Civil Power. The Warwickshire Regiment rendered most important services during the Birmingham Riots. The Westmoreland Regiment has been out at seven different periods in aid of the Civil Power. The Wiltshire Regiment was made "Royal," for its services in the Riots of 1830. The Worcestershire Regiment has been out ten times in aid of the Civil Power, and in 1842 was on duty from April to September. The Yorkshire Hussars have been out on various occasions in aid of the Civil Power. The 1st West York Regiment has been called out several times in aid of the Civil Power, and in 1805, at the expected invasion of the French; in 1817, 1820, and 1832, Riots at Sheffield; 1839, Rotherham and Sheffield; 1840, ditto; 1842, ditto. The 2d West York Regiment has been out on various occasions in aid of the Civil Power.

We are correct when we state, that there is not a Regiment or Corps of Yeomanry Cavalry but has been out in aid of the Civil Power. Many Corps, upon being disbanded, were supported at the entire expense of their Commandants. Amongst others, prominent for their patriotic devotedness, we may mention Captain Palmer, Commandant of the West Essex Yeomanry Cavalry; Alexander Mackinnon, Esq., M.P., Commandant of the Lymington Squadron of Yeomanry Cavalry, who equipped the Corps, at his own expense, from 1837 to 1844. For other particulars, we must refer to the respective Regiments in the Army List.

Colonel Lord de Ros, Major of Brigade, to the Inspecting General of Cavalry, writes:—

"Some Regiments of Yeomanry Cavalry, which have been long established, are on a footing of discipline hardly susceptible of improvement. Several Regiments of Yeomanry can number as many as six, eight, and even ten troops, a body so numerous as hardly to be within the management of a Regimental Staff of the usual establishment, and these, too, dispersed over a great extent of country.

"There are to be found in the ranks of the Yeomanry many

officers and non-commissioned officers, who from former service, in the Regular Forces, are perfectly competent to all points of Regimental duty and command. Another description of officer in the Yeomanry consists of gentlemen, who, from a natural military taste, or from a laudable desire to perform well whatever they take in hand, and to qualify themselves for the command which their position in their own neighbourhood leads them to assume in these Corps, have made themselves nearly or quite as much masters of their business as if they had gone through the whole gradation of instruction in the Regiments of the Line."

SECTION V.

ABSTRACT OF GOVERNMENT REGULATIONS FOR YEOMANRY CAVALRY.*

ALL matters not provided for in these Regulations must be referred to the Secretary of State for the Home Department, through the Lieutenant of the County.

Composition of Yeomanry Cavalry.

No Troop must consist of less than 40, or more than 100 Privates (Farriers included).

Troops under 70 men have 1 Captain, 1 Lieutenant, 1 Cornet, 1 Quartermaster, 1 Trumpeter; and Troops exceeding 70 have an additional Lieutenant.

A Sergeant and a Corporal are allowed to every 20 Privates; a Drill-Sergeant is included in the number.

A Corps of 120 Privates is allowed a Sergeant-Major.

A Regiment of 300 Privates is allowed an Adjutant instead of a Sergeant-Major.

A Corps or Regiment of 200 Privates is allowed 1 Lieutenant-Colonel and 1 Major.

A Regiment of 320 Privates is allowed a Lieutenant-Colonel Commandant, a Lieutenant-Colonel, and a Major.

Qualifications and Pay of Adjutant and Sergeant-Major.

ADJUTANT.—Four years' service as a Commissioned Officer or Sergeant-Major in the Regulars, Embodied Militia, Fencibles, or Honourable Company's Service. His pay is 6s. a-day, besides 2s. for forage, and commences from his first day's duty.

SERGEANT-MAJOR.—Three years' service as a Non-commissioned Officer in the Regulars, Embodied Militia, or Fencibles. His pay is 3s. 2d. a-day, besides 2s. for forage, and commences from his first day's duty. The application for permanent pay of a Sergeant-Major must be made to the War-Office, along with a statement of his service, and a certificate of his attestation, in the Yeomanry.

OFFICIAL CORRESPONDENCE.

On the following points application must always be made through the Lieutenant of the County, who, if he approves of the application, forwards it to the Home Secretary; No. 7 excepted, which he forwards to the Ordnance.

1. Alteration in the title or establishment of the Corps.
2. Permanent pay for an Adjutant.

* See " Yeomanry Regulations."

3. Assembly for *Exercise*. This must always be accompanied by a statement of the intended date and place of assembly, the number of men, and the days of exercise (not exceeding fourteen, nor less than five). On the Home Secretary notifying his assent, the Lieutenant of the County signs this statement, and sends it to the War Office, from whence forms of estimate and account are then sent to the Commandant.

4. Assembly for *Permanent Duty*. This application goes through the same form, and is accompanied by the same kind of return as the last.

5. Officers' commissions.

6. Application for permanent pay for an Adjutant (accompanied by a statement of service).

7. Supply or exchange of arms or accoutrements (accompanied by a return of the effective strength of the Corps).

On receiving through the Lieutenant of the County the authority for *Assembly for Exercise*, the Commandant transmits through the same channel a return, showing the intended date and place of assembly, the number of men, and the number of days.

An Officer on receiving his commission must without delay transmit to the *Gazette* writer, through the Clerk of the Peace for the County, the particulars of rank and date, signed by the Lieutenant for the County. The fee upon a commission is 5s.

Ordnance Supplies.

Carbines (12 per Troop).
Pistols, swords, belts, and sword-knots.
Trumpets or bugles, with strings.

Practice ammunition is supplied in the proportion of six rounds of ball, sixteen of blank cartridge, and three flints to each man, due March 25; and four rounds of ball, eight of blank cartridge, and two flints, due Sept. 29, every year. It is supplied half-yearly by the Ordnance Office, on a requisition being made before the 1st of August for the next Spring allowance, and before the 1st of December for the next Autumn allowance. If the requisition is delayed beyond those periods, the allowance is forfeited.

No ammunition must be transferred from one Corps to another.

When out on *actual service* the necessary ammunition must be obtained by application to the General commanding the District.

Commandants may buy clothing and appointments from the public stores, by application to the Ordnance.

A return of arms and stores in possession of the Regiment, Corps, Squadron, or Troop, must be sent on the 1st of November, yearly, to the Ordnance Office.

All correspondence regarding pay and allowances takes place with the Secretary at War.

Forms are every year sent from the War Office to the Commandants, to be filled up with the number of days of exercise and duty performed. They must be filled up and returned within one month after receipt.

Contingent Allowance Annually.

For each effective Non-commissioned Officer, Trumpeter, Farrier, and Private, on the establishment (including Drill-Sergeant's pay), but not that of the Sergeant-Major, 1*l*. 10*s*.

Clothing and Appointments Allowance.

Same as above, only *including* the Sergeant-Major.

Both these allowances, as well as the Adjutant and Sergeant-Major's pay, are issued half-yearly in advance, on the Commandant's filling up and returning the form sent him for the purpose from the War Office.

Three years of the contingent and clothing allowances will be advanced to new Regiments, Corps, Squadron, or Troops, and also to augmentations of old ones, on applying for filling up and returning a War Office form. But in both cases the men must be certified as enrolled and equipped within two months after the "Acceptance of Service."

Commandants of Regiments, Corps, or Squadrons, will receive all contingent and clothing balances from the Captains of Troops, and will draw for all arrears. This only applies to those Regiments or Corps formed of incorporated Troops.

Assembly.

The distinction between assembly for exercise, and assembly for permanent duty, must be carefully observed. In neither case must the actual assembly take place till the Lieutenant of the County has sent the Commandant, in writing, the consent of the Home Secretary.

For Exercise.

Yeomanry are not allowed to assemble for exercise for less than five consecutive days, nor must the whole of the days within the year exceed fourteen. Therefore, if they assemble more than twice in the year, special leave must be obtained, at one of the periods, to meet for four days in lieu of five.

The pay when assembled for exercise is 2*s*. for each man, and 1*s*. 4*d*. for each horse daily.

In ten days after the assembly for exercise is over, the Commandant sends to the Secretary at War an account of sums paid, and sums received, from whom he then receives either a form of bill, to draw for whatever has fallen short, or an order to pay whatever may have remained over in his hands to the Bank of England.

For Permanent Duty,

May be substituted for assembly for exercise. It must not exceed six consecutive days, besides the days of marching to and from the assembly. Immediately on receiving, through the Lieutenant of the County, the leave to assemble, estimates for the pay and allowances are to be sent to the War Office, on the forms supplied from thence; and in return a bill at ten days' sight is sent to the Commanding Officer. Within ten days after the duty is over, the account must be sent to the War Office; on which the Secretary-at-War, if he approves the account, either remits the balance due, if the bill did not suffice, or directs the balance over to be paid to Government, if the bill more than covered the expenditure. Yeomanry thus assembled are under the General of the District's orders, if there is one, or if in a garrison, under those of the Commandant, and are to conform to the Regulations for the Regulars. The Articles of War are to be read to the Yeomanry on these occasions.

Yeomanry when assembled on permanent duty, or in aid of the Civil Power, are billeted the same as regular Cavalry.

Aid of Civil Power.

The order of the Lieutenancy or Magistracy calling out Yeomanry, in aid of the Civil Power should state the reasons for so doing, and number of Troops required on these occasions.* The same daily rate of pay is allowed as when on "Permanent Duty."

A copy of the order is to be instantly sent by the Commandant to the Secretary-at-War, with an application for forms of estimate and account. After the duty is performed, and the account made up, it is to be transmitted to the Secretary-at-War with this certificate:—

We, the undersigned Magistrates for the   of   do hereby certify that   Troops of the   Yeomanry Cavalry were assembled in aid of the Civil Power on the   of   , and that the said Troops were actually and necessarily required by the Civil Authorities to remain on duty from that date until the   of

Magistrates for the
of
residing at

Destruction or Loss of Arms.

"The cause of all deficiencies should be particularly noted when they happen; and when arms become unserviceable, they are not, on that account, to be destroyed, but reserved to be returned to the Ordnance, when a convenient opportunity shall arise." Subjoined is a statement of some of the amounts fixed by the Ordnance, to be charged to individuals, in case of the *wilful destruction* or *loss* by *neglect*, of any of the accoutrements furnished by the Government, the same being recoverable by a summary process at law.

	s.	d.
For each carbine	40	0
For each sword	13	0
For each sword-scabbard	5	0
For each waist-belt	2	6
For each sword-knot	1	0
For each pistol	26	4
For each carbine ball-cartridge	0	0¼
For each pistol ditto	0	0½
For each flint	0	0¼

* Of course, when the case is immediate, a mere informality of the order in these respects would be no excuse for delay.

Offences and Fines.

Extract from an Act of 43d Geo. III., cap. 121, *intituled,* "*An Act, &c., &c., for the further regulating of Yeomanry and Volunteer Corps,*" sect. 14.

" And be it further enacted, that where any person enrolled in any such corps shall have neglected or refused, on demand made for that purpose, to pay any fines or penalties incurred under any of the rules and regulations thereof, then and in such case it shall be lawful for any Justice of the Peace, on application made for that purpose, and proof thereof by any Commanding Officer, &c., &c., to cause the same, together with double the amount thereof, as a penalty or forfeiture, to be levied by distress and sale of the defaulter's goods and chattels, by warrant under his hand and seal, &c., &c. And the sums so levied shall go to the general stock of such Corps, to be applied to such purposes relating to such Corps as the Commanding Officer thereof may think fit."

SCHEDULE of the Pay and Allowances of the Yeomanry Cavalry while doing Permanent Duty, or Duty in Aid of the Civil Power.

PAY.		Rates of Consolidated Pay and Allowances per Diem.			CONTINGENT ALLOWANCES.
		£	s.	d.	
	Colonel	1	12	10	To defray the expense of Postage and Stationery, and other Charges incidental to making up the Accounts, viz.—
An Allowance of 2s. 8d. a Day per Troop is also made to the Colonel, or to the Officer having a Commission as Commission.	Lieutenant-Colonel	1	3	0	
	Major	0	19	0	£ s. d.
	Captain (including his Allowance of 2s. 2d. per Diem)	0	16	9	For a Corps consisting of { 1 Troop, per Diem ... 0 1 0 2 Troops .... 0 1 1 3 or 4 Troops .... 0 1 7 For a Regiment consisting of 5, 6, or 7 Troops ... 0 1 10 For ditto consisting of 8 Troops or upwards 0 2 1
During a Vacancy in the command of a Troop, 2s. 2d. a Day will be allowed for the repair of Arms and other expenses, to which the Allowance to the Captain is applicable.	Lieutenant	0	9	0	
	Cornet	0	8	0	*Divine Service.*—No allowance is granted unless a separate Service is absolutely requisite. In such cases the Clergyman is to apply to the War Office for remuneration.
These Rates only to be allowed in the whole, whether the Officers hold other commission or not.	Adjutant (including constant Pay and Allowances)	0	10	0	*Ferries.*—The actual expense incurred in passing Ferries, supported by the proper Vouchers, will be allowed.
	Surgeon	0	11	4	
	Assistant-Surgeon	0	8	6	*Medicines furnished to the Sick.*—The actual expense thereof will be allowed, provided the Charge made be previously approved by the Director-General of the Army Medical Department, St. James's-place, London.
	Quarter-Master	0	5	6	
In lieu of every other Charge whatsoever	Sergeant-Major (including constant Pay and Allowances)	0	7	0	
	Sergeant	0	7	0	*Compensation for Horses.*—The value of the Horse, not exceeding Thirty pounds, will be granted to the owner thereof, upon the application of the Commandant of the Corps, provided the Secretary-at-War shall be satisfied that the loss was entirely and inevitably occasioned by the act of duty in the performance of which the Horse was injured.
	Corporal	0	7	0	
	Trumpeter	0	7	0	
	Private	0	7	0	
Including the allowance for Farriery	Allowance in lieu of Forage for each effective Officer's horse, not exceeding the proportions for each rank *	0	1	6	The application is to be accompanied by a detailed statement of the circumstances of the case, certified by the Commandant, and by a Certificate of the value of the Horse.

* Proportion of Horses for each Rank :—
Field Officer .. not exceeding 4
Captain .. .. ,, 3
Subaltern .. .. ,, 2
Adjutant .. .. not exceeding 3
Surgeon .. .. ,, 2
Assistant-Surgeon .. ,, 1
Quarter-Master ,, 1

OFFICERS

IN THE

YEOMANRY CAVALRY AND MILITIA,

Aides-de-Camp to the Queen.

GEORGE, MARQUIS OF HUNTLY, K.T.,
Aberdeen Militia.

T. WOOD,
Royal East Middlesex Militia.

ERNEST, EARL OF MOUNT EDGCUMBE,
Duke of Cornwall's Rangers.

THOMAS, EARL DE GREY, K.G.,
York Hussars Yeomanry Cavalry.

EDWARD BAKER,
Royal Wilts Yeomanry Cavalry.

CHARLES, DUKE OF RICHMOND, K.G.,
Royal Sussex Militia (*ext.*).

WILLIAM, LORD DINORBEN,
Royal Anglesea Militia.

G. H., MARQUIS OF DONEGAL, G.C.H.,
Antrim Militia.

INDEX

TO

REGIMENTS OF YEOMANRY CAVALRY,

ARRANGED ACCORDING TO COUNTY OR LOCAL DESIGNATION.

	Page		Page
Andover (see Hants)	2	Lothian, Royal Mid	21
Ayr	2	Lymington	13
Berks (see Hungerford)	2	Melford, Long (see Suffolk)	35
Bucks, 2d Royal	2	Middlesex, Uxbridge	22
Cambridge	3	Montgomery	23
Castlemartin	28	Northampton	24
Chaddesden (see Derby)	6	Newcastle and Northumberland	24
Chester, Earl of Chester's	4	Northumberland and Newcastle	24
Cumberland (see Westmoreland)	37	Nottinghamshire, Southern	25
Denbigh	5	Nottingham, Sherwood Rangers	26
Derby, Repton, and Gresley	6	Oxford, "Queen's Own"	27
Derby and Chaddesden	6	Pembroke, Castlemartin	28
Derby and Radborne	6	Radborne	6
Devon, Royal 1st	7	Repton	6
Devon, North	8	Salopian, North	29
Dorset, Queen's Own	9	Salopian, South	30
Essex, West	10	Somerset, North	31
Gloucestershire Hussars	11	Somerset, West	32
Gresley (see Derby)	6	Sherwood Rangers	26
Hants, Andover	12	Stafford "Queen's Own Royal"	33-4
Hants, Lymington	13	Suffolk, 1st Royal	34
Hants, North	12	Suffolk Borderers	35
Herts, North	13	Suffolk, Long Melford	35
Herts, South	14	Taplow	2
Hungerford	2	Uxbridge (see Middlesex)	22
Kent, East	15	Warwickshire	36
Kent, West	16	Westmoreland and Cumberland	37
Kettering, Royal	24	Wiltshire Royal	38
Lanark, Upper Ward	17	Worcestershire "Queen's Own"	39-40
Lanark, Lower Ward	17	Whittlesea (see Cambridge)	3
Lancaster's, Duke of	18	Yorkshire Hussars	41
Lancashire Hussars	18	York, 1st West	42, 3
Leicester, "Prince Albert's Own"	19	York, 2d West	44
Lothian, East	20		

INDEX TO REGIMENTS OF MILITIA.

	Page		Page
Anglesea, Royal Light Infantry	99	Berks, Royal	50
Antrim, Queen's Own Rifles	116	Brecon, Royal	73
Armagh	112	Bucks, Royal, or King's Own	76, 7
Aberdeen	126	Berwick, Haddington, Linlithgow,	
Argyll and Bute	156	and Peebles	110
Ayr, The Prince Regent's Royal Regiment of	154	Cambridge	105
		Cardigan Royal Rifle Corps	101
Bedford	60	Carmarthen, Royal Fusiliers	66

INDEX TO REGIMENTS OF MILITIA.

Regiment	Page
Carnarvon, Royal Rifle Corps	95
Cheshire, Royal	49
Cornwall's, The Duke of, Rangers	80
Cornwall, Royal, and Devon Miners	157
Cumberland, Royal	52
Carlow	107
Cavan	138
Clare	131
Cork City	149
Cork, North, Riflemen	155
Cork, South	124
Denbigh, Royal Rifle Regiment	87
Derby	100
Devon, East	82
Devon, North	57
Devon, South	67
Dorset	88
Durham	47
Donegal	139
Down, Royal North	114
Down, Royal South	151
Dublin, Royal City, Queen's Own Royal Regiment	137
Dublin County	148
Dumfries, Roxburgh, and Selkirk	118
Essex, East	56
Essex, West	61
Edinburgh	164
Flint, Royal Rifle Corps	73
Fife	115
Forfar and Kincardine	143
Fermanagh	108
Glamorgan, Royal	85
Gloucester, Royal North	106
Gloucester, Royal South	65
Galway	128
Hants, North	56
Hants, South	84
Hants, Isle of Wight	100
Hereford	92
Hertford	72
Huntingdon	46
Inverness, Banff, Elgin, and Nairn	113
Kent, East	90
Kent, West	79
Kerry	146
King's, The, Own Light Infantry	134
Kildare	125
Kilkenny	165
King's County	135
Kirkcudbright and Wigton	109
Lancashire, 1st Royal	86
Lancashire, 2d Royal	152
Lancashire, 3d Royal	163
Leicester	68
Lincoln, Royal North	51
Lincoln, Royal South	71
London, Royal	145
Leitrim	150
Limerick City	141
Limerick County	161
Londonderry	132
Longford	122
Louth	147
Lanark, Royal	111
Merioneth, Royal	99
Middlesex, Royal East	102, 3
Middlesex, Royal West	97
Middlesex, Royal Westminster	95
Monmouth, Royal	167
Montgomery, Royal	96
Mayo, North	159
Mayo, South	119
Meath, Royal	158
Monaghan	160
Norfolk, East	81
Norfolk, West	81
Northampton	89
Northumberland, Light Infantry	69
Nottingham	98
Oxford	91
Pembroke, Royal	70
Perth, Royal	123
Queen's County	142
Queen's Own, The, Light Infantry	120
Radnor, Royal	90
Rutland	48
Roscommon	130
Renfrew	167
Ross, Caithness, Sutherland, and Cromarty	133
Shropshire	94
Somerset, 1st	58
Somerset, 2d	88
Stafford, The King's Own	103
Suffolk, East	75
Suffolk, West	53
Surrey, 1st Royal	62
Surrey, 2d Royal	54
Sussex, Royal	93
Sligo	162
Stirling, Dumbarton, Clackmannan, and Kinross	127
Tipperary	121
Tyrone	117
Warwick	78
Westmoreland, Royal	59
Wiltshire, Royal	74
Worcester	104
Waterford	166
Westmeath	153
Wexford	136
Wicklow	129
York, East	55
York, North	64
York, 1st West	48
York, 2d West	63
York, 3d West	45

YEOMANRY CAVALRY OF GREAT BRITAIN.

AYR.
Ayrshire Regiment of Yeomanry Cavalry.

Lieut.-Colonels.—Commt. James Fairlie, 17 Nov. 1848. D.L.—*Holmes House.*
Sir Charles Lamb, Bart., 17 Nov. 1848. D.L.—*Beauport, Surrey.*
Major.—Sir James Boswell, Bart., 17 Nov. 1848. D.L.—*Auchinleck.*

	Date of Apointment to Present Rank.	Remarks exhibiting Services of Officers, whether L.L., D.L., M.P., or J.P., Country Seats, &c.
CAPTAINS.		
George Jas. Campbell	26 May 42	D.L.—*Tuesbanks.*
Robert Hunter	26 May 42	D.L.—*Hemlerston.*
Marquis of Ailsa	26 May 42	D.L.—*Culyear Castle.* Served in the 60th
Patrick Boyle	31 Aug. 42	D.L.—*Hewalton.* [Rifles and 17th Lancers.
James Ogilvie Farlie	20 March 43	D.L.—*Cordham.* Served in the 2d Life Guards.
Thos. S. Cuninghame	18 Dec. 48	D.L.—*Caprington Castle.*
LIEUTENANTS.		
Sir J. R. Cathcart, Bt.	22 July 37	D.L.—*Carleton.* Served in the 2d Life Guards.
John Joseph Burnett	26 May 42	D.L.—*Gadgirth.*
R. Robertson Glasgow	25 May 42	*Montgrennan.* [Navy.
John Hamilton	26 May 42	D.L.—*Lundnern.* Served in the E.I. Comp.
Sir T. Montgomerie Cuninghame, Bart.	11 Nov. 42	*L. Skeldon.* Served in the Army.
Patrick Warner	11 June 44	J.P.—*Ardeer.*
J. H. R. Crawford	2 Oct. 45	*Crawfordland Castle.* Served in the Austrian [Cavalry.
W. Cochrane Patrick	26 May 46	*Ladgland.*
Geo. M. Cuninghame	17 Nov. 46	*Barbieston.* Royal Navy.
Robert Gairdner	28 Dec. 46	
A. Cuninghame	18 Dec. 48	*Thornton.*
One vacant.		
CORNETS.		
Hon. G. F. Boyle	23 Jan. 47	*Cainrae.*
Andrew Cathcart	12 March 47	*Carleton.* Served in the 11th Hussars.
Walter F. Hamilton	18 Oct. 47	*Cairnhill.* Served in the Army.
Geo. James Campbell	19 Oct. 47	*Treesbanks.*
Lord Fergus Kennedy	17 March 48	E.I. Comp. Service.
Lord Nigel Kennedy	27 Feb. 49	
ADJUTANT.		
Augustus B. Calvert	10 July 44	Late 2d Dragoons.
SURGEON.		
William Whiteside	16 June 29	M.D. J.P.
ASSIST.-SURGEON.		
James L. Crawford	8 Oct. 49	M.D.
CHAPLAIN.		
Rev. J. C. Jamieson	10 July 44	

SERVICES OF THE REGIMENT.—The Regiment served at Paisley, in 1830, in aid of the Civil Power, and has done so repeatedly, for the last 56 years within the county. Volunteered to extend their services to any part of the Kingdom in 1848. No other military force kept in the county, which, for iron and coal, may be considered the Staffordshire of Scotland; having, as a matter of course, in the mining districts, a large turbulent population.

REGIMENTAL APPOINTMENTS.—Blue; facings, scarlet; lace, gold; Light Dragoon uniform; saddlery, old-pattern Heavy Dragoon.

EFFECTIVE STRENGTH.—Officers, 31; non-commissioned officers and privates, 475. Total, 506.

BERKS.—*Hungerford Corps of Yeomanry Cavalry.*

Captain-Commandant.—George Willes, 7 May 1844.
Lieutenant.—Henry Coe Coape, 29 Oct. 1844.
Second Lieutenant.—Alexander Hugh Popham, 10 May 1847.
Cornet.—Edward Morris, 6 May 1847.

BUCKINGHAMSHIRE.
2d *Royal Bucks Regiment of Yeomanry Cavalry.*

Colonel-Commandant.
His Grace the Duke of Buckingham and Chandos, 23 Sept. 1839. K. G., P. C. *Wotton House, Bucks; Avington House, Winchester.*
Lieut.-Colonel.
Thomas Tyringham Bernard, 9 Aug. 1843. J.P.—*Winchendon House, Bucks.*
Major.—George Lucas, 9 Aug. 1843.

	Date of Appointment to Present Rank.	Remarks exhibiting Services of Officers, whether L.L., D.L., M.P., or J.P.—Country Seats, &c.
CAPTAINS.		
Thos. Knox Holmes.	23 Sept. 39	
John Clode	16 Oct. 43	
Abraham G. Robarts	17 Feb. 44	
Wm. Fred. Farrar...	28 Dec. 44	
Marquis of Chandos.	27 Sept. 45	J.P., M.P.—*Wotton House, Bucks.*
Thos. Peers Williams	18 April 48	M.P.—*Temple House, Great Marlow.*
Henry Beauclerk	16 May 48	
Henry Smith	16 May 48	
LIEUTENANTS.		
Acton Tindal	3 Aug. 36	
Joseph Bailey	25 July 43	
John Garrard	18 May 44	
Frederick Bartlett...	20 Jan. 45	
Robert C. Walford...	27 Sept. 45	
Robt. Bateson Harvey	27 April 47	
Wm. Henry Bonsey.	16 May 48	
CORNETS.		
William Levi	22 Aug. 42	
Henry Sleath Trower	19 Nov. 48	
Wm. Fred. Northey.	27 April 46	
William Way Stone.	27 April 47	
H. Fleetwood Nash...	10 June 47	
ADJUTANT.		
Thomas Wells	15 Sept. 48	Served in the 4th Light Dragoons 11 years.
SURGEON.		
John Denne	26 Sept. 40	

SERVICES OF THE REGIMENT.—Under orders for Manchester, in aid of Civil Power, July, 1819. In London, Coronation of Geo. IV., from 16 to 22 July, 1821. At Otmoor Riots, from 6 to 10 September, 1830. At Hounslow Barracks, Great Marlow, High Wycombe, and Brill, from 22 November to 7 December, 1830, in aid of Civil power. In quarters in the neighbourhood of Aylesbury, during "Special Commission" for trial of agricultural labourers, from 9 to 15 January, 1831. At Chesham, from 25 to 27 May, 1835, to assist in carrying into effect the New Poor-law. In 1848, relieved the Life Guards in garrison at Windsor, and performed the Cavalry duties at that station, during the absence of the former, at the anticipated Chartist disturbances on the 10 April, in London. His Grace the Duke of Buckingham commanded on the occasion.

REGIMENTAL APPOINTMENTS.—Hussar; lace, silver. The officers', as well as the men's uniform, is made to correspond with the Hussar Regiments of the Regular Service, except a chaco being worn instead of a busby. Uniform.—Green cloth, black velvet facings; blue cloth overalls, and scarlet stripe.

EFFECTIVE STRENGTH.—365. The Regiment consists of 8 Troops, one of which is an Artillery Troop, with uniform exactly as the Horse Artillery.

Bucks.—*Taplow Troop of Yeomanry Cavalry.*

Captain-Commandant.

Earl of Orkney, 29 Dec. 1830. D.L.—*Taplow Court, Bucks. Glen App, Ayrshire.*

Lieutenant.—Edward Thomas Bradford, 15 April 1836.

Cornet.—John Parton, 24 May 1844.

Cambridge.

Whittlesey and Cambridgeshire Troop of Yeomanry Cavalry.

Captain-Commandant.

Charles Smith, 12 April 1831. Lieutenant in the Rifle Brigade, A.J.P. for the Isle of Ely, *Whittlesey.*

Lieutenant.—Daniel Boon Ground, 24 Sept. 1849.—*Whittlesey.*

Cornet.—Edward Zoomes, 24 Sept. 1849.—*Whittlesey.*

Quartermaster.—John Ground (Acting Quartermaster).

SERVICES OF THE REGIMENT.—This Troop formed the Military Escort in the autumn of 1835, on the occasion of the Duchess of Kent and Her Most Gracious Majesty (then the Princess Victoria), passing through Peterborough on their way from the Marquis of Exeter's into Norfolk, and received the thanks of the Committee who conducted the procession. The Troop also had the honour of escorting Her Majesty in October, 1843, on her visit to Cambridge and the Earl of Hardwicke's, on which occasion the Troop received an official letter from the Earl of Hardwicke (the Lord-Lieutenant of the County), by Her Majesty's command, expressing her satisfaction at the manner in which the services were performed. And also by special command from the Horse Guards, on the occasion of Her Majesty visiting Cambridge, in August, 1847, on the Installation of his Royal Highness Prince Albert, on which occasion the Lord-Lieutenant was again desired to express Her Majesty's approbation of the Troop; and Col. M'Dowal, Silver-Stick in Waiting, expressed himself in very complimentary terms as to the discipline and conduct of the Troop. The Captain has in his possession letters from Dr. Scrimshaw, of Peterborough, and the Mayors of Cambridge for the years 1843 and 1847, expressive of thanks for the services of the Troop.

REGIMENTAL APPOINTMENTS.—Heavy Dragoons: Officers' uniform, blue, scarlet facings, gold lace braiding. Privates' uniform blue, scarlet facings, braiding yellow; helmet. *Horse Appointments.*—Bridles, slip and chain, black; saddle and holsters brown; cover to holsters of black patent leather.

EFFECTIVE STRENGTH.—1 Captain, 1 Lieutenant, 1 Cornet, 1 Quartermaster Sergeants, 3 Corporals, 1 Trumpeter, and 60 Privates.

CHESTER.—*Earl of Chester's Regiment of Yeomanry Cavalry.*

Lieut.-Colonel-Commandant.
The Right Hon. Lord De Tabley, 1 Jan. 1836. J.P.—*Tabley House.*
Lieut.-Colonel.
Sir P. Egerton, Bart., 30 Nov. 1847. M.P., J.P., D.L.—*Oulton Park.*
Major.—H. Brooke, 12 Nov. 1831. D.L.—*The Grange.*

	Date of Appointment to Present Rank.	Remarks exhibiting Services of Officers, whether L.L., D.L., M.P., or J.P.—Country Seats, &c.
CAPTAINS.		
Egerton, W. Tatton	21 Feb. 27	M.P., J.P., D.L.
Antrobus, G. C.	25 July 27	J.P., D.L.—*Eaton Hall.*
Worthington, J. W.	24 Jan. 32	*Sharston Hall.*
Townshend, L. P. ...	23 Jan. 36	J.P.—*Wincham Hall.* Served as Subaltern in the 79th Highlanders, and as Captain and Major in the 49th Regiment.
Tatton, T. W.	9 July 36	J.P.—*Withenshaw Hall.*
Leycester, R. G.	25 Oct. 41	J.P., D.L.—*Toft Hall.*
Earl of Stamford and Warrington.	25 July 45	*Dunham Massey and Enville Hall.*
Earl Grosvenor	30 Nov. 47	M.P.
Legh, C. R. B.	20 March 48	J.P., D.L.—*Adlington Hall.*
Lyon, T.	4 Aug. 48	Served in 17th Lancers.
LIEUTENANTS.		
Palin, Wm.	16 May 29	
Richmond, Leigh ...	19 Sept. 40	
Marsland, Edward ...	27 March 41	J.P.
Nicholson, James ...	24 June 42	
Worthington, Wm.	25 July 45	
Antrobus, H. Lindsay	2 March 47	
Fenton, James	20 March 48	
Barker, Peter	22 March 48	
CORNETS.		
Pownall, William ...	22 Sept. 35	
Potts, Henry	29 June 39	*Grenrason.*
Gregg, E. H.	1 March 47	
Nicholls, W. D.	20 March 48	
Antrobus	5 Feb. 49	
Leigh	30 Nov. 49	*Belmont.*
ADJUTANT.		
Capt. H. Hill	11 July 36	Served in the Peninsula with the 11th Light Dragoons; was present in the action of El Bodon, 25th Sept., 1811; the investment of Badajoz, Battle of Salamanca, and the affair of cavalry on the following day; the investment of Burgos, as well as with the Advance and Rear-Guard to and from that place; and in the several affairs that occurred on that occasion. Served in the Campaign of 1815 with the 23d Light Dragoons, including the Battle of Quatre Bras, the affair of cavalry with the Rear-Guard on the 17th of June, the action of Waterloo, and on the advance to and capture of Paris.
SURGEON. Broadbent, Richard	21 April 32	
ASSISTANT-SURGEON. Deane, R. T.	21 April 32	

SERVICES OF THE REGIMENT.—18 May 1812.—1817, 13 March, 1 April (Manchester); 1818, July 14 (Stockport); 1819, Feb. 15 (Stockport); 1819, Aug. 16 (Manchester); Aug. 20 (Macclesfield); Dec. (Manchester); 1824, April 17—1826, April 28 (Manchester); 1830, Dec. (Hyde); 1837, July 26 (Stretford); 1839, July 22 (Macclesfield); 13 Aug. (Hyde); 18 Aug. (Chester and Macclesfield); 1841, July (Congleton); 1842, July 15 (Newcastle); 22 July (Congleton); 1842, Aug. 10 (Stockport, Macclesfield, Congleton, &c.); 1848, April 10 (Macclesfield).

REGIMENTAL APPOINTMENTS.—Light Dragoons, 1 Troop Hussars. *Officers' Uniform.*—Lace, silver. Full dress: blue Light Dragoon jacket, scarlet facings, silver lace epaulettes, gold sash, blue trowsers with oak-leaf silver lace, brass spurs; on chacoe and sabretash, as the Regimental Badge, the Earl of Chester's crest and coronet; gold line, black feather plume, silver pouch and sword-belts. *Field-Dress.*—Forage-cap, blue frock coat and scales, Oxford grey trowsers with red stripe, white patent leather pouch-belt, black sword-belt and sabretash. *Men's Uniform.*—Blue Light Dragoon jacket and scarlet facings, white lace (non-commissioned officers' silver lace), plated scales, white patent leather pouch-belt, Crimson and yellow sash, Oxford mixture trowsers with red stripe, chacoes with Regimental Badge. *Horse Appointments.—Officers'.*—Black Hussar bridle, breastplate, and crupper; Hussar saddle, blue shabraque, black sheep-skin with scarlet edge. *Men's.*—Black double-bitted bridle, old Light Dragoon pattern; ditto head collar and rein; last improved Heavy Dragoon pattern saddle; breastplate and crupper black; black sheep-skin with scarlet edge.

EFFECTIVE STRENGTH.—10 Quartermasters, 30 Sergeants, 30 Corporals, 10 Trumpeters, 6 Farriers, 491 Privates, 577 Horses. Total officers and men, 577.

DENBIGH.—*Denbighshire Regiment of Yeomanry Cavalry.*

Major-Commandant.

Sir William Lloyd, Knt., 1st March 1838, *Brynestyn, Wrexham:* Served in the East Indies, in the E. I. Co.'s Army, from 1800 to 1823. Commanded the Marines on board the *Bombay* frigate on a cruise, and at the storming and capture of Muckee, on the 26th, 27th, 28th, and 29th July 1804. Defeated a body of Pindarries with a small detachment of Cavalry 15th December 1810. Commanded the Residents' Escort at the battle of Sectubuldee, 26th and 27th November 1817. Wounded four times; twice severely; matchlock ball through the right shoulder, and one through the body; battle of Nagpoor, 16th December, and subsequent operations against the city of Nagpoor till its evacuation, 30th December 1817. Cadet of Infantry, 1799; Ensign, 6th November 1800; Lieutenant, 16th November 1802; Captain-Lieut., 3rd December 1813; Captain, 16th December 1814; Major, 7th November 1824. Magistrate of the county of Denbigh, Knt. Bach., creat. 1838.

	Date of Appointment to Present Rank.		Remarks exhibiting Services of Officers, whether L.L., D.L., M.P., or J.P.—Country Seats, &c.
CAPTAINS.			
Hugh Jones............	18 April	44	*Woodlands, Ruthin.*
Thomas Edgeworth..	1 May	47	*Wrexham.*
John Edwd. Madocks	1 Aug.	48	*Glennywern, Denbigh.* Served 7 months in the 18th Lt. Infantry, appointed August, 1837; 4 years in the 9th or Queen's Royal Lancers; and 6 years in the 13th Light Dragoons. Retired as a Captain in 1847. Magistrate and Deputy Lieutenant of the county of Denbigh.
LIEUTENANTS.			
John Roberts	18 May	43	*New Hall, Raubon.*
Thomas Humphries..	1 May	47	*Berse, Wrexham.*
Robert Lloyd	1 Aug.	48	*Ruthin.* Mayor of Ruthin.
CORNETS.			
William Rowland	18 April	44	*Wrexham.*
Richard Johnson	1 May	47	*Wrexham.*
SURGEON.			
Rd. L. Williams, M.D.	1 Feb.	24	*Denbigh.* Mayor of Denbigh, and a Magistrate for the county of Denbigh.

EFFECTIVE STRENGTH.—A Troop, 41 Privates, 1 Trumpeter, 1 Corporal, 1 Sergeant. B Troop, 41 Privates, 1 Trumpeter, 1 Corporal, 1 Sergeant. C Troop, 40 Privates, 1 Trumpeter, 1 Corporal, 1 Sergeant.

REGIMENTAL BADGES.—Plume, and Ich Dien.

REGIMENTAL APPOINTMENTS—Blue; colour of facing, scarlet; silver lace.

REGIMENTAL SERVICES.—Called out in aid of the Civil Power 27th December, 1831.

Head Quarters at Wrexham. First raised in the year 1794.

DERBY.—*Derby and Chaddesden Troop of Yeomanry Cavalry.*

Captain-Commandant.
Nathaniel Story, 12th April 1841; late of the 3rd Dragoon Guards.

Lieutenant.
Francis Sacheverel Wilmot, 12th June 1841.

Cornet.
John Gilbert Compton, 22nd Sept. 1842.

Quartermaster.
Samuel Weatherhead, 1st Nov. 1849.

REGIMENTAL APPOINTMENTS.—Hussar's blue jackets, bound with white lace; blue shabraques, bound with ditto; black wool skins.

EFFECTIVE STRENGTH.—2 Sergeants, 2 Corporals, 1 Trumpeter, 48 Privates.

DERBY.

Radborne Troop of Yeomanry Cavalry.

Captain-Commandant.
E. S. Chandos-Pole, 7th August 1813; late Lieut. and Captain 1st Foot Guards; J. P., D. L.; served at Walcheren, Spain and Portugal, &c.—*Radborne, Derbyshire.*

Lieutenant.
Francis Hurt, 12th Oct. 1838.

SERVICES OF THE CORPS.—Aid of the Civil Power in 1810, 16, 30, 31, 42, 43; Queen's Escort, &c.

REGIMENTAL APPOINTMENTS.—Light Dragoons: red, and facings with green.—Horse appointments: Hunting saddle, plain leather valisse, cloak rolled over holsters, plain Lt. Dragoon bridle.

ACCEPTED AND EFFECTIVE STRENGTH.—90 Non-Coms and Men; 4 Officers.

DERBY.

Repton and Gresley Corps of Yeomanry Cavalry.

Captain-Commandant.
Charles Robert Colisle, J.P., D.L., M.P., 25th July 1843.   *Lullington, Derbyshire.*

Lieutenants.
George Vandeleur, 25th July 1843; served in the 10th Hussars.
Mylles Cave Browne Cave, 25th Sept. 1843: served in the 11th Hussars.

REGIMENTAL APPOINTMENTS.—Light Dragoons.

EFFECTIVE STRENGTH.—Privates, 70; Sergeants, 3; Corporals, 3; Trumpeter, 1; Quartermaster, 1.

DEVON.—*Royal First Devon Regiment of Yeomanry Cavalry.*

Lieut.-Colonel Commandant.—J. W. Buller, 16 August 1842.

Lieut.-Colonel.—Baldwin Fulford, 16 August 1842.

Major.—Sir J. T. B. Duckworth, Bart., 24 July 1844.

	Date of Appointment to Present Rank.	Remarks exhibiting Services of Officers, whether L.L., D.L., M.P., or J.P.—Country Seats, &c.
CAPTAINS.		
John Guppy	29 Jan. 24	
Thomas Snow	10 Nov. 29	
John Barne	5 Feb. 31	
Lord Courtenay	31 Dec. 35	
Thomas Dyke Acland	17 Aug. 42	
Francis Baring Short	1 Sept. 42	
Edw. Andrew Sanders	29 July 44	
John Garratt	24 Dec. 45	
John N. Stevenson	25 Oct. 48	
LIEUTENANTS.		
William R. Bishop	27 Aug. 32	
John Henry Ley	1 Sept. 42	
Thomas M. Snow	19 June 43	
Edward Trood	24 Dec. 45	
William Barnes	24 Dec. 45	
John M. Wolcott	2 April 46	
Thomas Daniel	12 April 48	
S. H. Northcote	25 Oct. 48	
John Barnes Smith	2 Dec. 48	
CORNETS.		
Trehawke Kekewich	5 Oct. 42	
H. B. Swete	10 April 45	
J. B. Y. Buller	10 April 45	
Edmund Ethelston	2 April 46	
A. K. E. Hamilton	2 April 46	
W. M. Snow	20 March 48	
Montague Bere	12 April 48	
William Watts	2 Dec. 48	
ADJUTANT.		
Captain T. Rosser	22 June 41	
SURGEON.		
John Spettigue	11 Sept. 30	
VETERINARY SURGEON.		
Josias James Rogers	17 Nov. 40	

DEVON.—*North Devon Regiment of Yeomanry Cavalry.*

Colonel.—Lord Clinton, 10 Sept. 1834. D.L.—*Heanton Satchville.*

Lieut.-Colonel.
Sir Trevor Wheler, Bart., 2 Sept. 1842. P. W., J.P.—*Cross House.* Major in the army; served in the 16th Lancers, and 5th Dragoon Guards.

Major.—Viscount Ebrington, 2 Sept. 1842. M.P., D.L.—*Castle Hill.*

	Date of Appointment to Present Rank.		Remarks exhibiting Services of Officers, whether L.L., D.L., M.P., or J.P.—Country Seats, &c.
CAPTAINS.			
William Tardrew	14 Jan.	18	D.L., J.P.—*Annery House.*
John Nott	18 July	31	J.P.—*Bydown.*
L. Risden Heysett	14 April	32	*Bovacott.*
James Peard Ley	20 June	36	*Durrant.*
Charles C. Drake	27 May	37	*Springfield.*
George S. Buck	17 Sept.	44	D.L., J.P.—*Hartland Abbey.* Served in the [Royal Horse Guards Blue.
William Binford	25 Aug.	46	
George Braginton	14 Aug.	47	*Rows Moor.*
LIEUTENANTS.			
Wm. David Hornden	17 Sept.	44	*Callington.*
Alfred Robert Hole	17 Sept.	44	*Beam.* Cornet in the army; served in the
John Colwill Roe	25 Aug.	46	*Woolhanger.* [4th and 18th Light Dragoons.
Henry Ley	16 April	47	*Ley House.*
Adderly Wren	14 Aug.	47	*Len Wood.*
Wm. Anthony Deane	14 Aug.	47	*Webbery.*
C. E. Palmer	14 Aug.	47	[Light Dragoons.
H. St. George Pirault	25 Oct.	48	Lieutenant in the army; served in the 4th
CORNETS.			
Thomas Brydges	14 Aug.	47	*Marwood Hill.*
John C. M. Stevens	18 Feb.	48	*Winscott.*
Henry Thos. Cusack	18 Feb.	48	
Dotton Maycock	18 Feb.	48	Lieutenant in the army; served in the 16th [Lancers, and 6th Enniskillen Dragoons.
W. M. Marshall	18 Feb.	48	*Blagdon.*
John Johnson			*Wernworthy.*
ADJUTANT.			
James N. Macartney	9 Oct.	47	Capt. in the army; served in the 9th Lancers.
SURGEON.			
Edward H. Caddy	4 Nov.	24	
ASSIST.-SURGEON.			
Charles C. Turner		49	
CHAPLAIN.			
Rev. Peter Glubb	13 March 03		*Parsonage, Little Torrington.*

SERVICES OF THE REGIMENT.—Employed at different times in aid of the Civil Power, and in the protection of wrecks.

REGIMENTAL APPOINTMENTS.—Light Dragoons; silver; blue, facings scarlet, light Dragoon jacket; scarlet chacoe, black plume, French pattern: horse appointments the same as 14th Light Dragoons, with the exception of a pannel to the saddle instead of a blanket, and no sheepskin.

EFFECTIVE STRENGTH.—16 Sergeants, 16 Corporals, 8 Trumpeters, 320 rank and file. Band consists of 16.

DORSET.—"Queen's Own Regiment" of Dorset Yeomanry Cavalry.

Colonel-Commandant.
The Earl of Ilchester, 12 Feb. 1846. J.P., D.L.—*Melbury House.*

Lieut.-Colonel.
The Right Hon. Lord Rivers, 12 Feb. 1846. J.P., D.L.—*Rushmore Lodge.*

Major.
George Thomson Jacob, 6 June 1840. J.P., D.L.—*Shillingston Cottage.*

	Date of Appointment to Present Rank.	Remarks exhibiting Services of Officers, whether L.L., D.L., M.P., or J.P.—Country Seats, &c.
CAPTAINS.		
Henry Frampton	27 Jan. 31	J.P., D.L.—*Oaker's Wood, Dorchester.*
John Goodden	30 Jan. 31	J.P., D.L.—*Compton House, Sherborne.*
Harry Farr Yeatman	15 Aug. 40	J.P., D.L.—*Manston House, Blandford.*
Ed. St. Vincent Digby	14 Nov. 48	J.P., D.L.—*Mintau House, Dorchester.*
Hen. Jas. Farquharson	9 Nov. 49	*Langton House, Blandford.*
LIEUTENANTS.		
John Hussey	25 Jan. 31	J.P.—*Nash Court, Marnhall.*
John Floyer	27 Jan. 31	J.P., D.L., M.P.—*Stafford, Dorchester.*
Sir Wm. Cole Medlycott, Bart.	30 Jan. 31	J.P., D.L.—*Ven Sherborne.*
Henry Ker Seymer	28 Aug. 37	J.P., D.L., M.P.—*Hanford House, Blandford.*
Herbert Williams	21 Sept. 38	J.P.—*Shutsford, Dorchester.*
Thomas King	22 Sept. 38	*Olvediston, Shaftsbury.*
John Edw. Bradshaw	8 May 45	*Marn Hall.*
William Hooks	22 Aug. 46	*Sherborne.*
John Claval Mansel	22 April 47	J.P., D.L.—*Smedmore House.*
John Edward Bridge	9 Nov. 49	*Peddle Trenthide.*
CORNETS.		
Geo. Granville Glyn	7 Oct. 45	*Iwveme Minster.*
George Churchill	3 May 47	J.P.—*Buckland, Weymouth.*
Geo. Pleddle Mansel	4 Nov. 48	*Addens, Blandford.*
ADJUTANT.		
Joseph Firth	5 April 31	ℬ.—*Dorchester.*
SURGEON.		
Jas. Lush Buckland	13 April 41	*Shaftsbury.*
ASSIST.-SURGEON.		
William Highmore	13 April 41	*Sherborne.*

SERVICES OF THE REGIMENT.—In aid of Civil Power in 1831.

REGIMENTAL APPOINTMENTS.—Light Dragoons; lace, silver; cloth, scarlet.

EFFECTIVE STRENGTH.—330.

FORMER SERVICES OF THE OFFICERS.—1. Major Jacob joined the Grenadier Guards in 1814; Lieutenant 1815; exchanged to the 4th Dragoon Guards 1818; went on half-pay 3d Dragoon Guards 1819; was present at the battle of Quatre Bras; the retreat of the 17th June, 1818; led the attacking party at the storming of Peronne; and retired from the Service in 1838.—2. Captain Digby joined the 65th in 1825, the 9th Lancers as Lieut. in 1828, and left the Army in 1831.—3. Lieut. Bradshaw served in the 12th Lancers, and left them with the rank of Lieut.—4. Cornet Mansel joined the 53d as Ensign in 1836; Lieut. in 1840; Captain in 1843; exchanged into 60th Rifles, 1846; sold out in 1848.—5. Adjutant Firth served in the Blues twenty years: was with the Regiment on the Peninsula, and left them in 1831 on half-pay Quartermaster.

Essex.—*West Essex Corps of Yeomanry Cavalry.*

Captain-Commandant.

George Palmer, 8 Feb. 1831. J.P.—*Nazing Park.* Formerly in the London and Westminster Light Horse Volunteers, which Corps he entered in Jan. 1819.

	Date of Appointment to Present Rank.	Remarks, exhibiting Services of Officers, whether L.L., D.L., M.P., or J.P.—Country Seats, &c.
LIEUTENANTS.		
Joseph Jessop.........	1 Feb. 41	*Waltham Abbey.*
S. B. Edenborough...	26 July 43	*Waltham Cross.*
CORNET.		
John Round	26 July 43	J.P.—*Chelmsford.*
QUARTERMASTERS.		
R. Bullock Andrews .		*Epping.*
C. Rankin Vickerman		*Blackmore.*
SURGEON.		
James Stuart Dobson		*Harlow.*
ASSIST.-SURGEON.		
A. Chas. Merriman...		*Epping.*

SERVICES OF THE CORPS.—The West Essex Corps of Yeomanry Cavalry was raised by Captain Palmer in 1830, at the earnest request of the Right Hon. Lord Melbourne, Secretary of State for the Home Department, during the time of the agricultural riots. On the 26th Oct., 1832, kept the ground in Hatfield Park upon the occasion of His Grace the Duke of Wellington reviewing the whole of the Hertfordshire Yeomanry Cavalry, for whom they formed a Guard of Honour and escort. On the night of the 1st April, 1833, called out in consequence of an incendiary fire in the immediate neighbourhood of the Government powder-mills at Waltham Abbey. Reviewed by General Grosvenor in Nov., 1834. On 29th Oct., 1836, brigaded in Parnder Park with the Marquis of Salisbury's Hertfordshire Yeomanry Cavalry; the Brigade commanded by the Hon. Wm. Cooper, of the Royal Horse-Guards. Captain Palmer in 1838 volunteered the gratuitous services of the Corps to Her Majesty, which were accepted. In July, 1842, the West Essex Corps formed a Guard of Honour for H.R.H. Prince Albert. In July, 1843, the Corps escorted his Majesty the King of the Belgians from Lee-bridge to Wanstead and back. In July, 1844, escorted H.R.H. Prince Albert. On the 5th and 7th July, 1847, the Corps formed Guards of Honour, and had mounted escorts ready at the Tottenham and Hockerell stations of the Eastern Counties Railway for Her Majesty and H.R.H. Prince Albert. On the 12th of June, 1848, a Detachment was called out, under the command of Captain Palmer, in aid of the Civil Power at Waltham Abbey, in conjunction with a strong Detachment of the Royal Artillery, for the defence of the Government powder-mills at Waltham Abbey, and the small-arm manufactory at Enfield-loch, against the threatened Chartist insurrection. On the 18th June, 1849, the Corps brigaded with four squadrons of the South Herts Yeomanry Cavalry on Neying Marsh, near Broxbourne, and were reviewed by Major-General Fearon.

REGIMENTAL APPOINTMENTS.—*Uniform.*—Blue; lace, silver; red collar and cuffs; blue cloth breast, double row of buttons; sabretash, longsword. Men, white belts, armed with carbines; Light Dragoon chaco; red and white horse-hair plume; Oxford mixture overalls, broad red stripe; silver stripe for Court and evening dress; patent leather pouch belts, edged with red cord; white buckskin gloves; blue cloth shabraque and white sheepskin, red edging.

GLOUCESTERSHIRE.—*Gloucestershire Regiment of Yeomanry Cavalry.*

Lieut.-Colonel Commandant.
Duke of Beaufort, 21 April 1834. K.G., L.L.—*Hadminton House, and Troy House, Monmouth.*

Lieut.-Colonel.—Benjamin Chapman Browne, J.P., D.L., 14 May 1841.

Majors.
George William Blaithwaite, 26 March 1844.
Henry Wilmot Charleton, J.P., D.L. (Supy. without Pay), 19 Feb. 1847.

CAPTAINS.	Date of Appointment to Present Rank.	Remarks exhibiting Services of Officers, whether L.L., D.L., M.P., or J.P.—Country Seats, &c.
Sir Christ. Wm. Codrington, Bt.	1 Jan. 31	M.P., D.L.—*Doddington Park, Chippenham.*
Robert B. Hale	16 Dec. 36	J.P.
Walter Matthew Paul	10 March 41	D.L.
Hugh Vaughan	20 Jan. 43	J.P.
Rd. Castels Jenkins	23 April 47	
Thos. B. Lloyd Baker	21 March 48	J.P.
William Moore Adey	21 March 48	J.P.
LIEUTENANTS.		
J. Jasper Lee Bayley	15 Dec. 37	
Rbt. Stayner Holford	9 March 39	
Edward Hobson	10 March 41	
Sir Martin Hyde Crowley Boevey	22 April 45	J.P., D.L.
Charles William Jebb	22 Jan. 47	
Edw. Bloxsome, jun.	23 Nov. 47	
T. G. Parry	21 March 48	
J. L. Baldwyn	21 March 48	
CORNETS.		
William John Phelps	22 April 45	
W. O. Maclaine	12 April 47	
Viscount Canterbury	13 Aug. 47	J.P.
Henry Metcalfe Ames	13 Aug. 47	
C. Sydney Hawkins	21 March 48	J.P.
J. G. Colthorpe	17 May 48	
ADJUTANT.		
John Surman	23 April 34	
SURGEON.		
Henry Mills Grace	23 Jan. 43	J.P., M.D.
ASSIST.-SURGEON.		
J. C. Wickham	11 Feb. 45	M.D.
VETERINARY SURGEON.		
Samuel Hicks Withers	21 Jan. 43	

HANTS.—*North Hants Regiment of Yeomanry Cavalry.*

Lieut.-Colonel.
The Right Hon. Charles Shaw Lefevre, 19 Feb. 1831. M.P., D.L., J.P., and Speaker of the House of Commons.—*Heckfield Place.*

Major.
Sir Henry St. John Mildmay, Bart., 9 Oct. 1849. Late Capt. 2d Dragoon Guards. *Dogmersfield Park.*

	Date of Appointment to Present Rank.	Remarks exhibiting Services of Officers, whether L.L., D.L., M.P., or J.P.—Country Seats, &c.
CAPTAINS.		
Ed. St. John Mildmay	13 Dec. 30	J.P. Late Captain, 22d Light Dragoons.
Rt. Hn. Ld. Ashburton	19 Feb. 31	J.P.—*Grange Park.*
Melville Portal	27 Oct. 45	M.P., J.P.—*Freefolk Priors.*
John Willis Fleming	27 Oct. 45	D.L., J.P. Late Lieut. and Capt. Grenadier [Guards.—*Chilworth Manor House.*
LIEUTENANTS.		
Henry L. Hunter	15 Oct. 31	*Beech Hill.*
Francis Pigott	31 Dec. 38	M.P., J.P.
W. Theoph. Græme	8 Oct. 44	J.P.
T. Willis Fleming	Dec. 49	J.P.—*Stoneham Park.*
CORNETS.		
Wyndham Portal	18 June 42	
Thomas Baring	8 Oct. 44	
George Sclater	28 Dec. 47	
Henry Fleming	29 Aug. 49	
ADJUTANT.		
W. H. Toovey Hawley	8 Nov. 45	
SURGEON.		
Robert Southey Hill	2 Sept. 46	
REGIMENTAL SERGEANT-MAJOR.		
John Williams	22 Nov. 42	From 1st Royal Dragoons.

REGIMENTAL APPOINTMENTS.—Blue; lace, silver; Hussars, without pelisse.
HORSE APPOINTMENTS.—Officers, Hussars; men, Hussars, without shabraques.
EFFECTIVE STRENGTH.—Non-Commissioned Officers, Band, Rank and File, 198.

HANTS.—*Andover Troop of Yeomanry Cavalry.*

	Date of Appointment to Present Rank.	Remarks exhibiting Services of Officers, whether L.L., D.L., M.P., or J.P.—Country Seats, &c.
CAPTAIN.		
T. Assheton Smith	27 Dec. 30	
LIEUTENANT.		
Henry Thompson	27 Feb. 46	
CORNET.		
F. R. Loscombe	27 Feb. 46	

HANTS.—*Lymington Squadron of Yeomanry Cavalry.*

Commandant.
William Alexander Mackinnon, M.P., D.L., J.P., 22 August 1834.

From the year 1837 to the year 1844, the Lymington Squadron of Yeomanry was equipped and all the expenses paid by Mr. Mackinnon; all the other Squadrons of Yeomanry in the Forest and in South Hants were reduced except the Lymington Corps, which was allowed to remain on Mr. Mackinnon's engaging to pay all the expenses.

Lieutenants.
George St. Borbe, 18th September, 1837, *Lymington;* Alexander Mackinnon, Jun., J.P., 8 October 1839.

Cornet.—Frederick Augustus, Earl of Cavan, J.P., Oct. 1847.

Quartermaster.—Rd. Belbin.

SERVICES OF THE CORPS.—The Lymington Yeomanry was formed in 1831, in consequence of the lawless conduct of the labourers in the vicinity of the New Forest, who assembled to the amount of 2,000 men, and upwards, and levied contributions under threats of violence on the residences of several Noblemen and Gentlemen in the years 1830 and 1831, for which offences many were tried and capitally convicted. Since the formation of this Yeomanry no outrages whatever have occurred, and the lawless population about the New Forest has been kept in tolerable order and quiet.

REGIMENTAL APPOINTMENTS.—Light Dragoons.—Lace, gold; forest-green jacket, black velvet collar and cuffs, gold oak leaves and acorns on cuffs and collar, gilt buttons and epaulettes, gold lace girdle, patent leather cross-belt, &c.; trowsers same colour as jacket, with broad red cloth stripe; chacoe, with gilt ornaments and black plume.—The men's uniform the same, with brass epaulettes, web girdles, &c., &c.; patent leather sword-belts and sabretashes, &c.—Horse appointments: Bridle, collar and chain, breast-plate, saddle complete, and sheepskins; the officers', black, edged with red cloth; the men's, white.

EFFECTIVE STRENGTH.—1 Captain, 2 Lieutenants, 1 Cornet, 1 Quartermaster, 4 Sergeants, 3 Corporals, 1 Trumpeter, 39 Privates.

HERTS.—*Northern Herts Troop of Yeomanry Cavalry.*

Captain-Commandant.—Samuel H. Unwin Heathcote, 4 March 1831.

Lieutenant.—Wm. Curling, 3 May 1847.

Cornet.—George Devius Wade, 3 May 1847.

YEOMANRY CAVALRY.

HERTS.—*South Herts Regiment of Yeomanry Cavalry.*

Lieut.-Colonel.—James Walter, Earl Verulam, 4 June 1847. L.L.—*Gorhambury.*
Major.
James Brownlow William Gascoyne, Marquis of Salisbury, 4 June 1847. K.G., L.L.—*Hatfield House, Herts.*

	Date of Appointment to Present Rank.	Remarks exhibiting Services of Officers, whether L.L., D.L., M.P., or J.P.—Country Seats, &c.
CAPTAINS.		
Sir Henry Meux, Bart.	16 Aug. 47	M.P., J.P.—*Theobald's Park, Herts.*
Robert Wm. Gaussen	6 May 41	J.P.—*Brookman's, Herts.*
Geo. Smith Thornton	8 May 42	J.P.—*Amwellbury, Herts.*
T. Plumer Halsey...	6 Dec. 41	M.P., J.P.—*Great Berkhampstead, Herts.*
LIEUTENANTS.		
James Meyer	18 May 42	J.P.—*Enfield, Middlesex.*
Thomas Kemble	17 March 48	J.P.—*Leggatts, Herts.*
Frederick Gaussen	26 April 45	
John Branton	9 April 44	*Bush Hall, Hatfield, Herts.*
CORNETS.		
Sir Robt. Murray, Bt.	16 Aug. 47	J.P.—*Yardleybury, Herts.*
Edward Lewis	6 May 41	*Hertingfordbury, Herts.*
John Henry Pelly	26 April 45	J.P.—*Oak Hill, Southgate, Middlesex.*
John Kinder	9 April 44	J.P.—*St. Alban's.*
ADJUTANT.		
Wm. Hen. Sutton...	7 Feb. 31	J.P.—*Hertingfordbury, Herts.*
SURGEON.		
Wm. Lloyd Thomas	7 Feb. 31	*Hatfield, Herts.*
QUARTERMASTERS.		
John Christie		*Hoddesdon, Herts.*
Lord Robert Cecil...		*Hatfield House, Herts.*
William Parker		J.P.—*Ware Park.*
REGIMENTAL SERGEANT-MAJOR.		
Carter Fairbrother...	7 Nov. 29	Retired Quarterm. from Royal Horse Gds.

SERVICES OF THE REGIMENT.—On July 19, 1833, attended their late Majesties on their visit to Moor Park. On May 15, 1835, part of the Corps was called out in aid of Civil Power on a Poor-law Riot at Ampthill, Beds. On July 26, 1841, the Corps escorted Her Majesty from Great Berkhampstead to Dunstable, on her route to Woburn Abbey, and from Dunstable to Panshanger on July 29, and performed duty during Her Majesty's stay at Panshanger, and escorted Her Majesty to Rickmansworth on her return, July 31, 1841. On Dec. 7, 1843, provided escorts for Her Majesty, on her return from Birmingham, from the Watford Station to Rickmansworth. On Oct. 19, 1846, escorted Her Majesty from Rickmansworth to Cashiobury. On Oct. 22 escorted Her Majesty from Cashiobury to Hatfield House, and performed duty there during Her Majesty's sojourn, and escorted Her Majesty on her return from Hatfield to Windsor as far as Rickmansworth.

REGIMENTAL APPOINTMENTS.—The A B C Troops; Officers: Light Cavalry; green, scarlet facings; braided collar, with silver lace belts and sash, or girdle, and silver lace on trowsers, and chaco. Men: Light Cavalry; green, with scarlet facings; and black belts and chaco.

The D, or Cashio Troop, Heavy Dragoons—Officers' Uniform: scarlet, green facings; white leather belts; sash or girdle, silver lace; and silver lace trowsers; helmet; gauntlets. Men: scarlet, green facings; white belts; helmet; gauntlets.

EFFECTIVE STRENGTH.—4 Troops: 1 Lieut.-Colonel, 1 Major, 4 Captains, 4 Lieutenants, 4 Cornets, 1 Adjutant, 1 Surgeon, 4 Quartermasters, 1 Regimental Sergeant-Major, 8 Sergeants, 8 Corporals, 4 Trumpeters, 160 Privates. Total, 201.

KENT.—*East Kent Corps of Yeomanry Cavalry.*

Major-Commandant.

William Deeds, 20 Dec. 1830. J.P., D.L., M.P.—*Sandling Park.*

	Date of Appointment to Present Rank.	Remarks exhibiting Services of Officers, whether L.L., D.L., M.P., or J.P.—Country Seats, &c.
CAPTAINS.		
Sir Brook William Bridges, Bart.......	20 Dec. 30	J.P., D.L.—*Goodnestone Park.*
Right Hon. George Lord Harris	16 Sept. 37	J.P., D.L.—*Belmont.* Governor of Trinidad.
LIEUTENANTS.		
Wm. Creed Fairman .	3 March 48	J.P.—*Hales Place.* Captain by Brevet.
C. M. Lushington ...	11 Jan. 46	
Narberth H. D'Aeth..	12 Jan. 46	J.P.
Fred. M. Mulcaster...	26 May 48	Formerly Lieut. 12th Lancers.
CORNETS.		
Francis C. Hyde......	14 Jan. 46	*Syndale Park.*
Philip O. Papillon ...	26 May 48	
ADJUTANT.		
Capt. A. Heartley, Bt.	29 Dec. 30	Formerly Quartermaster Royal Horse Guards.
SURGEON.		
Amelius Sicard	27 May 42	

SERVICES OF THE REGIMENT.—Occasional aid of Civil Power.

REGIMENTAL APPOINTMENTS.—Light Dragoons; with silver lace.

Officers' Uniform.—Blue; double-breasted jacket, with light buff facings and turn-backs; beaded seams; silver epaulettes; crimson and gold sash; silver-embroidered belts; pouch and sabretash, embroidered with "White Horse, and Motto;" chaco, and dark green willow plume; trowsers, Oxford mixture, with two stripes of silver lace on each side.

Undress Appointments.—Shoulder scales; black belts, pouch, and sabretash; silver-mounted chaco, and horse-hair plume.

Light Dragoon.—Shell jacket and surtout; forage cap, silver band, and peak; trowsers, with buff cloth stripes, two on each side; blue cloth cloak.

Men's Clothing.—Blue; jacket, double-breasted, as above; sash, worsted, same colour as the officers; shoulder scales; white belts; Oxford mixture trowsers, with two buff stripes on each side; chaco, and horse-hair plume; stable jacket; forage cap; blue cloth cloak.

Officers' Horses.—Light Dragoon appointments, with black sheepskin shabraque, edged with buff; no furniture or housings.

Troop Horses.—Light Dragoon appointments, without horse furniture or housings.

EFFECTIVE STRENGTH.—2 Double Troops, forming 2 squadrons in the field; 2 Troop Quartermasters; 16 Non-commissioned Officers; 2 Trumpeters; 2 Farriers; 108 Privates.

Designation.—East Kent Yeomanry Cavalry.

KENT.—*West Kent Regiment of Yeomanry Cavalry.*

Lieut.-Colonel.
John Robert Viscount Sydney, 13 Dec. 1848. J.P., D.L.
Frognal, Foot's Cray, Kent.

Major.
James Chapman, 13 Dec. 1848. J.P.—*Paul's Cray Hill, Kent.*

CAPTAINS.	Date of Appointment to Present Rank.		Remarks exhibiting Services of Officers, whether L.L., D.L., M.P., or J.P.—Country Seats, &c.
John W. Shatford ...	22 July	48	J.P.—*St. Vincent's, Maidstone.*
Earl of Darnly	24 July	48	J.P.—*Cobham Hall, Rochester.*
Hon. C. S. Hardinge	25 July	48	J.P.—*South Park, Tunbridge.*
Wm. Joseph Berens .	13 Dec.	48	J.P.—*The Priory, Orpington, Kent.* Late [Capt. in the Carabineers.
LIEUTENANTS.			
Richard B. Berens ...	20 Dec.	30	*Nevington, Foot's Cray, Kent.*
William Gladdish ...	24 July	48	J.P.—*Cliff Cottage, Gravesend, Kent.*
Thomas H. Brenchley	24 July	48	*Wombwell Hall, Gravesend, Kent.*
Cuthbert J. Fisher...	25 July	48	J.P.—*Great Culverden, Tunbridge Wells.*
Viscount Neville......	22 May	49	J.P.—*Birling Manor, Kent.* Late 2d Life [Guards.
CORNETS.			
Evelyn Boscawen ...	20 July	48	J.P.—*Mereworth Castle, Kent.*
Henry Bowden	22 July	48	*Coopers, Chislehurst, Kent.* Late Lieut. and
Wm. Chebb Hayward	24 July	48	*Rochester.* [Capt. Scotch Fusr. Guards.
Neville Ward	2 Oct.	48	*Calverly Park, Tunbridge Wells.*
ADJUTANT.			
Lieut. George Albert	31 March	31	*Godden Green, Sevenoaks.* Peninsular and [Waterloo, late 15th King's Hussars.
SURGEON.			
Thomas R. Smith ...	2 Oct.	48	*St. Mary Cray, Kent.*

REGIMENTAL APPOINTMENTS.—Light Dragoons; uniform, blue; red facings; silver lace. Horse appointments, brown.

EFFECTIVE STRENGTH.—4 Quartermasters, 4 Sergeant-Majors, 13 Sergeants, 13 Corporals, 4 Trumpeters, 4 Farriers, 218 Privates.

YEOMANRY CAVALRY. 17

LANARK.
Upper Ward and Airdrie Corps of Lanarkshire Yeomanry Cavalry.

Major-Commandant.
Wm. Lockhart, 28 June 1849. M.P., D.L., J.P.—*Milton Lockhart, near Lanark.*

	Date of Appointment to Present Rank.	Remarks exhibiting Services of Officers, whether L.L., D.L., M.P., or J.P.—Country Seats, &c.
CAPTAINS.		
Alex. M. Lockart	24 April 33	D.L., J.P.
Archibald Gerard	17 April 48	J.P.—*Rochsoles, near Airdrie.* Late Capt. 92d Highlanders.
J. Thos. Brown, Jun.	18 April 48	J.P.—*Auchloshan, near Lesmehagow.*
Stephen Gray	25 Jan. 50	*Mansfield, near Lanark.*
LIEUTENANTS.		
George Vere Irving	26 April 42	J.P.—*Newton House, near Landhills.*
Robert Findley	5 Aug. 48	J.P.—*Battwrich Castle.*
Robert Monteith	8 Aug. 48	D.L., J.P.—*Carstairs House, near Carstairs.*
Robert Lockhart	25 Jan. 50	
CORNETS.		
John George Brown	1 Dec. 42	
John M'Lean	5 Aug. 48	
Douglas Baird	8 Aug. 48	J.P.—*Coats House, near Airdrie.*
D. C. R. C. Buchanan	25 Jan. 50	

REGIMENTAL APPOINTMENTS.—Light Dragoons; uniform, blue; facings, red; lace gold. Embodied in 1819.

LANARK.
The Queen's Own Royal Lower Ward Regiment of Yeomanry Cavalry.

Major-Commandant.
The Marquis of Douglas and Clydesdale, 14 Nov. 1848. *Hamilton, Douglas.*

	Date of Appointment to Present Rank.	Remarks exhibiting Services of Officers, whether L.L., D.L., M.P., or J.P.—Country Seats, &c.
CAPTAINS.		
James Merry	22 Dec. 48	
Sir Arch. I. Campbell, Bart.	25 Dec. 48	
George Baird	18 May 49	
LIEUTENANTS.		
Thomas M'Call	23 Dec. 48	
William Bruce	25 Dec. 48	
Donald Smith	18 May 49	
CORNETS.		
William Stirling	22 Dec. 48	
John Middleton	23 Dec. 48	
George Lumsden	18 May 49	
ADJUTANT.		
Capt. T. Paterson	22 June 49	Served in the Peninsula, and at Waterloo.

UNIFORM.—Blue, facings red, lace gold.

D

LANCASTER.—*Duke of Lancaster's own Regiment of Yeomanry Cavalry.*

Lieut.-Colonel.—The Earl of Ellesmere, 15 June 1847. J.P.—*Worsley Hall, Manchester, and Hatchford, Cobham, Surrey.*
Major.—Robert Tolver Gerard, 15 June 1847. (Late Capt. 6th Dragoon Guards.)

CAPTAINS.	Date of Appointment to Present Rank.	Remarks exhibiting Services of Officers, whether L.L., D.L., M.P., J.P.—Country Seats, &c.
John Langshaw	26 Sept. 35	
T. Y. P. Michaelson	17 May 40	J.P., D.L.
John Lord	12 May 41	J.P.
Albert Hudson Royds	27 Feb. 44	
Viscount Brackley	10 April 46	J.P., M.P.
LIEUTENANTS.		
John Fletcher	26 Sept. 35	J.P.
Alex. F. Haliburton	12 May 41	
T. Ainsworth Crook	27 Feb. 44	
Joseph Ridgway	11 Aug. 46	
George Loch	11 April 46	J.P.
CORNETS.		
William Gray	26 Sept. 35	
William Edw. Royds	27 Feb. 44	
John Jacson	11 April 46	J.P.
John Pickup Lord	24 April 46	
Hon. A. Egerton	17 June 47	SERVICES OF THE REGIMENT.—Occasional, in aid of the Civil Power.
SURGEON.		REGIMENTAL APPOINTMENTS.—Light Dragoons'
Thomas Howitt	3 June 45	uniform: scarlet; facings blue, lace gold.

EFFECTIVE STRENGTH.—31 Non-commissioned Officers, 15 Band, 219 Rank and file.

LANCASHIRE.—*Lancashire Hussar Regiment of Yeomanry Cavalry.*

Major-Commandant.
Sir John Gerard, Bart., 5 Sept. 1848. D.L.—*New Hall, Warrington.*

CAPTAINS.	Date of Appointment to Present Rank.	Remarks exhibiting Services of Officers, whether L.L., D.L., M.P., or J.P.—Country Seats, &c.
W. C. Yates	5 Sept. 48	J.P.—*Eccleston, Chorley.* Served as Capt. in the 1st or Royal Dragoons.
Wm. Ince Anderton	11 May 49	*Euxton Hall, Chorley.* Served in the 17th [Lancers.
LIEUTENANTS.		
Lionel Chas. Standish	1 Nov. 48	*Standish Hall, Wigan.* Served in the Rifle Brigade.
Fredk. Sewallis Gerard	16 Nov. 48	J.P.—*Aspull House, Wigan.* Served in the
Thos. D. B. D'Arcy	6 July 49	Served in the 89th Regiment. [9th Lancers.
CORNET.		
Hughes, G.	7 Nov. 49	REGIMENTAL APPOINTMENTS.—Hussar, lace gold. *Officers' Field-Dress.*—Blue jacket, with five loops of
SURGEON.		gold chain lace in front; collar, cuffs, and back
John Bullock Portus	24 May 49	seams braided Hussar fashion; trousers blue, with

gold cord on each outward seam; belts, gold; pouch and sabretache crimson cloth, edged with gold lace, with crown, Royal cipher, and the Lancashire rose embroidered in gold; cap crimson, with gold embroidery, gold ornaments, and gold cap-line; plume, black cock's tail; Hussar sash. *Undress.*—Blue jacket, with three loops of gold cord; collar, cuffs, and back seams with gold cord; trousers blue, with gold cord; forage cap, crimson; belts, black patent leather; pouch and sabretache, black patent leather, with crown and Lancashire rose. *Mess-Dress.*—Embroidered crimson waistcoat, crimson overalls, with gold lace on undress jacket. *Officers' Full-Dress.*—Blue Hussar jacket, fully laced with chain-lace in front, and braided on collar, cuffs, and back seams according to regimental pattern; pelisse, fully laced and trimmed with sable; pantaloons, crimson; Hessian boots; pouch-belt of stamped gilt metal; pouch gilt metal, with silver ornaments; busby, with gold cap-lines; sword-belt of gold lace, lined with crimson leather; sabretache, crimson, edged with gold lace, and embroidered with gold. *Horse Appointments.*—Shabraque, blue, edged with crimson vandykes and deep gold lace; the crown, Royal cipher, and Lancashire rose, embroidered in gold in front and on the points; leopard-skin saddle-cover; a black sheepskin worn in marching order; pelisse with five loops of gold chain lace: collar, cuffs, and edging of sable. *Men's Dress.*—Similar to the officers, except that a mixed worsted cord of blue and yellow is substituted for gold cord; chako, crimson, with horse-hair plume; pouch-belt, black patent leather; sword-belt, brown leather. Saddle and bridle, according to the regulations for Hussars, black sheepskin; shabraque, blue, edged with broad crimson lace and crimson vandykes; valise, blue, with crimson vandykes at the ends.

EFFECTIVE STRENGTH.—1 Sergeant-Major, 2 Troop Sergeant-Majors, 7 Sergeants, 7 Corporals, 2 Trumpeters, 140 Privates.

LEICESTER.
"Prince Albert's Own" Leicestershire Regiment of Yeomanry Cavalry.

Lieutenant-Colonel-Commandant.
G. A. L. Keck, 1 Nov. 1803. D.L.—*Staughton Grange.* Served in the 10th Hussars.
Lieutenant-Colonel.—Earl Howe, 1 Oct. 1831. J.P., D.L.—*Gopsal Hall.*
Major.—Chas. Wm. Packe, 18 Aug. 1840. J.P., M.P.—*Frestwold Hall.*

	Date of Appointment to Present Rank.	Remarks exhibiting Services of Officers, whether L.L., D.L., M.P., or J.P.—Country Seats, &c.
CAPTAINS.		
Edw. Basil Farnham	1 Sept. 26	J.P., M.P.—*Quorndon House.*
James Ley Douglas...	15 July 28	
Edward B. Hartopp	2 April 33	J.P.—*Dalby Hall.*
John B. Story	26 June 38	J.P.—*Lockington Hall.*
Sir W. W. Dixie, Bt.	22 Aug. 43	J.P.—*Bosworth Hall.*
Viscount Curzon	7 May 46	J.P.—*Penn House.*
Charles Thos. Freer	3 June 46	J.P. Served in the 7th Foot.
Geoffrey Palmer	4 May 47	J.P.
William Brooks	16 May 47	
LIEUTENANTS.		
Richard Gough	1 Sept. 18	J. P.
Colin C. Macaulay...	8 Aug. 29	
John Martin	6 March 39	
Henry C. Woodcock	18 April 42	
Viscount Campden...	22 Aug. 43	*Exton Park.*
Hampden Clements...	7 May 46	
Chas. S. Burnaby	3 June 46	
William Marshall	4 May 47	
Hon. Hy. D. Curzon	9 Nov. 47	
CORNETS.		
Sir F. W. Heygate, Bt.	1 May 40	
William Ward Tailby	31 Aug. 43	
Hon. E. S. Russell...	26 Sept. 44	M.P.
Thos. John Pares	17 Jan. 46	
Hon. W. H. Curzon	21 Oct. 47	
Henry St. J. Halford	9 Nov. 47	
Sir G. H. Beaumont, Bt	4 Aug. 48	*Coleorton Hall.*
Robert W. Arkwright	25 Aug. 48	J.P. Served in the 7th Dragoon Guards.
Cosmo Geo. C. Nevill	23 May 49	*Holt Hall.* Served in the 11th Foot.
ADJUTANT.		
Frederick Jackson	2 Aug. 34	Served in the "3d King's Own," Light Dragoons.
CHAPLAIN.		
Rev. A. R. Harrison	12 Jan. 47	
SURGEON.		
Gilbert Bridges	15 Dec. 24	
ASSIST.-SURGEON.		
Thomas Macaulay...	5 Oct. 43	
VET. SURGEON.		
William Burley	5 Sept. 13	

SERVICES OF THE REGIMENT.—Frequently in aid of the Civil Power.
REGIMENTAL APPOINTMENTS.—Light Dragoons; jacket, scarlet, double-breasted, collar, cuffs, and turnbacks, colour of regimental facings (Royal Blue), silver bullion back-pieces, skirts, cuffs and collar, ornamented with silver lace; epaulettes, plain lace straps, silver double bullion crescent; chako, black beaver with silver lace band, regimental ornaments in front " P. A. Own," and " L. Y. C.," plated chains with Lions' heads, and gold cord line with acorns; plume, white drooping feathers, gilt socket; trowsers, Royal Blue, with two stripes of silver lace an inch wide; waist belt, silver lace one inch wide, morocco lining and edging, with plated Lion's head ornaments, fastening in front with a snake; sabretache, leather, pocket edged round with silver lace, embroidered with " Prince Albert's Own, L. Y. C.," in centre and crown above, three rings at top for slings of belts in red morocco case; pouch-belt, silver lace, lining to correspond with waist-belt; pouch-box, red leather, red cloth face, silver lace edging round, embroidered with " Prince Albert's Own, L. Y. C.," and a crown in centre. *Field-Dress.*—Shoulder scales, German silver, lined with Royal Blue cloth; field trowsers, regimental pattern (Royal Blue), with two stripes scarlet cloth, frock coat, blue, single-breasted, with one row of uniform buttons, and Prussian collar with silver shoulder scales; forage cap, blue cloth, silver lace, black patent leather peak embroidered; cloak, blue, lined with scarlet, and scarlet collar. Hussar saddle and bridle and seal-skin.
EFFECTIVE STRENGTH—10 Quartermasters, 1 Sergeant-Major, 30 Sergeants, 26 Corporals, 10 Trumpeters, 10 Farriers, 519 Privates.

LOTHIAN.

East Lothian Regiment of Yeomanry Cavalry.

Major-Commandant.

James Maitland Balfour, 12 June 1848. J.P., D.L.—*Whittinghame.*

CAPTAINS.	Date of Appointment to Present Rank.		Remarks exhibiting Services of Officers, whether L.L., D.L., M.P., or J.P.—Country Seats, &c.
Jas. Wm. Hunter ...	26 June	46	J.P., D.L.—*Thurston.* Late Capt. 7th Dragoon Guards.
Wm. Sandilands ...	12 June	48	J.P.—*Barneyhill.* Late Capt. 7th Dragoon Guards.
J. Campbell Renton .	13 June	48	M.P., J.P.—*Mordington.*
LIEUTENANTS.			
T. S. M. Innes	25 June	46	*Phantassie.*
H. Marshall Davidson	12 June	48	*Holyn Bank.*
Alex. Mitchell Innes	13 June	48	*Ayton.*
CORNETS.			
Charles Balfour	26 June	46	*Newton Don.* Late Capt. Grenadier Guards.
Archibald Brown ...	12 June	48	*Johnstonburn.*
James Hall	13 June	48	*Dunglass.*
SURGEON.			
James Kellie, M.D.			

REGIMENTAL APPOINTMENTS.—Light Dragoons, clothing red, lace gold, facings blue.

LOTHIAN.—*Royal Mid-Lothian Regiment of Yeomanry Cavalry.*

Colonel-Commandant.
Sir John Hope, Bart., 11 Aug. 1828. M.P., V.L., J.P.—*Pinkie House.*

Lieutenant-Colonel.
Shatto W. D. Lord Aberdour, 19 April 1844. D.L., J.P.—*New Saughton House.*
Served in 71st Foot and 11th Hussars.

Major.
Wm. R. Ramsay, 20 July 1846. D.L., J.P.—*Burnton House and Sauchie House.*

	Date of Appointment to Present Rank.	Remarks exhibiting Services of Officers, whether L.L., D.L., M.P., or J.P.—Country Seats, &c.
CAPTAINS.		
Peter Ramsay.........	8 July 29	J.P.
Archibald Hope	5 July 45	D.L., J.P.
Richard Trotter	27 June 46	D.L., J.P.—*Morton Hall.*
John Wauchope	25 Jan. 47	D.L., J.P.—*Edmonstone House.*
Robt. B. W. Ramsay	25 Jan. 47	D.L., J.P.—*Whitehill.*
Sir J. G. Baird, Bart.	20 May 47	D.L., J.P.—*Saughton Hall.* Served in 10th
Stuart B. Hare	6 July 48	D.L., J.P.—*Calder Hall.* [Hussars.
LIEUTENANTS.		
Sir A. G. Maitland, Bt.	26 Jan. 46	D.L., J.P.—*Clifton Hall.* Served in 79th Regiment.
Andrew Wauchope...	26 Jan. 46	D.L., J.P.—*Niddry House.* Served in 17th Lancers.
Wm. S. Walker	25 Jan. 47	D.L., J.P.—*Bowland.*
William Baillie	6 July 48	J.P.
John W. Drummond	17 July 49	
CORNETS.		
Robert Dundas	13 June 43	D.L., J.P.—*Arniston House.*
Sir Graham Montgomery, Bart.	25 Jan. 47	D.L., J.P.—*Stobo Castle.*
George M. Innes ...	25 Jan. 47	*Ingliston.*
Alex. Cochrane	15 July 48	J.P.—*Linkfield Hall and Ashkirk.*
Andrew Gillon	6 July 48	J.P.—*Wallhouse.*
John M. Moubray ...	15 Sept. 48	J.P.—*Hartwood Lodge.*
John Borthwick	17 July 49	J.P.—*Crookston.* Served in 92d Regiment.
James Hope	17 July 49	
ADJUTANT.		
Capt. H. P. J. Harrison	27 May 45	Served in 10th Hussars and 4th Light Dragoons.
SURGEON.		
John G. M. Burt ...	25 Jan. 47	M.D.
ASSISTANT-SURGEON.		
Thos. Peacock	25 Jan. 47	M.D.

SERVICES OF THE REGIMENT.—The Royal Mid-Lothian Yeomanry Cavalry was originally formed in 1797, disembodied in 1837, and reformed in 1843. In the years 1819 and 1820 the Regiment was marched from Edinburgh to the undernamed towns, and quartered for several days to aid the Civil Power, viz., Glasgow, Hamilton, Bathgate, Mid-Calder, Falkirk, and Airdrie. On several occasions in Edinburgh the Corps has been under arms, and ordered out for the same purpose. In March, 1848, the regiment received orders from the Lord-Lieutenant to be in readiness to march to any place its services might be required, and on 31st July was ordered out by the Sheriff to aid the Civil Power, and remained under his orders during the night.

REGIMENTAL APPOINTMENTS.—Heavy Dragoons. *Officers' Uniform.*—Blue stable-jacket, silver lace, red facings, scales, red silk sash; overalls, blue, with red stripes; helmet, brass, with red plume. *Men's Uniform.*—Same as the officers, except the sash. *Horse Appointments.*—Hussar bridle, crupper, breastplate, and collar, with black skin.

EFFECTIVE STRENGTH. — 7 Quartermasters, 16 Sergeants, 16 Corporals, 5 Trumpeters, 320 Privates. Total, 364.

MIDDLESEX.—*Uxbridge Corps of Yeomanry Cavalry.*

Captain-Commandant.

Hubert De Burgh, 5 Jan. 1831. J.P., D.L.—*Drayton Hall, Middlesex.*

	Date of Appointment to Present Rank.	Remarks exhibiting Services of Officers, whether LL., D.L., M.P., or J.P.—Country Seats, &c.
CAPTAIN. Fredk. William Cox	10 Feb. 49	J.P.—*Hillingdon House, Middlesex.*
LIEUTENANTS. Chas. N. Newdegate	7 March 37	M.P., J.P.—*Harefield Park, Middlesex.*
Hugh Hammersly ..	30 Dec. 48	
CORNETS. Henry Boucherett ...	3 Aug. 47	*Market Rasen, Lincolnshire.* Served as Lieutenant 14th Light Dragoons, Captain 17th Lancers.
B. W. Arthur Sleigh	6 April 49	Entered the army as Ensign July 22, 1842; served in the West Indies, in 1843-4-5; promoted as Lieutenant, Nov. 10, 1844; exchanged to 77th Regiment, May, 1845; served in North America in 1846-7, at Nova Scotia, Cape Breton, and Lower Canada; appointed Adjutant of the depôt, February, 1847; served in Ireland on the Regimental Staff, until the return of the Regiment from foreign service, 1848.
QUARTERMASTER. George S. Corbett ...	17 Aug. 42	Late 14th Light Dragoons.

SERVICE OF THE CORPS.—Escorts,—William IV., 1833; Her Majesty, 1841, 1843, and 1846. In aid of Civil Power, February, 1832; February, 1844.

REGIMENTAL APPOINTMENTS.—*Officers' Full Dress.*—Dark green, black braid cords in seams of coatee, gold embroidery on collar and cuffs; lace gold; overalls dark green with gold lace; waist-belt, gold lace with bullion tassels; epaulettes; epaulettes, gold; sabretache, leather pocket, black velvet face, edged with gold lace, embroidered with crown and V. R.; pouch-belt, gold lace on black velvet; pouch-box, black velvet face, gold edging, embroidered with crown and V. R.; black beaver chacoe with gold cord lines and ornaments, in front, "Uxbridge Yeomanry Cavalry," plain scales; green cock's feathers drooping plume, gilt socket. *Field-Dress.*—Dark green frock; gold scales, double row of buttons; patent leather pouch-belt, gold ornaments; plain patent leather slings; overalls, with black oak-leaf braid; stable jacket, dark green, one row of gilt beads, black oak-leaf braid down centre, and frogs; forage cap, dark green, gold edging, gold-edged peak; cloak, dark green. Light Dragoon saddle, black sheep-skin, shabraque.

Montgomery.
Montgomeryshire Regiment of Yeomanry Cavalry.

Lieut.-Colonel.

Sir Watkin Williams Wynn, Bart., 26 Jan. 1840. Late Lieut. 1st Life Guards. J.P., M.P.—*Wynnstay, Denbighshire.*

Majors.

Viscount Seaham, 15 June 1848. Late Lieut. 1st Life Guards. J.P., M.P.—*Brynypys, Denbighshire.*

Rice Pryce Buckley Williames, 4 May, 1837. J.P.—*Pennant, Montgomeryshire.*

	Date of Appointment to Present Rank.	Remarks exhibiting Services of Officers, whether L.L., D.L., M.P., or J.P.—Country Seats, &c.
CAPTAINS.		
Robt. M. B. Maurice	13 Jan. 31	J.P.—*Bodynfol, Montgomeryshire.*
Chas. L. Tamberlain	31 Aug. 38	*Court Calmore, Montgomeryshire.*
Chas. W. W. Wynn	4 May 47	
Robert Davies Jones	5 May 49	J.P.—*Trefrefach, Merionethshire.*
LIEUTENANTS.		
David Jones	24 May 49	*Cyffronydd, Montgomeryshire.*
John Hamer	4 Jan. 50	*Glanyrafon, Denbighshire.*
CORNETS.		
Maurice E. Lewis	5 May 49	*Machynlleth, Montgomeryshire.*
Wm. B. Hewson	20 May 49	6, *King's Temple, London.*
ADJUTANT.		
Capt. N. Burlinson	7 Oct. 45	*Welshpool, Montgomeryshire.*
SURGEON.		
Maurice L. Jones	22 March 31	*Welshpool, Montgomeryshire.*
VET.-SURGEON.		
Pryce Davies	4 Jan. 50	

SERVICES OF THE REGIMENT.—The Montgomeryshire Regiment of Yeomanry Cavalry was raised in 1803 by its late Commanding Officer, the Right Hon. Charles Watkin Williams Wynn, under the name of the Montgomeryshire Volunteer Legion. The establishment consisted of 20 Companies of Infantry, and 3, afterwards increased to 6, Troops of Cavalry. The Infantry were disbanded, with all other Volunteer Regiments in the kingdom. The Cavalry remained on its old establishment until 1831, when it was consolidated into 4 Troops. The Regiment has been three times assembled on active service in aid of the Civil Power: 1st, in May, 1838; 2d, in December, 1838; 3d, during the greater part of May, 1839, in consequence of the Chartist disturbances. On this occasion Lord John Russell, then Home Secretary, communicated, through the Lord-Lieutenant, Her Majesty's warm approval of the prompt manner in which the whole Regiment assembled within a few hours of the requisition of the Magistrates, and also of their behaviour while on service.

REGIMENTAL APPOINTMENTS.—Light Dragoons; lace, silver. *Officers' Uniform.*—Scarlet dress jackets, silver epaulettes, blue overalls, scarlet stripe for field duty, silver for dress. *Men's.*—Ditto, without lace. *Horse Appointments.*—Black leathers and sheepskins.

EFFECTIVE STRENGTH.—17 Officers, 28 Non-commissioned Officers, 19 Band, 237 Privates; total 301.

The Montgomeryshire Yeomanry Cavalry Badge.—The Rouge Dragon; motto, Anorchfygol, "Unconquered."

NORTHAMPTON.—*Royal Kettering Corps of Yeomanry Cavalry.*

Captain-Commandant.
Thos. P. Maunsell, 3d February 1831. J.P., D.L., M.P.—*Thorpe Malsor, Kettering.*
Lieutenant.—John Booth, 6th Sept. 1831. J.P., D.L.—*Glendon Hall, Kettering.*
Cornet.—Wm. Thos. Maunsell, 6th Sept. 1831. J.P., D.L.—*Thorpe Malsor, Kettering.*
Quartermaster.—Thomas Wright Richards, 1831.

SERVICES OF THE REGIMENT.—Received Her Majesty and Prince Albert at Kettering, and escorted them on their route to and from Burghley House, in 1844.
EFFECTIVE STRENGTH.—3 Sergeants, 3 Corporals, 1 Trumpeter, 60 Rank and file.
REGIMENTAL APPOINTMENTS.—Scarlet, dark blue facings; gold epaulettes and lace; Light Dragoons' arms, swords, and percussion carbines.

NORTHUMBERLAND.
Northumberland and Newcastle Regiment of Yeomanry Cavalry.

Lieut.-Colonel.—Matthew Bell, 30 April 1826. M.P.—*Woolsington.*
Major.—Sir Matthew White Ridley, Bt., 15 Sept. 1848. J.P.—*Blagdon.*

	Date of Appointment to Present Rank.	Remarks exhibiting Services of Officers, whether L.D., D.L., M.P., or J.P.—Country Seats, &c.
CAPTAINS.		
Matthew Clayton	29 Aug. 37	*Newcastle-upon-Tyne.* [Guards.
Bryan Burrell	20 Aug. 39	*Broome Park.* Served in the 4th Dragoon
W. Hodgson Cadogan	20 Aug. 29	*Brinkburn Priory.* Served in the 5th Dragoon Guards.
Thomas Butler	30 Jan. 41	*Walwick.* Served in the 7th Fusiliers.
G. Clayton Atkinson	12 Aug. 43	J.P.—*Denton*
John Cookson	10 Sept. 46	*Benwell.*
Isaac Thos. Cookson	15 Sept. 48	*New Biggen.*
LIEUTENANTS.		
Thomas James	29 Aug. 37	J.P.—*Otterburn.*
William Cuthbert	20 Aug. 39	*Beaufront.*
Rt. Lambton Surtees	1 March 40	*Redworth.*
Chas. Edwd. Cookson	13 Sept. 45	*Swinburne Castle.*
Adam Atkinson	10 Sept. 46	*Lorbottle.*
Henry Geo. Liddell	18 Sept. 49	*Eslington.*
Hon. W. George Grey	18 Sept. 49	*Howick.*
CORNETS.		
Henry Wm. Fenwick	12 Aug. 43	*Newcastle.*
Rt. Calverly Bewicke	24 May 44	*Coally Manor.*
O. Baker Cresswell	13 Sept. 45	*Cresswell.*
John Anderson	18 Sept. 47	*Newcastle.*
Wm. Losh Anderson	15 Sept. 48	*Newcastle.*
James Delaval Shafto	18 Sept. 49	*Bavington.*
Wm. John Lawson	18 Sept. 49	*Longhirst.*
ADJUTANT.		
Capt. Wm. Woods	25 Aug. 23	*Newcastle.* Served in 48th Regiment, and 4th Dragoon Guards; received the Peninsula Medal; present at Albuera.
SURGEON.		
Henry Heath	29 Aug. 37	*Newcastle.*

SERVICES OF THE REGIMENT.—In aid of the Civil Power, from 15th Oct. to 16th Nov. inclusive, 1823, 23 days; ditto, 21st April to 21st May, 1831, 31 days.
REGIMENTAL APPOINTMENTS.—Light Dragoon pattern; facings and trowsers, light blue; epaulettes and lace, silver. *Horse Appointments.*—Plain, no shabraque for Non-commissioned Officers and Privates (Officers' shabraques, light blue); grey cloaks, and blue valises.
EFFECTIVE STRENGTH.—7 Troops.—7 Quartermasters, 1 Sergeant-Major, 21 Sergeants, 21 Corporals, 7 Trumpeters, 2 Farriers, 352 Privates; total, 411 Non-Commissioned Officers and Privates, Band of 28 included.
MEMORANDUM.—2 Troops are dismounted and trained to act as Light Infantry, being armed with Sergeants' percussion muskets.

YEOMANRY CAVALRY. 25

NOTTINGHAM.

South Nottinghamshire Regiment of Yeomanry Cavalry.

Lieut.-Colonel.
Robert Holden, 18 April 1848.—*Nuttall Temple*, near *Nottingham.*

Major.
John Sherwin Sherwin, 31 March 1845.—*Bramcote Hall, Nottingham.*

	Date of Appointment to Present Rank.	Remarks exhibiting Services of Officers, whether L.L., D.L., M.P., or J.P.—Country Seats, &c.
CAPTAINS.		
Robert Bromley	17 April 40	J.P., M.P.—*Stoke Hall, Newark.* Served as Lieut. in 1st Life Guards.
Thos. B. Charlton	30 Oct. 41	J.P.—*Chilwell Hall, Notts.*
Thos. B. T. Hildyard	30 Oct. 41	J.P., M.P.—*Flintham Hall, Newark.*
Henry Sherbrook	18 April 48	*Oxton Hall, Southwell.*
Thos. G. A. Parkyns	28 April 49	*Ruddington Hall*, near *Nottingham.*
LIEUTENANTS.		
John Hadden	11 March 31	J.P.—*Bramcote Lodge, Nottingham.*
George Rawson	12 Feb. 34	*Bestwood Hall*, near *Nottingham.*
James Morley	19 April 44	
Willingham Franklin	31 March 45	
R. D'A. T. Hildyard	5 Jan. 46	Served as Lieutenant in the Rifle Brigade.
John Savile Lumley	25 Jan. 47	*Rufford Park.*
Richard Milward	4 June 47	*Thurgarton Priory, Southwell.*
Robert Woodhouse	18 April 48	
Lord Arthur E. Hill	8 Aug. 48	M.P.—*Norwood Hall, Southwell.*
Richard Sutton	13 Nov. 49	*Skervington Hall.* Served as Lieut. in 1st [Life Guards.
CORNETS.		
William Watts	5 June 39	
Geo. Nathaniel Curzon	28 April 49	
Charles Sutton	13 Nov. 49	*Skervington Hall.* Served as Captain in the [12th Royal Lancers.
ADJUTANT.		
William Armstrong	1 May 41	Served as Cornet 6th Dragoons, 23 June 1814; Lieut. same Corps, 29 May 1817; Capt. 10th Royal Hussars, 26 June 1840; 27 years' Full-pay Service.
SURGEON.		
William Wright	13 July 26	

SERVICES OF THE REGIMENT.—The Regiment served in aid of the Civil Power during the Riots at Nottingham in 1831; assembled and remained on duty in aid of the Civil Power in 1839, and in April, 1848.

REGIMENTAL APPOINTMENTS.—Hussar; lace gold. *Officers' Dress.*—Full Dress: Blue jacket, with five Austrian loops of chain lace in front; collar, cuffs, and back-seams, braided Hussar fashion; overalls, blue, with two stripes of gold lace; Hussar sash; cap, scarlet, with gold ornaments and cap-line; black cock's-tail plume; belts, black morocco, with gold embroidery. Undress: Jacket, blue, with gold cord round collar, cuffs, and up back-seams; overalls, blue, with gold cord on outward seams; forage cap, blue, with embroidered peak. *Dress of Men.*—Similar to officers, but with yellow worsted cord; black patent leather pouch-belts; brown leather sword-belts. *Horse Appointments.*—Regulation Hussar saddle and bridle, black sheepskin; shabraque, edged with scarlet lace.

EFFECTIVE STRENGTH.—20 Sergeants, 5 Trumpeters, 365 Rank and file.

Designation.—South Notts Yeomanry Cavalry.

NOTTINGHAM.

Sherwood Rangers Regiment of Yeomanry Cavalry.

Lieut.-Colonel.

Sir Thomas Woollaston White, Bart., 29 April 1840. J.P.
Walling Wells Park.
Served in 16th Lancers, and 3d Light Dragoons, as Cornet.

Major.

Henry Pelham Pelham Clinton, Earl of Lincoln, 29 April 1840. J.P.

CAPTAINS.	Date of Appointment to Present Rank.	Remarks exhibiting Services of Officers, whether L.L., D.L., M.P., or J.P.—Country Seats, &c.
Wm. Samuel Welfitt	3 Nov. 35	J.P.—Served in 17th Lancers.
Lord W. P. Clinton .	11 April 38	
John H. M. Sutton...	3 Feb. 44	J.P.—*Kelham Hall.*
LIEUTENANTS.		
G. G. H. Vernon ...	8 Dec. 41	J.P.
Hon. S. H. Pierrepont	31 Oct. 44	
Wm. Leigh Mellish .	18 April 48	Served in Rifle Brigade as Captain.
Jonathan Alderson...	11 April 38	Served in 43d Regt. Foot.
Jonathan Hardcastle.	31 Jan. 45	
CORNETS.		
John Vessey Machin	31 Oct. 44	
James Thorpe.........	4 June 47	
Charles Thorold	14 April 48	
SURGEON.		
James Prior Lacy ...	25 Sept. 29	

SERVICES OF THE REGIMENT.—The Regiment has been out several times in aid of the Civil Power; also formed a Guard of Honour on the Queen's passing through Nottingham.

REGIMENTAL APPOINTMENTS.—Light Dragoons; dress, dark green, with gold lace; Light Hussar saddles, and boss bridles.

EFFECTIVE STRENGTH.—The Regiment consists of 3 Troops, each of 1 Quartermaster, 3 Sergeants, 3 Corporals, 1 Trumpeter, and 70 Privates.

Establishment of Regiment.—1 Lieut.-Colonel, 1 Major, 3 Captains, 6 Lieutenants, 3 Cornets, 1 Surgeon, 3 Quartermasters, 1 Sergeant-Major, 9 Sergeants, 9 Corporals, 3 Trumpeters, 210 Privates, and 1 Chaplain.

OXFORD.

"The Queen's Own" Oxfordshire Regiment of Yeomanry Cavalry (Light Dragoons).

Lieut.-Colonel-Commandant.
The Duke of Marlborough, 20 March 1845. L.L.—*Blenheim Palace.*
Lieut.-Colonel.—Lord Churchill, 5 April 1847. J.P.—*Combury Park.*
Majors.
Lord Norreys, 14 April 1847. M.P., J.P.—*Witham Park.*
Hon. G. C. Agar, 9 June 1837.—*Hartley Court*, near *Reading.*

	Date of Appointment to Present Rank.	Remarks exhibiting Services of Officers, whether L.L., D.L., M.P., or J.P.—Country Seats, &c.
CAPTAINS.		
Viscount Villiers	4 Jan. 31	M.P.—*Middleton Park.*
J. H. W. Jones	30 March 31	*Chastleton.*
Henry Peyton	30 March 31	*Stratten Audley.*
Viscount Parker	9 June 37	*Sherbourn Castle.*
Marquis of Blandford	22 April 47	*Blenheim Palace.*
Hon. H. Spencer	14 May 48	*Combury Park.*
LIEUTENANTS.		
Samuel Field	14 Oct. 30	*Deddington.*
P. J. H. Wykeham	26 Jan. 36	*Tythrup Park.*
B. J. Whippy	4 April 43	J.P.—*Charlbury.*
W. H. Dashwood	17 July 37	*Kistlington Park.*
John Shawe Phillips	6 April 41	*Crottam.*
William Evetts	21 June 47	*Woodstock.*
Hugh Montgomery	16 May 48	
CORNETS.		
Edward Wright	7 Nov. 38	*Turville House.*
John Stratton	3 July 42	*Farthinghoe.*
A. R. Tawney	21 June 43	*Sandford House.*
E. J. Abbott	22 April 47	
G. H. Barnett	21 June 47	*Glympton Park.*
F. H. Fitzroy	4 June 49	*Oxford.*
ADJUTANT.		
Lord Alfred Churchill	21 Oct. 48	*Blenheim Palace.* Served in 4th Light Dragoons, 1 July 1842 to April 1847; and 83d Foot, to April 1848.
PAYMASTER.		
Benjamin Holloway	10 May 46	*Woodstock.*
SURGEON.		
George Coles	14 Oct. 30	*Woodstock.*

SERVICES OF THE REGIMENT.—In aid of Civil Power in 1830, quelling Riots at Otmoor and other places; ditto, ditto, 1831, at Banbury and Otmoor; ditto, ditto, 1832, at Otmoor; ditto, ditto, 1835.

REGIMENTAL APPOINTMENTS.—*Officers' Uniform.*—Silver lace; crimson facings. *Men.*—Crimson facings.

STRENGTH OF THE REGIMENT.—1 Lieut.-Colonel Commandant, 1 Lieut.-Colonel, 2 Majors, 6 Captains, 7 Lieutenants, 6 Cornets, 1 Adjutant, 1 Surgeon, 1 Paymaster, 1 Regimental Sergeant-Major, 6 Troop Sergeant-Majors, 18 Sergeants, 18 Corporals, 6 Trumpeters, 315 Rank and file.

PEMBROKE.—*Castlemartin Regiment of Yeomanry Cavalry.*

Major-Commandant.
George Bowling, 10 April, 1843.—*Holyland*, near *Pembroke.*

	Date of Appointment to Present Rank.	Remarks exhibiting Services of Officers, whether L.D., D.L., M.P., or J.P.—Country Seats, &c.
CAPTAINS.		
Henry Leach	24 July 40	J.P., D.L.—*Corston House, near Pembroke, Pembrokeshire.* Served in the Scotch Fusilier Guards.
Thomas Mansell	24 Feb. 43	J.P., Borough of Pembroke.
Seymour P. Allen	28 June 43	J.P. County of Pembroke.—*Cresselly House, Pembrokeshire.* Served in 2d Life Guards.
LIEUTENANTS.		
J. Robertson Bryant	10 April 33	*Pembroke.*
George Parry	24 July 40	J.P., Borough of Haverfordwest.—*Honeyborough, Pembrokeshire.*
Edward Leach	26 May 43	J.P., Borough of Pembroke.—*Pembroke.*
CORNETS.		
James Broff Byers	1 July 43	*Northdown House, near Pembroke.*
Frederick Leopold Saephea Maunteffeil Baron de Rutzen and Baron Frentz	29 May 47	D.L., County of Pembroke.—*Slebech Hall, Pembrokeshire.*
John Leach	17 July 47	*Ivy Tower, Pembrokeshire, and Pembroke.*
ACTING-ADJUTANT.		
Stephen Rees		Served in the 9th, or Queen's Royal Lancers.
SURGEON.		
J. Whittaker Paynter	10 April 33	J.P., County and Borough of Pembroke.—*Town of Pembroke.*

SERVICES OF THE REGIMENT.—Called out the various times and places undermentioned, viz. :—To Fishguard, in the county of Pembroke, in 1797, where the French Troops had landed 1400 strong, who were compelled to surrender.—In 1817, at Fishguard aforesaid, to suppress Corn Riots, which they accomplished.—In 1839, at Tavernspite, county of Carmarthen, to suppress Turnpike Gate Riots, which they accomplished.—In 1843, at St. Clear's, county of Carmarthen, to suppress Turnpike Gate Riots. Out 26 days on duty on the breaking out of the Rebecca Riots.—From the 26th June, 1843, to the 18th November, same year, distributed over the counties of Carmarthen, Cardigan, and Pembroke, in the suppression of the Rebecca Riots, being 171 days in aid of the Civil Power in that year.

REGIMENTAL APPOINTMENTS.—Light Dragoon Hussars; lace, silver; jacket, blue; facings, buff; full silver lace Hussar jacket, with silver lace girdle; chaco; pouch and belt; sword and sabretache, with C. Y. C. ornaments.—Men, silver lace jackets; Light Dragoon appointments, with shabraque.

EFFECTIVE STRENGTH.—3 Troop Quartermasters, 1 Sergeant-Major, 6 Sergeants, 6 Corporals, Band 11, Rank and file, 112.

SHROPSHIRE.—*North Salopian Regiment of Yeomanry Cavalry.*

Colonel.
The Right Hon. Viscount Hill, 18 Aug. 1824. L.L.—*Hawkstone.* Served in the Royal Horse Guards.

Lieut.-Colonel.
Sir Robert Chamber Hill, 21 March 1831. C.B., J.P.—*Prees Hall.* Served in the Royal Horse Guards; commanded the Regiment in the Peninsula, and at Waterloo.

Major.
The Hon. Thomas Kenyon, 6 May 1834. D.L., J.P.—*Pradoe, Shrewsbury.*

	Date of Appointment to Present Rank.	Remarks exhibiting Services of Officers, whether L.L., D.L., M.P., or J.P.—Country Seats, &c.
CAPTAINS.		
John Edwards	19 Dec. 11	J.P.
Sir Andrew V. Corbet	26 July 20	D.L., J.P.—*Acton Reynold.*
John Whitehall Dod	26 May 23	D.L., J.P., M.P.—*Calver Hall.*
Richard Jones	4 July 29	
Sir John R. Kynaston	21 March 31	D.L., J.P.—*Hardwick Hall.*
George Harper	15 April 38	
John Croxon	15 April 38	
George Slavely Hill	15 April 38	J.P.
LIEUTENANTS.		
Robert Masefield	6 July 32	*Ellerton Hall.*
Richard Henry Kinchant	15 April 38	*Park Hall, Oswestry.* Served in the Army.
Robert Nicolls	15 April 38	
Thos. Dicken Browne	15 April 38	
Vincent R. Corbet	20 April 41	
George Stanton	22 April 43	
Richard Parry Jones.	18 April 44	
Jas. H. M. Martin	10 March 49	Former service, East India Horse Artillery.
CORNETS.		
Right Hon. Arthur Visc. Dungannon	15 April 38	*Brynkinalt, Chirk.*
Wm. S. Lawley	15 April 38	*Lee Gomery House.*
Isaac Scot Hodgson	20 April 41	
Andrew Geo. Corbet.	22 April 43	
Thos. Hugh Sandford	22 April 43	*Sandford Hall.*
Wm. H. Austen	18 April 44	
John F. F. G. Mytton	28 April 46	
B. H. B. Owen	10 March 49	
ADJUTANT.		
Capt. John Shirley	6 July 32	Served in the Royal Horse Guards, 25 years.
SURGEON.		
Edward Gwynne	4 July 29	
VET.-SURGEON.		
John Miles Hales	15 April 38	

SERVICES OF THE REGIMENT.—The Regiment called out in aid of the Civil Power at Oswestry, Jan., 1831; one Squadron on Escort duty with the Duchess of Kent and Princess Victoria, 1832; also one Troop each at Nantwich and Market Drayton in aid of the Civil Power in August, 1842.

REGIMENTAL APPOINTMENTS.—Coat, scarlet with silver lace; pantaloons, blue; facings, black velvet. Saddles, &c., as Heavy Dragoons. *Officers' Dress.*—Scarlet embroidered coat, epaulettes, laced pantaloons, and gold sash.

EFFECTIVE STRENGTH.—30 Officers and Staff, 420 Privates; total, 456.

Designation of the Corps.—First or North Salopian Regiment of Yeomanry Cavalry.

SHROPSHIRE.—*South Salopian Regiment of Yeomanry Cavalry.*

Lieutenant-Colonel.
Edward James Earl of Powis, 29 Feb. 1848.—*Powis Castle, and Walcot.*
Major.—The Hon. Henry Wentworth Powys, 26 Sept. 1837.—*Berwick Hall.*

	Date of Appointment to Present Rank.	Remarks exhibiting Services of Officers, whether L.L., D.L., M.P., or J.P.—Country Seats, &c.
CAPTAINS.		
John G. Weld Lord Forester	3 May 26	*Willey Park.*
Robert Burton	22 May 30	J.P.—*Longnor Hall.*
Thos. C. Whitmore...	7 April 38	M.P.—*Apley Park.*
Ralph M. Leeke	19 April 41	D.L.—*Longford Hall.*
O. G. C. Bridgeman, Viscount Newport	May 44	M.P.—*Weston Hall.*
Charles S. Lloyd......	18 April 49	*Leaton Knolls.*
LIEUTENANTS.		
Thos C. Eyton	7 April 38	J.P.—*The Vinery.*
John C. B. Borough	9 June 41	D.L.—*Chetwynd.*
Thomas J. Badger ...	April 47	*Kingsland House.*
Beriah Botfield	29 Feb. 48	*Norton Hall, Northamptonshire.*
Henry Whitmore ...	18 April 49	*Apley Park.*
CORNETS.		
J. R. Ormsby Gore	23 June 38	*Aston Hall.*
John Rocke............	19 Feb. 44	*Clungunford.*
Wm. Butler Lloyd...	29 Feb. 48	*The Whitehall.*
O. J. C. Bridgeman	18 April 49	*Cotsbrook.* Served in 11th Hussars.
Rowland Hunt	16 July 49	*Boreatton Hall.*
ADJUTANT.		
Gabriel Rollings......	1 May 41	Served in 4th Dragoon Guards.
SURGEON.		
David Crawford	24 May 36	
VETERINARY SURGEON.		
Henry Crowe	1 May 46	

REGIMENTAL APPOINTMENTS.—*Full Dress at Her Majesty's Levees and Drawing-Rooms.*—Coat, scarlet, single-breasted; collar, Prussian, black velvet, with two loops of gold lace; cuffs, black velvet; two buttons on waist behind: turnbacks, black velvet; skirts fastened by embroidered star: epaulettes, gold bullion, gilt scale strap, solid crescent; trowsers, dark blue, gold lace, oak-leaf and acorn pattern; sash dress regulation of the Heavy Dragoons; hat and feather, ditto ditto; sword, scabbard, knot, and belt, dress regulation of the Life Guards; boots, ankle; spurs, brass. *Field-Dress.*—Coat, scarlet, single-breasted; trowsers, Oxford-grey kersey, stripe of scarlet down outward seam; girdle, regulation of the Light Dragoons; helmet, steel with brass ornaments, and fastened with scale loop; sabretache, black patent leather, gilt ornament pouch-belt, white patent leather box, black patent leather, gilt ornament; gloves, white leather. *Undress.*—Coat, frock, dark blue, single-breasted; epaulettes, brass scales: trowsers, white drill; cap, dark blue cloth, edged with scarlet cord, gold lace band, black patent leather peak, edged with gold embroidery; sword-belt, white patent leather.

EFFECTIVE STRENGTH.—6 Troop Quartermasters, 15 Sergeants, 15 Corporals, 6 Trumpeters, 300 Rank and file.

YEOMANRY CAVALRY.

SOMERSET.—*North Somerset Regiment of Yeomanry Cavalry.*

Colonel.—Wm. Miles, 9 Aug. 1843. J.P., D.L., M.P.—*Leigh Court, Somerset.*

Lieut.-Colonel.
James Bennett, 9 Aug. 1843. Served in 12th and 14th Light Dragoons. J.P.—*Cadbury House.*

Major.—Montague Gore, 9 Nov. 1847. D.L.—*Barrow Court, Bristol.*

	Date of Appointment to Present Rank.	Remarks exhibiting Services of Officers, whether L.L., D.L., M.P., or J.P.—Country Seats, &c.
CAPTAINS.		
W. F. Knatchbull ...	14 May 27	J.P., D.L.—*Babington, Somerset.*
J. W. D. T. Wickham	29 Aug. 29	
P. W. Skynner Miles	27 April 39	J.P., M.P.—*Kingsweston, Somerset.*
R. C. Tudway.........	22 Aug. 39	J.P., D.L.
John Rees Mogg ...	2 Sept. 39	*High Littleton House, Somerset.*
John Harding.........	10 May 41	
W.H.P.Gore Langton	1 May 47	J.P.—*Newton Park, Somerset.*
P.H.St.JohnMildmay	24 Aug. 48	J.P.—*Hazlegrove House, Somerset.*
LIEUTENANTS.		
William M'Adam ...	7 July 30	*Ballochmorrie, Ayrshire, N.B.*
Henry Messiter	19 Jan. 31	
Wm. Benj. Naish ...	28 Sept. 39	[*House, Somerset.*
E. Berkeley Napier...	16 Nov. 39	Served in 59th Foot. D.L., J.P.—*Pennard*
John George Mogg...	24 Jan. 42	J.P.—*Manor House, Farrington Gurney.*
John William Miles	7 Nov. 43	
Henry St. John Maule	3 Feb. 44	
Philip J. W. Miles...	30 Jan. 49	
CORNETS.		
Bartholomew Smith	27 Jan. 40	
John Henry Blagrave	11 May 41	*Barrow House, Somerset.*
W. H. M. Colston ...	3 Feb. 44	J.P., D.L.
Lionel Helbert	17 Dec. 45	
Henry Lucas Bean...	23 Nov. 46	
Viscount Dungarvon	2 Feb. 48	
Arthur J. S. Paget...	30 Jan. 49	
Charles Fox Webster	8 May 49	
ADJUTANT.		
Capt. B. Leigh Lye	19 Feb. 21	B.UB. Served many years in the 11th Light [Dragoons.
SURGEON.		
John Soden...........	12 Dec. 44	
ASSIST.-SURGEON.		
Findlater Crang	9 Nov. 47	

SERVICES OF THE REGIMENT.—The Regiment has been assembled in aid of the Civil Power seven times, and the different troops and detachments have been called out for the same purpose sixty-four times.

REGIMENTAL APPOINTMENTS.—*Officers' Full Dress:* Same as the men's, excepting silver lace for cotton; green feather; double silver stripe down trowsers; silver sword-belt slings, and sabretache. *Men's Full Dress:* Blue coatee, red facings; white cotton lace round collar and cuffs; red breast; yellow and red girdle; blue overalls, narrow double red stripe; red inlaid in seams of jacket; chako, with black horsehair plume, chain plaited; gauntlets; sword-belt and slings, white (Ordnance); sword, straight (no sabretache); carbine, short Victoria (no pistols); blue cloak, red collar (no cape); black leather valise, round; shoulder scales to jacket.

Officers' Undress: Stable jacket; silver lace down front (with beading), round waist and cuffs; silver cord round collar and shoulder knot; overalls, blue, double red stripe; black sword-belt, slings, sabretache; short gloves; forage cap, blue crossed in silver cord; peak, embroidered silver. Walking dress: Blue frockcoat, braided; red waistcoat, embroidered silver. *Men's Undress:* Stable jacket, blue; no lace beaded down front, no buttons; seams inlaid red; red collar and cuffs; white cotton shoulder knot; overalls same as dress; short gloves.

HORSE APPOINTMENTS.—Light Cavalry (Cossack) saddle, headstall, chain, and biddoon; bridle-bit and rein; breastplate, all brass, embossed with "N. S. Y. C.;" interlaced'shabraque, blue bound with white cotton, and embroidered in two corners, Crown, initials of Regiment, V. R., &c., &c., in coloured worsted; black sheepskin; Light Dragoons.

SOMERSET.—*West Somerset Regiment of Yeomanry Cavalry.*

Colonel.
Charles Kemeys Kemeys Tynte, 25 July 1831. J.P.—*Halswell, Somerset, and Cafin Mabley, Monmouthshire.*

Lieut.-Colonel.
Edward Ayshford Sanford, 10 June 1849. J.P.—*Nynehead Court.*

Major.—William Pinney, 10 June 1849. M.P., D.L., J.P.—*Somerton.*

	Date of Appointment to Present Rank.	Remarks exhibiting Services of Officers, whether L.L., D.L., M.P., or J.P.—Country Seats, &c.
CAPTAINS.		
Martin Chas. Maher	25 July 31	*Obridge House.*
Augustus P. Browne	39 May 40	*Battleton House, Dulverton.*
Frederick W. Slade	20 Feb. 44	*Mansell Grange.*
James Hole	6 May 45	*Dunster.*
Wm. Henry Bernard	31 May 45	*Clatworthy.*
Wm. A. Sanford	9 Sept. 46	J.P.—*Nynehead Court.*
Charles N. Welman	10 Sept. 46	J.P.—*Norton Manor.*
James Randolph	22 May 48	*Milverton.*
Ralph Neville	10 June 49	J.P.—*Butleigh Court.*
LIEUTENANTS.		
P. Pleydell Bouverie	29 Oct. 44	*Brymour House.*
James Wm. Browne	6 May 45	*Swindon.*
Arthur Capel	6 May 45	J.P.—*Bulland Lodge.*
Thomas E. Clarke	10 Sept. 46	*Tremlett House.*
H. Cranston Adams	15 May 47	*Taunton.*
Stukeley Lucas	22 May 48	*Barrons Down.*
Theodore Thring	10 June 49	*Castle Carey.*
M. Valentine Maher	15 May 47	*Leycroft House.* An officer in the 10th Regiment.
CORNETS.		
Wm. Henry George	12 April 45	
Frederick C. Moore	4 June 46	*Taunton.*
Wyndham Slade	20 March 48	*Muntys Court.*
James Reynolds	29 May 48	*Wellington.*
ADJUTANT.		
Martin C. Maher	25 July 31	*Obridge House.* Entered the Army as Ensign in 1809; Lieutenant in Jan., 1811; Capt. 1830. Served in the 1st G. B. and 52d Regiment during the Peninsular War, and till after the Battle of Waterloo. Subsequently in the West Indies.
SURGEON.		
William Trevor	9 June 47	*Dulverton.*
ASSISTANT-SURGEON.		
Alfred Haviland	9 June 47	*Bridgwater.*
VETERINARY-SURGEON.		
James Channon	24 Oct. 32	*Taunton.*
CHAPLAIN.		
Rev. Jas. S. Broderip	10 April 48	*Cossington.*

SERVICES OF THE REGIMENT.—In aid of the Civil Power during the Bristol Riots, 1831; and from 10th to 25th of May, 1847.

REGIMENTAL APPOINTMENTS.—Regulation Light Dragoon pattern, blue jacket, scarlet facings, gold lace; chakoes, gold lace; gold epaulettes, sabertache, &c.; blue cloak, red collar. *Horse Appointments.*—Plain saddle, shabraque, black sheepskins, leather valises.

EFFECTIVE STRENGTH.—1 Colonel, 1 Lieut.-Colonel, 1 Major, 8 Captains, 8 Lieutenants, 8 Cornets, 1 Adjutant, 2 Surgeons, 1 Veterinary-Surgeon, 1 Chaplain, 8 Quartermasters, 1 Sergeant-Major, 24 Sergeants, 24 Corporals, 8 Trumpeters, 8 Farriers, 472 Privates. Total, 545 Non-commissioned Officers and Privates. 8 Troops. *Arms.*—Sabres, Light Dragoon pattern; carbines, short, percussion. Band, 32.

STAFFORDSHIRE.
The Staffordshire, or Queen's Own Royal Yeomanry Cavalry.

Lieut.-Colonel-Commandant.
Earl Lichfield, 10 April 1833.—*Shugborough and Ranton Abbey, Stafford.*
Lieut.-Colonel.—Edmund Peel, 25 April 1848. D.L.—*Bonehill House.*
Majors.—Hon. William Bagot, 25 April 1848. M.P., J.P., D.L.—*Blithfield.*
Earl of Granville, 12 Dec. 1848.—*Alderley Hall.*

	Date of Appointment to Present Rank.	Remarks exhibiting Services of Officers, whether L.L., D.L., M.P., or J.P.—Country Seats, &c.
CAPTAINS.		
Hon. Gilbert Talbot	1 Nov. 35	D.L., J.P.—*Ingestre.*
Frederick Tomlinson	5 May 36	D.L., J.P.—*Cliffville House.* [50th Regt.
Henry W. Desveaux	17 Sept. 41	J.P.—*Drakelow Hall.* Served as Capt. in
Geo. Holland Ackers	6 April 43	*Morton Hall.* Served as Capt. in the Royal
William D. Bromley	6 April 43	*Wootton Hall.* [Horse Guards.
Viscount Anson	16 Nov. 44	M.P.—*Shugborough.*
Sir Francis Scott, Bt.	7 Aug. 47	D.L., J.P.—*Great Barr Hall.*
Baron D. Webster	7 Aug. 47	J.P.—*Penn.*
John Pudsey	20 April 48	*Seisdon.*
Lorenzo K. Hall	25 April 48	D.L., J.P.—*Barton Hall.*
*LIEUTENANTS.		
George Grazbrook	30 Sept. 24	*Stourbridge.*
Robert J. Pell	29 Nov. 28	J.P.—*Burton-on-Trent.*
Michael Bass	12 Aug. 31	M.P., J.P.—*Holly Bush.*
William Mott	28 Oct. 37	J.P.—*Wall.*
Thomas Chawner	1 April 39	*Walsall.*
John Cruso	6 April 43	J.P.—*Leek.*
John William Sneyd	6 April 43	J.P.—*Basford Hall.*
Arthur Griffith	7 Sept. 45	*Lichfield.*
Ralph Thos. Adderley	9 May 46	*Ballaston Hall.* [Hussars.
Francis O. Bridgman	23 June 47	*Weston Hall.* Served as Capt. in the 10th
Robert Gurnet	7 Aug. 47	*Moor Hall.*
Hon. A. Wrottesley	20 Jan. 48	D.L., J.P.—*Wrottesley Hall.*
Hugo Meynell Ingram	25 April 48	*Hour Cross.*
Thos. Guy Gisborne	25 April 48	D.L., J.P.—*Croxall.* Served as Lieut. in
Thomas P. Heywood	27 April 48	*Domley's Hall.* [the 60th Rifles.
Frederick Peel	27 April 48	M.P.—*Drayton Manor.*
William F. Copeland	29 July 48	*Stoke.*
Edward D. Scott	21 May 49	*Great Barr Hall.*
*CORNETS.		
William Robertson	20 May 40	*Burton-on-Trent.*
Augustus E. Manley	7 April 45	*Manley Hall.*
William Challinor	17 Oct. 45	*Leek.*
Henry Lane	23 April 48	*King's Bromley.*
Morton Edwd. Buller	27 April 48	*Dilhorn Hall.*
Fredk. Augustus Peel	27 April 48	*Dosthill.*
Joseph Whitgreave	10 Sept. 48	*Talbot House.*
ADJUTANT.		
Major John R. Majendie	1 April 34	J.P.—*Pipe Grange.* Served as Capt. in the [92nd Highlanders. Major in the Army.
SURGEON.		
R. Wilson Lishman	25 June 35	*Shenstone.*
ASSIST.-SURGEON.		
Joseph P. Oates	6 Dec. 42	*Lichfield.*
VETY.-SURGEON.		
William Robinson	10 Jan. 16	*Fazeley.*

* 4 Lieutenants and 4 Cornets wanting.

SERVICES OF THE REGIMENT.—The Regiment was embodied in 1794, as the Staffordshire Yeomanry Cavalry. On Her Majesty's ascending the Throne, she was graciously pleased to permit the Regiment to assume their present designation, "The Queen's Own Royal Yeomanry." The Regiment has been repeatedly called out in aid of the Civil Power, to quell disturbances in the populous county of Stafford, and also into the adjoining counties, and has several times received the thanks of the Crown, through the Home Secretary. In the Riots which took place in 1842, the whole of the Regiment was called out in detachments, and remained on duty for a period of six weeks. On this occasion the county raised a subscription, and presented the Regiment with 12 magnificent Silver Trumpets, one for each Troop, and one to the Lieut.-Col.-Commandant, in gratitude for the services here performed. The Silver Trumpets each bear the following inscription :—" Presented by a grateful County to the Queen's Own Royal Yeomanry, for their Services in 1842."

REGIMENTAL APPOINTMENTS.—Equipped as Light Dragoons; clothing blue, facings, red; lace, silver; armed with swords and percussion carbines.—*Officers' Uniform*: Black helmet, with silver ornaments, and black plume; Light Dragoon jacket, with silver shoulder scales, and gold girdle; blue trowsers, with scarlet stripes; belts, black, with silver mountings. *Horse Appointments*: Black, with black sheepskin.—*Men's Uniform*: Black helmet, &c., with black plume; Light Dragoon jacket, with silver scales, blue and white girdle; blue trowsers, with scarlet stripes; buff belts. *Horse Appointments*: Brown, with black sheepskin. *Standards*:—1st, or Royal Standard, crimson and gold, with Royal Arms and designation, "The Queen's Own Royal Yeomanry."—2nd, 3rd, 4th, 5th, and 6th Standards, white and gold with Crown, and Staffordshire Knot, on silver ground, surrounded with a Garter, bearing the motto, "Pro Aris et Focis."

EFFECTIVE STRENGTH, &c.—1 Lieut.-Col.-Commandant, 1 Lieut.-Colonel, 2 Majors, 11 Captains, 22 Lieutenants, 11 Cornets, 1 Adjutant, 1 Surgeon, 1 Assist.-Surgeon, 1 Vety.-Surgeon, 1 Regimental Serjt.-Major, 11 Troop Quartermasters, 11 Troop Sergt.-Majors, 33 Sergeants, 44 Corporals, 11 Trumpeters, 11 Farriers, 770 Privates. Total, Non-Com. Officers and Privates, 892. The Regiment is composed of 11 Troops, forming 6 Squadrons.

SUFFOLK.

First Troop of Loyal Suffolk Yeomanry Cavalry.

Captain-Commandant.

Phillip Bennet, 31 March 1831. M.P., J.P.—*Hall Park, and Rougham, near Bury St. Edmund's.*

Lieutenant.—Peter Huddlestone, 30 May 1846. J.P.—*Norton.*

Cornets.—Fuller Maitland Wilson, 30 May 1846. J.P.—*Howlongtoff's.*

Surgeon.—William James Marshall, 31 March 1831.—*Nowton.*

REGIMENTAL APPOINTMENTS.—Green; gold lace.

EFFECTIVE STRENGTH.—2 Sergeants, 2 Corporals, 1 Trumpeter, 50 Privates.

SUFFOLK.—*Suffolk Borderers' Troop of Yeomanry Cavalry.*

Captain-Commandant.

Lieutenant-General Sir Edward Kerrison, Bart., K.C.B., M.P., 18 July 1831. *Oakley Park, Suffolk.* Colonel of the 14th Light Dragoons; late of the 7th Hussars. Sir Edward Kerrison served at the Helder in 1799; including the battles of Sept. 19, Oct. 2 and 6. Campaign of 1808-9 in Spain, under Sir John Moore, including the battle of Corunna. Commanded the 7th Hussars in the campaigns of 1813, 1814, 1815, and was present at the battles of Orthes and Waterloo, for which he has received medals. Sir Edward was severely wounded (his arm having been broken in two places) in Spain, Dec. 25, 1808; and slightly wounded at Waterloo, where he had also a horse shot under him. Sir Edward has received the War Medal and two clasps for Sahagun and Benevente and Toulouse.

Lieutenant.

Edw. Clarence Kerrison, 15 Aug. 1843. J.P.—*Brome Hall, Eye, Suffolk.*

Cornet.—James Drake, 15 June, 1837. *Billingford, Scole, Norfolk.*

Quartermaster.—Carleton Smythies, 1847. *Oak Lawn, Eye.*

Surgeon.—Thomas Edward Amyot. *Diss, Norfolk.*

SERVICES OF THE REGIMENT.—Several times called out to aid the Civil Power, and received the public thanks of the Magistrates of the counties of Suffolk and Norfolk.

REGIMENTAL APPOINTMENTS.—14th Light Dragoons; scarlet, with gold lace, chacoe and plumes, swords and pistols. Limited to 50 Non-commissioned Officers and Privates. Band 6, in blue uniform.

SUFFOLK.
Long Melford Troop of Yeomanry Cavalry, Lancers.

Captain-Commandant.—Vacant.

Lieutenants.

Nathaniel C. Barnardiston, 14 Nov. 1833. J.P.—*The Rye's, Henny, Essex.*
John Thomas Ord, 31 May 1837. J.P.—*Farnham, Bury St. Edmunds, Suffolk.*

Cornet.—John George Poly, 24 Feb. 1845. J.P.—*Boxted Hall, Suffolk.*

Quartermaster.—Thomas Goldsmith, *Sudbury.*

SERVICES OF THE REGIMENT.—The Long Melford Troop of Yeomanry Cavalry was established in 1831, under the command of Sir Hyde Parker, Bart., of Melford Hall; it was then a Light Dragoon Troop, established independently as recommended by Colonel Lord de Ros. The Troop was then 50 strong. In 1838, by directions of the Home Secretary, the Troop was disbanded, but, by application of the Magistrates, was allowed to be re-established without pay for clothing, &c. In 1840 the Troop was again placed on the Establishment by Government, Captain Hallifax having kept up the clothing and equipments in the mean time.

REGIMENTAL APPOINTMENTS.—*Officers.*—Lancer cap, scarlet cloth and black leather with white feathers; gold cap line; gold lace sash; white patent leather belts; steel spurs; bullion epaulettes, with silver crown and S. Y.; Light Cavalry sword; white patent gauntlets; dark green jackets, and overalls with scarlet cloth stripe; gold lace collar to jacket, and two rows of buttons on breast, and eight or ten on cuff, edged with scarlet cloth. *Undress.*—Frock coat, black braid facings; brass epaulettes, oilskin covered cap, peak patent leather, and gold lace edge. *Horse Appointments:* brown leather head collar and steel chain; bridle double, with brass mountings; breastplate ditto; Heavy Dragoon saddles, and dark green cloth shabraque, with broad scarlet cloth edge, and white sheepskins; cloak, dark mixed cloth, scarlet collar; Privates' uniform cap, worsted line, yellow; brass epaulettes; buff leather belts; jacket, imitation gold lace collar, brass; white horse-hair plume; pistols, flint.

EFFECTIVE STRENGTH.—1 Captain, 2 Lieutenants, 1 Cornet, 1 Quartermaster, 3 Sergeants, 3 Corporals, 1 Trumpeter, 61 Privates.

WARWICK.—*Warwickshire Regiment of Yeomanry Cavalry.*

Lieut.-Colonel Commandant.
Lord Brooke, 6 March 1848.   M.P., D.L., J.P.—*Warwick Castle, Warwick.*

Lieut.-Colonel.
Edward Bolton King, 25 Jan. 1848.   J.P.—*Chadshurst, near Kineton.*

Major.
Lord Guernsey, 23 Mar. 1848.   M.P.—"*The Bury,*" *Offchurch, near Leamington.*

	Date of Appointment to Present Rank.	Remarks exhibiting Services of Officers, whether L.L., D.L., M.P., or J.P.—Country Seats, &c.
CAPTAINS.		
H. C. Wise	8 Feb. 31	D.L., J.P.—*Woodcote,* near *Warwick.*
C. B. Adderley	10 Nov. 36	M.P., D.L., J.P.—*Hams Hall,* near *Coleshill.*
George Chetwynd ...	23 Feb. 38	D.L., J.P.—*Mancetter Lodge,* nr. *Atherstone.*
Darwin Galton	8 Aug. 45	J.P.—*Edstone,* near *Stratford-on-Avon.*
Robert J. Barnard ...	23 March 48	
Viscount Feilding ...	17 Oct. 49	D.L., J.P.
LIEUTENANTS.		
Matt. Wise	10 Jan. 38	J.P.—*Shrublands,* near *Leamington.*
George Unett	27 April 42	
William Wilmot......	25 March 45	
C. W. Hoskyns	7 July 47	*Wroxhall Abbey,* near *Warwick.* [*Avon.*
R. J. Atty	3 May 48	J.P.—*Ingon Grange,* near *Stratford-on-*
CORNETS.		[*Norton.*
Hon. W. H. Leigh...	12 April 44	J.P.—*Addlestrop House,* near *Chipping*
H. C. Okeover	20 Feb. 46	*Oldbury,* near *Atherstone,* and *Okeover Hall,*
John S. Parker	10 April 47	[near *Ashbourne.*
Robert Reid	7 July 47	
Wm. Henry Wilson	17 Oct. 49	*Knowle Hall.*
Henry Jas. Sheldon	17 Oct. 49	
ADJUTANT.		
Capt. Chas. Field ...	14 Sept. 41	Served in the 1st, or Royal Dragoons.
SURGEON.		
Josh. Willcox	13 April 36	

SERVICES OF THE REGIMENT.—This Regiment has repeatedly been on duty in aid of the Civil Power, more particularly during the Riots at Birmingham.

REGIMENTAL APPOINTMENTS.—Light Dragoons; scarlet jackets; blue overalls; silver lace; facings, white.

HORSE APPOINTMENTS.—Light Dragoon.

EFFECTIVE STRENGTH.—6 Troop Quartermasters, 1 Regimental Sergt.-Major, 18 Sergeants, 6 Trumpeters, 396 Rank and File.

WESTMORELAND.

Westmoreland and Cumberland Regiment of Yeomanry Cavalry.

Lieut.-Colonel.—Edward Williams Hasell, 30 May 1830. J.P.—*Dalemain.*

Major.
Sir Geo. Musgrave, Bart., 10 May 1847. J.P., D.L., served in the 15th Hussars.
—*Eden Hall.*

	Date of Appointment to Present Rank.	Remarks exhibiting Services of Officers, whether L.L., D.L., M.P., or J.P.—Country Seats, &c.
CAPTAINS.		
William Bushby	7 Nov. 36	J.P.—*Greystoke.*
James Salmond	17 Sept. 38	J.P., served in the 15th Hussars and 2d Dra-
Richard Burn	22 May 41	J.P.—*Orton Hall.* [goon Gds.—*Waterfoot.*
Robert Brisco	25 March 43	J.P.—*Low Mill House.*
George Edw. Wilson	10 May 47	J.P.—*Dalem Tower.* [*Lowther Castle.*
Henry Lowther	10 May 47	J.P., M.P., served in the 1st Life Guards.—
LIEUTENANTS.		[*Workington Hall.*
Edward S. Curwen	22 May 41	J.P., served in the 14th Light Dragoons.—
William Sleddale	16 May 42	*Rawhead.*
Joseph Studholme	25 March 43	*Wigton.*
Arthur Lowther	10 May 47	Served in the 6th Dragoons.—*Lowther Castle.*
J. Yeates Thexton	10 May 47	J.P.—*Beetham.*
Fred. John Graham	16 May 48	Served in the 1st Life Gds.—*Netherby Hall.*
CORNETS.		
Henry Spencer	7 May 44	*Whitehaven.*
G. R. G. Rees	20 Jan. 45	*Abbey, Carlisle.*
M. B. Harrison	20 Jan. 45	J.P.—*Ambleside.*
Barton E. Rees	10 May 47	*Abbey, Carlisle.*
Wordswth. Harrison	10 May 48	*Ambleside.* [*Villa.*
W. F. Hamilton	16 May 48	Served in the 79th Highlanders.—*Bowerbank*
ADJUTANT.		
Capt. Wm. Franklin	25 March 43 C. 26 May 48	Served in the 23d Lancers, 19th Lancers, and [7th Hussars.—*Victoria-place, Penrith.*
SURGEON.		
Joseph Wickham	10 May 47	*Penrith.*

SERVICES OF THE REGIMENT.—This Regiment was raised in 1819. In aid of the Civil Power, Appleby, March 23, 1829; Penrith, May 23, 1839; Carlisle, Aug. 14, 1839; Carlisle, Aug. 22, 1842; Penrith, Feb. 11, 1846; and Kendal, Feb. 24, 1846.

REGIMENTAL APPOINTMENTS.—Hussars, without the spare jacket on the shoulder; white silver lace. The dress and undress jackets of scarlet cloth; with white facings on the collar and cuffs; and blue cloth trowsers, with white stripes.

HORSE APPOINTMENTS.—The Hussars' saddle and bridle, with black skin and shabraque. The men's the same, but cotton lace on appointments. Full dress: chaco, silver mounted, with black full-dress feather. The men's, with cotton lace, and black horsehair plume.

EFFECTIVE STRENGTH.—6 Quartermasters, 1 Acting Sergeant-Major, 12 Sergeants, 13 Corporals, 6 Trumpeters, 6 Farriers, 287 Privates, 349 Horses. Total, 347.

WILTS.—*Royal Wiltshire Regiment of Yeomanry Cavalry.*

Lieut.-Colonel-Commandant.
Geo. W. F. The Earl Bruce, 30 June, 1837.—*Savernacke Lodge, Marlborough, Wilts.*
Lieut.-Col.—Chas L. Phipps, 20 May, 1840. Served in the 2nd Dragoon Guards.
Major.—Walter Long, 20 May, 1840. M.P.

	Date of Appointment of Present Rank.	Remarks exhibiting Services of Officers, whether L.L., D.L., M.P., or J.P.—Country Seats, &c.
CAPTAINS.		
William Wyndham .	27 May 25	
Charles J. Viscount Andover............	27 March 26	*Charlton Malmesbury, Wilts.*
Sir Frederick H. Bathurst, Bt.	5 Oct. 33	Served in the Grenadier Guards.
Thomas B. Sotheron.	28 Aug. 35	M.P.
Sir Edmund Antrobus, Bt.	23 Jan. 38	*Amesbury Abbey, Wilts.*
The Right Hon. Lord Ernest A. C. B. Bruce................	29 May 38	M.P.—*Tottenham Park, Marlborough.*
The Right Hon. Henry Earl of Shelburne .	30 May 38	M.P.—*Lansdowne House.*
The Right Hon. Sidney Herbert	6 May 40	M.P., P.C.—*Wilton House, Salisbury.*
Ambrose L. Goddard	12 Oct. 44	M.P.—*The Lawn, Swindon, Wilts.*
Richard P. Long	28 April 48	
LIEUTENANTS.		
Thomas R. Ward ...	27 Sept. 21	
Henry D. Seymore...	21 Nov. 40	
Edmund Antrobus...	27 April 43	*Amesbury Abbey, Wilts.*
John Astley............	27 April 43	
John Connolley	24 April 44	
The Hon. George Barrington	12 Oct. 44	*Beckett House, Farringdon, Berks.*
John Davis	5 May 45	
Horatio Earl Nelson .	16 April 47	*Trafalgar House, Wilts.*
Edwd. D. B. Escourt	28 April 48	
P. K. W. T. Keene...	27 July 48	
CORNETS.		
Nathaniel Barton ...	21 Nov. 40	
Wm. C. Merriman ...	2 May 43	
Daniel Bennett.......	5 April 45	
Alfred Morrison......	5 May 45	
Simon W. Taylor	16 April 47	
William E. Matcham	17 April 47	
Edward T. Clarkson .	28 April 48	
James C. H. W. E. Viscount Somerton	28 April 48	M.P.
ADJUTANT. John Johnson.........	30 Sept. 39	Served in the 15th Hussars, 7th Dragoon Guards, and 1st Foot, present at Waterloo.
QUARTERMASTER. John Iveson	2 May 43	
SURGEON. John Gardner.........	1 May 40	Served in the Grenadier Guards, present at [Waterloo.

SERVICES OF REGIMENT.—Frequently called out in aid of the Civil Power. Made Royal for good services during the Riots of 1830.
REGIMENTAL APPOINTMENTS.—Light Dragoons; blue; facings, scarlet.
EFFECTIVE STRENGTH.—9 Troop Quartermasters, 1 Regimental Sergt.-Major, 30 Sergeants, 28 Corporals, 10 Trumpeters, 330 Privates.

WORCESTERSHIRE.

Queen's Own Regiment of Worcestershire Yeomanry Cavalry.

Colonel.

The Hon. Robert Henry Clive, 12 Nov. 1833. J.P., D.L., M.P.—*Hewell Grange and Oakley Park.*

Lieut.-Colonel.

Lord Ward, 28 Dec. 1837.—*Witley Court and Himley Hall.*

Major.

John Joseph Martin, 24 May, 1831. J.P., D.L.—*Ham Court.*

	Date of Appointment to Present Rank.	Remarks exhibiting Services of Officers, whether L.L., D.L., M.P., or J.P.—Country Seats, &c.
CAPTAINS.		
Sir John Somerset Pakington, Bart.	24 May 31	J.P., D.L., M.P.—Chairman of Quarter Sessions.—*Westwood Park.*
Hon. W. J. Coventry	24 May 31	J.P., D.L.—*Earl's Croom.*
Richard Hickman ...	24 May 31	J.P.—*Oldswinford House.*
James Taylor	24 May 31	J.P., D.L.—*Moseley Hall and Strensham.*
William Bennitt ...	14 Feb. 32	J.P., D.L.—*Stourton and Portway Hall.*
John Howard Galton	22 April 34	J.P., D.L.—*Hadzor Hall.*
John Russell Cookes	28 Dec. 37	J.P.—*Woodhampton.*
Right Hon. Chas. S. Cox Lord Eastmore	31 Dec. 39	J.P.—*Eastnor Castle.*
Francis Rufford	6 Oct. 41	J.P., M.P.—*Yew Tree.*
Richard Temple	11 Aug. 46	J.P., D.L.—*The Nash.*
Robert Clive	1 July 48	J.P.—*Hewell.*
LIEUTENANTS.		
Joseph Smith	24 May 31	*Kemsey.*
Arthur Skey	24 May 31	J.P., D.L.—*Spring Grove.*
William Gist	24 May 31	J.P.—*Dixton House.*
Edward Dixon	14 Feb. 32	*Dudley.*
John Curtler	22 April 34	*Droitwich.*
Jas. Arthur Taylor...	2 Oct. 40	J.P.—*Moor Hall.*
Francis T. Rufford...	5 Oct. 41	*Prescott.*
William Yate Hunt .	31 Oct. 41	*Belle View.*
John Harwood	29 Oct. 44	*Stourbridge.*
Sir W. Smith, Bart. .	1 Aug. 46	J.P.—*Eardistone.*
Walter C. Hemming	1 Aug. 46	J.P.—*Bentley Lodge.*
Robert Berkeley......	1 July 48	*Spetchley.*
Wm. Francis Taylor .	1 July 48	*Moseley Hall.*
Edw. Grizley Stone .	19 Dec. 49	J.P.—*Chambers Court.*
Frederick Knight ...	19 Dec. 49	J.P., M.P.—*Wolverley.*
CORNETS.		
Edward Bearcroft ...	23 March 36	J.P.—*Mear Hall.*
Wm. C. Watson......	7 June 42	*Bronsil.*
John S. Pakington...	13 Sept. 43	J.P.—*Westwood Park.*
George H. Biggs ...	16 Oct. 44	J.P.—*Bromsgrove.*
Theodore H. Galton .	16 Oct. 44	*Hadzor House.*
Henry Carey Elwes...	18 March 45	*The Hook.*
Frederick Smith	18 Sept. 47	*Priory, Dudley.*
Robert Peel............	1 July 48	*Waresley.*

WORCESTERSHIRE.

Queen's Own Regiment of Worcestershire Yeomanry Cavalry.
(Continued.)

	Date of Appointment to Present Rank	Remarks exhibiting Services of Officers, whether L.L., D.L., M.P., or J.P.—Country Seats, &c.
CORNETS.		
Robert Mynors	1 July 48	J.P.—*Weather Oak House.*
Edward C. Rudge	19 Jan. 49	*Manor Abbey.*
George Dowdeswell	19 Dec. 49	*Pull Court.*
ADJUTANT.		
William Emmott	24 May 31	J.P.—Served in the Peninsula, and at Waterloo. *Tutnell Mount.*
QUARTERMASTERS.		
Thomas Jones		
Thomas Hillman		
Thomas Dixon		
Joseph Milton		
William Parkes		
Charles Turk		
Richard Smith		
John Skey		
Samuel Briggs		
Robert Preedy		
John Bateman		
SURGEON.		
Wm. Henry Ricketts	24 May 31	J.P., D.L—*Hill Court.* Served in the Peninsula, and at Waterloo.
ASSIST.-SURGEONS.		
Wm. E. Johnson	22 Sept. 43	*Dudley.*
Thomas Wm. Walsh	11 Aug. 46	*Worcester.*
VET.-SURGEON.		
John Rose	4 Oct. 32	*Worcester.*
CHAPLAIN.		
Hon. and Rev. Wm. Wentworth Talbot	11 Aug. 46	Vicar of Ombersley.

SERVICES OF THE REGIMENT.—In aid of the Civil Power, in 1831, at Dudley, Upton, and Tewkesbury; in 1832 at Dudley; in 1833 at Dudley; in 1834 at Dudley, and in 1835; in 1837 at Birmingham; in 1839 Birmingham riots, fires, &c., for six weeks, and kept in readiness from August, 1839, to February, 1840, to preserve the peace, and aid the Civil Power between Newport and Birmingham; in 1842 the Regiment called out in April in the vicinity of Dudley, and returned home 22 September.

REGIMENTAL APPOINTMENTS.—Light Dragoons; scarlet, with silver lace.

EFFECTIVE STRENGTH.—2 guns, ammunition, and spring waggon; 46 Officers, 692 Privates, 22 Artillery-men; total, 760.

YORKSHIRE:— *Yorkshire Hussar Regiment of Yeomanry Cavalry.*

Lieut.-Colonel-Commandant.—Earl de Grey, K.G., 22 Jan. 1819. *Studley Park.*
Lieut.-Colonel.—Wm. Beckett, 8 Oct. 1839. M.P.—*Kirkstall Grange.*

Major.
Sir John V. B. Johnstone, Bart., 22d April 1843. M.P.—*Hackness Park.*

	Date of Appointment to Present Rank.	Remarks exhibiting Services of Officers, whether L.L., D.L., M.P., or J.P.—Country Seats, &c.
CAPTAINS.		
Thos. E. Upton	14 June 25	*Leeds.*
Thos. Bischoff	7 Jan. 40	*Leeds.*
Hon. B. R. Lawley	13 April 42	*Escrick Park.*
Edw. H. Reynard	23 March 43	*Sunderlandwick.*
Viscount Downe	22 April 43	*Bookham Grove.*
John G. Smyth	2 Sept. 44	M.P.—*Heath Hall.*
Frederick Wood	2 Nov. 44	*Woollen Hall.*
Richard T. Lee	17 Nov. 46	*Grove Hall.*
M. W. Wilson	6 Oct. 49	*Eshton Hall.* Served in the 11th Hussars.
Viscount Lascelles	23 Oct. 49	*Goldsborough Hall.*
LIEUTENANTS.		
W. S. Morritt	6 July 41	*Rokeby Park.*
Thos. D. Bland	2 Aug. 42	*Rippon Park.*
Saml. J. Brown	23 March 43	*Lofthouse Hill.*
Henry Willoughby	22 April 43	*Settrington Hall.*
W. H. F. Cavendish	2 Sept. 44	*Codicote.*
Ralph Creyke	26 July 45	*Rawcliffe Hall.*
J. R. W. Atkinson	26 July 45	*Leeds.*
W. M. E. Milner	17 Nov. 46	M.P.—*Nunappleton.*
Hon. G. E. Lascelles	23 Oct. 49	*Harewood House.*
John D. Dent	13 Nov. 49	*Ribston Hall.*
CORNETS.		
Risley Fenton	12 Sept. 39	*Caldicote House.*
Chas. Reynard	4 May 43	*Hobb Green.*
Wm. H. Harrison	5 Sept. 43	*Norwood House.*
Edw. C. Taylor	2 Sept. 44	*Firby Hall.*
Viscount Goderich	2 Nov. 44	*Mowbray Lodge.*
Edw. Blayds	1 Dec. 46	*Oulton Hall.*
Thos. H. Preston	4 Feb. 47	*Moreby Hall.* Served in the 7th Hussars.
Godfrey W. Bosville	1 Dec. 47	*Thorpe Hall.* Served in the 7th Hussars.
Wm. Alcock	29 Feb. 48	*Airville.*
Hon. Francis Lawley	13 Nov. 49	*Escrick Park.*
ADJUTANT.		
Wm. Slayter Smith	18 June 22	*Ripon.* Served in the 13th Dragoons and 10th Hussars. Present at Waterloo.
SURGEON.		
Benj. Dodsworth	26 July 42	*York.*
ASSISTANT-SURGEON.		
William Short	2 Aug. 42	*Knaresborough.*

SERVICES OF THE REGIMENT.—Called out in aid of the Civil Power on various occasions.
UNIFORM.—Hussar, lace silver.
EFFECTIVE STRENGTH.—10 Troop Sergeant-Majors, 30 Sergeants, 30 Corporals, 10 Trumpeters, 10 Farriers, 411 Privates. Total, 501. One private allowed extra to aid as Regimental Sergeant-Major.

YORKSHIRE.—1st *West York Regiment of Yeomanry Cavalry.*

Colonel.—Viscount Milton, 4 May 1846. M.P.—*Wentworth House, Yorkshire,* and *Milton House, Northampton.*

Lieut.-Colonel.
J. E. G. Elmsall, 4 May 1846. J.P. Served 8¼ years in the 1st Dragoon Guards as Captain. Present at Waterloo.—*Woodlands,* near *Doncaster.*

Major.—Richard George Lumley, 11 May 1846. Served 6¼ years in the 7th Hussars.—*Teikhill Castle.*

	Date of Appointment to Present Rank.	Remarks exhibiting Services of Officers, whether L.L., D.L., M.P., or J.P.—Country Seats, &c.
CAPTAINS.		
Vincent Corbett	17 June 29	*Wortley.*
William Jeffcock	14 Aug. 33	J.P.—*High Hayles.*
Rich. H. Wrightson	14 Aug. 33	J.P.—*Warmsworth.*
James Brown	30 Aug. 37	J.P.—*Rossington,* and *Coss Grove.*
John Carver Athorpe	22 Sept. 43	J.P.—*Dinnington Park.*
Charles Preston	22 Sept. 43	*Askham.*
Hon. Charles Wentworth Fitzwilliam	4 May 46	*Wentworth House.*
Hon. Edw. Gambier Monckton	11 May 46	J.P.—Served 4 years in 50th Foot, and 9 years [in Rifle Brigade. *Felkirk.*
Thomas Walker	11 May 46	J.P.
Wm. Brook Naylor	24 April 47	
Wm. H. de Rodes	10 Nov. 47	*Barlbrough Hall.* Served 3 years in the 1st [Dragoon Guards.
Walter T. S. Stanhope	7 Oct. 47	J.P.—*Cannon Hall.*
LIEUTENANTS.		
Benjamin Biram	19 April 32	
John Jeffcock	20 April 40	*Cooley.*
Rowland Winn	26 June 42	J.P.—*Appleby, Lincolnshire.*
A. F. B. St. Leger	22 Sept. 43	*Parkhill,* and *Berkeley-square.*
Edward Jeffcock	22 Sept. 43	*Endcliffe.*
Samuel Alex. Cooke	11 May 46	*Loonsall.*
William Bamforth	7 Oct. 47	
Thomas Taylor	7 Oct. 47	
Charles Stanley	12 May 48	
William Fowler	16 Oct. 49	
Henry B. W. Milner	16 Oct. 49	*Nunappleton.*
CORNETS.		
Michael J. Ellison	20 June 40	
Henry Jas. Newbould	20 Oct. 45	
John Hartop	11 May 46	*Barmborough Hall.*
John Field Wright	11 May 46	*Bilham.*
Richard Ellison	11 May 46	
John Foster	11 May 46	*Lingotell.*
Samuel B. Jackson	7 Oct. 47	
Thomas Barff	7 Oct. 47	
Robert John Parker	15 April 48	*Selby.*
Charles E. S. Cooke	16 Oct. 49	*Wheatley Hall.*
Arthur J. Smith	16 Oct. 49	
ADJUTANT.		
Capt. Robert Cooke	13 May 42	Late Captain 9th Queen's Royal Lancers, in which Regiment he served 38 years. Expedition to South America in 1806, and Siege of Buenos Ayres. Expedition to Walcheren in 1809, and Siege and Capture of Flushing. Subsequently accompanied a Detachment to South Beveland.

YORKSHIRE—1st *West York Regiment of Yeomanry Cavalry.*
(*Continued.*)

	Date of Appointment to Present Rank.	Remarks exhibiting Services of Officers, whether L.L., D.L., M.P., or J.P.—Country Seats, &c.
SURGEON. Edward Taylor	10 Nov. 47	
ASSIST.-SURGEON. Henry B. Square ...	15 April 48	
VETY.-SURGEON. Benjamin Cartledge .	3 Nov. 49	
CHAPLAIN. Rev. John Shape......	29 Sept. 37	D.D.—*Vicarage, Doncaster.*

SERVICES OF THE REGIMENT.—15 Aug., 1803, first formation of the Regiment, consisting of 12 Troops. 15 Aug., 1805, the Regiment assembled, by order of his Royal Highness the Commander-in-Chief, at the expected Invasion of the French, and received the thanks of the Government for its services on the occasion. 22 Sept., 1806, the Regiment was inspected by his Royal Highness the Prince of Wales, and received his unqualified approbation for its appearance under arms. 17 Oct., 1806, the Regiment was again inspected by the Prince of Wales, on which occasion his Royal Highness was much pleased at its appearance. 5 July, 1814, the Regiment received the thanks of the House of Lords for its services during the War. 11 June, 1817, the Regiment received the thanks of the Secretary of State for the Home Department for its services during the late agitation in the West Riding. 21 April, 1820, the Regiment received the thanks of the King for its services on the 12th inst., while under the command of Major-General Sir J. Bing. 15 Dec., 1832, five troops of the Regiment called out, in aid of the Civil Power, for the suppression of Riots at Sheffield. 20 May, 1839, the Regiment assembled, in aid of the Civil Power, at Rotherham and Sheffield, for the suppression of Riots, and was thanked by the Major-General of the District and the Magistrates for its services on the occasion. 11 Jan., 1840, the Regiment assembled, in aid of the Civil Power, at Sheffield, Rotherham, &c., for the suppression of Riots, and for the purpose of escorting prisoners to York Castle, and received the thanks of the Secretary of State and the Magistrates for its efficient services on the occasion. 17 Aug., 1842, the Regiment assembled at Wakefield, Dewsbury, Doncaster, &c., in aid of the Civil Power, for the suppression of Riots, and received the thanks of the Queen, the Commander-in-Chief (his Grace the Duke of Wellington), the Secretary of State, and the Magistrates, for its efficient services. 14 June, 1844, the title of the Regiment was altered from "The *South*" to "The *First* West Yorkshire Yeomanry Cavalry." 10 April, 1848, the Regiment was held in readiness, by order of the Lord-Lieutenant of the West Riding, for immediate service, if required.

REGIMENTAL APPOINTMENTS.—*Officers' Full Dress.*—Chaco, silver band, with York rose in centre; plated chain, under strap; black plume, and gold line, with acorns; dress jacket, blue, no facings; silver lace across the chest, similar to the old Light Dragoon jacket; scarlet silk sash, with silver barrels; overalls, Oxford mixture, broad silver lace down the sides; white doeskin gloves; pouch and waist belts, silver lace; pouch and sabretache, covered with scarlet cloth, silver lace, and the York rose in the centre of each; straight sword; boots, and steel spurs; saddlery, Hussar pattern, brown leather; blue shabraque, without ornament; no sheepskin. *Men's Dress.*—Chaco, white band, plated York rose in the centre; plated chain, under strap; black plume, yellow line, with acorns; dress jacket, blue, white cotton cord across the chest; scarlet silk sash, with white barrels; overalls, sky-blue, four scarlet stripes down the sides; white cotton gloves; pouch-belt, white buff; black patent pouch; black leather sword belt; boots, and steel spurs; saddlery, brown leather, the old Light Dragoon pattern; no shabraque or sheepskin.

EFFECTIVE STRENGTH.—1 Sergeant-Major, 48 Sergeants, 36 Corporals; 12 Trumpeters, 515 Privates. Total, Non-commissioned Officers and Privates, 612. The Band (24) included in the above.

YORKSHIRE.—*2d West Yorkshire Regiment of Yeomanry Cavalry.*

Lieut.-Colonel.-Commandant.
George Pollard, 19 June 1844. J.P.—*Stannary Hall, Halifax.*
Major.—William Moore, 19 June 1844.—*Halifax.*

	Date of Appointment to Present Rank.	Remarks exhibiting Services of Officers, whether L.L., D.L., M.P., or J.P.—Country Seats, &c.
CAPTAINS.		
Henry Edwards	14 July 43	J.P., M.P.—*Hope Hall, Halifax.*
John Armitage	14 July 43	*Park Cottage,* near *Huddersfield.*
Samuel Waterhouse	19 June 44	*Green Heys,* near *Halifax.*
Thomas H. Horsfall	19 June 44	*Mount St. John,* near *Thirsk.*
LIEUTENANTS.		
Geo. Thos. Pollard...	14 July 43	*Stannary Hall, Halifax.*
Henry Akroyd	19 June 44	*Saville House, Halifax.*
George Haigh	19 June 44	*The Mount, Halifax.*
Joseph T. Armitage	1 June 46	*Birkby,* near *Huddersfield.*
George Addison	13 Sept. 47	*Chesnut Cottage,* near *Bradford.*
CORNETS.		
J. P. E. D'Arcy	19 June 44	*Hey,* near *Halifax.*
Courtenay K. Clarke	12 July 44	*Haugh End, Sowerby.*
Chas. Wm. Brook	1 June 46	*Greenhead,* near *Huddersfield.*
Francis Rouse	13 Sept. 47	*Belvidere House,* near *Bradford.*
ADJUTANT.		
John W. Johnson	19 June 44	*Halifax.* Served in the 15th King's Hussars.
SURGEON.		
Abraham Jubb	13 July 49	*Halifax.*

SERVICES OF THE REGIMENT.—After the Riots in 1842 (generally called the Plug Riots) this Regiment was formed, and went on permanent duty for 8 days, in September, 1843; do., do., 1844; do., do., 1845; do., do., 1846; do., do., 1847; 13 days on duty in aid of the Civil Power at Halifax, Bradford, and Huddersfield, during the Chartist disturbances in 1848, called out by order of Major-General Thorn, and the magistracy; 5 successive days' drill at Halifax, in July, 1849. Shortly after the formation of this Regiment, the ladies of Halifax, Huddersfield, and Bradford presented them with 1 Royal, and 3 Troop standards, embroidered and fringed with gold. The following highly gratifying correspondence took place between the Earl of Harewood, Lord-Lieutenant of the County of York, and Sir George Grey, Secretary for the Home Department, commendatory of the services of the second West Yorkshire Regiment of Yeomanry Cavalry, during the Chartist Riots:—

(*Copy*) " *Hanover-square, July* 13, 1848.

"My dear Sir,—I inclose you Sir George Grey's answer to my letter requesting leave for your Regiment not to go out on permanent duty this year; I think that if you were to insert in your Orderly Book, and convey to the Regiment, the first opportunity, the high sense he, as well as all who saw the 2d West York out on duty, entertain of their services, and the soldier-like appearance they made, which would have done credit to any regular regiment in the service, it would be advisable.

" I remain, yours most truly, " HAREWOOD.
" *To Lieut.-Colonel Pollard, Commandant 2d West Y. Y. Cavalry.*"

(*Copy*) " *Whitehall, July* 12, 1848.

"My Lord,—I have no hesitation in complying with the request transmitted to me by your Lordship from Colonel Pollard, that the 2d West Yorkshire Yeomanry Cavalry should be permitted not to go out for permanent duty this year, on the grounds stated in your Lordship's letter.

" I gladly avail myself of this opportunity of acknowledging the zeal and alacrity evinced by the officers and men of this Regiment on the late occasions on which they were called out, and I request that you will be so good as to express to Colonel Pollard the high sense I entertain of the valuable service which it rendered during the recent disturbances in Yorkshire.

" I have the honour to be, my Lord, your Lordship's obedient servant, " G. GREY.
" *To the Earl of Harewood, &c., &c., Hanover-square.*"

REGIMENTAL APPOINTMENTS.—Light Dragoons; lace, gold; blue and white facings; arms, clothing, and appointments similar to the 13th Light Dragoons, both for officers and troopers, also the horse appointments.

EFFECTIVE STRENGTH.—1 Lieut.-Colonel Commandant, 1 Major, 4 Captains, 5 Lieutenants, 4 Cornets, 1 Adjutant, 1 Surgeon, 4 Troop Sergeant-Majors, 12 Sergeants, 12 Corporals, 4 Trumpeters, 196 Privates. Total, 245.

FORMER SERVICES OF THE OFFICERS.—Lieut.-Colonel Pollard, and Major Moore served in the Local Militia, until the reduction of that force took place.

MILITIA OF THE UNITED KINGDOM OF GREAT BRITAIN AND IRELAND.

Head Quarters, Doncaster.] **1st, or 3rd West York Regiment of Militia.**

Colonel.
George Cholmley, 27 Jan. 1820.—*Howsham.* Served in the 7th Light Dragoons.
Lieut.-Colonel.
John Barnett, 28 Feb. 1846.—*Hutton Hall.*
Majors.
Christopher Clarke, 22 May 1820; Charles Stapleton, 28 Feb. 1846.

	Date of Appointment to Present Rank.	Remarks exhibiting Services of Officers, whether L.L., D.L., M.P., or J.P.—Country Seats, &c.
CAPTAINS.		
Stephen Donelan	8 July 08	
John Bainbridge	14 Jan. 10	
William Stainforth	28 Feb. 46	
J. S. McAdam	28 Feb. 46	
William Hepworth	28 Feb. 46	
S. S. Thelusson	28 Feb. 46	
LIEUTENANTS.		
C. Van Straubenzee	21 June 03	
John Mather	4 Dec. 08	
Thomas Wrightson	21 Oct. 10	
T. Buxton Vincent	31 Oct. 10	
Leonard Leaf	16 July 13	
Chas. Torina Houlton	19 July 12	
J. Lockwood Harrison	11 July 25	
Henry Whittaker	15 March 31	
William Waite	15 March 31	
E. F. E. Robinson	27 Feb. 32	
Justin Homfray	22 Nov. 38	
F. A. Laughton	28 Feb. 46	
ENSIGNS.		
Robert Mann	25 Aug. 12	
William Chambers	25 July 22	
ADJUTANT.		
William Rawson	7 Aug. 27	Served in the 35th Foot 21 years. Served at the siege and taking of La Valetta in Malta in 1800. Served with the British and Russian Army in Naples in 1805, and the subsequent occupation of Sicily. The second Egyptian campaign in 1807, including the capture of Alexandria and the second attack on Rosetta. At Walcheren and at the siege and reduction of Flushing in 1809. The campaign of 1814 in Holland, including both attacks on Merxem and bombardment of Antwerp. Campaign of 1815, including the Battle of Waterloo, taking of Cambray, and capture of Paris.
ASSIST.-SURGEON.		
Robert Mann	25 Aug. 12	

Facings, Green.

Head-Quarters, Huntingdon.] **2nd, or *Huntingdonshire Regiment of Militia*.**

Colonel-Commandant.

Thomas Wright Vaughan, 27 Sept. 1827. J.P., D.L.—*Woodstone House, Huntingdonshire.* Ensign and Lieut. 33rd Regiment, 1792; Captain 85th Regiment, 1794; Captain Yeomanry, 1802; Lieut.-Colonel Volunteers, 1804 (Peterborough Corps).

CAPTAIN.	Date of Appointment to Present Rank.	Remarks exhibiting Services of Officers, whether L.L., D.L., M.P., or J.P.—Country Seats, &c.
Lord R. Montague...	3 March 46	*Kimbolton Castle, Huntingdon.*
LIEUTENANT.		
Thomas C. Browne...	3 March 08	
ADJUTANT.		
Captain J. G. Green	16 March 25	J.P.—*Buckden, Hunts.* Captain, 26 March, 1825. Served in the 21st or Royal Scots Fusiliers; 2d Lieutenant, 26 Aug., 1804; 1st Lieutenant, 6 April, 1805; Captain, 31 May, 1810; exchanged to half-pay, and then to 1st or Royal Dragoons, 26 August, 1819.
SURGEON.		
Watton Isaacson ...	14 March 46	

EFFECTIVE STRENGTH.—The full establishment of the Huntingdonshire Militia is 6 Companies, and Colonel-Commandant: the peace establishment is 2 Companies, and Major-Commandant.

When the Duke of Manchester, who was the Colonel, retired, his Grace was pleased to lay before His Majesty, through the Secretary of State, the name of Thomas Wright Vaughan, Esq., as Colonel-Commandant, (and who had had the command from 1818,) and the following is the copy of the approval:—

"*Whitehall, Sept. 24, 1827.*"

"My Lord Duke,
"I have laid before his Majesty the King, your letter of the 21st inst., recommending Thomas Wright Vaughan, Esq., to be Colonel-Commandant of the Huntingdonshire Militia, and I am to acquaint you, that His Majesty approves thereof. "LANSDOWNE."

"*His Grace the Duke of Manchester, &c., &c., &c.*"

Facings, Black.

3rd, or Durham Regiment of Militia.

Head-Quarters, Barnard Castle.

Colonel.
Henry Duke of Cleveland, 16 May 1842. K.G., D.L.—*Raby Castle.* A Colonel in the Army (1838) unattached.

Lieut.-Colonel.
John Bowes, 14 Sept. 1835. *Streatham Castle, Durham.* Late M.P., Southern Division, Durham.

Major.—Sir William Eden, Bart., 9 Feb. 1846. *Windleston Hall, Rushford.*

	Date of Appointment to Present Rank.	Remarks exhibiting Services of Officers, whether L.L., D.L., M.P., or J.P.—Country Seats, &c.
CAPTAINS.		
Jos. R. Gunthorp	20 May 03	*Swansea, Wales.*
T. R. Gray	19 Oct. 42	J.P.—*Norton, near Stockton-on-Tees.*
Thos. M. Maude	23 March 46	J.P.—*Selaby Hall, Gainford, Durham.*
R. H. S. Jackson	3 Feb. 46	*Staincross Hall, Durham.* Adjutant. Late Capt. 97th Regiment.
LIEUTENANTS.		
George Nelson	7 Feb. 09	*Morpeth, Northumberland.*
Charles Milner	24 July 15	*Reddick, South Shields.*
George Allen	12 May 33	*Tees Cottage, Darlington.*
Thos. V. R. Dotton	19 Oct. 42	*Lovaine Row, Newcastle-on-Tyne.*
Edw. Kent Fairless	19 Oct. 42	*South Shields.*
Henry R. Webster	18 Feb. 43	*Sunderland.*
Charles Skinner	9 Feb. 46	*Stockton.*
Nicholas A. Spoor	23 March 46	*Whitburn, near Sunderland.*
J. R. Boulby	23 March 46	*Bishopwearmouth.*
ENSIGNS.		
Francis Beaumont	25 Sept. 12	
Thomas Green	24 Feb. 15	*Ravensworth, Gateshead.*
J. G. Frew	3 Jan. 23	*Dublin.*
ADJUTANT, PAYMASTER, AND QUARTERMASTER.		
Capt. R. H. S. Jackson	3 Feb. 46	
SURGEON.		
Edward Nixon	24 Sept. 21	*Holyrood, Edinburgh.*

SERVICES OF THE REGIMENT.—First raised in 1760. Has served since then in England and Scotland.

Facings, White.

Head-Quarters, Oakham.] **4th, or Rutland Light Infantry Regiment of Militia.**

Captain-Commandant.
Hon. W. M. Noel, 7 March 1840.—*Hetton Lodge, Rutland, and Clanna Falls, Gloucestershire.*

Facings, Yellow.

Head-Quarters, Leeds.] **5th, or 1st West York Regiment of Militia.**

Colonel.
John Stuart Lord Wharncliffe, 23 June 1846.—*Wortley Hall, Sheffield.*

Lieut.-Colonel.
Sir John Henry Lowther, Bart., 8 Jan. 1830.—*Swillington Hall, Leeds.*

Majors.
Joseph Allen, 25 June 1815. Late Lieut. 52d Regiment.
John Dyson, 9 Sept. 1815.

	Date of Appointment to Present Rank.	Remarks exhibiting Services of Officers, whether L.L., D.L., M.P., or J.P.—Country Seats, &c.
CAPTAINS.		
Bertie Markland	4 Nov. 04	
R. Mowbray Darnell	13 April 42	
Pat. Francis Durham	6 Sept. 48	Late Capt. 37th Foot.
LIEUTENANTS.		
John Hallen	28 Nov. 07	
Frederic Bromby	4 July 08	
David M. Pollock	29 July 15	
Benjamin Ainsworth	7 Dec. 15	
John Herbert	29 Nov. 18	Late Lieutenant 41st Foot.
Moffat Palmer	10 March 31	
James Mitchell	22 Oct. 40	
John Neale	22 Oct. 40	
ENSIGN.		
Thomas Pollock	4 Oct. 42	
ADJUTANT.		
Cuthbert A. Baines	2 May 46	Late Capt. 32d Foot.

SERVICES OF THE REGIMENT.—Served during the war in Great Britain and Ireland.

Facings, Dark Green.

6TH REGIMENT OF MILITIA. 49

Head-Quarters, Chester.] **6th (or Royal) Cheshire Regiment of Militia.**

Colonel.
The Hon. H. Cholmondeley, 30 August 1840. Late M.P. for Montgomery Boroughs, D.L., served in the 1st Life Guards.—*Vale Royal.*

Major.—Edwin Corbet, 13 April 1806. J.P.

	Date of Appointment to Present Rank.	Remarks exhibiting Services of Officers, whether L.L., D.L., M.P., or J.P.—Country Seats, &c.
CAPTAINS.		
T. C. Clutton	9 Jan. 04	J.P.
John Chelwood	2 Nov. 06	
Dumvill H. C. Poole	17 March 07	
John Sawry............	22 Sept. 12	
Geo. Cornwall Leigh	15 April 25	M.P., J.P.
Edward John Stanley	20 Dec. 30	J.P.
Jas. W. Hammond...	24 July 31	J.P.
Richard C. Leigh ...	9 Oct. 43	
LIEUTENANTS.		
J. J. Superscrutt ...	2 July 03	
Hugh Calveley	2 July 03	
William Haverkam...	22 May 09	
John Legh Sykes ...	6 July 12	
Fran. Pullon Mudd...	27 May 13	
Wm. Birch Sykes ...	26 Oct. 14	
James Gale	26 Oct. 14	
E. S. Harrison	2 June 25	
ENSIGNS.		
J. E. Errington	1 July 24	
Richard Biddulph ...	1 Feb. 31	
Thomas Ward.........	4 Feb. 31	

SERVICES OF THE REGIMENT.—The Regiment was embodied for active service, and served during the American War, preceding the French Revolutionary War, in the course of which they were three times encamped, viz., at Coxheath, Warley Common, and Stokes Bay, and were disembodied, and reduced to Peace Establishment, 1784. The Regiment was again embodied for active service, and marched from Chester on March 9, 1793, and was actively employed in various parts of Great Britain uninterruptedly until June 24, 1802, when it was disembodied, consequent on peace being concluded with France. During this period the Regiment was four times encamped, viz., Bexhill, 1794; Brighton, 1795; Blyth Bay, Northumberland, 1797; and Weymouth, 1798. In consequence, however, of the short duration of peace, the Regiment was again embodied at Chester, for permanent duty, on March 11, 1803, and continued in active service in various parts of Great Britain and Ireland until Feb. 24, 1816, when it was disembodied. During this period of service the monthly musters were taken at the following places:—March 24, 1803, Chester; June 24, 1803, Yarmouth; from July 24 to Nov. 24, 1803, encamped at Aberton; from July 24, 1803, to June 24, 1804, Chelmsford; July 24, 1804, Hull; from Aug. 24 to Sept. 24, 1804, camp, Ridgmount; from Oct. 24, 1804, to Feb. 24, 1805, Hull; from March 24, 1805, to June 24, 1805, Hailsham; from July 24, 1805, to June 24, 1806, Eastbourne; from July 24, 1806, to Dec. 24, 1807, Lewes; from Jan. 24, 1808, to Sept. 24, 1808, Portsmouth; from Nov. 24, 1808, to Oct. 24, 1809, Liverpool; Nov. 24, 1809, Plymouth; Dec. 24, 1809, Dartmoor; from Jan. 24, 1810, to July 24, 1813, Plymouth and Devonport; from Aug. 24, 1813, to Nov. 24, 1813, Lichfield; Dec. 24, 1813, Liverpool; from Jan. 24, 1814, to Aug. 24, 1815, Dublin; Sept. 24, 1815, Kilkenny; from Oct. 24, 1815, to Dec. 24, 1815, Tipperary; Jan. 24, 1816, Clonmel; Feb. 24, 1816, Chester, on which day the Regiment was disembodied, and the staff reduced to the Peace Establishment.

During the period from July, 1799, to Dec. 1813, 1,598 men volunteered from the Royal Cheshire Militia into various Regiments of the line; and in the year 1810 the whole Regiment volunteered to serve in Ireland, the terms of the men's service at that time not binding them to serve out of Great Britain.

Since the Regiment was disembodied in 1816 it has been assembled for twenty-eight days' training and exercise at four periods, viz., in the years 1820, 1821, 1825, and 1831.

Facings, blue.

Head-Quarters, Reading.] **7th, or Royal Berkshire Regiment of Militia.**

Colonel.
John Blagrave, 5 Sept. 1842. D.L., J.P.—*Calcot Park*, near *Reading*.

Lieut.-Colonel.—Charles Bacon, 31 Dec. 1842. D.L., J.P.

Major.
John Leveson Gower, 12 July 1845. D.L., J.P.—*Bill Hill*, near *Wokingham*.

	Date of Apointment to Present Rank.	Remarks exhibiting Services of Officers, whether L.L., D.L., M.P., or J.P., Country Seats, &c.
CAPTAINS.		
Henry Wm. Vincent	17 June 28	*Lilly Hill*, near *Bracknell*.
Henry Greenway	8 Sept. 37	J.P.—*Trunkwell House*, near *Reading*.
James J. Wheble	14 Sept. 37	J.P.—*Bulmershe Court*, near *Reading*.
Hon. E. P. Bouverie	23 Feb. 38	*Coleshill*.
Edward Blagrave	6 Aug. 45	*Magdalen College, Oxford*.
Edmund Wheble	29 Dec. 45	*Bulmershe Court*, near *Reading*.
Henry Pole	21 July 46	*White Waltham*, near *Maidenhead*.
LIEUTENANTS.		
Stephen Judd	26 Nov. 05	
William Coles	21 June 09	
John Norris	29 April 14	
James Hance	15 Oct. 14	
John Parker	16 Oct. 14	
William Rowe	22 Feb. 15	
Benjamin Hawkins	26 Sept. 18	
Henry Ince	2 July 21	
ENSIGN.		
Arthur Deane	3 May 31	
ADJUTANT.		
Alex. Nowell Sherson	19 Feb. 46	Captain Unattached. Late 72d Highlanders.
QUARTERMASTER.		
George Grey		
SURGEON.		
Charles Greenhead		
ASSIST.-SURGEON.		
Stephen Judd		

SERVICES OF THE REGIMENT.—Raised in 1758; disembodied at the Peace of Amiens. Called out again, after a few months, in 1803; embarked for Ireland May, 1813; and remained embodied until 1816.

Facings, Blue.

8th, or Royal North Lincoln Regiment of Militia.

[Head-Quarters, Lincoln.]

Colonel.—The Viscount Alford, 11 June 1836. M.P., J.P., D.L.
Harleston Lodge, Northampton; and *Belgrave-square, London.*

Lieut.-Colonel.—William Edward Tomline, 11 June 1836.
1, *Carlton-terrace, London;* and *Reby, Lincolnshire.*
Served in the 1st Life Guards.

Major.—Richard Ellison, 24 June 1836. J.P., D.L.—*Boultham Hall, Lincoln.*

	Date of Appointment to Present Rank.	Remarks exhibiting Services of Officers, whether L.L., D.L., M.P., or J.P.—Country Seats, &c.
CAPTAINS.		
John Brown	25 Dec. 06	
Joseph Clifton	16 May 11	
Henry Thorold	19 June 35	
Banks Stanhope	1 May 41	J.P., D.L.—*Reevsby Hall, Lincolnshire.*
Weston Cracroft	18 May 43	J.P., D.L.—*Hackthorn, Lincolnshire.* Served in the 1st Royal Dragoons.
John Tomline	15 Feb. 45	Served in the 59th Regiment.
Dudley Heneage	13 Feb. 46	
J. T. W. Sibthorp	13 Feb. 47	J.P., D.L.—*Branston, Lincoln.*
LIEUTENANTS.		
James Joseph Hayer	4 Oct. 09	
Samuel McDakin	19 Feb. 13	
Thomas Probart	14 July 13	
Thomas Chennell	10 Aug. 20	
Thomas Rayworth	15 Nov. 31	
John Swanton	15 Nov. 31	
George Gurley	16 Jan. 46	
ENSIGNS.		
Augustus L. Hamner	6 Sept. 32	
John P. Robinson	7 Feb. 46	
William B. Shepard	4 March 46	
Alex. E. Graydon	23 May 48	
ADJUTANT.		
Capt. F. Kennedy	21 April 24	Was present at the Siege and Capture of Flushing, 1809; Campaigns of 1811, 12, 13, 14, and 15, including the first Siege of Badajoz, and covering the second Siege, as also that of Ciudad Rodrigo, crossing the Esla; Retreat from Burgos; Actions of Val Moresco, Peyrehorade and Echalor; Battles of Fuentes d'Onor, Salamanca, Vittoria, Pampeluna, Pyrenees, Nive, Orthes, and Waterloo; and he led the column of attack at the Storming of Cambray. He has received the War Medal and six clasps.
SURGEON.		
William Rawlins	24 March 16	M.D.

Facings, Blue.

Head-Quarters, Whitehaven.] **9th, or Royal Cumberland Regiment of Militia.**

Colonel.
Hon. H. C. Lowther, 10 Sept. 1830. M.P.

Lieut.-Colonel.
J. K. Wilson, 8 June 1847. J.P.

	Date of Appointment to Present Rank.	Remarks exhibiting Services of Officers, whether L.L., D.L., M.P., or J.P.—Country Seats, &c.
CAPTAINS.		
T. A. Hill	14 July 12	
T. Brook	10 June 25	
S. W. Lacy	22 Feb. 31	
J. Willock	10 March 31	Served in the Army.
W. P. Meek	11 Sept. 38	Served in the Army.
W. G. C. Momnis	30 June 46	
LIEUTENANTS.		
J. Beaumont	21 April 09	
H. Denton	15 June 13	
J. N. Stephenson	4 Feb. 14	
W. Widdress	9 June 20	
J. Close	20 March 20	
ENSIGNS.		
R. Jameson	7 Nov. 16	
T. Metcalfe	22	
Hon. R. Barrington	10 June 25	
T. Powel	22 Feb. 31	
H. G. Humphries	25 June 41	
H. Humphries	30 March 46	
C. Hutton	31 March 46	
F. W. Brook	31 March 46	
ADJUTANT.		
Capt. R. Pennington	15 May 33	Served in the Peninsula from June, 1809, and during the greatest part of the subsequent campaigns, including the battle of Busaco, where he commanded one of the advance picquets of the 3d Division on the morning of the action, and was sharply engaged with the enemy; retreat to the lines of Torres Vedras, advance from thence, actions and affairs at Leria, Redinha, Pombal, Roblida, Condeixa, Foz d'Arouce, Guarda, and Sabugal; battles of Fuentes d'Onor, siege of Badajoz (wounded in the right thigh), actions at Campo Mayor, El Bodon, and Guinaldo; affairs and actions in the Pyrenees, St. Pé (contused wound), Hasparren, and Grassietta; battles of Nivelle, Nive, and Orthes (severely wounded), besides several other affairs of posts and picquets during the war. He has received the War Medal, and five clasps.
PAYMASTER.		
E. B. Harraden	25 May 03	
QUARTERMASTER.		
J. Jackson	25 May 03	
SURGEON.		
J. Simpson	25 May 03	
ASSIST.-SURGEON.		
P. M. Wilmot	22 Sept. 31	

Facings, Blue.

10th, or West Suffolk Regiment of Militia.

Head-Quarters, Bury St. Edmunds.

Colonel.—The Right Hon. the Earl Jermyn, 25 March 1846. D.L., M.P.

Lieut.-Colonel.—William Newton, 1 Nov. 1832.

Major.—William Wilde, 25 Dec. 1813.

	Date of Appointment to Present Rank.	Remarks exhibiting Services of Officers, whether L.L., D.L., M.P., or J.P.—Country Seats, &c.
CAPTAINS.		
George Bates	25 Oct. 10	
Thos. B. Western	22 June 24	
O'Neil Segrave	14 Oct. 30	
John G. Weller Poley	7 March 31	
Thomas Ross	14 April 46	
LIEUTENANTS.		
George Gooch	25 June 08	
John Garthorn	29 Feb. 11	
John Robt. Cuffley	2 Jan. 24	
David Dundas	24 May 27	
Danzie Carter	7 Feb. 31	
William Quarles	21 Feb. 31	
Paston Nicholls	15 March 31	
R. Harrison Black	1 July 31	
Lord Alfred Hervey	4 July 31	
Joseph St. John	1 Oct. 43	
John M'Grigor	25 Sept. 46	
ENSIGN.		
Samuel Chambers	9 May 31	
ADJUTANT.		
John M'Grigor	24 Jan. 46	Served 26 years in the Scots Fusilier Guards.
SURGEON.		
George Creed	22 June 24	

SERVICES OF THE REGIMENT.—Served during the whole of the period that the English Militias were embodied. In Ireland from Sept., 1798, to June, 1799, and from April, 1813, to Sept., 1814.

Facings, Yellow.   *Agents.*—Messrs. Cox and Co.

11th, or 2d Royal Surrey Regiment of Militia.

Head-Quarters, Guildford.

Colonel.
The Hon. Thomas Cranley Onslow, 16 March 1812.—*Upton House, Alresford, Hants.* Late of the 3d Foot Guards.

Lieut.-Colonel.
Sir Richard Frederick, Bart., 28 March 1809. J.P., D.L.—*Burwood Park, Esher, Surrey.* Capt. H. P. 9th Foot.

Major.—Viscount Cranley, 30 Oct. 1846. J.P.

	Date of Appointment to Present Rank.	Remarks exhibiting Services of Officers, whether L.I., D.L., M.P., or J.P.—Country Seats, &c.
CAPTAINS.		
Michael Barnes	25 April 08	
Wm. Tempest Wight	28 March 09	
W. Barclay Chadwick	30 May 10	
C. August Manning	12 Oct. 29	J.P., D.L. Governor of Portland Castle, &c.
Charles Mangles	14 Dec. 30	J.P.—*Poyle House, Farnham, Surrey.*
Augustus C. Onslow	28 Dec. 45	
LIEUTENANTS.		
John Blatch	26 Aug. 07	
John Daws	25 Dec. 07	
James Fitzwilliams	25 July 11	
John Hatch	19 July 13	
Charles O. Hodgson	25 June 19	
R. Weller Chadwick	1 Nov. 33	
Arthur Robinson	22 April 38	
ENSIGNS.		
Abraham Evanson	26 March 31	
Andrew Garden	31 March 31	
C. S. J. Longford	26 June 31	
Henry Dive Parrott	1 Nov. 33	
Fred. Thos. Durrell	31 July 41	
ADJUTANT.		
Francis Pyner	10 Dec. 19	Capt. H. P., 58th Regiment.
PAYMASTER.		
C. Orlando Hodgson	24 Nov. 19	
QUARTERMASTER.		
William Holl	24 July 19	
SURGEON.		
William Stevenson	15 Oct. 31	

SERVICES OF THE REGIMENT.—Served in Ireland, 1812 and 1813.

EFFECTIVE STRENGTH.—1 Colonel, 1 Lieutenant-Colonel, 1 Major, 8 Captains, 10 Lieutenants, 6 Ensigns, 1 Adjutant, 1 Paymaster, 1 Quartermaster, 1 Surgeon, and 668 Privates.

Facings, Blue.

12th, or York East Riding Regiment of Militia.

Head-Quarters, Beverley.

Colonel.—C. Grimston, 29 Oct. 1833. D.L., J.P.
Lieut.-Colonel.—G. H. Thompson, 15 November 1833. Served in the Army.
Major.—Sir H. M. Vavasour, Bart., 21 April 1838.

	Date of Appointment to Present Rank.	Remarks exhibiting Services of Officers, whether L.L., D.L., M.P., or J.P.—Country Seats, &c.
CAPTAINS.		
W. J. Lenthal.........	29 Dec. 09	Served in the Army.
F. L. Taylor	13 May 15	
S. J. Watson	8 June 21	
E. F. Coulson.........	21 May 31	
W. F. Bethel	2 Oct. 32	
J. J. Hopkinson	25 May 46	
F. Uppleby	25 May 46	
J. Todd	12 Jan. 47	
M. J. Grimston	12 Jan. 47	
R. Reynard............	21 Feb. 48	
LIEUTENANTS.		
W. Corrigan	2 May 10	
S. Ramsey	8 July 11	
J. Richardson.........	19 Jan. 16	
J. Kidd	30 Jan. 16	
T. Howard	2 June 20	
H. Raines	10 Dec. 31	
C. E. B. Dawson ...	13 March 46	
C. N. Hopkinson ...	25 May 46	
J. T. Buckle	25 May 46	
G. Holmes	22 Feb. 48	
ENSIGNS.		
E. Coupland	31 Aug. 15	
C. Watson	13 March 46	
J. S. Bell...............	13 March 46	
E. J. Inman	13 March 46	
H. W. Todd	16 Sept. 48	
ADJUTANT.		
J. Bell	20 July 24	
SURGEON.		
M. Chalmers	15 Oct. 14	M.D.
ASSIST.-SURGEON.		
E. Coupland	31 Aug. 15	En.

Facings, Buff.

13th, or North Hants Regiment of Militia.

Head-Quarters, Winchester.

Colonel.
The Right Hon. the Marquis of Winchester, 22 June 1842. J.P.—*Amport House.*

Lieutenant-Colonel.
Peter Hawker, 15 Nov. 1821. D.L.—*Longparish House.* Formerly of the 14th Light Dragoons; served in the Peninsula; was twice wounded, and received the War Medal.

Major.—Sir William Paulet, Bart.

Captains.
Henry Augustus Brander, 3 June 1825. Charles Popham Hill, 3 June 1825.

Lieutenant.—R. H. Fitzroy Somerset, 17 Nov. 1849.

Adjutant.—Joseph Tomlinson, 5 March 1846.

Surgeon.—William White, 13 July 1813.

Facings, Black.

14th, or East Essex Regiment of Militia.

Head-Quarters, Colchester.

Colonel.—Henry John Conyers, 29 Jan. 1828. J.P., D.L.—*Copt Hall, Epping.*

Lieut.-Colonel.
Jeremiah Kersteman, 2 June 1822. J.P., D.L.—*Loftman's,* near *Rochford.*

Major.—James Anderson, 13 Oct. 1831. J.P., D.L.—*Clifton, Bristol.*

	Date of Appointment to Present Rank.	Remarks exhibiting Services of Officers, whether L.L., D.L., M.P., or J.P.—Country Seats, &c.
CAPTAINS.		
William T. Maybey	14 Aug. 11	Colchester.
Edward G. Stone		*Loughton,* near *Tewkesbury.*
William Sanford		*Lambe, Ardleigh.*
Thos. J. Spitty	10 May 33	*Billericay.*
Denzel Ede		J.P.—*Brentwood.*
Arthur John Landon	10 Sept. 32	1, *Old Square, Lincoln's Inn.*
Robert J. Hansler	12 March 42	*Notting Hill, Bayswater.*
Cardinal Brewster	49	J.P.—*Halstead, Essex.*
LIEUTENANTS.		
John Lynch	2 Sept. 11	*Dromin, Killarney, Ireland.*
John Bell	30 June 12	*Rampant Horse-street, Norwich.*
Charles Rush	19 Jan. 13	*Braxted, Essex.*
John Light	2 June 13	*Ann Street, Wexford, Ireland.*
Charles Theedam	30 Sept. 31	*Frinton,* near *Walton, Essex.*
Henry Eustace	15 April 46	*Little Sanford, Essex.*
Henry Jones	16 April 46	Colchester.
W. H. L. Johnson	17 April 46	Colchester.
Philip Goldney	18 April 46	*St. Paul's Churchyard, London.*
ENSIGNS.		
Mark L. Light	19 April 46	*Ann Street, Wexford, Ireland.*
Samuel C. Kirby	20 April 46	*Little Clacton, Essex.*
ADJUTANT.		
Captain Jesse Jones	15 April 23	Colchester. Served with the Grenadier Guards at the defence of Cadiz and Isla de Leon, from 1st April, 1810, to May, 1811, and in the battle of Barrosa, for which he has received the War Medal and one clasp. In 1813 and 1814, he served in Holland, at the attack on Merxem, and storming of Bergen-op-Zoom. At the battle of Waterloo, the following year, he was severely wounded through the body by a musket-ball.
QUARTERMASTER.		
John Snell	8 July 19	77, *Little Britain, London.*
SURGEON.		
Thomas Calley	20 June 17	*Chudley, Devon.*

SERVICES OF THE REGIMENT.—Raised about the middle of the last century. Went to Scotland in 1805, and returned the following year. Went to Ireland in 1814, where they remained till 1816.

Facings, Green.

15th, or North Devon Regiment of Militia.

Head-Quarters, Barnstaple.

Colonel.
Right Hon. Lord Poltimore, 6 Dec. 1830. J.P., D.L.—*Poltimore*.

	Date of Appointment to Present Rank.	Remarks exhibiting Services of Officers, whether L.L., D.L., M.P., or J.P.—Country Seats, &c.
CAPTAINS.		
John May	3 Feb. 12	J.P., D.L.—*Broadgate, Barnstaple.*
Thomas Hole	16 June 15	D.L.—*Collipriest, Tiverton.*
William Hole	5 May 23	J.P. Served in the 36th Foot.
John Francis Worth	7 March 31	D.L.
M. R. N. Parker ...	15 April 31	J.P., D.L.—*Whiteway House, Chudleigh.*
Chas. H. Webber ...	25 April 46	*Buckland House, Barnstaple.*
William C. Rayer ...	25 April 46	
Richard Hall Clarke.	25 April 46	
LIEUTENANTS.		
John Atherley.........	3 Nov. 04	
William Johnstone...	27 Nov. 07	
Robert Hart	8 Aug. 10	
George Fortescue ...	29 July 11	
Thomas Smith	15 Sept. 18	
George Webb.........	16 June 15	
Robert Budd	19 June 15	J.P.
Thomas Harrison ...	16 Feb. 46	
Edward Moore	16 Feb. 46	
ENSIGNS.		
Thomas Sampson ...	25 Aug. 15	
Samuel Sampson......	6 April 32	
Sir Lawrence Vaughan Polk, Bart.	26 Feb. 35	J.P., D.L.—*Haldon House, Exeter.*
ADJUTANT.		
John Allen Ridgway.	7 June 31	Late Captain in the Rifle Brigade. Served in the Peninsula with the Rifle Brigade, from May, 1812, to the end of that war in 1814, including the battle of Vittoria, and various minor affairs. Served also the campaign of 1815, and was present at the battle of Waterloo. Severely wounded in the right shoulder by a musket-shot at the taking of Vera heights, and lost the forefinger of the left hand by a musket-shot at Waterloo. He has received the War Medal and three clasps.
QUARTERMASTER.		
William Arter.........	8 July 15	
SURGEON.		
John Beavis Bignell.	30 May 32	M.D., J.P.
ASSIST.-SURGEON.		
Edward Moore	17 July 46	M.D.

Facings, White.

16th, or First Somerset Regiment of Militia.

Head Quarters, Taunton.

Colonel.
John Earl Poulett, 23 Feb. 1819.—*Hinton St. George*, near *Ilminster*.

Lieut.-Colonel.
John Twyford Joliffe, 1 March 1839.—*Ammerdown Park*, near *Bath*.

Majors.
Vere Viscount Hinton, 3 April 1846.—*Hinton St. George.* Late Ensign in the 68th Regiment of Foot.
Robert James Elton, 4 April 1846.—*Whitestanton*, near *Chard*. Late Captain 17th Lancers.

	Date of Appointment to Present Rank.	Remarks exhibiting Services of Officers, whether L.L., D.L., M.P., or J.P.—Country Seats, &c.
Captains.		
Edward Day	31 March 14	
John Jones	15 June 14	
Henry Godfrey Marsh	2 March 31	
J. Hammet Beadon	11 May 31	
W. Vaughan Jenkins	11 Jan. 35	
C. Wane Loveridge	19 June 35	
Thomas Hussey	4 April 46	
J. Matthew Quantork	11 June 35	Served as Lieut. in the 4th Dragoon Guards.
John Randle Ford	6 April 46	
Lieutenants.		
John Eaton	24 Jan. 14	
Robert Jesse	27 Jan. 14	
W. Hutchings Chorley	26 Sept. 14	
John Gatehouse	27 Sept. 14	
Ed. Nagle Connellan	6 July 23	
Lewis Rooke	18 March 25	
Spencer Palmer	8 Oct. 27	
Chas. Trigge Chivers	7 July 29	
H. Burford Norman	25 Aug. 37	
Joseph Danl. Bishop	13 July 40	
Fred. C. S. Standert	3 April 46	
H. B. Batten	25 March 48	
Ensigns.		
Wm. Henry Powell	29 Jan. 12	
Wm. Robt. Steele	20 July 15	Served in the 48th Foot.
Fred. Barton Tench	21 March 31	
John Wright	21 March 31	
S. Ryder Dampier	3 April 46	
Henry Adney	4 April 46	
Henry Gully Foy	4 April 46	
Henry Cripps Wright	25 March 48	
Adjutant.		
William Surtees Cook	23 Feb. 46	Captain, unattached.
Surgeon.		
Charles Hugo	25 Dec. 17	
Assist.-Surgeons.		
Wm. Henry Powell	Nov. 11	
Henry Gulley Foy	4 April 46	

Facings, Black.

Head-Quarters, Appleby.] **17th, or *Royal Westmoreland Regiment of Militia*.**

Lieutenant-Colonel-Commandant.
William Earl of Lonsdale. L.L.—*Lowther Castle*, and *Whitehaven Castle*.

Major.
James Spedding, 2 Dec. 1828. D.L.—*Summer Grove*, near *Whitehaven*. Served in the 1st Foot Guards, as Lieutenant and Captain; was at the Helder, under Sir R. Abercromby, and Duke of York; present at landing and action, 27 Aug. 1799. Served in battles of 10 and 19 Sept. and 2 Oct. near Egmont-op-See, and severely wounded in the latter. Served in Sicily and Mediterranean, under Sir John Moore, in 1806 and 1807.

CAPTAINS.	Date of Appointment to Present Rank.	Remarks exhibiting Services of Officers, whether L.L., D.L., M.P., or J.P.—Country Seats, &c.
James Spedding......	11 March 39	
Geo. A. F. Bentinck	21 Aug. 44	
LIEUTENANTS.		Lieutenants Richardson, Mawbey, and Bell volunteered and served in 3d Provisional Battalion of Militia, in France, in 1814; in 7th Division of the Army, commanded by Sir Stapleton Cotton, now Lord Combermere.
James Richardson ...	28 March 13	
Joseph Mawbey	5 May 20	
John Bell	18 May 20	
ENSIGN.		
Joseph Moses	21 May 97	Served in the 3d Provisional Battalion, in 1814, in France, &c.
ADJUTANT.		
Edward H. Smith ...	7 May 46	Served in the 76th Regiment, and was in West Indies from 1834 to 1837.
PAYMASTER.		
James Bell	21 March 22	Served in the Regiment throughout the war, and served with 3d Provisional Battalion, in 1814, in France.
SURGEON.		
Orton Bradley	27 Jan. 13	

SERVICES OF THE REGIMENT.—This Regiment has served in all parts of the United Kingdom, and was one of the first to volunteer to serve in Ireland. In 1814, when volunteers were required to reinforce the army, this Regiment particularly distinguished itself. The strength of the Battalion consisted of 1 Major, 4 Captains, 4 Lieutenants, and 4 Ensigns; and of these, 3 Captains, viz., Bell, Sowden, and Richardson, and 2 Ensigns, Mawbey and Bell, volunteered to extend their services abroad, and formed part of the 3d Provisional Battalion commanded by Sir Watkyn Wynn, Bart., which landed at Bordeaux, and formed part of the 7th Division of the Duke of Wellington's army, commanded by Sir Stapleton Cotton, now Lord Combermere, owing to contrary winds, they arrived just too late for the battle of Toulouse, where the ground had been marked out for the Brigade to which they belonged.

EFFECTIVE STRENGTH.—1 Lieutenant-Colonel-Commandant, 1 Major, 4 Captains, 4 Lieutenants, 4 Ensigns, 1 Adjutant, 1 Paymaster, 1 Surgeon.

Facings, Blue.

18th, or Bedfordshire Regiment of Militia.

Head-Quarters, Bedford.

Colonel.
Richard Thomas Gilpin, 11 Sept. 1848. J.P., D.L.—*Hockliffe Grange.* Formerly of the 14th Light Dragoons.

Lieut.-Col.
William Bartholomew Higgins, 12 Sept. 1848. J.P., D.L.—*Picts Hill.*

Major.
Francis Charles Hastings Russell, 5 April 1849. M.P.—Formerly of Coldstream Guards.

	Date of Appointment to Present Rank.	Remarks exhibiting Services of Officers, whether L.L., D.L., M.P., or J.P.—Country Seats, &c.
CAPTAINS.		
John Harvey Astell	21 Feb. 46	
Chas. Hervey Smith	23 Feb. 46	
Robert H. Wilkinson	17 Nov. 47	
Wm. Cooper Cooper	13 June 48	J.P.—*Toddington Park.*
LIEUTENANTS.		
Fred. John Rix	30 Dec. 12	
Wm. C. R. Judd	20 Feb. 46	
Wm. K. Browne	24 Feb. 46	
John Lowden	4 Dec. 47	
William Stuart	13 June 58	
Charles Lindsell	19 Dec. 48	
ENSIGNS.		
George Ledger	21 Feb. 46	
Henry B. Richardson	9 Aug. 48	
Norborne G. Smith	20 Dec. 48	
ADJUTANT.		
Thos. Johnes Smith	6 Feb. 46	Captain, 7 Feb. 1846. Late Captain in the 56th Regiment.
SURGEON.		
Chas. Wright Hyne	7 Sept. 09	

SERVICES OF THE REGIMENT.—The Regiment was first embodied in the early part of 1760, and disembodied in Dec., 1761; embodied for the second time, 5th May, 1778, and were stationed at various quarters in the south of England; disembodied 17th Nov., 1782; embodied for the third time 4th Feb., 1793, and after serving in England and Ireland upwards of nine years, were disembodied in April, 1802; embodied for the fourth time, 25th March, 1803, and remained on actual service in England and Ireland nearly twelve years, being disembodied 1st Feb., 1815.

Facings, Dark green.

19TH REGIMENT OF MILITIA. 61

Head Quarters, Chelmsford.] 19th, or *West Essex Regiment of Militia.*

Colonel.
Sir John Tyssen Tyrrell, Bart., 27 April 1831. M.P.—*Boreham House.*
Lieut.-Colonel.—Quintin Dick, 11 Feb. 1846.
Major.—G. S. Sadler, 29 May 1829.

	Date of Appointment to Present Rank.	Remarks exhibiting Services of Officers, whether L.L., D.L., M.P., or J.P.—Country Seats, &c.
CAPTAINS.		
Charles Haselfoot	21 May 25	
W. M. Tufnell	11 Feb. 46	
Henry Bullock	12 Feb. 46	
John Wright	13 Feb. 46	
A. T. Schrieber	14 Feb. 46	
A. E. Williams	16 Feb. 46	
P. H. Meyer	17 Feb. 46	
Z. Button	17 Feb. 46	
LIEUTENANTS.		
Edward Gazeley......	31 Oct. 06	
Samuel Trigge.........	12 July 12	
John Watson..........	5 Dec. 12	
John Butcher	4 July 13	
A. N. Irwin............	8 Feb. 14	
John Wallis	1 Oct. 14	
Manasseh Brooke	1 Oct. 14	
John Humble..........	28 Oct. 15	
Henry Bird............	8 Aug. 20	
W. J. Lucas	25 Feb. 38	
ENSIGNS.		
J. T. Gilson	15 Sept. 31	
J. D. Trigge............	16 March 33	
H. Edinborough	11 Feb. 46	Served as a Volunteer in New Zealand during the operations in 1845, and was present in several of the skirmishes; he also volunteered his services in the Mounted Police in New South Wales on several occasions.
R. H. Lovell	11 Feb. 46	
ADJUTANT.		
Hugh Pearson.........		Served in China, (Medal) in the 49th; at Chusan and Canton (severely wounded).
PAYMASTER.		
Samuel Trigge.........		
SURGEON.		
Leonard Foaker		
ASSIST.-SURGEON.		
Henry Bird............		

Facings, Yellow.

20th, or First Royal Surrey Regiment of Militia.

Head-Quarters, Richmond.

Colonel.
James Bogle Delass, 4 July 1838. *Stoke Park, Guilford.*
Served in the King's Dragoon Guards as Captain (1812) some years.

Lieut.-Colonel.
William Holme Sumner, 2 Aug. 1838. *Hatchlands, Surrey.*

Major.—Thomas Budgen, 12 Sept. 1813.

CAPTAINS.	Date of Appointment to Present Rank.		Remarks exhibiting Services of Officers, whether L.L., D.L., M.P., or J.P.—Country Seats, &c.
Lyttleton Lyster	23 Dec.	12	*Union Hall, Roscaberry, Ireland.*
Alex. McDonald	14 Aug.	15	
Henry Laws Long	15 Oct.	16	*Hampton Lodge, Farnham.*
Edward Bray	18 Sept.	23	
Robert Taylor	6 Dec.	28	
Thomas G. C. Riley	20 Nov.	29	
Frederick B. Long	6 Dec.	38	
Wm. Paxton Jervis	12 Dec.	38	
LIEUTENANTS.			
Charles Friend	20 Jan.	12	
John Friend	5 July	14	
Charles F. Lyster	6 July	14	
Thomas Sparks	16 Aug.	15	Half-pay, Ensign 56th Regiment.
Charles Edw. Long	20 May	37	
Edmund Knapp	22 May	37	
Lyttleton H. Lyster	19 Nov.	38	
Thos. Lyon Thurlow	23 May	40	
James F. N. Daniell	25 May	40	
ENSIGNS.			
William Beckford	23 May	40	
Augustus Goldsmid	14 Oct.	41	
ADJUTANT.			
Henry E. Austen	22 Dec.	45	Half-pay Captain. Served 18 years in the 71st Regiment Light Infantry.
SURGEON.			
Thomas Cock	17 Dec.	31	
ASSIST.-SURGEON.			
Dr. Richard Hassall			M.D.—*Richmond.* In temporary charge of [Staff.

SERVICES OF THE REGIMENT.—In Ireland during part of the late War in 1811-12; and in England; the rest of its service in the different garrison towns.

Facings, Blue.

Agents, Messrs. Cox and Co., Craig's Court, Charing-cross.

21ST REGIMENT OF MILITIA. 63

Head-Quarters, York.] **21st, or 2d West York Regiment of Militia.**
Colonel.
William Markham, 5th March 1832. J.P., D.L.—*Becca Hall,* near *Aberford.*
Lieut.-Colonel.
Charles T. Brandling, 29 Jan. 1846. J.P., D.L.—*Middleton Lodge,* near *Leeds.*
Served in the 10th Royal Hussars as Cornet and Lieutenant.
Majors.
Jeremiah Bower, 14 Oct. 1820.—*Cheadle Lodge, Cheshire.* Served as Capt. during the war.
Joshua Saml. Crompton, 29 Jan. 1846. J.P., D.L.—*Sion Hill,* near *Thirsk.*

	Date of Appointment to Present Rank.		Remarks exhibiting Services of Officers, whether L.L., D.L., M.P., or J.P.—Country Seats, &c.
CAPTAINS.			
Joseph Newcombe ...	27 Jan.	31	*Upton, Slough.* Served on the Peninsula.
John Wilson	10 June	32	J.P.—*Seacroft Hall,* near *Leeds.*
Jeremiah Dyson	10 Sept.	36	
Rich. M. Milnes......	19 Nov.	40	M.P.—*Frystone,* near *Ferrybridge.*
William Linskill......	29 June	41	Served in the 28th Regt. as Ensign and Lieut., and in the 5th Dragoon Guards as Lieut., Adjutant, and Captain.
S. C. H. Ogle	22 April	43	M.P.—*84, Eaton-square, London.*
John Hardy	14 April	44	J.P., D.L.—*3, Portland-place, London,* and
Richard S. Carrol ...	29 Jan.	46	*Boston,* near *Tadcaster.* [*Yorkshire.*
F. W. D. Bland	29 Jan.	46	*Kippar Park,* near *Leeds.*
William Webster ...	19 Aug.	48	*Parthenon Club, London.*
LIEUTENANTS.			
Robert James	18 Jan.	03	
Jeremiah Kershaw...	6 July	08	
Edw. Thos. White ...	23 May	11	
William Walker......	3 April	32	
John Barstow	29 Dec.	38	*Nunthorpe,* near *York.*
Francis Watt	29 Dec.	38	*Walkington Lodge, Beverley*
W. E. Richardson ...	25 July	40	*Ricca Hall, Escrick, York.*
Thos. K. L. Walker...	26 Nov.	42	
C. J. Sherrard.........	29 Jan.	46	
John Sutton	19 Sept.	46	
H. H. Elrington ...	19 Sept.	46	
R. G. Walker	19 Aug.	48	
ENSIGNS.			
Charles Atkinson ...	5 Aug.	15	Served in the Royal Marines as 2d Lieut., [from 1811 to 1814.
Thomas Watson......	29 Jan.	46	
H. C. Wardle	29 Jan.	46	
Richard Alderson ...	29 Jan.	46	
Frederic Hope	29 Jan.	46	
Fred. Dodd.............	29 Jan.	46	
Strafford C. St. Leger	29 Feb.	48	
Cottswold Burdon ...	16 July	49	
ADJUTANT.			
Capt. A. Graves	27 Nov.	19	Capt. 32d Regiment, 13 April, 1813. Served in the expedition to Copenhagen in 1807; campaign in Portugal and Spain, including the battles of Roleia and Vimiera, advance into Spain, retreat to, and battle of Corunna. Expedition to Walcheren, Siege of Flushing, and ascent of the Scheldt, 1809. Peninsular campaigns from June, 1811, to Sept., 1813, including the siege of the Forts and battle of Salamanca (three wounds, two severe, one slight), siege of Burgos and retreat from thence, blockade of Pampeluna, battles of the Pyrenees, 28th, 29th, and 30th July (severely contused 28th), Maya Pass, advance into France, and various affairs of posts and piquets. He has received the War Medal and five clasps.
SURGEON.			
Wm. V. Hope.........	25 Feb.	15	
ASSISTANT-SURGEONS			
Thos K. L. Walker...	6 Aug.	31	
Richard Alderson ...	29 Jan.	46	

SERVICES OF THE REGIMENT.—In 1780, during the Gordon riots, encamped in the British Museum gardens, and acted against the rioters. In 1797, at Sheerness, and manned the batteries during the mutiny in the fleet; and a detachment of the Regiment brought Richard Parker a prisoner from the Sandwich. Served in Ireland 1798-9, and again 1814, 1815, and 1816. Gave 1,800 volunteers to the line during the war.
Facings, White. *Badge,* The White Rose.

Head-Quarters, Richmond, Yorkshire.] **22d, or North York Light Infantry Regiment of Militia.**

Colonel.

Francis Godolphin D'Arcy, his Grace the Duke of Leeds, 11 Feb. 1846. *Hornby Castle, Catterick, Yorkshire.*

Majors.

George Healey, 12 Aug. 1814.
Earl of Mulgrave, 18 Aug. 1846. M.P.—*Mulgrave Castle, Whitby, Yorkshire.*

	Date of Appointment to Present Rank.	Remarks exhibiting Services of Officers, whether L.L., D.L., M.P., or J.P.—Country Seats, &c.
CAPTAINS.		
J. P. H. Powles	25 Jan. 08	
Robert Colling	14 Oct. 08	
M. T. Lord Beaumont	18 April 24	*Carlton Hall, Yorkshire.*
Francis Morley	12 July 31	
John Jas. Robinson	2 July 46	
James Carter	30 Nov. 30	
LIEUTENANTS.		
Alexander White	1 Aug. 10	
Charles Paget	19 Feb. 13	
Richard Grillett	30 May 13	
Thomas Thompson	30 May 13	
Charles Allen	5 Aug. 14	
William Summers	25 Aug. 15	
Henry Porter	25 Sept. 15	
George Smith	16 July 31	
Robt. Ward Jackson	15 April 46	
ENSIGNS.		
George Ayre	22 April 17	
Richd. Bower Booth	15 April 46	
Walter W. Harland	15 April 46	
ADJUTANT.		
Capt. James Carter		

Facings, Black.

23d (Royal South Gloucester Light Infantry) Regiment of Militia.

Head Quarters, Gloucester.

Colonel.
Right Hon. William Earl Fitzhardinge, 22 Aug. 1810. L.L., J.P.—*Berkeley Castle.*

Lieut.-Colonel.
Robert Fitzhardinge Jenner, 29 Sept. 1842. D.L., J.P.

Major.
Edward Weight, 29 Sept. 1842. J.P.—Served in the 12th Lancers.

	Date of Appointment to Present Rank.	Remarks exhibiting Services of Officers, whether L.L., D.L., M.P., or J.P.—Country Seats, &c.
CAPTAINS.		
Robert Elton..........	25 May 10	
Humphrey Austin....	24 Oct. 25	J.P.
H. Wenman Newman	6 June 31	D.L., J.P.—*Thornbury Castle.* Served with the North Battalion of Regiment in Ireland, 1814; appointed to the South Battalion in 1830.
John Surman..........	26 Sept. 31	D.L., J.P.
M. Merryweather....	21 April 36	
Edward Owen Jones	8 March 39	J.P.
Duncome Pyrke.......	29 Sept. 42	J.P. Served in the 10th Light Dragoon's [Hussars.
Henry Chas. Harford	15 Sept. 43	
LIEUTENANTS.		
F. S. Thornton........	25 April 10	
James William Daniel	9 June 15	
William Leman.......	22 Aug. 31	
Isaac Nind	26 Sept. 31	J.P.—*Tewkesbury.*
Wm. Hamlet Millet .	21 April 36	
Thomas Earle.........	29 Dec. 38	
Arthur John Goldney	12 Aug. 43	
ENSIGNS.		
Edwd. Jas. Hobhouse	21 April 36	
William James Holt.	24 April 49	
ADJUTANT.		
Capt. George Henry Worthington	30 April 28	
SURGEON.		
George Tate	24 April 49	
ASSIST.-SURGEON.		
Wm. Philpot Brookes	24 April 49	M.D.

SERVICES OF THE REGIMENT.—Garrison and other duties. In Ireland in the years 1815 and 1816.

Facings, Blue.

Agents, Messrs. Cox & Co.

24th, or Royal Carmarthen Fusiliers, Regiment of Militia.

Head-Quarters, Carmarthen.

Colonel.—Hon. G. R. Trevor, 28 January 1831. M.P.

Major.—W. Rice, 4 February 1831.

	Date of Appointment to Present Rank.	Remarks exhibiting Services of Officers, whether L.L., D.L., M.P., or J.P.—Country Seats, &c.
CAPTAINS.		
L. Evans	1 Nov. 11	
D. T. B. Davies	21 Nov. 21	Served in the Army.
T. Thomas	4 Feb. 31	
S. Gwynne	27 April 31	
D. Davies	26 Jan. 39	
FIRST LIEUTENANTS.		
G. Horton	22 Jan. 12	
J. B. Gwynn	17 Nov. 31	
R. Benyon	26 Jan. 39	
T. Weir	23 May 39	
F. Green	24 May 39	
T. G. L. C. P. Gwynn	31 Jan. 43	
SECOND LIEUTENANTS.		
D. Thomas	26 Jan. 39	
M. Lewes	23 May 39	
M. Williams	24 May 39	
F. R. Cowel	7 Aug. 43	
ADJUTANT.		
Capt. E. J. Vaughan	8 Oct. 46	
PAYMASTER.		
Lieut. J. B. Davies	21 July 03	
QUARTERMASTER.		
J. Griffith	25 Nov. 14	Second Lieutenant.
SURGEON.		
H. Lawrence	3 Feb. 07	

Facings, Blue.

25th, or South Devon Regiment of Militia.

Head-Quarters, Plymouth.

Colonel.
Right Hon. the Earl of Morley, 8 Jan. 45. J.P., D.L.—*Saltram.*
Lieut.-Colonel.
Sir J. Buller Yarde Buller, Bart., 12 May 45. J.P., D.L., M.P.—*Lupton.*
Major.
Sir Henry Paul Seale, Bart., 12 May 45. J.P., D.L.—*Mount Boon.*

	Date of Appointment to Present Rank.	Remarks exhibiting Services of Officers, whether L.L., D.L., M.P., or J.P.—Country Seats, &c.
CAPTAINS.		
Thomas Oliver	20 March 11	*Bath.*
John D. I. Fortescue	22 Aug. 15	*Stratton.*
John Line Templer	20 May 20	J.P.—*Ivybridge.*
Sir J. Duckworth, Bt.	20 Jan. 20	J.P., D.L., M.P.—*Wear.*
John B. Y. Buller	12 May 45	J.P.—*Churston Court.*
Lawrence Palk	12 May 45	J.P.—*Haldon House.* Served in the Royal Dragoons five and a-half years.
Henry Richard Roe	11 April 46	J.P., D.L.—*Gnaton Hall.*
John Stevenson	11 April 46	J.P.—*Moreton.*
LIEUTENANTS.		
John Carne	22 Nov. 09	*Harrow.*
John Tucker	14 July 14	*Exeter.*
Charles T. Wright	9 Aug. 15	*Guernsey.*
Nichs. Gillard	1 Oct. 19	*Guernsey.*
Hon. J. A. Lysaght	10 April 43	*Southampton.*
Vincent Calmady	12 May 45	*Langdon Hall.*
Jeffery J. Edwardes	16 April 46	*Totness.*
John W. Walrond	16 April 46	*Knightshayes, Tiverton.*
John Bulteel	3 May 49	*Flete.*
ENSIGNS.		
John Feally	15 Feb. 14	*Bruff, Limerick.*
John Lampeer	2 Oct. 19	*Plymouth.* (Paymaster.)
Joseph Ralph	16 April 46	*Plymouth.* (Quartermaster.) Capt. h. p.
John Beer	16 April 46	*Holbeton.*
John Leader	16 April 46	*Cork.*
John Limbrey Toll	16 April 46	*Exeter.*
ADJUTANT.		
Wm. Hawley Fisk	22 Sept. 36	*Plymouth.* Captain on half-pay. Twenty-one years' former service in Cavalry and Infantry, including ten years in India and Mediterranean.
PAYMASTER.		
John Lampeer	22 Jan. 20	*Plymouth.* (Ensign.)
QUARTERMASTER.		
Joseph Ralph	16 April 46	*Plymouth.* (Ensign.) Captain on half-pay. Twenty-four years' former service in Infantry, principally in St. Helena, East Indies, and Persia.
SURGEON.		
John Butter	22 Nov. 11	M.D., F.R.S., F.L.S., &c.—*Windsor Villa, Plymouth, and Summerswood, South Brent, Devon.*
ASSIST.-SURGEON.		
John Tucker	5 Jan. 11	(Lieutenant.)

SERVICES OF THE REGIMENT.—With the Grand Coast Encampment in Sussex and Kent, 1793, 4, 5. Volunteered for service in Ireland during the Rebellion, and proceeded to Waterford under the immediate command of Colonel Lord Rolle; in reward for the exemplary conduct of the Corps whilst in Ireland, the Mayor and inhabitants of Waterford presented to every Non-commissioned Officer and Private a handsome silver medal, "In testimony of merit," and which was permitted to be worn. The Regiment was subsequently marched to distant parts of England, having been quartered in Yorkshire and in Kent.

Facings, White.

Head-Quarters, Leicester.] **26th, or Leicester Regiment of Militia.**

Colonel.
John Duke of Rutland, 21 May 1898. K.G., L.L.—*Belvoir Castle.*

Lieut.-Colonel.
John King, 24 July 1839. J.P., D.L.—*Stretton Hall, Leicestershire.*

Major.
The Marquis of Granby, 24 July 1839. M.P.—*Belvoir Castle.*

	Date of Appointment to Present Rank.	Remarks exhibiting Services of Officers, whether L.L., D.L., M.P., or J.P.—Country Seats, &c.
CAPTAINS.		
James Harrison	2 Aug. 03	
Robert Ralph Noel .	30 Jan. 21	
Chas. C. Morris	1 June 25	*Loddington Hall.*
Thomas Pochen	2 Feb. 31	
Richard Cheslyn......	22 Feb. 31	Formerly in the 7th Hussars.
Jonathan W. Bryan .	6 April 31	
Thos. S. Sadler	18 Aug. 45	
Fred. Thos. Fowke...	4 June 46	
LIEUTENANTS.		
Jonathan Singleton...	20 April 09	
Geo. Oakley Sanders	9 July 30	Commandant of H.M.'s fort and settlement of Dixcove, Gold Coast, Western Africa.
C. M. Cooke	22 Feb. 31	
George Fred. Hurst .	22 Feb. 31	
Benjamin Sutton ...	27 Sept. 33	
Lord John Manners .	24 Feb. 40	
James Edw. Webb...	30 April 40	
Henry David Erskine	4 June 46	
Joseph Knight	4 June 46	
ENSIGNS.		
Henry Wakeman ...	27 Sept. 33	
Robert Harrington...	27 April 46	
Augustus Lafarque...	27 April 46	
Walter Lafarque......	27 April 46	
Edward H. Sanders .	23 May 49	
ADJUTANT.		
Henry F. Hawker ...	26 Aug. 43	B.M. Served twenty-two years in the 19th Foot as Ensign, Lieutenant, Captain, and Adjutant.

SERVICES OF THE REGIMENT.—Served in Ireland 1798.

Facings, Yellow.

27th, or Northumberland Light Infantry Regiment of Militia.

Head-Quarters, Alnwick.

Colonel.
The Earl of Beverley, 17 May 1804.

Lieut.-Colonel.
John Blenkinsopp Coulson, 3 April 1807. J.P., D.L.—Served in 43d Regiment.

Major.—Robert Ogle, 31 August 1819. J.P., D.L.

CAPTAINS.	Date of Appointment to Present Rank.	Remarks exhibiting Services of Officers, whether L.L., D.L., M.P., or J.P.—Country Seats, &c.
William Lewes	4 Nov. 06	
Edward Dale	4 Nov. 06	J.P.—Served in the 45th Regiment.
Robert Charleton	28 March 17	
Charles V. Loraine	4 March 31	
John Richard Scott	4 March 31	
John Potts	29 April 31	J.P.
Edward W. Riddell	15 March 34	
Hon. Lord Lovaine	19 April 42	Served in the Grenadier Guards.
Charles A. Monck	20 Aug. 45	J.P.
Adam Atkinson	29 June 46	
LIEUTENANTS.		
Charles F. Charleton	17 May 04	Paymaster.
Robert Bell Reed	4 March 13	
William Walker	24 Sept. 13	
Cuthbert Shafto	28 March 17	
James Maxwell	28 March 17	
Chas. Bulmar Ridley	28 March 17	
Robert Falder	4 March 31	
Bowes Todd Wilson	4 March 31	
ADJUTANT.		
Capt. J. N. Frampton	25 Nov. 45	Served in the Rifle Brigade.
PAYMASTER.		
Lieut. C. P. Charleton	11 Nov. 04	
SURGEON.		
Philip Dennis	8 Aug. 12	

Facings, Buff. *Agents,* Messrs. Cox and Co.

Head-Quarters, Haverfordwest.] **28th, or Royal Pembrokeshire (Rifle Corps) Regiment of Militia.**

Lieut.-Colonel.
Hugh Owen Owen, 16 Sept. 1830. D.L.—*Landshipping.*

Major.
William Henry Lewis, 21 May 1846.—*Clanfiew.*

	Date of Appointment to Present Rank.	Remarks exhibiting Services of Officers, whether L.L., D.L., M.P., or J.P.—Country Seats, &c.
CAPTAINS.		
James Mark Child ...	6 Jan. 20	*Begelly, Pembrokeshire.*
James Higgon	12 June 20	*Scolton.*
George Bowen Jordan Jordan	21 May 46	*Pigeonsford.*
LIEUTENANTS.		
Edward Davenport...	23 Sept. 18	
George James	13 Oct. 31	*Haverfordwest.*
Robert Child	13 Oct. 31	*Newton, Pembrokeshire.*
ADJUTANT.		
Capt. John Holland .	6 April 46	*Haverfordwest.* Served in the Royal Marines.
PAYMASTER.		
William Butler	8 June 28	*Haverfordwest.*
SURGEON.		
Thomas Dumayne	25 March 11	*Milford.*

SERVICES OF THE REGIMENT.—The Royal Pembrokeshire Militia was embodied the first time, during the last War, on the 2d January, 1793. The Regiment volunteered for Ireland, and embarked on the 6th April, 1799. The Regiment volunteered its service to go with General Moore to be employed in Spain and Portugal, and to be attached to the 43d Regiment, and received a letter from the Right Honourable the Secretary at War, dated 12th July, 1808; also another, dated 21st July, 1808, from the same office, conveying His Majesty's most gracious thanks thereupon. The Regiment was made a Light Infantry Regiment on the 30th March, 1810. The Regiment volunteered again for Ireland, and embarked on the 8th Sept., 1811, and was made a Rifle Regiment on the 17th July, 1811.

Uniform, Green.

29TH REGIMENT OF MILITIA.

Head-Quarters, New Sleaford.] **29th, or South Lincoln Regiment of Militia.**

Colonel.—Earl of Brownlow, 20 June 1811.

Lieut.-Colonel.—C. D. L. W. Sibthorp, 8 Oct. 1822.   Served in the Army.

Major.—G. L. Welby, 3 Feb. 1846.

	Date of Appointment to Present Rank.	Remarks exhibiting Services of Officers, whether L.L., D.L., M.P., or J.P.—Country Seats, &c.
CAPTAINS.		
H. Brown	23 June 08	
L. L. B. Ibbetson	23 May 29	
W. Torkington	7 April 31	
F. Hopkinson	6 Dec. 36	
M. Johnson	7 June 38	
Sir F. Whichcote, Bt.	5 Jan. 41	
Grantham	18 Nov. 39	
G. B. Tathwell	19 Feb. 47	
LIEUTENANTS.		
H. Lucas	19 April 1799	
R. Wyche	26 May 03	
C. Parker	7 June 05	
H. S. Hawes	9 March 10	
T. J. Davis	10 Aug. 12	
J. Taylor	14 May 14	
S. Brailford	24 Jan. 46	
J. B. Lousada	19 Feb. 47	
E. H. Peel	19 Feb. 47	
H. H. Tennant	19 Feb. 47	
ENSIGNS.		
P. M. Pell	1 Nov. 31	
A. Andrews	5 Feb. 32	
W. S. Clark	19 Feb. 47	
W. W. Hett	30 May 48	
PAYMASTER.		
Ens. F. Bowman		
SURGEON.		
J. S. De Merveilleax	18 June 18	

Facings, Blue.

Head-Quarters, Hertford.] 30th, or Hertford Regiment of Militia.

Colonel.
Marquis of Salisbury, 9 May 1815. K.G.

Lieut.-Colonel.
C. H. Strode, 12 March 1840. Served in the Army.

Major.
E. Hampson, 12 March 1840.

CAPTAINS.	Date of Appointment to Present Rank.	Remarks exhibiting Services of Officers, whether L.L., D.L., M.P., or J.P.—Country Seats, &c.
J. Holmes	29 May 11	
J. Lomax	29 May 20	
J. C. Strode	9 June 40	
C. W. Wilshere	1 Sept. 41	
J. C. Phelips	27 July 46	
LIEUTENANTS.		
S. Fairman	2 June 20	
F. B. Alston	16 July 42	
A. Tunstall	16 July 42	
ADJUTANT.		
Capt. E. S. James	4 June 46	Served in the Army.
SURGEON.		
J. Davies	28 Oct. 26	

Facings, Goslin Green.

31st, or Royal Brecon Regiment of Militia.

Head-Quarters, Brecon.

Lieutenant-Colonel.
Lloyd Vaughan Watkins, 16 Nov. 1847. M.P., J.P., L.L., D.L.—*Pennoyre Park, Brecknockshire*, and *Broadway, Carmarthenshire.*

Major.
William Richard Stretton, 17 March 1846. *Dan-y-Park, Crickwell.* Served in the 23d Fusiliers.

	Date of Appointment to Present Rank.	Remarks exhibiting Services of Officers, whether L.L., D.L., M.P., or J.P.—Country Seats, &c.
CAPTAIN. David W. Lloyd	20 Oct. 38	*Llandilo Vane.*
LIEUTENANTS. William Nalbon	17 Dec. 39	
George Davis	6 Jan. 46	
William Bridgwater	17 March 46	
R. W. Williams	27 July 46	
ADJUTANT. D. J. Dickinson	7 Feb. 46	*Landefaurg.*—Served in the 2d Foot, and the 7th Royal Fusiliers. Served with the Queen's Royals throughout the campaign in Affghanistan and Beloochistan, in 1838 and 1839, and was present at the assault and capture of the fortresses of Ghuznée and Khelat, at which last he was severely wounded by a musket-shot,—leg broken. Medal for Ghuznée.
SURGEON. Arthur Lawrence	7 June 20	

SERVICE OF THE REGIMENT.—Served in Ireland during the Rebellion.
Facings, Blue.

32d, or Royal Flintshire Regiment of Militia (*Rifles*).

Head-Quarters, Mold.

Colonel.
Sir Richard Puleston, Bart., 24 Feb. 1846. J.P., D.L.—*Enoral Park, Flintshire.* Captain Shropshire Militia, Dec. 1807.

Major.—C. J. W. D. Dundas, 24 Feb. 1846.

	Date of Appointment to Present Rank.	Remarks exhibiting Services of Officers, whether L.L., D.L., M.P., or J.P.—Country Seats, &c.
CAPTAINS. P. M. H. Jones	24 Dec. 46	
Richard P. Puleston	7 May 46	
FIRST LIEUTENANT. W. Hancock	2 May 46	
SECOND LIEUTENANT. John Simon	14 Feb. 16	
SURGEON. Thomas Griffith	8 Nov. 15	

Uniform, Green.

33D REGIMENT OF MILITIA.

Head-Quarters, Marlborough.] **33d, or Royal Wiltshire Regiment of Militia.**

Colonel.—Sir J. Hobhouse, Bart., 13 Feb. 1840. M.P.—*Erlestoke, Wilts.*

Lieut.-Colonel.

Lord Methuen, 15 May 1845. M.P., J.P.—*Corsham, Wilts.* Served in the Army.

Major.

W. C. Grove, 15 Feb. 1836. J.P.—*Odstock, Wilts.* Served in the Army.

CAPTAINS.	Date of Appointment to Present Rank.		Remarks exhibiting Services of Officers, whether L.L., D.L., M.P., or J.P.—Country Seats, &c.
M. Gore	13 June	28	*Mount-street, Berkeley-square.*
H. N. Goddard	1 Feb.	31	J.P.—*Manor House, Cliffe, Wilts.*
W. P. Shuckburgh	16 Feb.	31	J.P.—*Downton, Wilts.*
H. T. Grove	22 March	31	J.P.—*Odstock, Wilts.*
W. Vince	2 Dec.	36	*Ashley Box, Wilts.*
A. H. Tonge	19 Sept.	38	*7, Lansdowne Villa, Cheltenham.*
W. A. Heathcote	18 June	39	*Rollestone, Shrewton.* Served in the Army.
Hon. H. St. John	2 May	42	*Sidmouth, Devon.*
Hon. St. J.P. Methuen	21 May	42	*Corsham, Wilts.*
T. Gaisford	15 May	47	*Trowbridge, Wilts.*
LIEUTENANTS.			
J. Smith	20 Feb.	08	*Moate, Ireland.*
T. W. Wadley	9 April	11	*Bath.*
J. V. Perriman	14 Feb.	10	*Bath.*
T. Hooper	14 Feb.	10	*Reading.*
T. Theobald	5 Sept.	11	*Almonsbury Hill, Bristol.*
J. McKinlay	12 Sept.	15	*St. Filian's, N. B.*
H. F. Bythesea	27 Jan.	27	*Wellington-street, Woolwich.*
F. Pearson	18 June	32	*Sackville-street, London.*
W. Long	15 March	46	*Trowbridge.*
G. Gould	16 March	46	*Trowbridge.*
E. H. Mortimer	17 March	46	*Trowbridge.* Served in the 67th Regt., as Lieut., in Ireland, the Mediterranean, and West Indies, four years. In the 46th Regt., in the East Indies, upwards of six years.
ENSIGNS.			
G. Theobald	14 Sept.	31	*Almonsbury Hill, Bristol.*
G. H. Goddard	15 March	46	*Trowbridge.*
ADJUTANT.			
Capt. D. Price	5 Feb.	24	Entered the Army as Ensign in the 36th Regt., in 1805, whilst a Cadet at Marlow; embarked for Portugal in 1808, and served in the Peninsula until 1814; was severely wounded at Salamanca, and has received a Medal and six Clasps. On Half-pay, as Captain 36th Regiment, since 1814.
PAYMASTER.			
T. W. Wadley	25 June	15	*Bath.*
SURGEON.			
William Tucker	28 May	46	
ASSIST.-SURGEON.			
T. Hooper	14 Feb.	10	*Reading.*

SERVICES OF THE REGIMENT.—First raised in the year 1759. Embarked for Ireland 24th March, 1814; disembarked from Ireland, 1816.

Facings, Blue.

34th, or East Suffolk Light Infantry Regiment of Militia.

Head-Quarters, Ipswich.

Colonel.
Henry Bence Bence, 3 May 1844. J.P., D.L.—*Thonington Hall.* Served in 16th Light Dragoons during the Peninsular War; wounded at Talavera.

Lieut.-Colonel.
Charles Blois, 3 May 1844. *Cockfield Hall.* Served in the Royal Dragoons; wounded at Waterloo.

Major.—Thomas Pytches, 24 May 1827. J.P., D.L.

Captains.	Date of Appointment to Present Rank.		Remarks exhibiting Services of Officers, whether L.L., D.L., M.P., or J.P.—Country Seats, &c.
Anthony Collett	15 June	27	*Bury St. Edmund's.*
Hector Munro	3 Oct.	31	*Halsmere, Surrey.*
J. W. C. Whitbread	21 July	32	*Sandham Hall.*
John Patrick Perry	27 Aug.	32	
Chas. Henry Rooke	14 April	46	*Didham, Essex.*
James Mill Walker	19 June	46	*Levington Hall, Suffolk.*
John Geo. Sheppard	14 July	46	*Ash High House.*
Lieutenants.			
John Jenkins	1 July	15	*Gosport, Hants.*
J. S. Foster	1 July	16	
R. H. Sheppard	17 March	25	*Investiff, Suffolk.*
Frederick Robinson	2 May	31	*Danwich, Suffolk.*
Charles Groton	1 April	46	*Beddingham, Suffolk.*
Henley T. Dakins	7 March	47	
Bodkin J. Cobbold	7 March	47	
Adjutant.			
Horatio Beckham	7 July	20	K.S.F.—Half-pay Captain 43d Light Infantry; served in the British Legion in Spain, as Colonel, commanding 7th Royal Irish Light Infantry, during which period he was twice wounded: received the Order of St. Fernando, which he has permission to wear, together with two Medals.
Assistant-Surgeon.			
John Jenkins	1 March	13	

Services of the Regiment.—First raised in the year 1757. The Regiment, after serving two years in Scotland, volunteered its services to Ireland, in which country it served two years; and during the war, from 1803 to 1813, sent 1,119 volunteers to the Line, the greatest part of whom went to the 43d Light Infantry, and 83 more volunteered for service in the Peninsula, in the 2d Provisional Battalion of Militia, making together 1,202, being more than twice its establishment, which is 521 men. Motto, "*Pro Aris et Focis.*"

Facings, White.

Head-Quarters, High Wycombe.

35th, or Royal Bucks King's Own Regiment of Militia.

Colonel.
Right Hon. Lord Carington, 7 March 1839. L.L.—*Wycombe Abbey, Bucks.*

Lieut.-Colonel.
George Grenville Pigott, 7 June 1836. J.P., D.L.—*Doddershall Park, Bucks.* Late of Her Majesty's 14th Foot. Served with the 2d Battalion from 1812 in the Mediterranean, at Malta, Genoa, and in 1815 with the Allied Army then serving in France; from thence to the Ionian Islands until the reduction of the 2d Battalion in 1817.

Major.
George Fitzroy, 5 August 1846. J.P.—*Grafton Regis, Stony Stratford, Bucks.* Late of Her Majesty's Regiment of Foot Guards.

	Date of Appointment to Present Rank.	Remarks exhibiting Services of Officers, whether L.L., D.L., M.P., or J.P.—Country Seats, &c.
CAPTAIN.		
Robert M. Bates ...	8 Oct. 07	*Worksop,* near *Nottingham.* Served in France with the 1st Provisional Battalion of Militia.
Hon. George Ives Irby	7 Feb. 31	J.P.—*Hedsor,* near *Maidenhead, Bucks.*
John W. B. Brown .	7 Feb. 31	Late of the Line.
Edmund Morgan ...	15 Sept. 31	*Tenby, Pembrokeshire.*
John Robe	7 June 33	*Biddenham,* near *Bedford.*
Wm. G. Cavendish...	13 June 46	M.P.—*Burlington House, London.*
Robert Smith	13 June 46	*Endsleigh-street, Tavistock-square, London.*
LIEUTENANTS.		
Michael Macnamara .	15 May 98	*Buckingham.* Served in France with the 1st Provisional Battalion of Militia.
Walter Carington ...	7 July 12	*U. S. Club, London.* Served in France with the 1st Provisional Battalion of Militia.
John Harland.........	8 July 12	*Richmond, York.* Served in France with the 1st Provisional Battalion of Militia.
James Grove	5 Nov. 12	*Dawlish, Devon.* Served in France with the 1st Provisional Battalion of Militia.
John Bridger	5 July 23	*Mansfield-road, Notts.* Served in France with the 1st Provisional Battalion of Militia.
John Moore	31 Jan. 27	77, *Camden-road Villas, London.*
ENSIGNS.		
John Clark	24 March 26	
Wm. H. Chapman ...	13 June 46	*St. John's Wood, Regent's Park.*
Frank Hatchard......	5 Aug. 46	50, *Lower Belgrave-place.*

35th, or Royal Bucks King's Own Regiment of Militia.

(*Continued.*)

	Date of Appointment to Present Rank.	Remarks exhibiting Services of Officers, whether L.L., D.L., M.P., or J.P.—Country Seats, &c.
ADJUTANT.		
Capt. Chas. T. Grove	21 May 25	*High Wycombe.* In the Royal Bucks Militia from 1807 to 1812; was appointed to the 14th Regiment, and served with the 2d Battalion in Sicily, Malta, Genoa, and in 1815 with the Allied Army then serving in France; from thence to the Ionian Islands; was acting Adjutant until the reduction of the 2d Battalion in 1817. In 1821 was appointed Captain; was appointed in the Royal Bucks Militia, and succeeded to the Adjutancy of the Regiment 21 May, 1825.
SURGEON.		
Joseph Rose Holt ...	5 Aug. 46	M.D.—*High Wycombe.*
ASSIST.-SURGEONS.		
John Moore		77, *Camden-road Villas, London.*
Frank Hatchard......	5 Aug. 46	50, *Lower Belgrave-place.*

SERVICES OF THE REGIMENT.—In 1794 the Regiment was encamped near Weymouth during the period His Majesty George III. visited that place, on which occasion the Regiment had the honour to form the personal Guard of His Majesty, and for this distinguished service, on the 26th September of that year, His Majesty conferred the title on the Regiment of Royal Bucks King's Own Militia. In June, 1798, the Regiment volunteered with the Colonel, the Marquis of Buckingham, to serve in Ireland, that country being then in a state of rebellion; their offers of service having been accepted, the Regiment embarked at Liverpool for Dublin, and arrived on the 2d of July following; their reception by the public authorities was highly complimentary to the Regiment, it being the first English Militia Regiment that had landed in Ireland; other Regiments soon after followed their gallant example. In the spring of 1799 the Regiment returned to England, and in the same year a volunteering to the Line took place from all the Militia Regiments, and on this occasion the Royal Bucks K. O. Regiment furnished 400 men, including Sergeants, Corporals, and Privates, with the regulated proportion of Officers, all of whom joined the 4th, or King's Own Regiment of Infantry. The Regiment afterwards furnished yearly (principally to the 14th Regiment of Infantry), its full quota of men during the war. In the year 1808 the Regiment again, with the Noble Colonel, then Lord Temple, volunteered to serve in Spain during the period the French armies invaded that country. The Ministry did not avail themselves of this offer, but the proposal met the highest consideration for the gallantry thus displayed by the Corps. The Regiment in 1813 again served in Ireland, *as hen by law established;* during this period the intention of Government to form Provisional Battalions of Militia was promulgated; another opportunity presented itself to call forth the gallantry of the Regiment, which was made fully apparent on forming the 1st Provisional Battalion of Militia, and this was mostly composed of the Royal Bucks King's Own Regiment, and commanded by their Noble Colonel, the late Duke of Buckingham and Chandos, who embarked with the Battalion in 1813 for Bourdeaux, and served in France during the time the Allied Armies were in possession of that country.

Facings, Blue.

36th, or Warwickshire Regiment of Militia.

Head-Quarters, Warwick.

Colonel.
The Earl of Warwick, 19 Sept. 1803. K.T., L.L.—*Warwick Castle.*

Lieut.-Colonel.
J. M. Boultbee, 29 May 1847. D.L.—*Springfield Knole.*

	Date of Appointment to Present Rank.	Remarks exhibiting Services of Officers, whether L.L., D.L., M.P., J.P.—Country Seats, &c.
CAPTAINS.		
George Stevenson	28 May 11	Late R. Staff Corps.
R. H. Lamb	29 Jan. 14	*Brayborough, Daventry.*
William Arden	9 Nov. 15	*Barton, Lichfield.*
Henry Elliott	12 March 25	
William Hooper	26 Dec. 36	*Ashley Hill.*
M. E. Ferrers	2 Feb. 47	*Badgley Hall.*
Henry Arnold	15 Feb. 47	*Ashby Lodge.*
T. W. Biddulph	26 Dec. 48	*Bordenbury Park.*
LIEUTENANTS.		
H. Hammond	2 June 08	
John Gem	24 July 08	
J. H. Law	9 Feb. 31	Capt. Unattached. (Late 36th Regiment.)
Thomas Miles	26 June 12	
William Powell	10 Aug. 13	
Samuel Wiggins	9 Feb. 14	
C. B. Thomas	1 March 14	
C. Du Moulin	24 Oct. 31	
J. A. Mitchell	22 Feb. 32	
C. Greenway	24 Oct. 32	
ENSIGNS.		
E. Forster	22 Feb. 31	
H. Wilson	28 Feb. 31	*The Abbey, Cumberland.*
O. Mills	9 March 31	
Henry Bannister	13 Jan. 38	
C. Dickenson	5 Jan. 41	
ADJUTANT.		
Thos. Cassan	18 Feb. 46	Late Capt. 37th Regiment.
SURGEON.		
John Wilmshurst	18 May 04	
ASSISTANT-SURGEON.		
Philip Trauter	18 Nov. 10	

SERVICES OF THE REGIMENT.—The Warwickshire Militia volunteered and served in Ireland during the rebellion, 1798; also served in that country from 1812 to 1814.

Facings, Yellow.

37TH REGIMENT OF MILITIA.

Head-Quarters, Maidstone.] **37th, or *West Kent Regiment of Militia*.**

Colonel.
Sir John Kenward Shaw, Bart., 2d March 1832. J.P., D.L.—*Maidstone*.
Lieut.-Colonel.—Vacant.

Majors.
Thomas Gybbon Monypenny, 20 Jan. 1846. J.P., D.L.—*Rolvenden*. Late Lieut. in the 80th Regiment. Served under Sir Thomas Graham in 1814, at the Blockade of Antwerp, and afterwards at Quatre Bras and Waterloo. Wounded.
Thomas Twisden Hodges, 21 Jan. 1846. M.P., J.P.—*Hempsted*, near *Cranbrook*.

	Date of Appointment of Present Rank.	Remarks exhibiting Services of Officers, whether L.L., D.L., M.P., or J.P.—Country Seats, &c.
CAPTAINS.		
Thos. Charles Evans	28 Dec. 13	*Dover*. Late Assist.-Surgeon in the 4th Foot.
Sir T. M. Wilson, Bt.	4 April 31	J.P.—*Charlton House*, near *Blackheath*.
John Whitehead	4 April 31	*Barnjet, Maidstone:*
James Whatman	15 May 38	J.P.—*Vinters, Maidstone*.
Wm. Peel Croughton	26 Jan. 39	J.P.—*Heronden, Tenterden*.
M. Hammond Dalison	20 Jan. 46	*Hamptons*, near *Tonbridge*.
Fred. Francis Morrice	21 Jan. 46	*Betshanger*, near *Deal*.
George Perkins	22 Jan. 46	*Chipstead Place, Sevenoaks*.
M. Herbert Jenner...	23 Jan. 46	*Chislehurst, Bromley*.
LIEUTENANTS.		
John M'Gregor	15 Feb. 13	
Joseph Wakeford	7 Feb. 14	
Edward Hinde	2 May 15	Late Lieutenant Rifle Brigade; H.P.
George Henry Dansey	29 Nov. 15	
Edwd. Chamberlayne	8 March 16	
Decimus Woodgate	26 Feb. 31	
Henry Johnson	30 April 31	
Sir Walter Charles James, Bart.	18 May 38	
F. Amilius Hodgson	7 Aug. 39	Cornet, late Royal Waggon Train; H.P.
James Coveney	20 Jan. 46	
Chas. Jarrard King...	21 Jan. 46	
ENSIGNS.		
Arthur Foulks	7 Dec. 33	
William Allen	7 Aug. 39	
H. Squires Shrapnell	7 Aug. 39	
R. T. Gybbon Gybbon Monypenny	20 Jan. 46	Late Ensign 86th Regiment.
James M'Gregor	5 Feb. 46	
C. Augustus Abbott	6 Feb. 46	
Frederick Thompson	7 Feb. 46	
ADJUTANT.		
Capt. John Eley	12 July 17	
QUARTERMASTER.		
Thomas Fancett	29 April 18	
PAYMASTER.		
Edwd. Chamberlayne	19 Feb. 17	
SURGEON.		
William Sankey	31 Jan. 46	

SERVICES OF THE REGIMENT.—Served in Ireland during the War, and volunteered several hundred men to the Line.

Facings, Kentish Grey.

38TH REGIMENT OF MILITIA.

Head-Quarters, Torpoint.] **38th, or (*Duke of Cornwall's Rangers*) Regiment of Militia (*Rifles*).**

Colonel.

Right Hon. Earl Mount Edgcumbe, 17 Feb. 1821.—*Mount Edgcumbe.* Served in the campaign of 1815, and was present at the Battle of Waterloo.

Lieut.-Colonel.—Thomas John Phillipps, 1 April 1840.—*Lander.*

Major.—Hon. George Edgcumbe, 7 Feb. 1826.

	Date of Appointment to Present Rank.	Remarks exhibiting Services of Officers, whether L.L., D.L., M.P., or J.P.—Country Seats, &c.
CAPTAINS.		
Thos. Trick............	14 May 17	
J. B. Messenger......	21 Aug. 29	*Heath Cottage, Brighton.*
Samuel Borlase	11 Sept. 20	J.P.—*Castle Horneck, Penzance.*
Richard Johns	30 Aug. 25	J.P.—*Trevince Tregony.*
Nicholas Kendall ...	22 Oct. 26	J.P.—*Pelyn, Lostwithiel.*
Henry P. Andrew ...	1 May 32	J.P.—*Truro.*
John S. Trelawney...	1 April 40	J.P.—*Harewood House, Cornwall.*
W. H. P. Carew......	17 Sept. 40	M.P., J.P.—*Antony House, Cornwall.*
C. G. P. Brune	2 May 46	J.P.—*Place House, Padstow.*
William B. Call	2 May 46	J.P.—*Whiteford House, Callington.*
LIEUTENANTS.		
John Bartlett.........	12 Oct. 07	
William Hurden......	21 July 12	
Thomas Peter.........	17 June 14	
Rich. F. Rattenbury	9 Dec. 15	
T. S. Beachamp	31 Dec. 18	
Daniel Thackeray ...	21 June 20	
Henry O'Neil	2 May 46	
George A. Hicks......	2 May 46	
Jas. Bennett Rodd...	2 May 46	
Fred. John Trick ...	2 May 46	
John Wm. Peard ...	2 May 46	
SECOND LIEUTENANTS.		
Edwin Eveleigh	7 July 31	
Richard G. Bennett	5 Jan. 43	
W. H. H. Messenger	2 May 46	
Edward Carthew ...	2 May 46	
Hon. S. K. Lysaght	2 May 46	
Samuel Hext	2 May 46	
Richard P. Johns ...	2 May 46	
ADJUTANT.		
John Brockman	28 Aug. 21	Served in the Rifle Brigade.
QUARTERMASTER.		
Mathew Semple	25 Sept. 19	
SURGEON.		
John Ward............	6 Jan. 23	

Uniform, Green.

39TH AND 40TH REGIMENTS OF MILITIA. 81

Head-Quarters, Norwich.] *39th, or West Norfolk Regiment of Militia.*

Colonel.—Horatio Walpole, Earl of Orford, 26 June 1822. J.P., D.L.—*Wollerton and Blandford.*
Lieut.-Colonel.—George Nelthorpe, 2 April 1799. D.L.
Major.—William Earle Lytton Bulwer Heydon, 6 July 1825. J.P., D.L.

	Date of Appointment to Present Rank.	Remarks exhibiting Services of Officers, whether L.L., D.L., M.P., or J.P.—Country Seats, &c.
CAPTAINS.		
H. F. Eustace.........	9 May 29	
Charles Bedingfeld...	27 Aug. 31	
LIEUTENANTS.		
Matthew Goode	27 Sept. 03	
William H. Harper...	10 June 13	
Gordon Calthrop ...	11 Aug. 15	
Thomas S. Clarke ...	23 Aug. 15	
ENSIGN.		
Thomas E. Baker ...	11 Aug. 15	
ADJUTANT.		
James Powley.........	23 July 19	
ASSIST.-SURGEON.		
Thomas E. Baker ...	11 Aug. 15	

SERVICES OF THE REGIMENT.—Served in England, Ireland, and Scotland, during the war.
Facings, White.

Head-Quarters, Yarmouth.] *40th, or East Norfolk Regiment of Militia.*

Colonel.—Hon. Berkeley Wodehouse, 9 Sept. 1842. D.L.—*Athgarven Lodge, Ireland.* Late Major 8th Hussars.
Lieut.-Col.—William Mason, 6 May 1824. D.L., J.P.—*Necton Hall, Norfolk.* High Sheriff of the County, 1849.
Major.—Sir E.H.K.Lacon, Bart., 6 July 1839. D.L., J.P.—*Hopton Court, Suffolk.*

	Date of Appointment to Present Rank.	Remarks exhibiting Services of Officers, whether L.L., D.L., M.P., or J.P.—Country Seats, &c.
CAPTAINS.		
John Longe	7 April 30	D.L.—*Spixworth Hall, Norfolk.*
Hon. B. Wodehouse	7 April 30	
LIEUTENANTS.		
Edward Steele	31 May 11	
E. Boardman	5 Sept. 12	
Robert Berham	23 Feb. 14	
William Sharpe	3 Dec. 21	
James Roper	5 May 25	
ENSIGNS.		
William Gedge	23 Jan. 12	
Henry Postle	11 March 31	
William Morrill	7 Feb. 38	
ADJUTANT.		
W. P. K. Browne ...	2 April 46	Served throughout the war with China (Medal) as Adjutant of the 49th Regiment, and latterly as a Brigade-Major, and was present at Canton, Amoy, Chusan, Chinhae, Ningpo, Segoan, Chapoo (wounded), Woosung, Chin Kiang Foo, and Nankin.
SURGEON.		
George Bateman......	20 Nov. 17	

SERVICES OF THE REGIMENT.—In Camp and Garrison duty in Great Britain, from the 11th December, 1792, to 24th April, 1802. In Camp and Garrison duty in Great Britain and Ireland, from the 21st March, 1803, to 24th June, 1814. The Training periods at Head-Quarters, Yarmouth, in the years 1820, 1821, 1825, 1826, and 1831.
Facings, Black.

41st, or First East Devon Regiment of Militia.

Head-Quarters, Exeter.

Colonel.—Hugh, Earl Fortescue, 20 May 1816. L.L.—*Castle Hill, Southmolton.*
Formerly in 9th Foot.

Lieut.-Colonel.
Sir James Hamlyn Williams, 24 April 1846. J.P., D.L.—*Clovelly Court.*
Formerly in Rifle Brigade.

Major.—Hon. John William Fortescue, 24 April 1846. J.P., D.L.—*Castle Hill.*
Half-pay 7th Fusiliers.

	Date of Appointment to Present Rank.	Remarks exhibiting Services of Officers, whether L.L., D.L., M.P., or J.P.—Country Seats, &c.
CAPTAINS.		
Paul Oury Treby ...	24 Nov. 10	J.P.—*Goodamoor,* near *Plympton.*
Henry Marsh	12 June 11	*Grosvenor-place, Bath.*
Ervine Clarke.........	8 May 15	J.P.—*Elford Manor,* near *Plymouth.*
Sir E. M. Elton, Bart.	2 June 31	J.P., D.L.—*Widworthy Court.*
Francis Baring Short	13 Jan. 46	J.P.—*Bickham,* near *Exeter.*
George Fursdon	13 Jan. 46	J.P.—*Fursdon.*
John Crichton Harris	18 Feb. 46	J.P.—*Radford,* near *Plymouth.* Formerly [70th Foot.
Shilston C. Hamlyn .	20 Aug. 46	J.P.—*Leawood.*
LIEUTENANTS.		
Richard Cornish......	5 Sept. 10	
Wm. Lyfe Pearce ...	10 Dec. 13	
Philip Lardner	26 May 32	Naval War Medal and Clasp.
Richard Wake	21 Oct. 33	
Charles Rumley	13 Jan. 46	Formerly 30th Foot.
Percy C. Lipyeatt ...	13 Jan. 46	Formerly 24th Foot.
Henry Churchill......	31 March 46	
Edward H. Marsh ...	21 May 46	
ENSIGNS.		
Charles R. Ellicombe	13 Jan. 46	
Frederick G. Young .	26 Jan. 46	
George Lane Dacie...	11 Feb. 46	
Henry Thos. Hartnoll	24 April 46	
Chas. Corbyn Wills .	19 March 46	
ADJUTANT.		
Capt. Chas. Holman .	27 March 20	D.L.—Half-pay 52d Light Infantry. Served in the Peninsula from Nov. 1811, attached to the Portuguese service, and was present with Lord Hill's corps covering the siege of Badajoz, advance on Llerena, siege and storm of the three fortified convents of Salamanca,—led the storming party to the gate of San Vincente at its capture; battle of Salamanca,—slightly wounded by a musket shot in the leg; siege of Burgos, and storming the works and the White Church; several skirmishes on the retreat from thence near Torrequemada, and blowing up the bridge of Duenas; battles of the Pyrenees on the 28th, 29th, and 30th July; night attack and defeat of a French battalion on the heights of Urdax, action near Zugarrimundi,—severe contused wound; battles of the Nivelle and the Nive, actions at Ustaritz and Villa Franque, battles of St. Pierre and Orthes, actions at Aire, Vic Bigorre, and Tarbes, and battle of Toulouse. Served the campaign of 1815, including the battle of Waterloo; also with the army of occupation in France. He has received the War Medal and six clasps.
SURGEON.		
Frederick G. Farrant	7 Sept. 46	

SERVICES OF THE REGIMENT.—Served in Ireland in 1816.

Facings, White.

42d (Dorset) Regiment of Militia.

[Head-Quarters, Dorchester.]

Colonel.
John James Smith, 15 Jan. 1846. J.P., D.L.—*The Down House, Blandford.*

Lieut.-Colonel.
George Thompson Jacob, 8 Feb. 1846. J.P.—*Shillingbone House, Blandford.* Served in the Foot Guards at Waterloo.

Major.
George Colly Loftus, 7 Oct. 1846. J.P.—*Wolland House, Blandford.* Served in the Foot Guards.

	Date of Appointment to Present Rank.	Remarks exhibiting Services of Officers, whether L.L., D.L., M.P., or J.P.—Country Seats, &c.
CAPTAINS.		
Thomas Gould	22 April 14	[*Somerset.*
George Emery	8 Dec. 19	D.L. of Somerset.—*The Grove, Banwell,*
W. L. Henning	9 June 20	*Frome House.*
Samuel Cox	31 Oct. 37	J.P.—*Dorset House.*
Chas. A. Emery	7 Aug. 43	*Banwell, Somerset.* Served in the Commissariat Department at the Battle of Waterloo.
LIEUTENANTS.		
Thomas Layton	3 April 06	*Eton, Bucks.*
Charles West	13 Feb. 15	*Sherborne, Dorset.*
John Davis	7 Oct. 46	*Yetminster.*
W. A. Biddle	16 Oct. 46	*Wimborne.*
Giles Symonds	7 July 47	Late 4th Light Dragoons.
ENSIGN.		
John Gollop	16 Oct. 46	*Beaminster.*
ADJUTANT.		
Capt. St. Geo. Wyatt	27 March 23	*Dorchester.*
SURGEON.		
William Small	13 Nov. 12	*Brighton.*

SERVICES OF THE REGIMENT.—The Dorset Regiment was raised by ballot in 1757, and the command given to the Hon. George Pitt, afterwards Lord Rivers, whose commission was dated Oct. 25 in that year, and was of a prior date to any other Militia Colonel. This Militia also had their arms and clothing previous to any other corps, which accounts for "No. I." being still retained on their button. In 1798 the Regiment embarked for Ireland, and disembarked at Waterford. In 1799, the Mayor, Corporation, and inhabitants of Carrick-on-Suir presented to the Earl of Dorchester, the then Colonel of the Regiment, a valuable sword, and to the officers of the Regiment a present of plate for the use of their mess, as a token of gratitude for their services, and the kind feeling entertained by the town, during the Regiment being quartered there. Between 1798 and 1814, 48 officers, with their quota of non-commissioned officers and men, volunteered into various Regiments of the line, Artillery, Marines, &c., for general service. Served in Ireland in 1798, 1813, and 1815. Embodied for training, May, 1820; May, 1821; May 1825; Sept., 1831. Disembodied at Dorchester, Colonel Richard Bingham commanding.

Facings, Green.

Head-Quarters, Southampton.] **43d South Hants Light Infantry Regiment of Militia.**

Colonel.
Sir John Walters Pollen, Bart., 25 June 1827. J.P., D.L.—*Redenham Park, Andover.*

Lieut.-Colonel.
Edward Hulse, 22 March 1831.—*New Burlington-street.*

Major.
Edward Gilbert, 5 Dec. 1812.—*Bently Lodge, Lyndhurst.*

	Date of Appointment to Present Rank.		Remarks exhibiting Services of Officers, whether L.L., D.L., M.P., or J.P.—Country Seats, &c.
CAPTAINS.			
Peter Pole	29 Aug.	24	*Manchester-square, London.*
William Kingsmill	25 June	29	*Sidmonton House, Newbury.*
Charles Brett	8 July	31	*Royal Yacht Club, Cowes.*
Edw. Wm. St. John	1 July	39	
Thomas W. Fleming	1 July	39	*Stoneham Park, Southampton.*
LIEUTENANTS.			
Thomas Palmer	29 June	09	
John Hutchinson Lee	8 July	39	*Elms Bedhampton, Herts.*
W. Wyne Tyndell	8 July	36	
John Hamborough	7 June	43	
John Beardmore	18 May	46	
ENSIGNS.			
John Gompertz	28 Jan.	14	
Thos. Wm. Swan	10 Sept.	23	
William W. Lee	8 July	31	
ADJUTANT.			
Capt. J. R. Norton	21 Jan.	46	*Southampton.* Served in 15th and 63d Regiments twenty years.
QUARTERMASTER.			
Joel Bennett			*Bernard-street, Southampton.*

SERVICES OF THE REGIMENT.—Raised in the year 1779, disembodied 1787; embodied 1792, disembodied 1802; embodied 1803, disembodied 1814; embodied 1815, disembodied 1816. Served in Hyde Park during the riots of 1780. Made Light Infantry 1811. Served in Scotland from May, 1813, to May, 1814.

Facings, Yellow.

44th Royal Glamorgan Light Infantry Regiment of Militia.

Head-Quarters, Cardiff.

Colonel.
C. J. Kemeys Tynte, 4 January 1849. M.P., D.L., J.P.—*Cefer Mably, Glamorganshire.* Served as Lieut.-Colonel Somersetshire Yeomanry Cavalry.

Lieut.-Colonel.—J. N. Lucas, 3 April 1849. D.L., J.P.

Major.
Sir Chas. Morgan, Bart., 3 April 1849. J.P., D.L.—*Ruperra, Glamorganshire; Tudigan Park, Monmouthshire.* Served in the Glamorganshire Yeomanry Cavalry.

	Date of Appointment to Present Rank.	Remarks exhibiting Services of Officers, whether L.L., D.L., M.P., or J.P.—Country Seats, &c.
CAPTAINS.		
F. Fredricks	18 April 26	D.L., J.P.
Henry Seymour	5 Jan. 27	D.L., J.P.
T. T. Wheatley	18 April 32	
John Hewitt	10 Feb. 46	D.L., J.P.—*Tyr.Mab Ellis, Glamorganshire.* Served in the Royal Marines in the American War, &c.
Henry Lewis	13 Feb. 46	D.L., J.P.
H. Lucas	23 March 46	
Captain-Lieut. John Langley	2 May 98	
1ST LIEUTENANTS.		
Thomas Rowe	28 Sept. 12	
Gerald Fitzgerald	17 July 15	
Tobias Fitzgerald	17 Feb. 46	
Thomas Place	23 Feb. 46	
Wm. Morgan Harris	25 Feb. 46	
Henry Goldfinch	27 Feb. 46	
2D LIEUTENANTS.		
James Bird	26 June 26	
George Chapman	17 Feb. 46	
Webster Austin	20 Feb. 46	
Windham Lewis	28 Feb. 46	*The Heath, near Cardiff.*
Windham Lewis	21 March 46	
ADJUTANT.		
Captain John Henry Armstrong	21 March 46	Served with the 98th Regiment in the Caffre War.
PAYMASTER.		
Captain-Lieut. John Langley	2 May 98	
QUARTERMASTER.		
George Steele	7 July 22	
SURGEON.		
Richard Reece	26 June 26	
ASSIST.-SURGEON.		
James Bird	26 June 26	

SERVICES OF THE REGIMENT, FROM 1800.—1800, Regiment served 6 months in Ireland and 6 in England; 1801-2, in Wales; 1803 to 1813, in England; 1814, disembodied; 1815, embodied, and served in Ireland from Sept.; 1816, disembodied in July, served in Ireland to that period; remained disembodied, but assembled annually for training till 1831. Staff reduced in 1835.

Facings, Blue.

Agents, Messrs. Cox & Co.

Head-Quarters, Lancaster.] **45th Royal Lancashire, or Duke of Lancaster's Own Regiment of Militia.**

Colonel.
John Plumbe Tempest, 4 Nov. 1819. D.L., J.P.—*Tong Hall.*

Lieut.-Colonel.
Lawrance Rawstorne, 4 Nov. 1819. D.L., J.P.—*Penwortham.*

Majors.
Edward Every Clayton, 14 April 1846. *Carr Hall.*
George Oned, 21 March 1846.

	Date of Appointment to Present Rank.	Remarks exhibiting Serv'ces of Officers, whether L.L., D.L., M P., or J.P.—Country Seats, &c.
CAPTAINS.		
Edward Jones.........	5 July 15	
James Rigby	11 Feb. 31	
Peter Stanley Lowe .	12 Feb. 31	
R. J. T. Williamson .	25 Nov. 31	
R. F. Shuttleworth .	31 Dec. 32	
J. R. Shaw	31 May 33	
Henry M. Feilden ...	15 Nov. 42	
Wm. A. Cross	13 Dec. 42	
Robert W. Ffrance...	13 Dec. 42	
LIEUTENANTS.		
Godfrey Rawstone ...	21 Feb. 20	
C. Horatio Carey ...	5 Feb. 31	
R. Maingay............	5 March 31	
S. H. Oughton	25 April 31	
C. P. Williams	26 May 31	
F. W. Rutledge	19 May 32	
H. C. Irvine	29 April 36	
Richard P. Dawson .	27 Dec. 45	
John French Slegg...	31 Dec. 45	
ENSIGNS.		
Bennett Smith	7 May 10	
Wm. Howett	23 March 31	
PAYMASTER.		
Bennett Smith	7 May 10	
ASSIST.-SURGEON.		
Wm. Howett	23 March 31	

Facings, Blue.

46th, or Royal Denbighshire Rifle Regiment of Militia.

Head-Quarters, Wrexham.

Lieut.-Colonel-Commandant.
Robert Myddleton Biddulph, 5 March 1840. L.L., J.P.—*Chirk Castle.*

Major.
Richard Miles Wynne, 1 June 1832. D.L., J.P.—*Eyarth House.* Served in the 3d Provisional Battalion of Militia.

	Date of Appointment to Present Rank.	Remarks exhibiting Services of Officers, whether L.L., D.L., M.P., or J.P.—Country Seats, &c.
CAPTAINS.		
Thomas Jones.........	25 March 13	
Richard V. Kyrke ...	1 Dec. 26	
John J. Ffoulkes ...	1 Dec. 34	J.P.—*Eriviatt.*
Thomas Kenrick......	1 May 31	
Simon Yorke	13 Oct. 43	J.P.—*Erddig.*
FIRST LIEUTENANTS.		
Thomas Roberts......	1 Sept. 15	*Hafod y Dré.*
Thos. L. Fitzhugh ...	9 Feb. 46	D.L., J.P.—*Plas Power.* Late Lieutenant in the Grenadier Guards.
John Hughes	9 Feb. 46	
H. R. Sandback	21 Feb. 46	J.P.—*Hafodynos.*
Richard A. Price ...	18 Dec. 48	
Sir T. Erskine, Bart.	7 Dec. 49	*Pwll y Crochon.* Late Lieutenant in the 71st Highlanders.
SECOND LIEUTENANTS.		
Griffith J. Morris ...	25 Aug. 15	
Edw. Lloyd Ward ...	9 Feb. 46	
Robert H. Hughes...	18 Dec. 48	
Robert Wm. Wynne.	14 Jan. 50	*Bronynendon, Abergavenny.*
ADJUTANT.		
Ebenezer Jones	2 April 31	Captain ½. ½. Unattached. Late of the Royal Artillery Royal Staff Corps, and 43d Light Infantry.
PAYMASTER.		
Griffith J. Morris ...	25 Aug. 15	Captain ½. ½. 22d Foot.
SURGEON.		
Richard S. Perkins...	9 Feb. 46	

SERVICES OF THE REGIMENT.—In 1813 the late Colonel, Sir Watkin Williams Wynn, Bart., and the greater part of the Regiment volunteered into the 3d Provisional Battalion of Militia, and served with the Duke of Wellington's army in the south of France. The regiment was made Light Infantry in 1809, and was armed and equipped as a Rifle Corps in 1814.

EFFECTIVE STRENGTH.—344 Privates.

Uniform, Dark Green; *Facings,* Blue.

47th, or Second Somerset Regiment of Militia.

Head-Quarters, Bath.

Colonel.—William Pinney, 18 Jan. 1850. M.P.

Lieut.-Colonel.

Francis Fownes Luttrell.—🎖. Was wounded at the Battle of Waterloo, when serving as Lieut. and Captain in the Grenadier Guards; is a D.L. and Magistrate for the county of Somerset.

CAPTAINS.	Date of Appointment to Present Rank.	Remarks exhibiting Services of Officers, whether L.L., D.L., M.P., or J.P.—Country Seats, &c.
William Dawbin	2 Feb. 14	
Robt. John Bisdee	23 May 31	
A. G. Lethbridge	17 June 34	
H. B. Strangways	3 Aug. 34	
T. J. Thackeray	10 Jan. 42	
W. S. Farquharson	10 June 45	
John Halliday	7 May 46	
J. P. Lethbridge	7 May 46	
J. G. Evered	8 May 46	
H. N. S. Shrapnell	18 June 46	*Gosport, Hants.* Served in the 3d Dragoon [Guards.
LIEUTENANTS.		
F. R. L'Estrange	18 May 31	
Wm. Chivers	16 Nov. 32	Served as Second Lieut. in Royal Marines.
Edmund Callanan	29 April 43	
Charles Tucker	2 Feb. 44	
William Barker	29 Nov. 44	
David De Charms	4 May 45	
Thomas Salmon	18 July 46	
William Perham	22 July 39	🎖. as First Lieut. Royal Marines.
R. E. Perrott	7 May 46	
G. C. Montague	7 May 46	
I. W. S. Johnstone	7 May 46	
C. W. Kinglake	8 May 46	
Charles W. Fuller	8 May 46	
ENSIGNS.		
William Newberry	28 Feb. 46	
Daniel Williams	7 May 46	
E. Harwood	7 May 46	
J. F. Nicholls	7 May 46	
C. G. Homer	8 May 46	
R. Hetherington	8 May 46	
T. B. Wright	8 May 46	
ADJUTANT.		[Regiments.
Capt. A. J. M'Pherson	25 March 46	Served in the 64th Foot, 77th and 6th Royal

SERVICES OF THE REGIMENT.—First raised in the year 1797. Served in the west, east, and north of England and Ireland.

Facings, Yellow.

Head-Quarters, Northampton.] **48th, or Northamptonshire Regiment of Militia.**

Colonel.—Thomas Philip Maunsell, 2 April 1845. J.P., D.L., M.P.
Thorpe Malsor, Northamptonshire.

Lieut.-Colonel.—Lord Burghley, 9 Jan. 1846. M.P.

Major.—Quintus Vivian, 26 March 1846. J.P.—Served in the 8th Hussars.

	Date of Appointment to Present Rank.	Remarks exhibiting Services of Officers, whether L.L., D.L., M.P., or J.P.—Country Seats, &c.
CAPTAINS.		
William Davison ...	24 Jan. 24	
John Chris. Mansell .	9 Oct. 33	J.P.—*Cosgrove Hall, Northamptonshire.*
Charles Hill	29 June 39	J.P.
Vernon Wentworth .	28 April 43	
Philip P. Duncombe.	1 May 45	D.L.—*Great Buckhill, Bucks.*
Thomas Rose	27 Feb. 46	Adjutant. Served in the 15th Foot.
Richard T. Clarke ...	4 April 46	J.P.—*Welton Place, Northamptonshire.*
Fitzpatrick H. Vernon	11 April 46	
William Christie......	18 April 46	
John B. Maunsell ...	28 May 48	Served in the 60th Rifles and 12th Lancers.
LIEUTENANTS.		
Thomas Wage.........	3 March 98	
W. R. Adcock.........	13 Jan. 07	
W. M. Kingsbury ...	26 Aug. 07	
Hon. G. A. F. J. Fane	6 Nov. 41	
ENSIGNS.		
Edward Griffin	5 April 46	
Huntley R. Fletcher .	21 May 46	
ADJUTANT.		
Capt. Thomas Rose ..	27 Feb. 46	Served in the 15th Foot.
QUARTERMASTER.		
James Ingle............	30 May 23	
SURGEON.		
Henry Terry	4 Dec. 24	" Waterloo."
ASSIST.-SURGEON.		
George J. Gates	22 May 46	

SERVICES OF THE REGIMENT.—The Regiment occupied Lambeth Palace during the Lord George Gordon Riots. In 1793 they were embodied, and disbanded in 1802. In 1803, re-embodied, and went to Ireland in 1811. In 1813, removed to Scotland, and were finally disbanded in 1814.

Facings, Yellow.

49th, or East Kent Regiment of Militia.

Head-Quarters, Canterbury.

Colonel.—Samuel Elias Sawbridge, 14 April 1808.—*Olanteigh.*
Lieut.-Colonel.—Charles Henry Tyler, 9 April 1835.—*Lynstead Lodge.*
Major.—John Price Ladd, 9 April 1835.

	Date of Appointment to Present Rank.	Remarks exhibiting Services of Officers, whether L.L., D.L., M.P., or J.P.—Country Seats, &c.
CAPTAINS.		
J. S. W. S. E. Drax	30 Dec. 17	M.P.
Chas. George Dering	28 Aug. 26	J.P.—*Barham Court.*
Fredk. J. Cumming	27 June 39	
Ed. G. L. Perrott ...	27 June 39	
William Love	27 June 39	*Summerhill.*
W. Augustus Munn	20 Jan. 46	J.P.—*Throwley House.*
LIEUTENANTS.		
Philip Parsons	6 Sept. 11	
William Mount	11 Feb. 14	J.P.
Chas. Alfred Mount	21 Jan. 46	
Walter Leith	22 Jan. 46	
Henry Maxwell	23 Jan. 46	
ENSIGNS.		
Silas Newman.........	19 Nov. 13	
Alexander Leigh......	7 June 39	
Alexander Cumming	24 May 43	
Theodosius Abbott...	29 Jan. 46	
James Abbott.........	30 Jan. 46	
ADJUTANT.		
Charles Winter	31 Dec. 45	Served as Capt. in the 66th and 76th Regiments.

SERVICES OF THE REGIMENT.—Raised in the year 1779. Served in Ireland from September 13, 1811, to October 8, 1813. Disembodied June, 1814.

Facings, Kentish Grey.

50th, or Royal Radnor Regiment of Militia.

Head-Quarters, Presteigne.

Major-Commandant.
Brevet Major John Abraham Whittaker, 21 March 1846. J.P.—*Newcastle Court.*
Served formerly in the 28th Regiment as Capt.

	Date of Appointment to Present Rank.	Remarks exhibiting Services of Officers, whether L.L., D.L., M.P., or J.P.—Country Seats, &c.
CAPTAIN.		
John P. Severn	28 March 46	J.P.—*Penybort.*
LIEUTENANTS.		
Thomas Meredith ...	12 Feb. 14	*Pentry,* near *Kington.*
Henry Ricketts	21 March 46	*Coombe.*
ADJUTANT.		
Capt. F. P. Sanders	31 Dec. 45	Served formerly as Capt. in the 43d Light Infantry.

SERVICES OF THE REGIMENT.—The Royal Radnor Militia served in England and Wales at different periods, and in Ireland from 1811 to 1813.

Facings, Blue.

51st, or Oxfordshire Regiment of Militia.

Head-Quarters, Oxford.

Colonel.
Charles Oldfield Bowles, 3 April 1847. J.P., D.L.—*North Aston House.*

Lieutenant-Colonel.
John William Fane, 6 April 1847. J.P., D.L.—*Shirburn Lodge, Oxon.*

Major.
The Honourable Henry George Spencer, 24 April 1847.

Captains.	Date of Appointment to Present Rank.		Remarks exhibiting Services of Officers, whether L.L., D.L., M.P., or J.P.—Country Seats, &c.
Michael E. Impey ...	5 Sept.	31	
Anthony M. Storer...	5 April	34	
P. A. Holloway	10 Jan.	46	
George A. S. Fane ...	12 Jan.	46	
A. M. Matthews......	23 Jan.	46	
Samuel W. Gardiner	2 April	46	D.L.—*Coombe Lodge, Oxon.*
The Hon. Thomas E. Stonor	14 April	46	J.P.
Lieutenants.			
William Davis.........	4 Nov.	07	
William Scott	6 Nov.	13	
William Brown	1 April	14	
Sweeten Grant	7 Sept.	14	
Bernard L. Watson..	3 Nov.	20	
Charles J. Preedy	7 May	30	
Arthur F. Shum......	18 Feb.	46	
Wm. W. Holloway...	18 Feb.	46	
Thomas Kemp Story	3 Dec.	46	
Ensigns.			
Robert Roberts	4 Aug.	12	
John James Ireland	7 May	25	
Adjutant.			
George Cuming	3 Feb.	46	Served eight years in the 63d Regiment, and twenty-one in the 71st Light Infantry.
Surgeon.			
George N. Robinson.	25 July	10	M.D.
Assist.-Surgeons.			
Robert Roberts	4 Aug.	12	
John James Ireland	7 May	25	

Services of the Regiment.—Served in Ireland, in the years 1813 and 1814.

Facings, Yellow.

52d (*Herefordshire*) Regiment of Militia.

Head-Quarters, Hereford.

Colonel.
The Earl Somers, 16 Jan. 1836. L.L.—*Eastnor Castle*, near *Ledbury*. Late Capt. 2d Dragoon Guards.

Lieut.-Colonel.
J. L. Scudamore, 15 Feb. 1836. D.L., J.P.—*Kent Church Court.*

Major.
Sir John C. Walsham, Bart., 1846. D.L., J.P.—*Knill Court, Kingston.*

	Date of Appointment to Present Rank.	Remarks exhibiting Services of Officers, whether L.L., D.L., M.P., or J.P.—Country Seats, &c.
CAPTAINS.		
J. G. Beavan	16 May 31	J.P.—*Island House, Kington.*
W. Unett	10 May 32	J.P.—*Venwood, Boodnham.*
J. Parkinson	17 Feb. 36	J.P.—*Kinnersley Court, Herefordshire.*
J. K. Symonds	20 June 38	J.P.—*Pengethley,* near *Ross.*
Sir V. Cornewall, Bt.	3 July 46	J.P.—*Morcas Court, Herefordshire.*
H. E. C. Stanhope	4 Aug. 46	
R. B. Mynors	4 Aug. 46	
J. Berrington	4 Aug. 46	11, *St. James's-street, Westminster.*
LIEUTENANTS.		
J. Hawkins	22 June 10	*Harbour-place, Birmingham.*
M. Parker	24 Aug. 12	*St. Heliers, Jersey.* H.P. Lieut. 3d P. Battalion.
C. M. Gamber	16 April 14	*Grey's Inn-square, London.* H.P. Lieut. 3d P. Battalion.
C. Chamberlain	3 June 14	
W. Bennett	14 Aug. 15	*Ash Grove, Marden, Hereford.*
T. Palmer	3 July 17	*Wittington, Worcestershire.*
J. E. Acton	25 Sept. 36	H.P. Lieut. 3d P. Battalion.
Henry Symonds	20 June 38	
Daniel Evans	24 June 46	
ENSIGNS.		
W. F. Hill	12 Jan. 16	
Joseph Seward	2 July 31	
J. Linton	24 June 46	
E. Williams	24 June 46	
R. Richards	24 June 46	
ADJUTANT.		
Capt. J. E. Money-Kyrle	27 April 16	Late 32d Foot.
PAYMASTER.		
W. F. Hill	12 Jan. 46	
SURGEON.		
John Morris	17 July 46	

Facings, Goslin Green.

53D REGIMENT OF MILITIA. 93

Head-Quarters, Chichester.] **53d, or Sussex Light Infantry Regiment of Militia.**

Colonel.
His Grace Charles Duke of Richmond, 4 Dec. 1819. R.G., L.L.—*Goodwood*.

The Duke of Richmond joined the Army in Portugal, on the 24th July, 1810, as Aide-de-Camp and Assistant Military Secretary to the Duke of Wellington, with whom he remained until the close of the war in 1814, and was present in all the skirmishes, affairs, general actions, and sieges, which took place during that period, amongst which were the battles of Busaco and Fuentes d'Onor, storming of Ciudad Rodrigo, storming of Badajoz, battles of Salamanca, Vittoria, and the Pyrenees, the first storming of San Sebastian, action at Vera, and battle of Orthes. He was sent home with duplicate Dispatches of the battle of Salamanca, and the capture of Astorga by the Spaniards; and with the Despatches of Vera and the entrance of the army into France. In Jan., 1814, being desirous of obtaining a practical knowledge of Regimental duty in the Field, he left the Duke of Wellington's Staff to join the first battalion of his Regiment, the 52d Light Infantry, and was present with it in the battle of Orthes, where he was severely wounded in the chest by a musket-ball, which has never been extracted. At the end of 1814, he was appointed Aide-de-Camp to the Prince of Orange, and was with him in the battles of Quatre Bras and Waterloo;—after the Prince of Orange was wounded the Duke of Richmond joined the Duke of Wellington as Aide-de-Camp, and remained with his Grace during the remaining part of that campaign. His Grace has received the War Medal and eight clasps.

Lieut.-Colonel.—John Paine, 28 Nov. 1845.

Majors.
Robert Henry Hurst, 10 Jan. 1840.   George Kirwan Carr, 19 Feb. 1847.

	Date of Appointment to Present Rank.	Remarks exhibiting Services of Officers, whether L.L., D.L., M.P., or J.P.—Country Seats, &c.
CAPTAINS.		
Richard Witherell	19 Sept. 25	
Charles Dorrien	12 Dec. 31	
Ed. Earl of Winterton	12 Dec. 31	
Richard B. Newland	12 Dec. 31	
Thos. E. Swettenham	20 March 37	
Henry Wm. Bates	20 March 37	
John Hamlin Borrer	21 April 46	
Frederick Moor	21 April 46	
James S. D. Scott	21 April 46	
Rush Martin Cripps	21 April 46	
LIEUTENANTS.		
William Kipping	14 May 03	
Francis J. Forth	20 July 08	
William Anderson	14 Dec. 16	
W. W. M. Walker	20 March 37	
Hon. Keys Turnour	21 Jan. 40	
Hon. Spencer Lord Templemore	21 April 46	
Hon. F. A. Chichester	21 April 46	
Henry David Cole	21 April 46	
Sir P. F. Shelly, Bart.	21 April 46	
Charles C. Bates	21 April 46	
Edw. Thos. Shiffner	21 April 46	
George Weeks	21 April 46	
ENSIGNS.		
Richard Shawe	21 April 46	
John George Willis	21 April 46	
Edwyn E. Dormer	21 April 46	
James Dennis	21 April 46	
Thos. Geo. Walker	17 Oct. 46	
Wm. Boyer Watson	22 May 48	
Wm. Adams Nash	22 May 48	
John Sanctuary	22 May 48	
ADJUTANT.		
Capt. John Smith	2 Oct. 12	
ASSIST.-SURGEON.		
Lieut. Geo. Weeks	21 April 46	

Facings, Blue.   *Agents*, Cox and Co.

54th, or Shropshire Regiment of Militia.

Head-Quarters, Shrewsbury.

Colonel.
Viscount Rowland Hill, 4 June 1849. L.L.—*Hawkestone, Salop.* Served in Royal Horse Guards Blue, from 20 July, to 1824. Lieut.-Colonel N. Salop Yeomanry Cavalry, 18 Aug. 1824.

Lieutenant-Colonel.
Richard F. Hill, 30 Jan. 1846. *Zante, Ionian Islands.* Served as Lieut.-Colonel 53d Regiment; retired in 1842.

Major.—Edward Lloyd Gatane, 8 May 1846. *Coton Bridgenorth.*

	Date of Appointment to Present Rank.	Remarks exhibiting Services of Officers, whether L.L., D.L., M.P., or J.P.—Country Seats, &c.
CAPTAINS.		
John Quin Pardy	29 Jan. 49	Adjutant.
Edward F. Acton	12 Jan. 32	*Galacre Park, Bridgenorth.*
Henry C. Taylor	13 Jan. 46	*Chicknell, Wolverhampton.* Served as Cornet
John Whitmore	13 Jan. 46	*Cheltenham.* [17th Lancers; retired 1842.
LIEUTENANTS.		
Charles Prince	21 April 06	*Wem.* Half-pay.
Thomas B. Dorset	21 July 10	*Oswestry.* Half-pay.
William Arkenstall	21 March 14	*Newport, Salop.* Half-pay.
Thomas Boyce	20 Oct. 17	Paymaster. Served as 2d Lieutenant Artillery Drivers, from 1813 to 1815.
J. M. K. Chadwick	11 July 32	*Bristol.*
Thomas Hardwick	12 July 32	*Bridgenorth.*
Thomas Mathews	12 July 32	*Ludlow.*
William Lovett	30 Jan 46	*Belmont, Oswestry.*
ENSIGNS.		
Charles Fraser	12 July 32	*Cashel, Tipperary.*
Walace Bayce	30 Jan. 44	*Salop.*
Peter A. Beck	30 Jan. 47	*Salop.*
ADJUTANT.		
Captain J. Q. Pardy	29 Jan. 49	Served in the Army. Peninsula Medal and clasp.
PAYMASTER.		
Thomas Boyce	20 Oct. 17	Served as 2d Lieutenant Artillery Drivers, from 1813 to 1815.
SURGEON.		
T. N. Heathcote	8 May 46	*Shrewsbury.*

SERVICES OF THE REGIMENT.—The Regiment was first raised in the year 1762. Its establishment consisted of 8 Companies, under the command of the Earl Bath, and was raised to serve three years. Facings, Buff.—1776, embodied for actual service, by Warrant 28th March. 1778, marched for Maidstone from Shrewsbury, to encamp at Coxheath. Facings changed to Green, 1776, and the Regiment divided into 10 Companies. From 1778 to 1783, doing duty in various parts of England, returned to Shrewsbury, disembarked on the 15th March, 1783. The Regiment again embodied 28th Jan., by Warrant 1st Jan., 1793, under command of Lord Clive. From 1793 to 1797, the Regiment was moved to various places in England.—1795, received an addition of an Artillery Company of 1 Captain, 1 Lieutenant, 3 Sergeants, 65 Rank and File.—1797, marched to Scotland, being the first English Regiment of Militia sent there.—1798, the Regiment increased by 341 from the Supplementary Militia. The establishment was 1 Colonel, 1 Lieutenant-Colonel, 2 Majors, 8 Captains, 14 Lieutenants, 10 Ensigns, 1 Paymaster, 2 Adjutants, 1 Quartermaster, 1 Surgeon, 2 Assistant-Surgeons, 2 Staff-Sergeants, 50 Sergeants, 50 Corporals, 28 Drummers, 2,112 Privates.—1799, marched to Weymouth, to do duty as Guards over His Majesty's Establishment; reduced to 45 Sergeants, 45 Corporals, 735 Rank and File.—From 1801 and 1802, marched to Isle of Wight, Southampton, &c.—1802, returned to Shrewsbury, to be disembodied, retaining a permanent Staff of 1 Adjutant, 1 Sergeant-Major, 33 Sergeants, 33 Corporals, and 13 Drummers.—1808, embodied at Shrewsbury, 28th March; did duty in various Towns and Garrisons in England, until 1808. Strength of Regiment, 12 Companies.—1811, two Companies ordered to be trained as Rifle Companies.—1813, embarked at Plymouth, for Cork, Ireland; did duty in various places there.—1814, marched to Dublin, and did duty in that Garrison until 1815, when the Regiment embarked for Liverpool, and returned to Shrewsbury; disembodied 18th February, 1815—Called out for training and exercise, 11th May, 1820; and again in 1825, for twenty-eight days.—Strength of Disembodied Staff, as per War-Office Circular, No. 954, dated 1st Dec., 1845, 1 Adjutant, 1 Sergeant-Major, 12 Sergeants. Discharged, not filled up.—Discharged, 1 Sergeant-Major, and 6 Sergeants, —Total, 1 Adjutant, 6 Sergeants, present strength.

Facings, Green.

55th, or Royal Westminster Middlesex Regiment of Militia.

Head-Quarters, Hammersmith.

Colonel.—H. C. C. Viscount Chelsea, 6 Dec. 1841.
Lieut.-Colonel.—Edward Richard Bagot, 10 June 1846. Served in the 60th Rifles.
Majors.—Hon. C. Lennox Butler, 25 Feb. 1846.
Robert Cannon, 24 July 1846.

CAPTAINS.	Date of Appointment to Present Rank.	Remarks exhibiting Services of Officers, whether L.L., D.L., M.P., or J.P.—Country Seats, &c.
Robert Brailsford	8 June 07	
Charles Ralfs	8 Feb. 14	
John Cook	29 April 31	
Henry Price	26 March 32	
R. Monkhouse Piper	23 Sept. 34	
R. Tappin Claridge	7 June 42	
John James Glossop	25 Feb. 46	
Henry Penton	25 Feb. 46	
LIEUTENANTS.		
George Edward Cook	28 May 40	
Francis Crozier	28 May 40	
H. St. John Corbett	5 March 46	
George Samuel	19 Dec. 46	
Charles Villiers Bayly	19 Dec. 46	
ENSIGNS.		
Charles Henry Sirr	9 May 42	
James Haggard	19 Dec. 46	
ADJUTANT.		
Robert M'Ewen	4 April 46	Served in the Scots Fusilier Guards.
SURGEON.		
William Ralfs	18 March 17	

SERVICES OF THE REGIMENT.—Served in England, Ireland, Scotland, and Jersey.

Facings, Blue.

Head-Quarters, Carnarvon.

56th, or Royal Carnarvon Rifle Regiment of Militia.

Major-Commandant.
O. J. E. Nanney, 10 Oct. 1831. J.P., D.L.—Served in the Army.

Captain.—T. E. Roberts, 11 Jan. 1839.

Lieutenant.—J. E. Lloyd, 4 Feb. 1839.

Second Lieutenants.
W. Turner, 23 July 1831.
A. D. Willoughby, 11 Aug. 1841.

Paymaster.—Lieut. T. Church, 25 Sept. 1808.

Surgeon.—J. Williams, 30 Aug. 1842.

Uniform, Green.

57th (*the Royal Montgomeryshire*) Regiment of Militia.

Head-Quarters, Welshpool.

	Date of Appointment to Present Rank.	Remarks exhibiting Services of Officers, whether L.L., D.L., M.P., or J.P.—Country Seats, &c.
CAPTAINS.		
W. P. Daykin.........	29 July 05	
Robert Owen Tudor	7 April 12	
LIEUTENANTS.		
Charles Necrassoff ...	20 Aug. 03	
Charles Brown	15 May 13	
Walter O. Smith ...	13 Oct. 13	
H. J. Evans	14 March 31	
ENSIGNS.		
C. H. Garratt	5 Jan. 32	
Pryce Turner	1 July 36	
ADJUTANT.		
Capt. E. Dwen	29 June 46	Served 25 years in the 43d Light Infantry.

SERVICES OF THE REGIMENT.—First called out for training in the year 1772. Commanded by the Right Hon. Viscount Hereford. Left the county 1776, and stationed in Kent, and encamped with many other Regiments on Coxheath. In 1779 returned home and re-embodied; left the county, and returned again at the end of the American War in 1783. In the spring of 1787 they were embodied again for annual training, and in May, 1793, they marched out of the county for active service, and did duty in several counties in England. The Regiment volunteered for service in Ireland in 1811, and served in that country till 1813. The Regiment returned to Welshpool, Montgomeryshire, in the year 1814, and were disembodied.

Facings, Blue.

58TH REGIMENT OF MILITIA.

Head-Quarters, Uxbridge.] **58th, or Royal West Middlesex Regiment of Militia.**

Colonel.
The Right Hon. the Viscount Enfield, 29 April 1844. D.L., M.P., J.P.—95, *Eaton-square*, and *Cople House, Bedford*. Served as Capt. in the Rifle Brigade.

Lieut.-Colonel.
Charles Ramsden, 22 Jan. 1846. D.L., J.P.—*Belgrave-square*, and *Cantley Hall, Doncaster*. Served in the Rifle Brigade.

Majors.
Sir John Gibbons, Bart., 22 Jan. 1846.
George Viscount Cantalupe, 16 June 1847. D.L., J.P. Served as Captain in the Grenadier Guards.

	Date of Appointment to Present Rank.	Remarks exhibiting Services of Officers, whether L.L., D.L., M.P., or J.P.—Country Seats, &c.
CAPTAINS.		
William Griffiths ...	3 April 21	
George Miles	12 Dec. 25	
Henry W. Marriott .	8 Aug. 29	*Grove House, Bayswater.*
Hon. G. H. C. Byng.	25 Feb. 46	
Jas. G. De Burgh ...	25 Feb. 46	
Wm. Capel Clayton .	23 April 46	
F. C. H. Russell......	9 Aug. 47	
Henry Tufnell.........	11 Feb. 48	M.P.
Chas. Wm. Grenfell .	18 April 48	M.P.
LIEUTENANTS.		
Charles Alavoine......	10 May 09	
T. C. Parker	25 April 10	Assistant-Surgeon.
William Myers	11 Sept. 10	
Fred. Burchell	25 March 12	
John Forster	6 Sept. 13	
Galbraith Johnston .	7 Sept. 13	
William Brew.........	23 March 14	
Charles Brew	2 April 14	
F. C. Phillips	7 Nov. 15	
Charles Hewitt	27 Nov. 19	Paymaster.
Henry T. Bradfield...	9 Nov. 29	
Henry Bliss	12 July 45	
Arthur C. Tupper ...	25 Feb. 46	
Wm. Bird Parker ...	23 April 46	
Arch. R. Ridgway ...	23 April 46	Assistant-Surgeon.
Edward Day	20 May 46	
Churchill Proby	8 Nov. 47	
Ernest O. Coe.........	11 Feb. 48	
ENSIGNS.		
T. W. Austin	15 Jan. 20	
William Wheatley ...	25 March 25	
J. Le Poer Bookey...	22 Jan. 46	
Henry Austin.........	23 April 46	
ADJUTANT.		
Capt. J. H. Evelegh .	17 Dec. 45	
PAYMASTER.		
Charles Hewitt	27 Nov. 19	Lieutenant.
ASSIST.-SURGEONS.		
T. C. Parker	25 April 10	Lieutenant.
Arch. R. Ridgway ...	23 April 46	Lieutenant.

SERVICES OF THE REGIMENT.—Volunteered for and went to France in the year 1814. Served two years in Ireland.

EFFECTIVE STRENGTH.—1 Colonel, 1 Lieut.-Colonel, 2 Majors, 10 Captains, 22 Lieutenants (including Paymaster and 2 Assist.-Surgeons), 8 Ensigns, 1 Paymaster, 1 Adjutant, 1 Quartermaster, 1 Surgeon, 2 Assist.-Surgeons. Wanting to complete: 1 Captain, 4 Lieutenants, 4 Ensigns, 1 Quartermaster, and 1 Surgeon.

Facings, Blue.

o

59th, Nottingham, or Royal Sherwood Foresters Regiment of Militia.

Head-Quarters, Newark.

Colonel.
L. Rolleston, 11 April 1843. M.P.

Lieut.-Colonel.
Sir T. W. White, Bart. 1 June 1833.

Major.
S. Sherwin, 22 July 1833.

	Date of Appointment to Present Rank.	Remarks exhibiting Services of Officers, whether L.L., D.L., M.P., or J.P.—Country Seats, &c.
Captains.		
T. Matthews	8 Dec. 13	
J. Overend	14 Jan. 14	
T. D. Hall	14 Feb. 31	
H. P. Lowe	27 June 33	
J. B. Taylor	27 June 33	
G. Walker	6 Aug. 33	
J Franklin	11 Nov. 33	
W. Taylor	1 Oct. 36	
T. Need	18 Jan. 48	
Lieutenants.		
J. Martin	1 March 09	
W. Stubbs	25 Aug. 10	
J. Bodhill	26 May 13	
E. Wakefield	16 July 13	
R. Bigsby	15 Sept. 28	
G. G. G. Cooper	25 Jan. 31	
R. T. Hewitt	14 Oct. 31	
R. H. Bigsby	21 April 48	
A. Lowe	21 April 48	
Ensigns.		
W. Price	5 May 16	
J. G. Hewitt	28 June 31	
C. Calvert	16 Feb. 32	
Adjutant.		
J. Barth	24 Oct. 12	
Quartermaster.		
J. Collins	25 Feb. 20	
Surgeon.		
J. Anders	28 April 13	

Facings, Blue.

60TH AND 61ST REGIMENT OF MILITIA.

Head-Quarters, Dolgelly.] **60th, *Royal Merioneth Light Infantry Regiment of Militia.***

Colonel.—Hon. E. M. L. Mostyn, 17 Dec. 1847.

	Date of Appointment to Present Rank.	Remarks exhibiting Services of Officers, whether L.L., D.L., M.P., or J.P.—Country Seats, &c.
CAPTAIN. W. W. E. Wynne ...	10 June 20	
1ST LIEUTENANTS. R. J. Price	1 Jan. 31	
R. B. Phillipson	2 Jan. 31	
E. L. Edward	2 Jan. 34	
H. H. L. Clough......	28 Feb. 48	
2D LIEUTENANT. E. Barker	18 Jan. 48	
ADJUTANT. W. Anwyl...............	17 Nov. 17	
PAYMASTER. Lieut. R. M. Richards	18 Jan. 48	
SURGEON. T. Parry	26 April 16	

Facings, Blue.

Head-Quarters, Beaumaris.] **61st (*Royal Anglesea Light Infantry*) *Regiment of Militia.***

Colonel.
William Lewis Hughes Lord Dinorben, 7 Sept. 1808.—*Kenmel Park, St. Asaph.*

	Date of Appointment to Present Rank.	Remarks exhibiting Services of Officers, whether L.L., D.L., M.P., or J.P.—Country Seats, &c.
CAPTAINS. Lord Dinorben	4 April 94	One company is commanded by the Commandant, of whatever rank he may be.
Thos. Peers Williams	10 April 35	M.P.—*Temple House, Berkshire; Craigg Dow, Anglesea.*
LIEUTENANTS. Thos. Gray	5 July 03	Acting Paymaster.
Sir R. W. Bulkeley .	20 June 30	M.P.—*Baron Hill, Anglesea.*
ENSIGNS. John Horton	10 June 11	
Henry Jones , ...	11 Feb. 11	Late Adjutant.
ADJUTANT. Capt. C. S. Jones. ...	7 Sept. 32	Late Captain 59th Regiment. Served 17 years in the Regular Army, in the 43d, 62d, 58th, and 59th Regiments; returned on appointment to the Adjutancy of the Royal Anglesea Militia.
SURGEON. Robt. Wynne Jones .	12 Aug. 35	

SERVICES OF THE REGIMENT.—England and Ireland during the War, but volunteered in a body for Foreign Service in 1813.

Facings, Blue.

62d, or Derby Regiment of Militia.

Head-Quarters, Derby.

Colonel.—Lord H. M. Waterpark, 12 April 1832. D.L., J.P. *Doveridge Hall, Staffordshire.*

Lieut.-Colonel.—Richard Becher Leacroft, 8 July 1844. D.L.

Major.—Edw. Thomas Coke, 17 June 1842. J.P.—Served in the 45th Regiment.

	Date of Appointment to Present Rank.	Remarks exhibiting Services of Officers, whether L.L., D.L., M.P., or J.P.—Country Seats, &c.
CAPTAINS.		
Henry F. Hunter	3 Feb. 31	
Hugh Bateman	7 July 46	
Thomas Cox	7 July 46	
LIEUTENANTS.		
John Emery	4 Nov. 09	
John Lambert	10 Feb. 13	
Henry Wragg	10 Feb. 14	
Gaven Miller	25 Nov. 14	Served in the 19th Regiment of Foot.
Wm. Edw. Woodd...	23 Oct. 15	
William Morley	8 March 31	
Moreton L. Brooke...	14 July 46	
ADJUTANT.		
Francis Dixon	28 Aug. 15	D., U. Served in 1st Grenadier Guards.
SURGEON.		
William Bennet	16 March 07	

SERVICES OF THE REGIMENT.—Served in Ireland in the years 1813 and 1814. A part of the officers, non-commissioned officers, and privates, served in France, in the 3d Provisional Battalion of Militia, in the year 1814.

Facings, Yellow.

63d, or Isle of Wight Light Infantry Regiment of Militia.

Head-Quarters, Newport.

Captain-Commandant.
Percy Scott, 20 July 1832. J.P.—Lieut. Half-pay, late 98th Regiment. Served in the Peninsula with the 2d Queen's.

Lieutenant.—Francis Worsley, 5 Nov. 1844.

Ensign.—Robert Jacobs, 5 Nov. 1844.

SERVICES OF THE REGIMENT.—The Isle of Wight Militia, originally numbering 60 men, was first raised in 1757, at which time the population of the Island did not probably exceed 14,000; for, 20 years afterwards, namely, in 1777, according to an authentic enumeration made by the parochial clergy of its 30 parishes, the population amounted to but 18,024. In 1770 this Militia was first embodied. Subsequently, at different periods, its numbers were greatly extended, and, in 1797, was formed into a Corps of three Companies, with a Major-Commandant. It was disembodied in 1802. In 1803, it was again embodied, but on the reduced establishment of 1 Captain-Commandant, 2 Lieutenants, 1 Ensign, and 60 Privates, which was its strength when last called out for training in 1831. Thus it will have been observed, that when the population of the island in 1757 might have been estimated at 14,000, the number of its Militia was 60 Privates; and when the population, in 1831, amounted to 42,552, the number of its Militia was the same as in 1757, namely, 60 men. The further anomalous position of the Isle of Wight, with regard to its present quota of Militia, in reference to the extent of its population, and as compared with some of the smaller counties of England, will be seen by the following statement:—

	No. of Population, According to the last Census.	Strength of Militia.
County of Rutland	21,344	85
,, Radnor	25,186	140
,, Merioneth	39,238	121
Isle of Wight	42,552	60

Facings, Yellow.

Head-Quarters, Aberystwith.] *64th, or Royal Cardigan Rifles Regiment of Militia.*

Lieut.-Col.

W. E. Powell. L.L., D.L., M.P., J.P.—*Manteos, Cardiganshire.* Major, Dec. 3, 1811; Colonel, Dec. 15, 1823; Royal Horse Guards (Cornet), May 9, 1803; Lieut., Sept. 5, 1805; Retired, 1809; Ensign, H. P. Bradshaw's Levy, May 21, 1811; Full-pay Ensign, 57th Regiment, July 11, 1822; Cornet, H.P. 18th Hussars, Sept. 12, 1822.

Major.

J. Lloyd Phillips. Capt., 15 Oct. 1821; Major, 22 March 1833.

	Date of Appointment to Present Rank.	Remarks exhibiting Services of Officers, whether L.L., D.L., M.P., or J.P.—Country Seats, &c.
CAPTAINS.		
C. A. Pritchard	30 Oct. 22	D.L., J.P.
R. O. Powell	4 Dec. 23	J.P.
W. H. W. Parry ...	9 June 25	D.L., J.P.
R. Wagner	3 July 38	J.P.
LIEUTENANTS.		
W. Watkins	23 Jan. 09	
J. Brinley	10 Oct. 10	
H. Mostyn	25 Feb. 11	
P. Evans	4 March 11	D.L., J.P.
ADJUTANT.		
Capt. Vere Webb ...	29 Aug. 31	Served with the Rifle Brigade during the campaigns of 1814 and 1815 in Holland, the Netherlands, and France, including both the Actions at Merxem, bombardment of Antwerp, and battle of Waterloo, at which last he was slightly wounded.
SURGEON.		
Thomas James	18 Feb. 46	

SERVICES OF THE REGIMENT.—Opposed the landing of the French at Fishguard on 22d February, 1797; served in Ireland from 8th August, 1811, to 17th Sept., 1813; and was disembodied on the 3d July, 1814.

Uniform, Green.

Head-Quarters, Hampstead.] **65th, or Royal East Middlesex Regiment of Militia.**

Colonel.—Thomas Wood, 12 April 1803.
Lieut.-Colonel.—Thomas St. Leger Alcock, 8 Feb. 1850.
Majors.
Guy Parsons, 7 August 1849.
Edward Dewes, 8 Feb. 1850.

	Date of Appointment to Present Rank.	Remarks exhibiting Services of Officers, whether L.L., D.L., M.P., or J.P.—Country Seats, &c.
CAPTAINS.		
James Stuart	22 April 37	
Geo. John Stone	10 June 39	
H. S. M'Clintock	4 April 40	
Geo. Thos. Lowth	11 Aug. 40	
Jacob Wm. Hinde	11 Aug. 40	
Thos. Meyer Carrick	22 April 44	Late Lieutenant 78th Highlanders.
Hon. W. J. P. Gore	25 Feb. 46	
Mark Jas. Gambier	25 Feb. 46	
John Gilbert Ogilvie	25 Feb. 46	
Henry Spicer	25 Feb. 46	
Nath. Cumberlege	25 Feb. 46	
William Reed	19 Dec. 46	
LIEUTENANTS.		
Charles Miller	23 April 03	
Alex. M'Gregor	31 March 13	
Alex. Noble	14 April 13	
James Prince	11 Feb. 14	
Wm. Sutherland	5 April 14	
James M'Gregor	12 Nov. 14	
John Harris	1 July 15	
George Carnaby	26 Oct. 15	
T. Hodges	24 July 17	
Geo. De la Motte	18 Aug. 20	
Wm. Middlemiss	19 Aug. 20	
J. R. Moriarty	20 Aug. 20	
Edw. Hodges	22 Aug. 20	
R. B. Pitman	23 Aug. 20	
Wm. Phillips Snell	22 Jan. 46	
Ed. Berry O. West	22 Jan. 46	
John Cocking	22 Jan. 46	
F. G. H. G. Williams	22 Jan. 46	
Edward D. Cole	22 Jan. 46	
Milo V. Maher	22 Jan. 46	
Samuel May	25 Feb. 46	
Horace Wood	25 Feb. 46	
Chas. Tunstal Hyde	25 Feb. 46	
Herbert Rice	25 Feb. 46	
Francis Dalton	25 Feb. 46	
Edw. Jas. Dyson	27 Nov. 46	
ENSIGNS.		
W. B. Bromehead	20 May 25	
E. B. Mayhew	10 Feb. 29	
John Pinjean	24 May 32	
A. K. Orm	6 March 36	
T. W. Creaser	4 April 40	
Frederick A. Fox	25 Feb. 46	
Edward Keily	11 June 34	
Geo. Mignon Innes	26 March 46	
Chris. Charles Horne	4 May 46	

65th, or Royal East Middlesex Regiment of Militia.
(*Continued.*)

	Date of Appointment to Present Rank.	Remarks exhibiting Services of Officers, whether L.L., D.L., M.P., or J.P.—Country Seats, &c.
ADJUTANT.		
Capt. F. W. Hamilton	7 Feb. 46	
PAYMASTER.		
Charles Miller	23 April 03	Lieutenant.
QUARTERMASTER.		
W. N. Bull	1 Oct. 18	
SURGEON.		
John Phillips	18 Dec. 22	
ASSISTANT-SURGEON.		
W. B. Bromehead	20 May 25	Ensign.

Facings, Blue.

Head-Quarters, Stafford.] 66th, or "King's Own" Staffordshire Regiment of Militia.

Colonel.—William, the Earl of Dartmouth, 15 April 1812. J.P.—*Sandwell Park.*
Lieutenant-Colonel.—Thomas William Giffard, 4 April 1846. *Chillington Hall.*
Major.—The Hon. Wellington Patrick Manvers Chetwynd Talbot, 4 April 1846.

	Date of Appointment to Present Rank.	Remarks exhibiting Services of Officers, whether L.L., D.L., M.P., or J.P.—Country Seats, &c.
CAPTAINS.		
Richard Riddlesden	21 June 15	
John Fitzherbert	27 June 15	*Swynnerton Park, Stafford.*
Charles Coyney	18 June 28	D.L.— *Weston Coyney, Stafford.*
William H. Smith	23 April 31	
Honourable W. W. Wrottesley	20 Feb. 40	
William Walter Viscount Lewisham	10 June 43	M.P., J.P.—*Patshall Hall.*
William Haig	14 Feb. 46	
Edw. P. Mainwaring	23 April 47	*Whitmal Hall.*
Francis Chambers	4 April 48	*Seighford Hall, Stafford.*
LIEUTENANTS.		
William Meadows	2 May 08	
Augustus Alderman	8 Aug. 11	
Askew J. Hilcoat	25 Dec. 11	
William Landor	28 March 14	
James Underhill	16 Aug. 15	
George H. Davis	30 Sept. 15	
William Worsey	8 Nov. 15	
James Jackson	29 April 16	
William Legge	29 April 16	
William Booth	14 May 21	
John Jenkins	20 June 21	
Joseph Bunney	21 June 21	
John P. Nuttall	8 March 31	
Samuel Adams	23 May 31	
John Scott Green	14 July 31	*Lichfield.*
Edward Cope	4 Feb. 47	*Birmingham.*
John Taylor	4 April 47	
ENSIGN.		
Edmund Astle	14 March 33	

SERVICES OF THE REGIMENT.—In Ireland, from Sept., 1815, to April, 1816. Staff called out occasionally in aid of Civil Power. Body-guard to King George III., several years, and for which service, the badge "Windsor" was granted by Royal permission.

Facings, Blue.

67th (Worcester) Regiment of Militia.

[Head-Quarters, Worcester.]

Colonel.
Thomas Henry Bund, 19 June 1843. J.P. Served in the 13th Light Dragoons.

Lieut.-Colonel.
Thomas Clutton Brock, 10 March 1848.

Major.
Thomas Clowes, 10 March 1848. Served in the 8th King's Foot.

	Date of Appointment to Present Rank.	Remarks exhibiting Services of Officers, whether L.L., D.L., M.P., or J.P.—Country Seats, &c.
CAPTAINS.		
G. C. Vernon	29 Dec. 36	
Samuel Wheeley	14 Jan. 41	
John C. Dent	3 July 43	
Robert Blayney	17 July 43	
C. S. Hawkins	30 Jan. 46	
John W. Martin	30 Jan. 46	
E. B. Marriott	30 Jan. 46	
Charles Bernerd	30 Jan. 46	
LIEUTENANTS.		
Samuel Galindo	30 June 12	
Henry Jefferies	15 Feb. 16	
Percy Galindo	3 Feb. 21	
W. W. Woodward	15 June 31	
R. F. Crosse	30 March 38	
C. H. Maund	20 May 39	
T. W. Kinder	30 Jan. 46	
Gervase Clifton	30 Jan. 46	
Thomas F. Peel	30 Jan. 46	
Septimus Sanderson	2 Oct. 46	
ENSIGNS.		
John Q. Palmer	2 Oct. 46	
S. S. Burton	2 Oct. 46	
Henry D. Mitchell	2 Oct. 46	
E. H. Courtney	2 Oct. 46	
H. Giles	10 March 48	
ADJUTANT.		
Capt. Ernest Lavie	10 June 46	Served in the 8th King's Foot.
QUARTERMASTER.		
Lieut. John Garmston	12 July 10	
SURGEON.		
Matthew Pierpoint	19 May 15	
ASSIST.-SURGEONS.		
H. D. Mitchell	2 Oct. 46	
H. Giles	10 March 48	

Facings, Buff.

Head-Quarters, Ely.] **68th, or Cambridge Regiment of Militia.**

Lieut.-Colonel.—T. Vatchell, 25 May 1808.

Major.—E. H. Green, 7 June, 1832.

	Date of Appointment to Present Rank.	Remarks exhibiting Services of Officers, whether L.L., D.L., M.P., or J.P.—Country Seats, &c.
CAPTAINS.		
C. Beauchamp	25 Dec. 07	
T. S. Dixon	25 Jan. 14	
Lord Godolphin	15 Jan. 31	
W. P. Hammond ...	16 Jan. 31	
J. C. Daintree.........	6 July 31	
R. J. Eaton	1 Nov. 36	M.P.
W. H. Campbell......	10 Dec. 41	
LIEUTENANTS.		
G. Draycott	25 Dec. 08	
B. Warburton.........	25 Dec. 11	
C. Leeder	25 Jan. 14	
W. Gayfer	26 Jan. 26	
B. Possin.........	25 March 31	
C. C. Bailz	20 April 46	
ENSIGNS.		
T. Yorke	7 July 20	
G. Cole	18 Aug. 32	
PAYMASTER AND QUARTERMASTER.		
W. Gayfer	26 Jan. 26	
SURGEON.		
G. Eaton...............	25 Jan. 10	
ASSISTANT-SURGEON.		
G. Cole	18 Aug. 32	

Facings, Yellow.

Head-Quarters, Cirencester.] **69th, or Royal North Gloucestershire Regiment of Militia.**

Colonel.
T. H. Kingscote, 28 Feb. 1840.
Lieut.-Colonel.
Sir M. H. H. Beach, Bart., 17 Feb. 1844.
Major.
Hon. A. H. Morton, 15 March 1831.

	Date of Appointment to Present Rank.	Remarks exhibiting Services of Officers, whether L.L., D.L., M.P., or J.P.—Country Seats, &c.
CAPTAINS.		
W. Holbrow	17 Sept. 13	
F. Vaughan	14 Jan. 14	
J. M. P. Hopton	11 July 31	
J. G. Welch	26 March 33	
R. A. F. Kingscote	17 Feb. 44	
G. Austen	20 Feb. 46	
J. Haythorne	20 Feb. 46	
A. B. Rooke	5 May 46	
J. Parkinson	19 May 46	
H. Bold Williams	11 May 47	
LIEUTENANTS.		
A. W. Burkett	14 Feb. 31	
A. F. G. Hornsby	25 March 31	
J. Prosser	28 July 31	
R. W. N. Vaughan	28 Oct. 33	
E. W. A. Vaughan	2 March 38	
E. Hopkins	3 Aug. 38	
L. Sawyer	21 July 43	
S. Robertson	5 May 46	
ENSIGNS.		
W. R. Watson	9 Feb. 38	
A. Jones	5 May 46	
W. A. Chamberlain	5 May 46	
ADJUTANT.		
Captain Tobin	46	
PAYMASTER.		
W. Hames	27 June 21	Lieutenant.
QUARTERMASTER.		
J. Mosley	25 Aug. 19	Lieutenant.
SURGEON.		
R. Fitkin	25 June 08	M.D.

Facings, Blue.

Head-Quarters, Carlow.] **70th, or County Carlow Regiment of Militia.**

Colonel.
Henry Bruen, 16 May 1816. M.P.
Lieut.-Colonel.
Robert La Touche, 7 Sept., 1808.
Major.
Harman H. Cooper, 15 Nov. 1841.

	Date of Appointment to Present Rank.	Remarks exhibiting Services of Officers, whether L.L., D.L., M.P., or J.P.—Country Seats, &c.
CAPTAINS.		
Thomas H. Watson	11 Oct. 14	
George Burton	10 March 15	
Bury Doyne	22 Aug. 22	
Skeffington Daly	1 April 38	
William P. Butler	27 May 41	
Philip J. Newton	15 Nov. 41	
LIEUTENANTS.		
John Sherlock	26 Aug. 06	
Michael Thorowgood	26 Aug. 06	
Nicholas Bishop	26 July 09	
Robert Byrne	6 Aug. 13	
John Lecky	1 March 30	
Sir Robt. Harty, Bt.	15 Dec. 43	
ENSIGNS.		
George Grey Watson	30 March 46	
Thos. Benj. Bunbury	30 March 46	
James Butler	30 March 46	
John C. Brady	30 March 46	
William Clarke	30 March 46	
CAPTAIN AND ADJUTANT.		
Vacant		
QUARTERMASTER.		
Owen Cary	30 March 46	
SURGEON.		
Thomas Rawson	15 Aug. 35	
ASSIST.-SURGEON.		
Richard King	30 March 46	

Facings, Yellow.

Agents, Messrs. Cane & Co., Dublin.

Head-Quarters, Enniskillen.] **71st, or Fermanagh Regiment of Militia.**

Colonel.
The Earl of Enniskillen, 24 Oct. 1834. D.L., J.P., M.P.—*Florance Court.*

Lieut.-Colonel.
Hon. Henry Cole, 19 Jan. 1846. M.P.—Late Capt. 6th Enniskillen Dragoons. Served afterwards in the 7th Hussars.

Major.
Hon. Henry Crichton, late Major Enniskillen Dragoons.

	Date of Appointment to Present Rank.	Remarks exhibiting Services of Officers, whether L.L., D.L., M.P., or J.P.—Country Seats, &c.
CAPTAINS.		
Henry Irvine	3 Oct. 06	
H. M. Richardson	11 May 31	D.L., J.P.
Alex. Nixon	10 March 36	D.L., J.P.—Lieut. in the 27th, or Enniskillen Regiment of Foot during the Peninsular War; served also in America. Has Peninsular medal, with clasps, for the battles of Vittoria, Pyrenees, St. Sebastian, Nivelle, Nive, Orthes, and Toulouse.
Francis Hassard	2 Nov. 40	D.L., J.P.
John Gerard Irvine	10 Feb. 47	D.L., J.P.
Thomas Nixon		D.L., J.P.
LIEUTENANTS.		
Henry Hetherington	17 Aug. 11	
John Crozier	17 Aug. 11	J.P.
George Wilkinson	10 Jan. 12	
George Shegogg	27 May 14	J.P.
Fred. R. Magenis	18 May 38	
Robert Faussett	1 Jan. 40	
Edward Barton	24 Sept. 47	
ENSIGNS.		
Edward Thompson	20 May 12	
James Hyde	22 Oct. 12	
James Scott	10 March 40	
Gartside Tipping		J.P.
H. Perceval		
ADJUTANT.		
Capt. W. Corry	26 Sept. 21	J.P.
SURGEON.		
Baptist G. Frith	30 May 22	J.P.

SERVICES OF THE REGIMENT.—Served in England and Ireland from April 26, 1793, until April 3, 1816.

Facings, Buff.   *Agents*, Sir E. R. Borough, Bart., and Co., Dublin.

Head-Quarters, Kirkcudbright.] **72d, or *Kirkcudbright Light Infantry Regiment of Militia*.**

Colonel.
Sir David Maxwell, Bart., 25 April 1820. D.L., J.P.
Cardoness, by *Gatehouse.*

Lieut.-Colonel.
Sir William Maxwell, Bart., 1 February 1841. D.L., J.P.
Monreith, by *Stranraer.*

Major.
William Stewart, Esq., 31 March 1846. D.L., J.P.
Shambelly, by *Newabby.*

	Date of Appointment to Present Rank.	Remarks exhibiting Services of Officers, whether L.L., D.L., M.P., or J.P.—Country Seats, &c.
CAPTAINS.		
George Fullarton	21 Dec. 21	*Irvine, Ayrshire.*
Chas. W. D. Thomson	21 Feb. 24	J.P.—*Mackermore*, by *Newton Stewart.*
Robert Hannay	18 Oct. 31	D.L., J.P.—*Rusko*, by *Gatehouse.*
Edw. H. Maxwell	10 June 46	*Penninghame House*, by *Newton Stewart.*
LIEUTENANTS.		
John McCracken	24 April 04	*Glenluce.*
George Burnet	24 April 04	74, *New City-road, Glasgow.*
David Hannah	24 March 46	12, *West Cross Causeway, Edinburgh.*
ENSIGNS.		
Anthony Laurie	12 Aug. 15	10, *Rermford-place, Chapel-street, Liverpool.*
Walter Laurie	18 April 31	*Union Bank, London.*
John Denniston	18 April 31	*Australia.*
George James D. Hay	22 April 46	*Dunragget*, by *Glenluce.*
PAYMASTER.		
John McCraken	31 May 03	Lieutenant. *Glenluce.*
QUARTERMASTER.		
Robert Donaldson	25 Nov. 08	*Glasgow.*
SURGEON.		
David Blair	3 July 20	J.P.—*Kirkcudbright.*

Facings, Yellow.

Head-Quarters, Dunse.] **73d, or Berwick, Haddington, Linlithgow, and Peebles Regiment of Militia.**

Colonel.
William Hay, 4 April 1831.

Major.
James Pringle, 7 July 1832.

Captains.	Date of Appointment to Present Rank.	Remarks exhibiting Services of Officers, whether L.L., D.L., M.P., or J.P.—Country Seats, &c.
Sir G. Hamilton	1 Feb. 34	
A. H. Baillie	7 July 36	
G. Park	7 July 36	
J. C. Renton	7 July 36	
J. Hume	7 July 36	
W. C. Sandilands	27 Sept. 36	
Thomas Shairp	19 Aug. 41	
Lieutenants.		
William Home	27 Sept. 36	
John Dodds	18 Aug. 37	
William S. Bond	18 Aug. 37	
James W. Murray	20 May 38	
John D. Martin	30 June 39	
F. C. Davidson	14 Sept. 47	
B. M'Laren	14 Sept. 47	
Ensigns.		
R. Cunningham	27 Sept. 36	
George Wilson	27 Sept. 36	
John Salton	27 Sept. 36	
James Sawers	27 Sept. 36	
George Hood		M.D.
Paymaster.		
R. Cunningham	8 June 34	
Adjutant.		
Captain J. Cox	17 Sept. 30	
Surgeon.		
M. Turnbull	2 Aug. 41	
Assistant-Surgeon.		
G. Hood	3 May 42	M.D.

Facings, Yellow.

74th, or Royal Lanarkshire Regiment of Militia.

Head-Quarters, Hamilton.

Colonel.
The Marquis of Douglas and Clydesdale, 23 Jan. 1834. *Hamilton Palace.*

Lieut.-Colonel.
Right Hon. Lord Belhaven, 21 Nov. 1833. D.L.—*Wishaw House, Lanarkshire.* Formerly of 2d Life Guards. Served in the Peninsular War. Has Medal, and one clasp.

Major.—Sir Windham Carmichael Anstruther, Bart., 23 March 1846.

	Date of Appointment to Present Rank.	Remarks exhibiting Services of Officers, whether L.L., D.L., M.P., or J.P.—Country Seats, &c.
CAPTAINS.		
H. C. J. Hamilton	29 April 03	
William Roberton	28 March 31	*Lauchup, Lanarkshire.*
Charles Horrocks	21 March 46	Formerly Captain of the 6th Foot.
W. C. J. Anstruther	23 March 46	*Westraw House.*
William M. Cochrane	24 March 46	
Hugh H. R. Aikman	14 May 46	*Ross House, Hamilton.*
George Aug. Irving	15 May 46	
LIEUTENANTS.		
Lindsay Bennet	25 Oct. 08	
John Kidd	15 July 11	
Daniel McKenzie	12 Aug. 11	
A. K. Fotheringham	16 Jan. 32	
Hon. C. A. Murray	19 April 38	Consul-General, *Cairo.*
Douglas Hamilton	23 March 46	J.P.
Robert Dixon	24 March 46	
Aug. Fred. Lindley	14 May 46	
William Golly	8 March 47	
ENSIGNS.		
William McCririe	23 July 10	
John Strang	3 Sept. 23	
Andrew Tennent	24 April 34	
William Mitchell	20 March 46	
John Naismith	21 March 46	
Eugené E. Vaughane	23 March 46	
R. G. M. McDonald	25 June 46	
ADJUTANT.		
Herbert H. Vaughan	7 Sept. 31	Served 22 years in the 67th Regiment, in the Peninsula and East Indies; present at the siege of Cadiz and battle of Barossa, the Mahratta campaigns of 17, 18, and 19, at the taking of Ryghen-Amilnan, and at the storming of the Petta and Fort of Assargur, also in the latter part of the Nepaul campaign in 1815, under Colonel the late Sir Jasper Nichols. Has a Medal and one clasp for the battle of Barossa, 5th March, 1811.
SURGEON.		
John Thomson	11 July 46	M.D.

SERVICES OF THE REGIMENT.—Served all over England and Scotland, and also in Ireland, on the interchange of Militia Corps.

Facings, Blue.

Head-Quarters, Market Hill.] **75th, or Armagh Regiment of Militia.**

Colonel.—The Earl of Gosford, 19 Nov. 1834.—*Gosford Castle, Market Hill.*
Lieut.-Colonel.—William Blacker, 5 Nov. 1812. J.P.—*Carrick, Portadown.*
Major.—Thomas Fulton, 10 Feb. 1835. J.P.

CAPTAINS.	Date of Appointment to Present Rank.	Remarks exhibiting Services of Officers, whether L.L., D.L., M.P., J.P.—Country Seats, &c.
Henry Caulfield	18 March 44	
Hugh Harris	18 March 44	
LIEUTENANTS.		
Edward Maunsell	15 Nov. 08	
George Woodhouse	9 Aug. 12	
Walter J. Dawson	28 Sept. 12	
William Kay	18 Feb. 14	
Thomas J. Simpson	10 May 15	
William L. Patterson	3 June 15	
ENSIGNS.		
Edward Turner	3 May 15	*Turner's Grove, Newry.*
Joshua Paul Barker	3 June 15	
SURGEON.		
William Lodge Kidd	12 March 19	Served as Assistant-Surgeon, Royal Navy.
ASSISTANT-SURGEON.		
James S. Hueston	25 Jan. 20	

Facings, White.

Agents.—Sir Edward R. Borough, Armit, and Co.

76th, or Inverness, Banff, Elgin, and Nairn Regiment of Militia.

Head-Quarters, Inverness.

Colonel.
Earl of Seafield, 21 June 1803. L.L.—*Cullor House, Banff.*

Lieut.-Colonel.
Thomas Gordon, 30 June 1812.—*Park, Banffshire.*

Major.
Charles Lennox Cumming Bruce, 1 Feb. 1810. M.P.—*Dumphail, Elginshire.*

CAPTAINS.	Date of Appointment to Present Rank.	Remarks exhibiting Services of Officers, whether L.L., D.L., M.P., or J.P.—Country Seats, &c.
William Duff	15 July 12	
John Macleod	27 Oct. 15	Served in Royal Marines.
Eneas Macpherson	22 July 20	
A. J. Robertson	25 April 25	*Inshes, Inverness-shire.*
A. Macpherson	5 May 25	
William Grant	7 Jan. 31	
Alexander Grant	7 Jan. 31	
John Gordon	22 April 46	*Cairnfield Buckie.*
Hon. James Grant	21 May 46	Served in 42d Royal Highlanders.
LIEUTENANTS.		
Alexander Weir	18 Feb. 04	
Peter Wilson	27 Feb. 05	
John Leith	8 Sept. 12	
James Lobban	12 March 13	
George Alexander	4 Sept. 15	
John Leslie	19 March 22	
James Cameron	6 April 29	
ENSIGNS.		
C. Macpherson	12 March 13	
Alexander Allan	11 May 13	
John Forsythe	1 Sept. 20	
John Peter Cooper	19 April 25	
James Macpherson	7 May 31	
R. T. Mackenzie	8 Oct. 33	
A. R. M'Donell	8 May 25	
ADJUTANT.		
Robert Goldie	16 March 46	Served in 23d Royal Welsh Fusiliers and [Royal Horse Guards.
SURGEON.		
James Bayne	1 Aug. 15	

Facings, Green.

Head-Quarters, Newton Ards.] **77th, or *Royal North Down Regiment of Militia*.**

Colonel.
Viscount Frederick William Robert Castlereagh, 1 Sept. 1837.

Lieut.-Colonel.
John P. Nugent, 9 Aug. 1836.

Major.
William Read, 2 Nov. 1836.

CAPTAINS.	Date of Appointment to Present Rank.	Remarks exhibiting Services of Officers, whether L.L., D.L., M.P., or J.P.—Country Seats, &c.
Richard Dunne	29 Aug. 12	
Hugh Carleton	15 Feb. 16	
H. J. Johnston	14 July 28	
Thomas G. Knox	11 June 32	
Isaac Corry	2 Nov. 36	
Francis C. Forde	14 Aug. 47	
LIEUTENANTS.		
William Hickland	1 Dec. 03	
Hans Hendrick	7 May 10	
Alexander Crozier	19 Dec. 12	
Richard Kerr	24 June 43	
John Reilly	24 June 43	
John Craig	3 Feb. 45	
Robert F. Gorden	10 Dec. 45	
ENSIGNS.		
William Henery	11 April 14	
Henery Mercer	5 April 15	
Mathew Forde	10 Dec. 45	
Arthur Brown	10 Dec. 45	
Gilbert H. Howe	18 Dec. 47	
ADJUTANT.		
William Howe	25 Aug. 15	
SURGEON.		
Pinkston Blackwood	16 Feb. 05	
ASSISTANT-SURGEON.		
John Johnston	4 March 46	

Facings, Blue.   *Agents*, Sir Edward Richard R. Borrough, Armit, and Co.

78th, or Fifeshire Regiment of Militia.

Head-Quarters, Cupar.

Colonel.—James Lindsay, 11 June 1835. D.L., J.P.—*Balcarras*. Served in the Grenadier Guards.

Lieut.-Colonel.—John Balfour, 22 Nov. 1843. D.L., J.P.—*Balbirnie*. Served in the Grenadier Guards.

Major.—James Wemyss, 6 Oct. 1845. J.P.—*Wemyss Hall*. Served in the Line.

	Date of Appointment to Present Rank.	Remarks exhibiting Services of Officers, whether L.L., D.L., M.P., or J.P.—Country Seats, &c.
CAPTAINS.		
John Christie	16 May 09	
Wm. Graham Bonar	20 Dec. 24	J.P.—*Greyston*.
Robert Moubray	27 Oct. 31	J.P.—*Cockairne*.
John Purvis	17 July 46	*Kinaldy*.
James Inglis	17 July 46	*Kirkmay*.
Alexander Bethune	21 May 49	J.P.—*Blebo*. Served in the 42d Highlanders.
LIEUTENANTS.		
Peter Scott	14 May 08	
John Beath	26 Dec. 08	*Balcruvie*.
P. M. Richardson	14 April 09	
Wm. Lawson	9 Oct. 10	J.P.—*Pitlethie*.
Charles Graham	26 Dec. 13	
Vans Craigie Baird	19 June 20	
J. D. Fyffe	7 Nov. 32	
George Hannah	17 July 46	
Richard Rennie	17 July 46	
J. H. Ebowern	7 Oct. 49	
ENSIGNS.		
Robert Sutter	24 March 13	
Wm. Bouthron	19 June 20	
Andrew Walker	11 Oct. 31	
Andrew Mabon	11 Oct. 31	
Andrew Duncan	17 June 46	
ADJUTANT.		
William Scott (Brevet Captain)	16 July 33	**W.M.**—Served in the Peninsula from March, 1813, to the end of the war in 1814, including the Battle of Vittoria, siege of San Sebastian, passage of the Bidassoa, the Nive, and the Adour, investment of Bayonne, and repulse of the sortie, where he received a bayonet wound. Served also the campaign of 1815, and was present at the battles of Quatre Bras and Waterloo. He has received the War Medal and two clasps for Vittoria and Nive. Served in the Scots Fusilier Guards.
PAYMASTER.		
Wm. Lawson	24 Dec. 07	*Pitlethie*.
SURGEON.		
James Moore Graham	12 March 14	
ASSIST.-SURGEON.		
W. Bouthron	19 June 20	

SERVICES OF THE REGIMENT.—Served in Great Britain and Ireland during the War.

Facings, Yellow.

Head-Quarters, Randalstown.] **79th, or Queen's Own Royal Rifles Antrim Regiment of Militia.**

Colonel.
George Hamilton, Marquis of Donegal, 3 April 1841. G.C.H., D.L.—*County Antrim.* Served in the 7th and 18th Hussars, Peninsula.—*Orman Park.*
Lieut.-Colonel.—Thomas Verner, 11 June 1842. J.P.—*Cadogan-place, London.*

Majors.
George Ferguson, 3 Aug. 1841.—*Donegal-place, Belfast.*
Frederick Seymour, 27 Dec. 1845.—*St. James's-square, London.* Served in the 7th Hussars.

	Date of Appointment to Present Rank.	Remarks exhibiting Services of Officers, whether L.L., D.L., M.P., or J.P.—Country Seats, &c.
CAPTAINS.		
H. D. Peers	14 April 25	Served in 2d Dragoon Guards.
Chas. B. Carrothers	10 June 34	Served in 28th Regiment, Waterloo.
Thomas Vernor	16 June 43	*Orman Park.*
John M'Gildowney ..	7 Feb. 44	*Clare Park, County Antrim.*
William Murry	13 June 44	*Belgrave-square, London.* Served in 8th
Hon. Geo. Handcock	29 April 45	*Randalstown.* [Hussars.
Henry Kean	28 Jan. 46	*Orman-road.* Served in 86th Regiment.
J. W. H. Wray	28 Jan. 46	*Bush Mills, County Antrim.* Served in 97th
Right Hon. Earl of Belfast...............	29 June 48	Regiment.
LIEUTENANTS.		
Sir J. E. Tennent ...	30 March 35	
Stephen Rice	27 June 38	*Carrickfergus.*
N. Alexander	10 Aug. 39	D.L., M.P.—*Port Glenone House, County*
R. D. Coulston	12 June 43	[*Antrim.*
Hon. A. Kerr	16 June 43	*Brighton.*
E. A. C. Macartney	21 Nov. 43	*Hollywood.*
Richard Maunsell ...	16 June 46	*Brecart, Toombridge.* Served in the 7th
Henry M'Mill.........	24 Aug. 49	*Park Mount, County Antrim.* [Fusiliers.
Henry Kennedy	29 Aug. 49	*Hollywood.*
ENSIGNS.		
Abraham Sims	17 June 13	*New Ross.*
John M'Donnell......	4 Oct. 33	*Cushindall.*
James Durham	18 Dec. 13	*Allsop-terrace, London.*
W. C. Magrath	12 June 16	*Dublin.*
H. B. Ferguson	27 June 38	*Athonary Castle, Navan.*
Thomas Stannus......	29 Aug. 49	*Lisburn.*
ADJUTANT AND PAYMASTER.		
Capt. C. B. Carrothers	10 June 34	Served in the 28th Regiment in the Peninsula from June, 1809, to Sept., 1811, and again from March, 1813, to the end of the war in 1814, including the battle of Busaco, action at Campo Mayor, first siege of Badajoz, battles of Albuera, Nivelle, and Nive, affair at St. Palais, battle of Orthes, affair at Lambeige, and battle of Toulouse. Served also the campaign of 1815, and was present at the battles of Quartre Bras and Waterloo, at which last he was severely wounded. He has received the War Medal and seven clasps.
QUARTERMASTER.		
Alexander Markham	18 June 34	Lieut.—*Randalstown.*
ASSISTANT-SURGEON.		
Wilson Ramsay	28 June 46	*Dublin.*

SERVICES OF THE REGIMENT.—The Queen's Own Royal Rifles, or Antrim Militia, served in England, Ireland, and Scotland. In England and Scotland from May, 1813, till July, 1814. All their other service in Ireland.

Agents.—Sir E. R. Borough, Armit, and Co., Dublin.

80th, or Royal Tyrone Regiment of Militia.

Head-Quarters, Caledon.

Colonel.
The Right Hon. the Earl of Caledon, 1 May 1839.—*Caledon House.*
Served in the Coldstream Guards.

Lieut.-Colonel.
James Molyneux Caulfield, 1 May 1846. M.P., J.P.—*Hockley, Armagh.*

Major.
John Irvine, 1 May 1846. D.L., J.P.—*Rockfield, Enniskillen.*

	Date of Appointment to Present Rank.	Remarks exhibiting Services of Officers, whether L.L., D.L., M.P., or J.P.—Country Seats, &c.
CAPTAINS.		
Lord Claude Hamilton	1 May 46	J.P., D.L., M.P.—*Baron's Court.*
Lord Visc. Northland	1 May 46	J.P., D.L., M.P.—*Dungannon Park.*
Charles Eccles	1 May 46	J.P.
Robert M. Moore	1 May 46	J.P., D.L.
Joseph Greer	1 May 46	J.P.
Burleigh Stuart	1 May 46	
G. W. Vesey	1 May 46	
LIEUTENANTS.		
Thomas Young	1 March 06	
Roger C. Anketell	22 May 06	
Alfred G. Richardson	2 Oct. 08	
John L. Speer	14 April 14	
William Moore	1 May 46	
Thomas Simpson	1 May 46	
William Hyde	1 May 46	
William Irwin	1 May 46	
Richard Alex. Shaw	26 March 47	
ENSIGNS.		
Daniel Mansergh	20 Aug. 13	
John Byers	20 Aug. 13	
Robert G. Falls	27 Nov. 15	
Thomas Greer	1 May 46	
James Bourrieu	1 May 46	
ADJUTANT.		
Capt. Wm. Lundie	5 March 46	Served in the Coldstream Guards.
PAYMASTER.		
Capt. Andrew Millar	3 Dec. 26	
SURGEON.		
Joseph H. Scott	17 Jan. 25	

SERVICES OF THE REGIMENT.—In Ireland during the War.

Facings, Blue.   *Agents.*—Messrs. Richard Cane and Co.

Head-Quarters, Dumfries.] **81st, or *Dumfries, Roxburgh, and Selkirkshire Regiment of Militia.***

Colonel.
The Marquis of Queensberry, 26 Dec. 1837. L.L.—*Kinmount.*

Lieutenant-Colonel.
William Grierson, 1 June 1835. *Dumfries.*

Major.
The Honourable H. Buller Johnstone, 30 March 1846. *Bath.*

	Date of Appointment to Present Rank.	Remarks exhibiting Services of Officers, whether L.L., D.L., M.P., or J.P.—Country Seats, &c.
CAPTAINS.		
John Morice	17 Aug. 20	*Dumfries.*
George Hoggan	3 April 31	
John Scott	19 March 44	*Edinburgh.*
G. Rutherford	17 Feb. 46	D.L.—*Jedburgh.*
The Hon. D. Murray	9 April 46	*Edinburgh.*
LIEUTENANTS.		
Peter Dodds	2 May 09	*Edinburgh.*
John Taylor	29 Aug. 09	*Lander.*
James Fair	25 March 11	*Melrose.*
Robert Thorburn	25 March 11	*Kelton.*
Thomas Markie	27 March 21	*Edinburgh.*
W. Thompson	4 March 46	*Dumfries.*
Gideon Curl	4 March 46	*Edinburgh.*
Richard Rimmer	5 Nov. 47	*Marchmount.*
ENSIGNS.		
William Scott	11 Dec. 21	*Edinburgh.*
John Gilfillan	14 May 22	*Edinburgh.*
John Bevan	8 June 27	*Tierport.*
William T. Barker	18 Dec. 45	*Dumfries.*
Richard Carson	9 April 46	*Dumfries.*
Charles Charteris	4 March 46	
ADJUTANT.		
Captain R. C. Noake		*Dumfries.* Served in the Royal Dragoons and 44th Regiment.
SURGEON.		
James Grieve	18 Dec. 45	M.D.—*Dumfries.*
ASSISTANT-SURGEON.		
W. T. Barker	18 Dec. 45	M.D.—*Dumfries.*

SERVICES OF THE REGIMENT.—The Regiment was first raised and embodied at Dumfries, 24th June, 1798; disembodied, 24th April, 1802. Re-embodied at Dumfries, 5th April, 1803; embarked for England, in 1810. Served in Ireland during 1811 and 1812, and was again disembodied, 18th August, 1814. The Regiment was assembled for training and exercise for a month, in the years 1820, 1821, and 1825.

Facings, Yellow.

82d, or South Mayo Regiment of Militia.

Head-Quarters, Westport.

Colonel.
The Marquis of Sligo, 5 July, 1841. J.P.—*Westport House.*

Lieut.-Colonel.
Dominick Brown, 31 Dec. 1805. J.P., D.L.—*Brown Hall.*

Major.
P. C. Lynch, 4 March 1848. J.P.—*Hollybrook House.*

	Date of Appointment to Present Rank.	Remarks exhibiting Services of Officers, whether L.L., D.L., M.P., or J.P.—Country Seats, &c.
CAPTAINS.		
A. C. O'Malley	30 Jan. 06	J.P.—*Newcastle Park.*
Robert Browne	12 May 10	J.P.
G. Clendinny	20 Jan. 38	*Thomas Town.*
F. Blake Knox	5 July 41	J.P.
LIEUTENANTS.		
Peter O'Malley	9 June 08	
Martin Kirwan	27 Oct. 10	
H. P. Workman	1 Nov. 11	
Francis Crean	19 Feb. 13	J.P.—*Prospect House.*
Denis O'Conor	11 May 13	
C. F. Higgins	7 Aug. 38	J.P.—*Trafalgar Park.*
Charles G. Mahon	27 April 39	J.P.—*Mount Pleasant.* High Sheriff.
ENSIGNS.		
Robert Bodkin	1 May 36	J.P., D.L.—*Anna House.*
W. H. Parker	20 May 38	J.P.
Ouseley Higgins	9 May 39	J.P.—*Kellmore.*
W. H. Sirr	4 May 41	
M. F. Eames	22 April 48	
ADJUTANT.		
Capt. F. Higgins		J.P.
PAYMASTER.		
John D. Brown	14 Jan. 25	J.P., D.L.—*Mount Browne.* Late M.P. for Mayo.
SURGEON.		
Thomas Dillon		M.D.

Facings, White.

Agents, Messrs. R. Cane and Co.

Head-Quarters, Bethnal-green.] *83d, or 2d Tower Hamlets Queen's Own Regiment of Militia.*

Colonel.
The Earl of Wilton, 12 Nov. 1840.

Lieut.-Colonel.
J. S. North, 8 Jan. 1836.

Major.
L. S. Dickenson, 17 July 1846.

	Date of Appointment to Present Rank.	Remarks exhibiting Services of Officers, whether L.L., D.L., M.P., or J.P.—Country Seats, &c.
CAPTAINS.		
M. O'Shaughnessay	8 March 14	
A. Sayer	2 Sept. 15	
W. H. Armstrong	25 April 31	
Visc. Glentworth	25 Nov. 36	
H. C. Curtis	17 July 46	
S. Souvin	17 July 46	
H. T. Vanheythusen	17 July 46	
G. Michell	17 July 46	
LIEUTENANTS.		
J. Orpwood	21 June 05	
J. Hubbard	25 Sept. 07	
A. F. Squire	25 Sept. 10	
J. Wigfield	7 April 12	
R. Butler	25 Oct. 12	
J. Hudson	15 July 24	
T. Chalmers	16 March 32	
A. Thomas	16 March 32	
J. Burgess	28 Aug. 46	
G. F. Richardson	26 Aug. 48	
ENSIGNS.		
J. Stone	10 Nov. 31	
B. Bayle	10 April 39	
G. Mitchell	10 April 39	
J. Brash	10 April 39	
ADJUTANT.		
Capt. L. Cowell		
ASSIST.-SURGEON.		
J. Smartt	18 May 08	

Facings, Blue.

84TH REGIMENT OF MILITIA.

Head-Quarters, Cahir.] **84th, or Tipperary (Duke of Clarence's) Regiment of Militia.**

Colonel.—Richard Earl of Glengall, 21 Nov. 1826. D.L., J.P.—*Cahir Castle, Cahir.*

Lieut.-Colonel.—Richard J. Lord Viscount Suirdale, 24 July, 1849. D.L., J.P.—*Knocklofty, Clonmel.* Served in the 98th Regiment.

Majors.—John C. Bloomfield, 21 Feb. 1817.—*Castle Caldwell, Ballyshannon.*

	Date of Appointment to Present Rank.	Remarks exhibiting Services of Officers, whether L.L., D.L., M.P., or J.P.—Country Seats, &c.
CAPTAINS.		
Mathew Penefather...	6 Aug. 03	D.L., J.P.—*New Park, Cashel.*
Charles Elliott	16 Oct. 04	
Benjamin Bunbury...	29 Oct. 07	
James Archer Butler	29 June 29	J.P.—*Garnavilla, Cahir.*
William Quin	5 Nov. 35	J.P.—*Loughlohn Castle, Cahir.*
John Trant	21 March 38	D.L., J.P.—*Dovea, Templemore.*
Lancelot Bayly	2 May 38	*The Farm, Nenagh.* Served in the 68th
Richard Gason	18 April 44	J.P.—*Richmond, Nenagh.* [Regiment.
Henry Moore	28 May 46	*Barn, Clonmel.*
Henry W. Massy....	10 Nov. 49	J.P.—*Rosana, Tipperary.*
LIEUTENANTS.		
James O'Connor......	8 March 00	
William Brogdon ...	7 Jan. 07	
Edward Daly	27 March 07	J.P.—*Mornington, Mutifornham.*
George Riall	1 Jan. 10	
Maurice O'Donnell...	28 March 11	
David McO'Boy......	2 Sept. 11	
Walter Lambert	10 June 18	J.P.—*Castle Lambert, Oranmora.*
Richard White	22 Nov. 31	
John Chaytor.........	31 March 39	
Thos. Lord Manners	31 March 39	*The Grove, Suffolk.*
Henry Sargint.........	17 April 49	
Henry Sheppard......	10 Nov. 49	
ENSIGNS.		
A. De Coursey Daunt	17 June 12	
E. M. Mulcahy	3 Dec. 12	J.P.—*Ballymakee, Clonmel.*
Finch White..........	7 March 14	
James Keating	23 July 27	
Denis O'Brien.........	31 March 39	*Waterloo Cottage, Cahir.*
Theobald B. Aldwell	29 April 39	
Edmond S. Mulcahy	26 July 39	
John Mulcahy	20 Sept. 39	
ADJUTANT.		
Capt. Hugh Daniell...	17 Oct. 31	
PAYMASTER.		
William Moore	13 Dec. 23	*Loughtally, Clonmel.*
QUARTERMASTER.		
Lieut. Wm. Brogdon	1 Dec. 98	
SURGEON.		
James Dempster	30 Sept. 47	J.P.—Served in the 42d, 93d, and 94th Regts.
ASSIST.-SURGEON.		
Richard Milbank ...	21 April 18	

SERVICES OF THE REGIMENT.—The Regiment was first embodied on the 1st April, 1793. Served in Ireland till 1802, when disembodied. Re-embodied in March, 1803; and served in England and Ireland till 24th April, 1816, when again disembodied.

Facings, Yellow.   *Agents*, Sir E. R. Borough, Bt., Armit, and Co.

R

85TH REGIMENT OF MILITIA.

Head-Quarters, Newtown Forbes.] **85th, or *Prince of Wales' Royal Longford Regiment of Militia.***

Colonel.
Henry White, 9 Jan. 1837. L.L.—*Woodlands, Dublin.*

Lieut.-Colonel.
Sir George Ralph Fetherstone, Bart., 1 Jan. 1833. D.L., J.P.—*Ardagh.*

Major.
Samuel Wenslow Blackall, 1 Jan. 1833. D.L., M.P., J.P.—*Colamber.*

CAPTAINS.	Date of Appointment to Present Rank.	Remarks exhibiting Services of Officers, whether L.L., D.L., M.P., or J.P.—Country Seats, &c.
Mark Kerr	30 Dec. 06	*Bracklow, Co. Cavan.*
Thomas Barnewall	25 July 11	
William Ledwith	25 July 38	*Ledwithstown.*
John Dopping	25 July 38	*Derrycassan.*
LIEUTENANTS.		
Ross Carthy	6 Dec. 09	
Wm. G. Atkinson	30 July 11	*Forgeny.*
William Murray	28 June 13	*Cloncallow.*
John Alex. Fearns	6 Dec. 13	
Morgan O'Connell	6 Dec. 38	
John Wm. Brown	25 Feb. 46	
ENSIGN.		
Andrew Brock	30 Aug. 13	*Race Park.*
ADJUTANT.		
Capt. W. Walker	6 Dec. 09	
PAYMASTER.		
John Hart	31 Dec. 22	
QUARTERMASTER.		
Henry Hazlewood	2 March 40	
SURGEON.		
S. F. Crawford	3 Aug. 13	M.D.

SERVICES OF THE REGIMENT.—Engaged with the French Troops at Castlebar, August 27, 1798. The Light Company served through the whole of the Rebellion of that year.

Facings, Yellow.   *Agent,* Mr. J. Atkinson, Dublin.

86th, or Royal Perth Regiment of Militia.

Head-Quarters, Perth.

Colonel.—Earl of Kinnoull, 3 May 1827.
Lieut.-Colonel.—Sir T. Moncreiffe, Bart., 4 Aug. 1829.
Major.—John Gardiner, 3 Sept. 1827.

	Date of Appointment to Present Rank.	Remarks exhibiting Services of Officers, whether L.L., D.L., M.P., or J.P.—Country Seats, &c.
CAPTAINS.		
George Wright	4 Aug. 22	
D. W. Bissett	9 May 22	
Thos. Elder Baird	7 Sept. 24	
Samuel Barrett	7 Sept. 24	
Hon. John Rollo	7 Sept. 24	
Robert Graham	8 Aug. 25	
F. N. Menzies	8 Aug. 25	
LIEUTENANTS.		
Duncan Fletcher	4 May 32	
Geo. Mackenzie	3 July 35	
Robt. Steuart	4 May 35	
Alex. Pattullo	3 March 36	
John Gibbons	8 March 36	
Steuart Robertson	4 July 38	
Thomas Nicholl	4 July 38	
J. Isdale	8 Sept. 39	
J. D. M'Gregor	9 Aug. 39	
David Blair	7 Sept. 41	
ENSIGNS.		
Robert Thomson	7 Sept. 41	
John Robertson	7 Sept. 41	
Robert Menzies	8 Aug. 45	
J. R. Prentice	9 Sept. 45	
SURGEON.		
P. Peridies	3 Sept. 33	M.D.
ASSIST.-SURGEON.		
R. Thomson	4 Aug. 44	

Facings, Blue.

87th, or South Cork Regiment of Militia (Light Infantry).

Head-Quarters, Rathcormac.

Colonel.
Viscount Doneraile, 18 April 1848. M.P.—*Doneraile House.*

Lieutenant-Colonel.
William H. St. Leger Alcock Stowell, 18 April 1848. J.P.—*Kilbrittain Castle.*
Served as Captain in H.M.'s 23d Regiment.

Major.
John Crone, 11 June 1813. *Byblox Doneraile.*

CAPTAINS.	Date of Appointment to Present Rank.	Remarks exhibiting Services of Officers, whether L.L., D.L., M.P., or J.P.—Country Seats, &c.
Henry Wallis	20 March 10	D.L., J.P.—*Drisbane Castle, Kanturk.*
Philip Somerville	19 March 11	J.P.—*Union Hall, Cork.*
James N. Crone	6 Jan. 16	*Doneraile.*
The Earl of Shannon	3 Aug. 30	J.P.—*Castle Martyr.*
Sampson French	15 July 34	J.P.—*Ouskinney, Queenstown.*
Hewett Poole	9 Aug. 34	*Mayfield, Bandon.*
Robert Heard	8 July 46	*Kinsale.*
George Bowles	2 Nov. 46	*Ahern.*
LIEUTENANTS.		
Francis Heard	5 Sept. 08	*Cork.*
Samuel Loyde	9 Sept. 08	*England.*
Samuel Godsell	11 March 11	*Mallow.*
John Walton	19 Aug. 12	*Kinsale.*
William F. Austin	10 Oct. 12	J.P.—*Grange House, Fermoy.*
Francis Jones	12 Jan. 46	*Midleton.*
Carew C. Townsend	12 Jan. 46	*Woodside, Cork.*
Joseph Dean Freeman	29 Jan. 46	*Mallow.*
George Robt. Bruce	30 Jan. 46	*Prohurst, Charleville.*
John Lucas	2 Nov. 46	*Fermoy.*
ENSIGNS.		
Pascho Coggin	26 March 14	*Mallow.*
Hugh Norcott	2 April 14	*Doneraile.*
John Milward	2 May 14	*Doneraile.*
William Bowles	12 Jan. 46	*Ahern.*
William Ryder	12 Jan. 46	*Rathcormac.*
ADJUTANT.		
Arthur Hyde Lucas	12 Feb. 46	J.P.—Served as Capt. in H.M.'s 45th Regiment.
SURGEON.		
John Glover Gregg	5 March 46	M.D.—*Cork.*
ASSISTANT-SURGEON.		
John Nagle	9 April 46	M.D.—*Midleton.*

SERVICES OF THE REGIMENT.—The South Cork Regiment was embodied in 1793; was employed against the Insurgents in 1798, and took part in the engagement of the 21st June, 1798, at Vinegar Hill, which ended in the total dispersion of the Insurgent force. Served in England from June, 1812, to October, 1814.

EFFECTIVE STRENGTH.—Eight Companies.

Facings, White. *Agents,* Messrs. Cane and Co., Dublin.

Head-Quarters, Naas.] **88th, or Kildare Regiment of Militia.**

Colonel.
The Marquis of Kildare, 6 June 1849. J.P., D.L., M.P.—
Carton, Maynooth, Co. Kildare.

Lieut.-Colonel.
Robert Moore, Dec. 1835. *The Grove, Monasterevan, Co. Kildare.*

Major.
Sir Gerald G. Aylmer, Bart., 4 Sept. 1837. J.P., D.L.—
Donadea Castle, Co. Kildare.

	Date of Appointment to Present Rank.	Remarks exhibiting Services of Officers, whether L.L., D.L., M.P., or J.P.—Country Seats, &c.
CAPTAINS.		
William Ryder	22 Dec. 05	*Riverstown, Co. Kildare.*
Henry Ridgeway	6 March 06	
Edward Beauman	2 March 39	J.P.—*Furnace, Co. Kildare.*
Robt. L. W. Moore	4 March 39	*The Grove, Co. Kildare.*
Lord Naas	2 Dec. 40	J.P., M.P.—*Palmerstown, Co. Kildare.*
George P. Mansfield	22 Feb. 49	*Morristown Lattice.*
LIEUTENANTS.		
Arundel Carpenter	20 Sept. 06	
William Sherlock	26 July 09	
Henry Rice	18 Jan. 11	
Richard Irwin	13 Jan. 12	
Thomas C. Bagot	6 July 13	
Richd. Higginbotham	8 July 13	
Lucius Von Barle	20 Dec. 13	
ENSIGNS.		
George Sutcliffe	8 July 13	
William Beatty	19 July 13	
Somers Johnson	36	
Henry J. Ridgeway	9 March 46	
George W. Bourke	9 March 46	
ADJUTANT.		
Capt. Hercules G. R. Robinson	7 Feb. 46	J.P.—*Castlewarden, Naas, Co. Kildare.* Late 87th Royal Irish Fusiliers.
QUARTERMASTER.		
John Thos. Pellett	22 Feb. 48	
ASSIST.-SURGEON.		
Robert Huson	15 Jan. 16	

Facings, Black.

Agents, Sir Edw. R. Borough, Bart., Armit, and Co., Leinster-street, Dublin.

89th, or Aberdeenshire Regiment of Militia.

Head-Quarters, Aberdeen.

Colonel.
The Marquis of Huntley, 23 May 1798. K.T., D.L., J.P.—*Aboyne Castle.* Served in the Guards.

Lieut.-Colonel.
John Gordon, 6 June 1820. D.L., J.P.—*Cluny Castle.*

Major.
Henry Knight Erskine, 9 Feb. 1849. D.L., J.P.—*Pittochree.* Served in the 33d Regiment.

	Date of Appointment to Present Rank.	Remarks exhibiting Services of Officers, whether L.L., D.L., M.P., or J.P.—Country Seats, &c.
CAPTAINS.		
Charles Fraser	5 July 25	J.P., D.L.—*Williamstone.*
George Gordon	20 Nov. 31	J.P., D.L.
William Davidson	3 March 32	*Kabbaty.*
John Paton	19 Feb. 48	J.P., D.L.—*Grandholm House.* Served as Lieut. 91st Regiment.
James Forbes	4 Sept. 49	Late Capt. 11th Regiment.
LIEUTENANTS.		
John Fleming	14 June 08	
John Dick	14 June 08	
George Cameron	29 Dec. 08	
Ewen M'Pherson	15 Feb. 11	
James Ferguson	22 Nov. 22	
John Greig	20 Jan. 34	
William Duguid	22 March 34	
Thomas Gordon	22 March 34	
James Will	8 March 49	M.D. Assistant-Surgeon.
ENSIGNS.		
George Menzies	29 Jan. 17	
William Priest	12 July 31	
Alexander M'Nab	12 July 31	
James M'Kenzie	22 March 34	
Charles Sebright	17 Sept. 36	
ADJUTANT.	12 July 31	
Capt. James Bland	27 March 34	Captain (1st, or) The Royal Regiment.
QUARTERMASTER.		
James Roy	4 April 11	
SURGEON.		
Niel Sutherland	6 March 03	M.D.—Assistant-Surgeon to the Forces.
ASSIST.-SURGEON.		
James Will	March 49	M.D.

SERVICES OF THE REGIMENT.—The Regiment was embodied at Aberdeen 20th July, 1798; served in different garrisons in Scotland until 30th April, 1802, when it was disembodied at Aberdeen. Re-assembled at Aberdeen 21st April, 1803; served in Scotland until 12th Dec., 1812, when it marched to England, where it continued to serve until 17th Sept., 1814, when it arrived in Aberdeen, and was disembodied there. It was again embodied at Aberdeen 25th July, 1815, and disembodied there 24th Feb. 1815. It assembled for training for twenty-eight days from 25th June, 1820; also for twenty-one days from 4th July, 1821; for twenty-eight days from 5th July, 1825; and for twenty-one days from 19th July, 1831. The Regiment furnished at different times during the late war 647 Volunteers to the Regiments of the Line.

Facings, Yellow.

90th (*Stirlingshire, Dumbarton, Clackmannan, and Kinross*) Regiment of Militia.

Head-Quarters, Stirling.

Colonel.
Jas. Graham, Duke of Montrose, 12 Oct. 1827. K.T., L.L.—*Buchanan House.*

Lieut.-Colonel.
Wm. David Murray, Earl of Mansfield, 4 May 1828. D.L.—*Scone Palace.*

Major.
James Henry Callander, 2 April 1829. *Craigforth* and *Ardkinglas.*

	Date of Appointment to Present Rank.	Remarks exhibiting Services of Officers, whether L.L., D.L., M.P., or J.P.—Country Seats, &c.
CAPTAINS.		
James Skelton	26 July 28	Served in the 19th Dragoons.
R. S. M'Gregor	26 Oct. 44	Served in the Royal Navy to the end of the [War, and then in the Indian Army.
James Christie	22 Jan. 46	
T. M. M. Weller	4 Jan. 46	
H. M. Urmston	25 June 46	
LIEUTENANTS.		
John Macnab	26 June 02	
James Clark	10 July 11	
Coll Turner	28 April 13	
James Reddie	5 Oct. 13	
John Donaldson	1 Aug. 22	
James Stuart	6 April 32	
D. B. Shaw	4 Jan. 46	Served in the British Auxiliary Legion as 1st Lieut. of Artillery from 1836 to 1838, and was present at the general actions on the 10th to 16th March, 1837; at the taking of Hernanii by escalade; at the assault and capture of Yrun by storm, for which he received the cross of the Military Order of San Fernando and a gold medal; at the capitulation of Fuenterabia; the attack of Andonin, when the Artillery of the Legion received the thanks of the Commander-in-Chief (Espartero) in covering his advance to intercept Don Carlos re-crossing the Ebro; besides several minor affairs which were, for the most part, severely contested.
ENSIGNS.		
Alexander Black	3 Aug. 46	
James Campbell	7 Jan. 46	
W. M'A. Douglas	7 Jan. 46	
ADJUTANT.		
John Fraser	7 March 16 C. 19 Sept. 16	Served in the 72d Foot.

SERVICES OF THE REGIMENT.—Served in Scotland and England during the late War.

Facings, Yellow.

91st, or Galway Regiment of Militia.

Head-Quarters, Ballinasloe.

Colonel.—The Marquis of Clanricarde. K.P.

Lieut.-Colonel.—Earl of Clancarty, 20 Dec. 1830.

Major.—Thomas Mahon, 29 Nov. 1811.

	Date of Appointment to Present Rank.	Remarks exhibiting Services of Officers, whether L.L., D.L., M.P., or J.P.—Country Seats, &c.
CAPTAINS.		
Edward Kirwan	11 Dec. 13	
Thomas Seymour	15 July 15	
Charles P. Trench	18 Oct. 32	
John Eyre	31 March 34	
Henry J. Gascoyne	31 March 34	
William Gregory	4 March 42	M.P.
Elliott B. Warburton	4 March 42	
— Kirwan		
LIEUTENANTS.		
Frederick Groome	1 Aug. 01	*Moat.*
Joseph Pilkington	18 Sept. 06	*Furbore.*
Walter Rosengrave	28 Sept. 08	*Gort.*
Philip Daly	10 Aug. 09	*Cloonea.*
Eyre Seymour	5 Sept. 10	*Eyrecourt.*
William Collis	18 Sept. 10	
John Davies	11 Nov. 11	*Gort.*
John Egan	21 Dec. 11	*Mayo.*
John Kelly	29 May 12	*Limerick.*
James Evans	15 Jan. 14	*America.*
ENSIGNS.		
Stephen Blake	15 Feb. 14	*Dublin.*
Patrick O'Connor	21 Feb. 14	*Roscommon.*
Bartholomew Brown	7 March 14	
Thomas Woods	26 March 14	
Henry Kirwan	3 Sept. 33	
PAYMASTER.		
Saml. S. Harrison	30 June 23	*Woodbury.*

Facings, Yellow.

92d, or Wicklow Regiment of Militia.

Head-Quarters, Arklow.

Colonel.
Sir R. Howard, Bart., 1 Oct. 1834. M.P., J.P., D.L.—*Bushy Park.*

Lieut.-Colonel.
William Acton, 30 April 1833. J.P., D.L.—*Westaston.*

Major.
William P. Hoey, 15 July 1839.

	Date of Appointment to Present Rank.	Remarks exhibiting Services of Officers, whether L.L., D.L., M.P., or J.P.—Country Seats, &c.
CAPTAINS.		
William Blackford	7 Sept. 29	
George B. Hoey	15 July 33	
Edward Grogan	14 July 34	
R. A. G. Cunninghame	16 April 40	J.P.—*Mount Kennedy.*
Richard Hoey	10 March 42	
John Proby	2 June 47	
LIEUTENANTS.		
John Cairey	10 March 08	
George Hornidge	7 May 12	
John Minchin	22 Aug. 12	
Joseph Lefebure	15 Jan. 13	
John Wisdom	5 Aug. 13	
Nicholas Goodall	8 Feb. 45	
William Grogan	2 June 47	
ENSIGNS.		
Benjamin Scott	31 March 14	
Nicholas Gray	12 Feb. 25	
Charles Coats	2 Feb. 28	
Sir W. Frazer, Bart.	8 Feb. 45	
Charles Frizell	2 June 47	J.P.—*Castle Kevin.*
ADJUTANT.		[and 76th Regts.
Geo. A. Bayley	8 April 46	Lieut. ℔.℔. 57th Regt. Served in the 71st
QUARTERMASTER.		
Robert Martin	19 Sept. 13	
SURGEON.		[tugal, &c., &c.
David Wright	18 Oct. 20	M.D.—Served in 48th Regt. in Spain, Por-
ASSIST.-SURGEON.		
Hants Lloyde	15 Sept. 15	

SERVICES OF THE REGIMENT.—The Wicklow Regiment was embodied on June 10, 1793, by the enrolment of volunteers. On June 24, 1798, the Regiment retook the town of Castlecomer from the rebels, and saved it from being burned, it having been set fire to in several places. On the 26th of the same month the Regiment attacked 4,000 rebels near Kilcomney Hill, killed nearly 1,000, and took 14 pieces of cannon, with a large quantity of stores. The Regiment received public thanks, through General Asgill, for their conduct on both these occasions. In May, 1802, the Regiment was disembodied; on March 25, 1803, the Regiment was re-embodied. On Aug. 2, 1814, the Regiment was again reduced. On May 25, 1815, the Regiment was again raised, and disbanded on March 29, 1816.

Facings, Black.   *Agents*, Messrs. R. Cane and Co., Dublin.

93d, or Roscommon Regiment of Militia.

Head-Quarters, Boyle.

Colonel.
General The Viscount Lorton, 24 Nov. 1797. L.L.—*Rockingham, Boyle.*

Lieut.-Colonel.
John Cauldfeld, 7 May 1840. J.P.—*Bloomfield, Mullingar.*

Major.
James Kelly, 12 January 1806.

	Date of Appointment to Present Rank.	Remarks exhibiting Services of Officers, whether L.L., D.L., M.P., or J.P.—Country Seats, &c.
CAPTAINS.		
Edward Mitchell	23 June 01	J.P.—*Castlestrange, Athleague.*
John Kelly	27 May 05	
Edward Roper	22 Nov. 06	
Owen T. Lloyd	11 Oct. 10	J.P.
Christopher St. Geo. French	25 Jan. 23	J.P.—*Clooneyquin, Tulsk.*
William Lloyd	28 Jan. 29	D.L.—*Rockville, Drumsna.*
Hon. L.H.K. Harman	12 Feb. 46	D.L.—*Newcastle, Ballymahon.*
Rchd. Joynt Annesley	12 Feb. 46	
LIEUTENANTS.		
Nathaniel Dudgeon	15 Feb. 08	
Gilbert Hogg	15 Feb. 09	
Henry H. O'Hara	4 Jan. 42	J.P.—*Crebilly House, Ballmeena.*
Geo. Lefroy	10 Jan. 42	
William J. French	12 Feb. 46	
Thos. William Lloyd	12 Feb. 46	
John Comy	12 Feb. 46	
James Hewett	12 Feb. 46	
William Duckworth	12 Feb. 46	
Robert Barry	10 March 48	
ENSIGNS.		
Thomas Stoyle	26 Nov. 13	
Thomas Hardy	5 March 42	
Christopher French	13 Sept. 46	
John Robertson	12 Feb. 46	
Henry K. Irwin	12 Feb. 46	
Henry Fry	12 Feb. 46	
ADJUTANT.		
Capt. G. R. Cummin	4 May 46	J.P.—Served in the 7th Royal Fusiliers.
QUARTERMASTER.		
John W. Flanagan	Aug. 49	J.P.—*Drimdoo, Boyle.*
SURGEON.		
Lodge Hall	12 July 05	M.D.
ASSIST.-SURGEON.		
William M'Gill	12 May 12	M.D.

Facings, Black.   *Agents*, Sir E. R. Borough, Armit, and Co.

94th, or Clare Regiment of Militia.

Head-Quarters, Clare Castle, Ennis.

Colonel.
Crofton Moore Vandeleur, 24 June 1843. D.L., J.P.—*Kilrush House.*

Lieut.-Colonel.
Most Noble The Marquis of Conyngham, 28 Dec. 1825.

Major.
Simon Geo. Purdon, 25 Oct. 1847. J.P., D.L.—*Tinerana, Killaloe.*

	Date of Appointment to Present Rank.	Remarks exhibiting Services of Officers, whether L.L., D.L., M.P., or J.P.—Country Seats, &c.
Captains.		
Hugh Massy	5 May 12	Late Capt. 16th Regiment.
Augustine Butler	3 Nov. 32	J.P., D.L.—*Ballyline, Crusheen.*
Michael Finucane	4 Nov. 32	J.P.—*Stamer Park, Ennis.*
Robert W. Studdert	1 Jan. 47	J.P.—*Cullane, Newmarket-on-Fergus.*
Marcus Paterson	16 July 47	J.P.—*Lacknabranner, Killaloe.*
Robert A. Studdert	1 Nov. 47	J.P.—*Kilkishen House, Kilkishen.*
Lieutenants.		
Geo. Wm. Hodges	3 Aug. 08	*Donagrogue Castle, Knock.*
W. F. Paterson	28 Aug. 11	J.P.—*Violet Hill, Broadford.*
Saml. E. Johnson	2 June 12	
Thomas Hewitt	13 June 12	*Granahan, Newmarket-on-Fergus.*
Robert Mahon	17 Jan. 14	*Ashline Park, Ennis.*
Charles Mahon	1 Aug. 46	J.P.—*Cragbrian Castle, Ennis.*
J. Fitzwilliam Scott	2 Aug. 46	J.P.—*Knopogue Castle, Quin.*
Ensigns.		
Robert Fitzgerald	7 June 12	*Kilkee.*
Anthony R. King	18 Jan. 14	
Godfrey Massy	7 Aug. 15	
Hon. S. K. Daly	11 Jan. 40	
William Spaight	12 Jan. 40	J.P.—*Derry Castle, Killaloe.*
Adjutant.		
Capt. C. Wm. Gore	1 June 46	Late Capt. 72d Highlanders.
Paymaster.		
Charles Mahon	16 Sept. 11	*Cahircalla, Ennis.*
Surgeon.		
Thomas Burton	1 June 46	M.D.
Assistant-Surgeon.		
Charles A. Brew	1 June 46	

Services of the Regiment.—Served in Ireland during the Rebellion, and in England during the Peninsular war.

Facings, Yellow.

Agents.—Sir E. R. Borough, Bart., Armit, and Co.

Head-Quarters, Londonderry.] **95th, or Londonderry Regiment of Militia.**

Colonel.
Sir Robert A. Ferguson, Bart., 24 June 1839. L.L., M.P.—*The Farm, Londonderry.*

Lieut.-Colonel.
Alexander Robert Stewart, 11 Oct. 1822. D.L., J.P.—*Ards House, Co. Donegal.*

Major.
William Fitzwilliam Lenox Conyngham, 14 April 1848. *Springhill, County Derry.* Late Lieut. 88th Foot.

	Date of Appointment to Present Rank.	Remarks exhibiting Services of Officers, whether L.L., D.L., M.P., or J.P.—Country Seats, &c.
CAPTAINS.		
Rowley Miller.........	20 July 03	D.L., J.P.—*Moneymore.*
Conolly Skipton	28 Feb. 06	D.L., J.P.—*Beech Hill, Co. Derry.* Late [Marines.
Abraham Pilkington.	8 Dec. 09	
William Graves	27 June 15	J.P.—*Gravesend, Co. Derry.* Late Marines.
Stewart Bruce.........	26 Aug. 39	D.L., J.P.
Samuel Bateson	7 May 44	
Croker Miller	20 April 47	Late 17th Foot.
John Henderson......	21 April 47	Late 14th Light Dragoons.
John K. M'Clintock.	22 April 47	J.P.—*Hampstead Hall, County Derry.*
LIEUTENANTS.		
Samuel Graves	28 Feb. 06	
Richard Williams ...	4 May 07	
William Jones	4 May 07	
John Alexander	15 Aug. 09	
ENSIGNS.		
John Jones	4 April 09	
John Sinclair	12 Sept. 10	
James Taylor	1 April 13	
John Rodgers.........	18 Aug. 15	J.P.
Charles Lever	18 July 40	
G. F. H. M'Clintock	30 Oct. 45	
ADJUTANT.		
Capt. Jas. M'Clintock	18 July 24	Late 88th Foot.
QUARTERMASTER.		
J. Campbell............	19 April 47	Lieut. Half-pay.
SURGEON.		
John R. Furguson ...	19 April 47	M.D.
ASSIST.-SURGEON.		
Alexander Skipton ...	31 Jan. 15	M.D.

SERVICES OF THE REGIMENT.—Embodied in 1793; served in Ireland until 1802. During the Rebellion of 1798 the Regiment was stationed in the counties of Dublin, Wicklow, Kildare, Carlow, and Wexford. The greater part of the Regiment was engaged in the battles of Gorey, Arklow, New Ross, Folk's Mill, Blackmore Hill, and Vinegar Hill. It was disembodied in 1802, and re-embodied in 1803, and served in Ireland and England until 1815, when it was again disembodied. Towards the close of the war, the entire of the Regiment volunteered, with the exception of one Private, for foreign service, and it was notified to the Commanding Officer that their services would have been accepted had the war continued.

Facings, Blue.

Agents, Sir E. R. Borough, Bart., and Co., Dublin.

96th, or Ross, Caithness, Sutherland, and Cromarty Regiment of Militia.

Head-Quarters, Dingwall.

Colonel.
Charles Fraser, 7 May 1821. Lost a leg at the siege of Burgos, when serving in the Foot Guards. He has received the War Medal and one clasp for Salamanca.

Lieut.-Colonel.
The Honourable James Sinclair, 7 May 1831.

Major.
Sir G. G. Monro, Bart., 4 Aug, 1834.

CAPTAINS.	Date of Appointment to Present Rank.	Remarks exhibiting Services of Officers, whether L.L., D.L., M.P., or J.P.—Country Seats, &c.
Rod. Mackenzie	7 May 21	
Hugh S. Clarke	8 Aug. 33	
Hon. R. Dunbar	8 Aug. 33	
Thomas Mackenzie	9 Sept. 34	
James Gillanders	10 Sept. 34	
T. F. Sinclair	8 Aug. 36	
C. A. Sinclair	8 Aug. 36	
H. M. Fowler	9 Feb. 39	
LIEUTENANTS.		
F. Munro	7 May 21	
Zach. Macauley	8 Aug. 33	
John Mackenzie	8 Aug. 33	
Daniel Gilchrist	9 Sept. 34	
Simon M'K. Ross	8 Aug. 35	
ADJUTANT.		
Captain A. Mackenzie		

Facings, Buff.

Head-Quarters, Stoke Newington.] **97th, or King's Own Light Infantry Regiment of Militia.**

Colonel.—The Marquis of Dalhousie, 8 April 1845. *Dalhousie Castle, N. B.* Governor-General of India.

Lieut.-Colonel.—John Caske Gant, 15 Feb. 1814. J.P.—*Middlesex.*

Major.—Nicholas Willard, 15 Feb. 1814. J.P.—*Sussex.*

	Date of Appointment to Present Rank.	Remarks exhibiting Services of Officers, whether L.L., D.L., M.P., or J.P.—Country Seats, &c.
CAPTAINS.		
James Gillett	5 May 18	
James A. Bailey	9 Oct. 26	Served in the 65th Foot.
John Ogle	24 Feb. 31	
F. F. Courtenay	11 June 45	
LIEUTENANT.		
Henry Stanton	25 June 10	
ENSIGN.		
— Walsh	17 May 34	
ADJUTANT.		
Capt. R. Berford	25 May 25	Served with the 5th Regt. in Portugal and Spain in 1808-9, and was present at the battles of Roleia and Vimiera, action at Lugo, retreat to and battle of Corunna. Subsequently on the expedition to Walcheren and at the siege of Flushing. Served afterwards in the Peninsula with the 2d Queen's Royals, from 1812 to the end of that war in 1814, and was present at the battle of Vittoria, blockade of Pampeluna, actions in the Pyrenees from 25th to 31st July; with the covering army at San Sebastian and also at its capture; affair at the convent of St. Antonia, actions on the Nivelle and the Nive, and with the four companies of the Queen's which led the advance to the assault and capture of the principal redoubt in front of Sarre; and in all the affairs in the vicinity of St. Jean de Luz, Bayonne, and the Adour; also at the battles of Orthes and Toulouse, and the various affairs of posts and picquets in which the fourth Division were engaged. He has received the War Medal and nine clasps.
PAYMASTER.		
David H. Stable	19 Nov. 00	

REGIMENTAL APPOINTMENTS.—The White Tower, and the Queen's Crest.

98TH REGIMENT OF MILITIA. 135

Head-Quarters, Parsonstown. *98th, or King's County Regiment of Militia.*

Colonel.—The Earl of Rosse, 19 June 1834. L.L.—*Birr Castle.*
Lieut.-Colonel.—The Hon. Laurence Parsons, 24 Dec. 1847. D.L.—*Brighton.*
Major.—The Earl of Charleville, 28 June 1831. *Charleville Forest, Tullamore.*

	Date of Appointment to Present Rank.	Remarks exhibiting Services of Officers, whether L.L., D.L., M.P., or J.P.—Country Seats, &c.
CAPTAINS.		
J. W. Tibeaudo	10 April 09	J.P.—*Tenehinch.*
J. H. Drought	6 Dec. 21	D.L.—*Lettybrook House.* Served in the 13th [Light Dragoons.
William Darley	20 July 32	
Edmund L'Estrange	25 April 34	J.P.—*Moystown Cottage.*
W. B. Buchanan	25 Nov. 44	J.P.—*Shannongrove.*
Garrett O'Moore	1 Aug. 46	D.L.—*Cloghan Castle.*
Richard W. Bernard	27 Dec. 46	
John A. Drought	12 Dec. 49	*Whigs Borough.* Served as Capt. 65th Regt.
LIEUTENANTS.		
William Dowling	7 July 06	
John Wetherelt	8 Nov. 08	*Dove Grove.*
Percival Roche	12 March 09	
Arthur Mosse	30 March 11	
Christian Poe	14 Sept. 13	
James Grant	14 Dec. 33	
John Blake	25 June 38	*Garbally.*
Francis De Burgh	1 March 44	
Thomas Edw. Cox	4 May 48	
Philip Warburton	1 Jan. 49	
ENSIGNS.		
Nicholas Brown	11 Nov. 12	
William Abbott	20 March 13	
Edmond Shawe	14 Dec. 13	
William L'Estrange	4 May 14	
Hon. Otway Toler	1 Jan. 48	
George Wetherelt	1 Jan. 48	
ADJUTANT.		
Capt. Thos. Cox	8 April 26	Served as Lieut. of the Royal Artillery in Sir John Moore's campaign in the north of Spain and battle of Corunna, from 1808 to 1809. Joined the Portuguese army in 1811; present at the siege and capture of Badajoz in 1812, battle of Castella, both sieges of Tarragona in 1813, and blockade of Barcelona in 1814; and he continued to serve with the Portuguese army till 1819. He has received a gold cross for four campaigns from John VI., late King of Portugal; also the War Medal, with two clasps.
SURGEON.		
John Waters	1 Aug. 46	M.D.
ASSIST.-SURGEON.		
Thomas H. Baker	1 Aug. 46	M.D.

SERVICES OF THE REGIMENT.—The King's County Regiment of Militia was raised by the late Earl of Rosse, in the year 1793; remained principally in the south and west of Ireland till the Rebellion of 1798, when it was removed to the county Wexford, and fought at the battle of Vinegar Hill under the late Colonel L'Estrange, and afterwards a Wing of the Regiment successfully defended the town of Newtown Barry. The Regiment subsequently served in the island of Guernsey and in different parts of England, and was finally disembodied in the year 1816.

Agents, Sir E. R. Borough, Armit, and Co., Dublin.

99th Regiment of Militia.

Head-Quarters, Wexford.] **99th, or Wexford Regiment of Militia.**

Colonel.—Hon. Robert S. Carew, 5 April 1847.
Lieut.-Colonel.—William P. Pigott, 21 July 1801.
Major.—William Jacob Blacker, 1 Nov. 1845.

	Date of Appointment to Present Rank.	Remarks exhibiting Services of Officers, whether L.L., D.L., M.P., or J.P.—Country Seats, &c.
Captains.		
John Gray	11 June 07	
Charles Hewson	16 Sept. 13	
George P. Pigott	30 May 42	
John B. Graves	30 May 42	
Augustus Kennedy	30 May 42	
Lord A. Loftus	13 Oct. 42	
Lovick Reade	5 July 44	
Benjamin Wilson	2 Sept. 44	
C. C. Cookman	2 June 47	
Anthony John Cliffe	12 Nov. 47	
Lieutenants.		
Robert Brown	17 Feb. 06	
Jos. Thetford	2 Feb. 09	
John Sheppard	2 Feb. 09	
George Wade	19 June 09	
Stern Philips	29 Jan. 10	
John Hawkes	11 Aug. 12	
Matthew W. Palliser	11 Aug. 12	
Henry Hatton	24 Nov. 12	
George Sheppard	11 June 13	
J. W. C. Redmond	30 May 42	
Edward W. Nunn	13 June 45	
Lord Stopford	14 Jan. 48	
Ensigns.		
Aug. A. Nunn	26 Nov. 14	
George W. Ogle	30 May 42	
Samuel Tench	30 May 42	
Henry L. Tottenham	30 May 42	
John Sparrow	20 July 42	
Cornwallis Tottenham	3 June 43	
Lord Henry Loftus	5 July 44	
John Thomas Beatty	12 Nov. 47	
Adjutant.		
Capt. David Beatty	27 Feb. 46	
Surgeon.		
Richard H. Verling	4 Dec. 46	
Assist.-Surgeon.		
Thomas Lane	18 July 11	

Facings, Yellow.

Agents, Sir E. R. Borough, Bart., and Co., Dublin.

100th, or Royal Dublin City Regiment of Militia.

Head-Quarters, Dublin.

Colonel.—David Charles Le Touche, 8 April 1849. D.L., J.P.—*Luggelaw, Co. Wicklow;* and *Marlay, Co. Dublin.*
Lieut.-Colonel.—Robert Shaw, 8 April 1849. J.P.—*Kimmage House, Co. Dublin.*
Major.—Sir E. R. Borough, Bt., 8 April 1849. J.P.—*Coolock Lodge, Co. Dublin.*

	Date of Appointment to Present Rank.	Remarks exhibiting Services of Officers, whether L.L., D.L., M.P., or J.P.—Country Seats, &c.
CAPTAINS.		
George Faulkner	12 Nov. 01	*Lower Gloucester-street, Dublin.* Served at the Battle of Vinegar Hill.
John Ussher	9 Feb. 08	Canada.
Samuel Sankey	12 Oct. 19	*Upper Mount-street, Dublin.* A Major in the Army; served in the Peninsula, in the 9th Regiment; received a Medal and one Clasp for Roleia.
Garrett Wall	6 Jan. 27	*Wall's Court, Co. Dublin.*
Henry Shaw	14 Feb. 39	*Palmerston, Co. Dublin.*
G. E. Powell	25 Nov. 42	*Camolin Park, Co. Wexford.*
Sir B. B. M'Mahon, Bart.	30 Aug. 45	D.L., J.P.—*Fitzwilliam-square, Dublin,* and *Facarry House, Mountfield, Co. Tyrone.* Served as Captain in the Foot Guards.
Hon. St. John Butler	8 April 49	J.P.—*Turnerville, Co. Dublin.*
LIEUTENANTS.		
James Montgomery	17 Sept. 05	*Cork-street, Dublin.*
R. G. Murray	12 Sept. 06	*Hillsborough, Co. Down.*
D. Hautenville	4 Aug. 10	*London.*
Charles Fletcher	14 Oct. 13	*College-street, Dublin.*
Charles Warren	22 Dec. 13	*Ormond Quay, Dublin.*
R. E. Bourne	12 March 39	*Terenure House, Co. Dublin.*
Francis Ellis	9 Sept. 39	J.P.—*Facary House, Omagh, Co. Tyrone.*
Henry Farran Darley	30 Aug. 45	*Fitzwilliam-street, Dublin.*
Richard Moore	16 June 46	*Hermitage Co., Dublin.*
ENSIGNS.		
Edward O'Rielly	14 Oct. 13	*Drumbad, Co. Donegal.*
Thomas Jones	23 March 14	*Cracon, New Ross, Co. Wexford.*
William Horan	25 April 14	*Douglas, Isle of Man.*
John Lees	8 April 35	*Black Rock House, Co. Dublin.*
William M'Kay	9 Sept. 39	*Stephen's-green, Dublin.*
Shapland Swiney	16 Aug. 44	*Dublin.*
ADJUTANT.		
Capt. Saml. William Russell	26 Jan. 46	*Upper Baggot-street, Dublin.*—Served as Captain in the 98th Regiment in the Expedition to the North of China in 1842, and was present at the Storming of the City of Chin Kiangfoo, at the Attack and Capture of the Tartar entrenched Camps on the Heights outside the City, and at the landing before Nankin; received a Medal for China.
PAYMASTER.		
Lieut. James Montgomery		
SURGEON.		
Cathcart Lees	4 Feb. 46	M.D.—*Fitzwilliam-street, Dublin.*
ASSIST.-SURGEON.		
Jonathan Leech	12 Feb. 46	M.D.—*Minnow Bank, Co. Dublin.*

SERVICES OF THE REGIMENT.—Served at the Battle of Vinegar Hill.
Facings, Blue. *Agents,* Sir E. R. Borough, Bart., Armit, and Co., Dublin.

101st, or Cavan Light Infantry Regiment of Militia.

Head-Quarters, Cavan.

Colonel.—Alexander Saunderson, 1 Nov. 1838.

Lieut.-Colonel.—Joseph Pratt, 3 May 1799.

Major.—H. Pratt De Montmorency, 6 March 1843.

	Date of Appointment to Present Rank.	Remarks exhibiting Services of Officers, whether L.L., D.L., M.P., or J.P.—Country Seats, &c.
CAPTAINS.		
M. James Boyle	25 June 27	
Hon. Rich. Maxwell	6 March 43	
Saml. Moore, jun.	5 Feb. 44	
Michael Phillips	Feb. 48	
James Story	5 July 48	
H. Dean Edwards	16 March 49	
LIEUTENANTS.		
John Francis Elliott	20 July 10	
John Gumley	22 Feb. 13	
John Webb	26 March 14	
Samuel Martin	25 Oct. 15	
John Wilson	4 Dec. 15	
John Thompson	4 Aug. 32	
J. Albert Nesbit	21 Oct. 48	
ENSIGNS.		
Richard Moore	1 Sept. 15	
William Cochrane	25 Oct. 15	
Edward Cosby	5 Jan. 16	
George Waring	1 May 34	
William Smith	6 March 43	
ADJUTANT.		
Capt. N. Gosselin	21 March 46	
SURGEON.		
Charles Halpin	Feb. 46	

Facings, Black.

Agents.—Sir E. R. Borough, Bart., and Co., Dublin.

102d, or the Prince of Wales' Donegal Regiment of Militia.

Head-Quarters, Ballyshannon.

Colonel.
Right Hon. Nathaniel, Earl of Leitrim, 22 June 1796. K.P., P.C. (Ireland), L.L., C.R.—*Manorhamilton, Co. Leitrim; Killadoon. Celbridge;* 2, *Grosvenor-place, London; Kilmacrenan, Donegal.*

Lieut.-Colonel.
George Henry, Earl of Mountcharles, 5 Jan. 1849. *Mountcharles, Donegal; Slane Castle, Slane, Co. Meath.*

Major.
Sir James Stewart, Bart., 20 April 1812. V.L., J.P.—*Fort Stewart, Ramelton.* Late Cornet in 6th Dragoon Guards.

	Date of Appointment to Present Rank.	Remarks exhibiting Services of Officers, whether L.L., D.L., M.P., or J.P.—Country Seats, &c.
CAPTAINS.		
John Wray	20 May 05	*Derrygonelly.* Late Capt. 69th Foot.
John Jones	25 June 05	*Cahir, Tipperary.*
William Benson	4 May 07	*Dublin.*
Johnston Mansfield	7 Sept. 09	J.P.—*Killygordon, Castlefin.*
Daniel Chambers	1 Feb. 12	J.P.—*Letterkenny.*
John Stewart	8 April 40	*Letterkenny.*
Henry Bradley	8 April 40	
William Stewart	15 Jan. 42	
Hon. C. S. Clements	17 April 45	M.P., J.P.—*Killadoon* and *Grosvenor-square.* Served in the Army.
LIEUTENANTS.		
Thomas Perry	8 Jan. 99	*Kilcoram, Youghal.*
John Clarke	30 Nov. 01	*Tubberkeene, Dungloe.*
William O'Brien	8 Feb. 08	*Bildoyle, Dublin.*
Robert Lindsay	18 March 11	*Cherrymount, Enniskillen.*
William Cooper	16 Sept. 11	*St. Helier's, Jersey.*
Fras. H. Nesbitt	16 Sept. 11	*Londonderry.*
John Dick	19 Sept. 11	*Ballynamallard, Fermanagh.*
Henry Benison	1 Feb. 12	*Dublin.*
John Chambers	15 Aug. 12	J.P.—*Foxhall, Letterkenny.*
Alexander Knox	31 March 13	*Castlefin, Co. Donegal.*
Geo. W. Carlton	2 Dec. 13	*Rossbeg, Mohile.*
John Lavens	22 Jan. 14	*Newtownstewart, Tyrone.*
Daniel Patton	29 Jan. 14	*Sion Strabane.*
ENSIGNS.		
Thomas Benison	2 April 13	*Bundoran.*
William Thompson	17 Dec. 13	*Altaghderry, Londonderry.*
Robert Mansfield	12 Jan. 14	*Castlefin, Donegal.*
William Lindsay	22 Jan. 14	*Milwood, Enniskillen.*
Robert Reynolds	29 Jan. 14	*Mullins, Ballyshannon.*
Samuel Roulston	23 Feb. 14	*Castlegay Letterkenny.*
John Knox	8 Oct. 14	*Castlefin, Donegal.*
ADJUTANT.		
Samuel Searle	8 April 46	Served in the 70th Regt. 24½ years.
SURGEON.		
Roper Little	8 April 46	*Ballinamore, Leitrim.*

102d, or "*The Prince of Wales*'" Donegal Regiment of Militia.
(*Continued.*)

SERVICES OF THE REGIMENT.—The Donegal Regiment of Militia was raised at Lifford, in April, 1793, by the Right Hon. Colonel William Burton Conynghame, and through him styled the "Prince of Wales';" was inspected there by Major-General Stopford, 14th Oct., 1793; marched to Derry, 1st Dec., 1793; to Birr, and reviewed by Major-General Crosbie, 11th Aug., 1793; to Athlone, 15th Aug., 1794; to Drogheda, 30th June, 1795, and reviewed there by Major-General Eustace, 9th Sept., 1795. Marched for Loughlins-town camp, 21st April, 1796, about which time Colonel Conynghame died. The command of the Regiment was then given to Lord Clements, the present Earl of Leitrim. The Regiment was reviewed at camp, 1st Nov., 1796, by Major-General Crosbie; marched for Cork, in Dec., and returned to Loughlins-town camp, on 16th Jan., 1797; reviewed at New Geneva Barracks, 28th Sept., 1797, by Major-General Fawcett. The Regiment was engaged with the Rebels, at Three Rocks, Wexford, in May, 1798; at New Ross, 5th June, and at Vinegar Hill. The Light Company was also engaged at Enniscorthy, under the command of Captain Harvey; Sergeant Finch was promoted to a commission into the Line, for his bravery when surrounded by Rebels, previous to the battle of Ross; and Sergeant Hamilton, for his gallantry at the battle of Ross. In July, 1798, the Regiment marched to Youghal; and on 22d Oct., to Camden and Carlisle Forts; to Baltinglass, Oct., 1799; Dundalk, May, 1800. Reviewed at Lisburn, 20th Nov., 1800. The Regiment was inspected by Brigadier-General Hart, at Lifford, 12th May, 1802, and disbanded. The Regiment was again embodied by Colonel Lord Clements, at Lifford, 15th March, 1803, and inspected there by General Hart, 10th May; marched to Mullingar, August, 1803; Naas, June, 1804; Camp Kildare, 23d July; Naas, Sept., 1804; Dublin, July, 1805; Prosperous, 18th July, 1806; Cavan, Dec., 1806; Cork, June, 1807; Tuam, 6th Jan., 1808; Camp Kildare, June, 1808; Dublin, Aug., 1808; Tuam, April, 1810; Castlebar, April, 1811; Boyle, July, 1812; Dublin, June, 1813; Ballyshannon, July, 1814; Tullymore, Aug., 1815; Mullingar, March, 1816; and to Ballyshannon, March, 1816, and disbanded.

LETTER ON THE CONDUCT OF THE DONEGAL MILITIA.

(Copy.) "*Dublin Castle,* 5 *May,* 1802.

"My Lord,—Having directed a Warrant and Letter of Instructions to be transmitted to you for disembodying the Regiment of Militia, of which your Lordship is Colonel, the first and most gratifying part of the duty I have to discharge, is to communicate, in obedience to the King's commands, to the officers, non-commissioned officers, and men through you, the high sense with which His Majesty is impressed of their uniformly good conduct since they have been embodied, and of their truly meritorious zeal and public spirit, under all the trying occurrences which have arisen to call forth their loyal exertions, during the long and arduous contest in which we have been engaged.

"It is particularly gratifying to me, that from a return of peace having occurred during my administration, I am not only called upon to signify to your Lordship, *His Majesty's gracious approbation of the meritorious services of the Donegal Regiment of Militia*, but that His Majesty should also be enabled by the fortunate event, to which I have referred, to relieve the Corps from those arduous duties, in which they have been so long and so honourably employed; and I cannot doubt that the loyal and patriotic spirit by which your Lordship and the officers of your Regiment have been actuated, will make a due impression upon the minds of the inhabitants of your county, and will continue to produce the most salutary effects in regard to peace and tranquillity. "I have, &c.,

"HARDWICKE.

"*Colonel the Lord Viscount Clements, Donegal Regiment of Militia.*"

Facings, Black.   *Agents,* Messrs. Cane and Co., Dublin.

103d, or Limerick City Regiment of Militia.

Head-Quarters, Limerick City.

Colonel.
Lord Viscount Gort, 7 Dec. 1842. J.P.—*Roxborough, Limerick; Lough Cooter Castle, Gort.*

Lieut.-Colonel.
Hon. Charles Smyth Vereker, 30 June 1837. *Chesham-place, London.*

Major.
Hon. Standish Prendergast Vereker, 10 Sept. 1842. J.P.—*Gort.*

	Date of Appointment to Present Rank.	Remarks exhibiting Services of Officers, whether L.L., D.L., M.P., or J.P.—Country Seats, &c.
CAPTAINS.		
Exham Morony	29 March 02	
Sir H.D. Massey, Bart.	20 Nov. 19	J.P.—*Doonas, Clare.*
Chris. St. George	7 April 34	J.P.—*Tyrone, Galway.*
Ralph Westropp	15 Oct. 38	J.P.—*Coolreagh, Clare.*
Wm. Dent Farrer	2 March 42	J.P.—*Brooklyn Park, Queen's Co.*
Thomas N. Royse	27 May 42	J.P.—*Nautenan, Limerick.*
LIEUTENANTS.		
Daniel Smyth	4 Oct. 06	*Limerick.*
Robert M'Craith	1 Nov. 10	*Co. of Limerick.*
Godfrey Massy	9 Sept. 11	*Turrets, Co. of Limerick.*
Chris. Hemsworth	29 April 13	*Tipperary.*
Edmond Morony	15 June 13	*Ballyclogh, Limerick.*
Henry V. Watson	8 Sept. 38	*Limerick.*
James Spaight	29 Aug. 40	*Limerick.*
ENSIGNS.		
Amos Vereker	23 March 13	*Limerick.*
J. S. B. Peffard	8 May 13	
Charles Smyth	28 June 39	
Burton Smyth		
Richard Taylor		
ADJUTANT.		
Thomas Jervis	12 June 24	*Limerick.* Served in the 6th Dragoon Gds.
SURGEON.		
John Wilkinson	27 Dec. 17	M.D.—*Limerick.*

SERVICES OF THE REGIMENT.—This Regiment highly distinguished itself for its loyalty in the Irish Rebellion, more especially when a portion of the French Army under General Humbert, one of Napoleon's favourite Generals, landed at Killala Bay in the year 1798; being there joined by a numerous body of rebels, he marched on to Castlebar, where he put to flight a superior force of the King's Troops, and the battle was called, in derision, "The Races of Castlebar." Elated with his success, General Humbert then pushed on to Sligo, his army at that time amounting to upwards of five thousand men, including rebels; the town was garrisoned by the Limerick City Militia, commanded by the second Viscount Gort, then Colonel Vereker, and a troop of Dragoons. Upon the first alarm the Colonel at once determined to oppose their advance; and, marching out at the head of four hundred of his own Regiment and about thirty Dragoons, placed himself so cleverly in a defile at Coloony, about five miles from Sligo, that he opposed their further progress, made them change their route, and threw them into the hands of the Marquis of Cornwallis. The Limerick Militia lost about twenty-seven killed and forty wounded, and the French and rebels about twice that number. The Regiment was rewarded by the thanks of Parliament; the Colonel got an honourable augmentation to his arms, with the motto, "Coloony," and medals were struck upon the occasion, and handed by the Corporation of Limerick to those engaged. The battle was fought upon the 5th of Sept., 1798, and lasted four hours. The Colonel, 1 Captain, and 1 Lieutenant, wounded; and 1 Lieutenant and 1 Ensign killed.

Facings, Buff. *Agents*, Sir E. R. Borough and Co., Dublin.

Head-Quarters, Mountrath.] **104th, or Queen's County Regiment of Militia.**

Colonel.
Sir Charles H. Coote, Bart., 1825.

Lieut.-Colonel.
Francis P. Dunne, 15 February 1846. M.P.

Major.
Richard Dunne, 24 July 1839.

	Date of Appointment to Present Rank.	Remarks exhibiting Services of Officers, whether L.L., D.L., M.P., or J.P.—Country Seats, &c.
CAPTAINS.		
Lodge Philips.........	25 Dec. 15	
William W. Despard	25	
Robert White....... .	6 Sept. 46	
Henry Pigott	18 Feb. 46	
LIEUTENANTS.		
John Elly	12 Jan. 07	
Richard Lodge	7 March 08	
Thomas Hovendeu...	4 Nov. 08	
George Long	11 July 09	
William B. Cowley...	12 Dec. 11	
ENSIGNS.		
William Clarke	18 July 11	
William Cooke	15 April 14	
PAYMASTER.		
Thomas White	4 Aug. 17	
SURGEON.		
James Smith	18 Aug. 13	

Facings, Blue.

Agents, Sir E. R. Borough, Bart., and Co., Dublin.

105TH REGIMENT OF MILITIA. 143

Head-Quarters, Montrose.] **105th, or Forfar and Kincardine Regiment of Militia.**

Colonel.—Donald Ogilvy, 28 Feb. 1828. D.L.—*Clova*, and *Balnaboth*.

Lieutenant-Colonel.
Sir Alexander Ramsay, Bart., 11th Nov. 1834. *Balmain.* Ensign 14th Sept. 1803; Lieutenant 1st Oct. 1804.

Major.—James Rait, 27th May 1842. D.L.—*Armiston.*

CAPTAINS.	Date of Appointment to Present Rank.	Remarks exhibiting Services of Officers, whether L.L., D.L., M.P., or J.P.—Country Seats, &c.
Thomas Brown	2 July 11	Ensign 20th August, 1805; Lieutenant 8th May, 1807.
David Laird	3 March 31	D.L.—*Strathmartin.* Ensign 84th Foot, July, 1826; Lieutenant in June, 1827; served till June, 1830.
Alexander B. Higgins	10 March 31	Ensign 36th Foot, 21st June, 1801; half-pay, 24th June, 1802; full pay, 70th Foot, Jan., 1804; Lieutenant in 2d Foot, March, 1804; sold out in March, 1805; and in May, 1806, appointed Captain and Adjutant City Dublin Militia, and served till 1809; Ensign 54th Foot, October, 1809; Lieut. 4th Garrison Battalion, 1st June, 1810; Lieut. in 1st, or Royals, Dec., 1810, and served till Dec., 1818, and is now on half-pay from same Corps.
Alexander Gordon	15 March 31	
John Ramsay L. Amy	7 Dec. 44	J.P.—*Dunkenny.*
Duncan S. Robertson	31 Dec. 45	
Hugh Alex. Kennedy	31 Aug. 44	Half-pay late Lieutenant 14th Regiment Madras Native Infantry; served in the Madras Army from 1826; Lieutenant 21st May, 1803.
D. W. Balfour Ogilvy	26 May 48	J.P.—*Tannadice.*
LIEUTENANTS.		
William Middleton	22 March 08	J.P.—Ensign 18th Nov., 1807, in the Forfarshire Militia.
James Thomson	12 Feb. 13	Ensign 5th Sept., 1811, in the Forfarshire Militia.
George Hull	6 Feb. 26	Ensign 29th April, 1814; has also been Assistant-Surgeon since April, 1814.
James Smith	22 May 30	Ensign 2d March, 1816, in the Forfarshire Militia.
John Brown	15 July 31	Ensign 13th March, 1816, in the Forfarshire Militia.
John Hay	19 Feb. 33	
Edward K. Murray	30 May 35	
Thomas Scott	17 Feb. 46	
William P. Scott	17 Feb. 46	
William D. Fyfe	11 June 32	

105th, or Forfar and Kincardine Regiment of Militia.
(Continued.)

	Date of Appointment to Present Rank.	Remarks exhibiting Services of Officers, whether L.L., D.L., M.P., J.P.—Country Seats, &c.
ENSIGNS.		
Alex. Dickson	20 June 46	
David Brewster	20 June 46	
William Smart	20 June 46	
Louis Turnskie	23 June 46	
William Cruikshank	18 Oct. 47	
PAYMASTER.		
James Thomson	25 Nov. 14	Ensign 5th Sept., 1811; Lieut. 12th Feb., 1813.
ADJUTANT.		
Archibald Macneill	18 April 27	J.P.—*Brakie*. Ensign 91st Foot 18th Aug., 1804; Lieut. 15th Aug., 1805; Adjutant 15th June, 1809; Capt. 25th Nov. 1813; on half-pay 24th Dec., 1815, till April, 1826.
QUARTERMASTER.		
James Jack	30 Oct. 19	
SURGEON.		
Henry Hoile	25 Dec. 05	On retired half-pay from 25th June, 1829.

SERVICES OF THE REGIMENT.—In Montrose, from 6th April, 1803, to 1st July, 1803; Musselburgh camp, till 9th Nov., 1803; Musselburgh town, till 13th Oct., 1806; Glasgow Barracks, till 5th March, 1807; Stirling Castle, till 11th June, 1808; Edinburgh Castle, till 19th May, 1809; Berwick-on-Tweed, till 7th May, 1810; Dunbar, till 28th May, 1810; Newcastle-on-Tyne, till 10th June, 1811; Tynemouth, till 2d Nov., 1812; Stockport, till 27th Jan., 1813; Manchester, till 28th March, 1814; Clonooney Barracks, Ireland, till 6th July, 1814; Naas Barracks, till 12th Sept., 1815; Downpatrick, till 2d March, 1816. It may be noticed here, that when the Forfar Militia were first embodied, in 1798, the Regiment was the 8th North British Militia. When embodied in 1803, it was then the 11th British Militia; when the Militia were renumbered, it was made the 105th. The original establishment of the Regiment in 1803 was 647 privates; on 21st June, 1803, it was raised to 970; and on 12th July, 1805, it was again reduced to 647; and on 14th Nov., 1807, it was raised to 1,049; and on 17th Sept., 1811, it was again reduced to 647, at which it still remains.

EFFECTIVE STRENGTH.—1 Colonel, 1 Lieut.-Colonel, 1 Major, 8 Captains, 10 Lieutenants, 6 Ensigns, 1 Adjutant, 1 Paymaster, 1 Surgeon, 2 Assistant-Surgeons, 1 Quartermaster, 1 Sergeant-Major, 1 Quartermaster-Sergeant, 1 Drum-Major, 21 Sergeants, 22 Corporals, 10 Drummers and Fifers:—

    From Forfarshire......... 511 Privates
     „ Kincardineshire... 136 „
             647

Facings, Yellow.

Head-Quarters, Euston-square.] 106th, or *Royal London Regiment of Militia.*

Colonel.
Sir Claudius Stephen Hunter, Bart. and Ald., 23 Aug. 1820.

Lieut.-Colonel.
William Thompson, Ald., 25 March 1835. M.P.

Major.
John Belshes Horne, 4 Feb. 1846. Late of the 6th Royal Regt.; served in India.

	Date of Appointment to Present Rank.	Remarks exhibiting Services of Officers, whether L.L., D.L., M.P., or J.P.—Country Seats, &c.
CAPTAINS.		
Thomas Allen.........	7 Sept. 30	
Edward Tickner......	3 June 35	
Richard Hicks	5 June 35	
James Berkley	14 June 39	
C. F. Mackenzie......	4 Feb. 46	Late Lieut. in the 41st Regiment. Served in [India.
James Thomson	5 Feb. 46	
Cl. S. Paul Hunter...	5 Nov. 46	
George Platt	9 Feb. 47	
LIEUTENANTS.		
George Cressall	30 Sept. 30	
William Maunder....	3 Oct. 30	
John Steele............	10 Oct. 30	
Robert Dallinger	3 June 35	
James Deans	4 June 35	
John Thos. Coleman	14 June 35	
Wm. Thos. Hall......	4 Feb. 46	Late in the 6th Regiment.
Thomas Heath	5 Feb. 46	
Wm. Tomlin Walker	6 Feb. 46	
James Quallette	7 Feb. 46	
ENSIGNS.		
Geo. Borlase Childs .	5 Feb. 46	
John Harrison Allan	7 Feb. 46	
ADJUTANT.		
Wm. Thos. Hall......	4 Feb. 46	Lieut., with Brevet Rank of Captain. Served in India with the 6th Foot.
ASSIST.-SURGEON.		
Geo. Borlase Childs .	5 Feb. 46	F.R.C.S., Surgeon in Chief to the City Police [Force.

SERVICES OF THE REGIMENT.—By Acts of 34 Geo. 3, c. 81, and 35 Geo. 3, c. 27, the old trained Bands of the City of London were regulated and formed into six Regiments of Militia, the Services of which were limited to 12 miles from the City. By Act 36 Geo. 3, c. 92, the six Regiments were reduced to two Regiments of 600 men each; and again by Act of 1 Geo. 4, c. 100, the two Regiments were reduced to one Regiment only, and the Services extended to any part of Great Britain. From its limited services the London Militia has only been enabled to perform duty at the Dockyards of Woolwich and Deptford; but was called out and did efficient service in the suppression of the Riots in 1780, and on various other occasions of civil disturbance in London and its vicinity, such as the Spafields Riots, the Chartist Meetings, and on other occasions in maintaining the peace of the City.

Facings, Blue.

107TH REGIMENT OF MILITIA.

Head-Quarters, Tralee.] **107th, or Kerry Regiment of Militia.**

Colonel.
Earl of Kenmare, 24 Jan. 1837. K. St. P.

Lieut.-Colonel.
Hon. Thomas Browne, 12 March 1849.

Major.
Charles George Fairfield, 31 May 1849.

	Date of Appointment to Present Rank.	Remarks exhibiting Services of Officers, whether L.L., D.L., M.P., or J.P.—Country Seats, &c.
CAPTAINS.		
William Collis		
Patrick Fitzgerald	16 Oct. 07	
Maurice Collis	1 Sept. 13	
John Bateman	16 Aug. 16	
Francis Chute		
B. Thompson	3 Oct. 34	
Valentine Brown	11 Dec. 44	
LIEUTENANTS.		
George Hilliard	11 Nov. 07	
Pierce Leslie	11 May 35	
Francis Twiss	1 Sept. 35	
Rowland Chute		
John Cronin	30 Aug. 41	
Chas. D. O'Connell	3 March 43	
Leslie Julian	31 July 43	
David Mahoney	14 March 45	
George Sandes	19 June 35	
Thomas O'Connell	15 April 47	
ENSIGNS.		
George Foster	1 Sept. 14	
Samuel Croker		
John M'Carthy		
John Fitzmaurice	29 Jan. 46	
Bastable Hilliard	29 Jan. 46	
Daniel J. O'Connell	26 Sept. 49	
ADJUTANT.		
Capt. D. A. Curtayne	5 Feb. 46	
SURGEON.		
Francis Crumpe	30	M.D.

Facings, Yellow.

Agents, Sir E. R. Borough, Bart., and Co., Dublin.

Head-Quarters, Dunleer.

108th Louth Regiment of Militia.

Colonel.
Right Hon. Lord Bellew, 17 Nov. 1843.   L.L., J.P.—*Barmeath, Dunleer.*

Lieut.-Colonel.
Lord Viscount Massareene, Oct. 1847.—*Oriel Temple, Collon,* and *Antrim Castle.*

Major.
John M'Clintock, 24 July 1827.   J.P.—*Collon.*

CAPTAINS.	Date of Appointment to Present Rank.	Remarks exhibiting Services of Officers, whether L.L., D.L., M.P., or J.P.—Country Seats, &c.
Latham Hamlon......	1 Feb. 06	
Thomas Phipoe	20 June 08	
George M'Entagert ..	5 Oct. 13	
Lewis Upton	16 April 47	
LIEUTENANTS.		
James H. Bunburry	25 March 11	
William P. Brabazon	17 March 12	
Benjamin Atkinson ..	14 Nov. 12	
David Atkinson	26 Dec. 12	
William Ruxton......	16 April 47	
ENSIGNS.		
John Forster	9 Feb. 14	
Hon. E. J. Bellew ...	16 April 47	
Tarquel Macneill ...	2 Feb. 49	
ADJUTANT.		
Capt. H. L. Pendleton	24 June 20	
SURGEON.		
Robert Pentland ...	2 Feb. 49	*Drogheda.*

Facings, Light Green.

Agents.—Sir Edw. R. Borough, Bart., Armit, and Co., Dublin.

Head-Quarters, Lucan.] **109th, or Dublin County Regiment of Militia.**

Colonel.
William Viscount Brabazon, 10 May 1847. D.L., J.P.—*Kilruddery.*

- Lieutenant-Colonel.
Samuel White, 18 Dec. 1836. J.P.—*Killikee.*

Major.
Baron de Robeck, 16th July 1832. D.L., J.P.—Served in the 7th Hussars.

CAPTAINS.	Date of Appointment to Present Rank.	Remarks exhibiting Services of Officers, whether L.L., D.L., M.P., or J.P.—Country Seats, &c.
John Wilson	13 May 13	
James Gandon	18 Aug. 24	J.P.—*Lucan.*
James Annesley	26 Sept. 25	
Robert B. Smith	8 Nov. 44	
Manners M'Kay	11 Feb. 46	J.P.—*Moreen.* Served in the 3d Dragoon Guards.
Hon. James Butler	19 April 48	
Charles Colthurst		J.P.—*Lucan House.*
LIEUTENANTS.		
William B. Picknell	8 March 00	
Thomas Mangan	18 Sept. 09	
Robert Burnett	8 Sept. 12	
William H. Kellett	13 May 13	
Isaac Humphries	14 Oct. 13	
Stephen J. Ardagh	16 Dec. 15	
William Tennant		
ENSIGNS.		
Samuel Lapham	8 May 28	
Augustus Sheil	20 April 38	
Alex. T. E. Malpas	24 Jan. 44	
Samuel Duff	1 May 46	
Arthur P. Graves	11 Nov. 46	
Luke M'Donnell	19 April 41	
ADJUTANT.		
Henry J. V. Kemble	1 June 45	Served as Captain 67th Regiment.
PAYMASTER.		
Chaworth Lyster	18 Jan. 22	
SURGEON.		
Augustus Heron	28 April 96	
ASSISTANT-SURGEON.		
William A. Duke	5 Aug. 46	

SERVICES OF THE REGIMENT.—Served in Ireland during the Rebellion.

Facings, White.   *Agents,* Messrs. Cane and Co., Dublin.

110th, or City of Cork Regiment of Militia.

Head-Quarters, Cork.

Colonel.
Lord Viscount Bernard, 5 Sept. 1846. L.L., D.L., M.P., J.P.—*Castle Bernard.*

Lieut.-Colonel.
Sir Augustus Warren, Bart., 13 April 1829. J.P.—*Warren Court.*

Major.
Thomas Wall Hewitt, 5 Nov. 1812.

	Date of Appointment to Present Rank.	Remarks exhibiting Services of Officers, whether L.L., D.L., M.P., or J.P.—Country Seats, &c.
CAPTAINS.		
Elias Pearse	2 April 03	
Poole Hickman	30 Sept. 06	
Anthony Morgan	27 Jan. 13	
Francis Rowland	3 Dec. 18	
Richard Beare	26 April 27	
Hon. W. White	10 June 35	L.L., D.L., J.P.—*Macroom.*
John C. Kearney	19 July 41	
A. F. G. Ansley	23 Aug. 47	
LIEUTENANTS.		
William Nash	23 Oct. 13	
Nicholas Parker	19 Aug. 26	
Charles Good	7 Sept. 26	
William Barter	14 Dec. 26	
Richard B. Robinson	16 Jan. 27	
Emmanuel B. Bass	14 Nov. 45	*Cork.*
Frederick W. Corker	27 Jan. 46	
John J. Jones	5 Sept. 46	*Bengaskeddy.*
Charles Ottley	23 Aug. 47	*Macroom.*
Isaac Morgan	28 April 48	*Tivoley.*
ENSIGNS.		
Michael Parker	19 Aug. 26	
John Bass	27 Sept. 26	
Richard Evanson	3 Nov. 26	
John S. Dunscomb	27 Jan. 37	J.P.—*Mount Disiart.*
Thomas B. Barter	25 Jan. 46	J.P.
Thomas Gath	23 Aug. 46	
ADJUTANT.		
Augustus Warren	9 Feb. 46	Served in the 99th and 72d Regiments.
SURGEON.		
Stephen Cuddy	3 April 26	J.P.
ASSIST.-SURGEON.		
Horace N. Meade	30 March 46	M.D.

Facings, Blue.

Agents, Messrs. R. Cane and Co., Dublin.

Head-Quarters, Mohill.

111th, or Leitrim Regiment of Militia.

Colonel.
Lord Viscount Clements, 2 Feb. 1843.

Lieut.-Colonel.
Henry Theo. Clements, 11 Nov. 1842.

Major.
George Faris, 2 Sept. 1812.

CAPTAINS.	Date of Appointment to Present Rank.	Remarks exhibiting Services of Officers, whether L.L., D.L., M.P., or J.P.—Country Seats, &c.
Johnston Moreton	17 Dec. 04	
Joseph Johnston	5 April 06	
Acheson O'Brien	14 July 12	
J. H. Peyton	1 Dec. 15	
G. H. C. Peyton	27 Feb. 18	
LIEUTENANTS.		
Edward Harrison	9 Dec. 07	
H. L. Montgomery	3 Nov. 41	
ENSIGNS.		
Adam Rutherford	16 Nov. 12	
John Halfpenny	16 Nov. 12	
ADJUTANT.		
William Rose	1 Sept. 46	
ASSIST.-SURGEON.		
John Duke	2 April 13	M.D.

Facings, Yellow. *Agents,* Sir E. R. Borough, Bart., and Co., Dublin.

Head-Quarters, Hillsborough.] **112th, or** *Royal South Down Regiment of Militia.*

Colonel.
Most Noble the Marquis of Downshire, 30 July 1845.

Lieut.-Colonel.
Lord A. Edwin Hill, 30 July 1845.

Major.
James Baillie, 16 Nov. 1830.

	Date of Appointment to Present Rank.	Remarks exhibiting Services of Officers, whether L.L., D.L., M.P., or J.P.—Country Seats, &c.
CAPTAINS.		
Marcus J. Annesley	14 Nov. 12	
Thomas John Tighe	8 Dec. 12	
Thomas Laur. Ward	20 April 19	
Vere Essex Ward	2 Feb. 31	
Wm. Robert Ward	24 Feb. 31	
Wm. Brownlow Ford	3 Jan. 49	
LIEUTENANTS.		
Alex. Montgomery	11 Nov. 08	
Adward F. Noland	12 March 12	
John Symes	16 May 29	
John Temple Reilly	1 March 35	
Thomas Gregg	30 June 41	
James M'Clelland	21 Feb. 44	
ENSIGNS.		
D. Barry Hewitson	8 Nov. 14	
Geo. Fleming Echlin	1 Nov. 33	
R. T. Bunbury Isaac	8 Nov. 41	
Fitzherbert D. Lucas	14 Feb. 44	
John Stewart	3 Feb. 45	
ADJUTANT.		
Capt. J. A. Hodgson	30 March 19	
PAYMASTER.		
Charles Birch	19 Nov. 07	
SURGEON.		
John Wilson	25 May 17	

Facings, Blue.

Agents, Messrs. Cane & Co., Dublin.

Head-Quarters, Liverpool.] **113th, or 2d Duke of Lancaster's Own Regiment of Militia.**

Colonel.—Hon. C. J. Fox Stanley, 3 March 1848.
Lieut.-Colonel.—J. H. Ford, 2 March 1846.
Majors.
Sir F. G. Hesketh, Bart., 27 February 1846.
T. M. Steel, 12 May 1846

	Date of Appointment to Present Rank.	Remarks exhibiting Services of Officers, whether L.L., D.L., M.P., or J.P.—Country Seats, &c.
CAPTAINS.		
W. Leigh	15 Dec. 27	
N. Blundell	5 March 31	
R. B. Clayton	12 June 31	
H. F. Rigge	27 Oct. 38	
J. Weld	22 Nov. 39	
J. Bourne	14 April 46	
R. Johnson	22 May 46	
R. A. A. Aspinal	29 May 46	
E. J. Stanley, jun.	28 May 47	
R. Phibbs	31 May 47	
LIEUTENANTS.		
J. Grant	6 July 03	
R. J. Halsall	25 May 23	
C. Jones	21 March 31	
W. P. T. Temperley	6 May 34	
J. Withers	15 Sept. 36	
T. S. G. B. Lennard	8 Jan. 39	
T. B. Molyneux	12 May 40	
J. T. Bourne	18 April 43	
A. T. Knight	28 Nov. 45	
T. Lane	17 March 48	
W. C. Davies	1 April 48	
ENSIGNS.		
J. F. Morgan	21 Oct. 13	
S. Marshall	12 March 14	
J. M. Clementi	12 March 47	
W. Ayrton	13 March 47	
ADJUTANT.		
Capt. J. Weir	20 Feb. 46	

Facings, Blue.

Head-Quarters, Mullingar.] **114th, or (*Westmeath*) *Regiment of Militia*.**

Colonel.
The Marquis of Westmeath, 7 Jan. 1815. L.L.—*Clonyn, Castletown, Delvin.*
Served in Coldstream Guards, Egyptian Battalion.

Lieut.-Colonel.
Sir Richard Levinge, Bart., 3 Jan. 1846. J.P.—*Knockdrin Castle Mullingar.*
Served in 43d Light Infantry.

Major.
William Pollard, 7 July 1843. D.L.—*Castlepollard.*

CAPTAINS.	Date of Appointment to Present Rank.	Remarks exhibiting Services of Officers, whether L.L., D.L., M.P., or J.P.—Country Seats, &c.
Thomas Stubbs	1 Aug. 08	
Richard Levinge	4 Aug. 12	J.P.—*Levington Park, Mullingar.*
Charles John Lyons	1 Sept. 15	D.L.—*Ladistown, Mullingar.*
Sir P. Nugent, Bart.	29 June 40	M.P., D.L.—*Donore.*
Hon. C. Handcock		*Athlone.*
J. M. Berry		J.P.—*Ballinagall, Mullingar.*
LIEUTENANTS.		
Philip Greene	1 July 97	
Charles Pilkington	3 March 06	*Dalystown.*
Arthur Chaigneau	21 Sept. 40	J.P.—*Bennown, Ballymahon.*
William Levinge	8 Nov. 41	
Samuel Vignoles	7 Sept. 42	J.P.—*Tyrrell's Pass.*
John Malone	4 Aug. 49	J.P.—*Ballymore.*
ENSIGNS.		
C. W. Hamilton	1 March 42	*Dublin.*
Samuel A. Reynell	7 March 42	J.P.—*Archerstown.*
Arthur Upton	3 Jan. 48	
Charles Roche	12 Jan. 48	*Drumcree.*
PAYMASTER AND ADJUTANT.		
Capt. Hen. Robinson	2 Jan. 47	J.P.—Served in 60th Royal Rifles.
SURGEON.		
Robert Barlow		*Mullingar.*

Facings, Yellow.   *Agents*, Sir E. R. Borough, Bart., and Co., Dublin.

Head-Quarters, Ayr.] **115th, or Prince Regent's Royal Ayrshire Regiment of Militia.**

Colonel.

Earl of Eglinton and Winton, 4 June 1836. L.L.—*Eglinton Castle, Ayrshire.*

Lieut.-Colonel.—W. S. Neill, 10 Jan. 1837. D.L., J.P.—*Swindrige House, Ayrshire.* Served in the 69th Regiment.

Major.—Sir J. M. Cunningham, Bart., 17 April 1837.—*Crosshill, Steuarton, Ayrshire.* Served in the 94th Regiment.

	Date of Appointment to Present Rank.		Remarks exhibiting Services of Officers, whether L.L., D.L., M.P., or J.P.—Country Seats, &c.
CAPTAINS.			
C. S. M'Allester	6 June	20	J.P.—*Kennox, Steuarton, Ayrshire.*
James Hood	15 March	25	J.P.—*Jersey.* Served in the 91st Regiment.
Charles Lamb	17 April	37	*Beauport Park, Battle, Sussex.*
R. T. Kennedy	17 April	37	J.P.—*Daljerrock, Ayrshire.*
W. F. Hamilton	19 Jan.	46	J.P.—*Cairnhill, Ayrshire.* Served in the 83d
Thomas Davidson	8 April	46	J.P.—*Drumley, Tarbolton.* [Regiment.
Patrick Warner	8 April	46	J.P.—*Ardeer, Tarbolton.*
LIEUTENANTS.			
Duncan M'Intyre	1 Dec.	02	
Geo. Phillips	19 Dec.	09	
John Belram	5 April	14	*Ayr, N.B.*
Chas. M'Vitie	20 June	25	
Lauchlam Campbell	30 July	42	
William Gemmell	20 May	45	*Lady Kirk, Ayr, N.B.*
Robert M'Kay	8 April	46	*Ayr, N.B.*
W. C. Gemmell	18 Feb.	48	*Dale.*
ENSIGNS.			
Quinten M'Adam	19 Jan.	46	*17, Shandwick Place, Edinburgh.*
John Crichton	19 Jan.	46	*Linn, Ayrshire.*
W. F. Fullarton	19 Jan.	46	*Irvine, N.B.*
Robert Crichton	11 June	46	*Linn, Dalsy, Ayrshire.*
Patrick Blair	3 Feb.	48	
Nathan M'Neel	4 April	49	
ADJUTANT.			
James Miller	3 Feb.	46	Served in the Scots Fusilier Guards.
PAYMASTER.			
Duncan M'Intyre	25 June	03	
SURGEON.			
J. J. M. Abercromby	19 Jan.	46	*Burntisland, Fife, N.B.*

SERVICES OF THE REGIMENT.—In Nov. 1802, the Regiment was embodied under the command of Colonel Lord Montgomarie; and in August, 1808, it volunteered, unanimously, to serve with the Regular Army in Spain: their service was not accepted.—August, 1811. The Regiment extended its service, and was enrolled for the Militia of the United Kingdom.—February, 1813. The Regiment expressed its abhorrence of the conduct of several men in some Regiments of Scotch Militia, and disclaimed any knowledge of or participation in, their proceedings. The Regiment received the approbation of the Commander of the Forces in Scotland in General Orders, dated Adjt.-General's Office, Edinburgh, 25th February, 1813, and that of Major-General Scott, commanding the Brigade, in Brigade orders, 26th February, 1813. The thanks of the Lord-Lieutenant of the County, 10th March, 1813; and the approbation of the Commander-in-Chief, for its uniform zeal and good conduct, dated Adjt.-General's Office, Horse Guards, 16th March, 1813.—June, 1813. His Royal Highness the Prince Regent was pleased in the name, and on behalf of his Majesty, to approve of the Regiment being styled, "The Prince Regent's Royal Regiment of Ayrshire Militia." The Regiment served in Scotland, England, and Ireland; and upon all occasions the men shewed a peculiar willingness to extend their service. The strength of the Regiment was only 436 men, and during the period it was embodied it gave 11 officers and 694 men as Volunteers to the Line.

116th, or North Cork Regiment of Militia (Rifles).

Head-Quarters, Fermoy.

Colonel.
W. H. M. Hodder, 1 March 1831.

Lieut.-Colonel.
William T. French, 3 Feb. 1832.

Major.
John Roe, 6 June 1812.

	Date of Appointment to Present Rank.	Remarks exhibiting Services of Officers, whether L.L., D.L., M.P., or J.P.—Country Seats, &c.
CAPTAINS.		
Thomas Crooke	10 May 15	
Cooper Penrose	21 Nov. 21	
Joseph Coghlan	25 Oct. 34	
Robert Maxwell	25 Oct. 34	
Robert Atkins	22 Dec. 45	
Nicholas P. Leader	22 Dec. 45	
Robert Aldworth	19 Jan. 46	
Spencer Price	19 Jan. 46	
LIEUTENANTS.		
David Kirby	9 July 11	
Robert Starkey	6 Dec. 12	
Rich. G. Annesly	26 March 38	
Thomas Newenham	4 Jan. 44	
Pepper Roberts	19 Jan. 46	
Edward Lane	19 Jan. 46	
Edward Hoare	19 Jan. 46	
Charles Lyster	19 Jan. 46	
Richard Pennefather	19 Jan. 46	
ENSIGNS.		
Arthur Huband	17 Jan. 42	
Hodder Roberts	19 Jan. 46	
Wm. Robt. Starky	19 Jan. 46	
James Roe	19 Jan. 46	
Thos. Edw. Freeman	19 Jan. 46	
Hon. Henry Bernard	19 Jan. 46	
SURGEON.		
Thomas Page	27 May 18	

Facings, Black.

Agents.—Sir E. R. Borough, Bart., and Co., Dublin.

Head-Quarters, Campbeltown.] 117*th, or Argyll and Bute Regiment of Militia.*

Major.
C. George Campbell.

	Date of Appointment to Present Rank.	Remarks exhibiting Services of Officers, whether L.L., D.L., M.P., or J.P.—Country Seats, &c.
CAPTAINS.		
Allan Ross		
Sir John P. Orde		
William Robertson		
Sir A. Campbell, Bart.		
C. Campbell		
M. Campbell		
D. Campbell		
LIEUTENANTS.		
Alex. Anderson		
John MacNicol		
Colin MacLachlan		
A. E. MacDonald		
A. Kerr		
J. Campbell		
ENSIGNS.		
Arch. MacArthur		
James Grant		
A. M'Laine		
G. M'Neil		
ADJUTANT.		
C. A. Campbell		
SURGEON.		
James Broun		

Facings, Yellow.

118th, or Royal Cornwall and Devon Miners' Regiment of Militia (Light Infantry).

Head-Quarters, Truro.

Lieutenant-Colonel-Commandant.
Edward William Wynne Pendarves, 16 Nov. 1843. M.P., D.L., J.P.—*Pendarves.* Deputy-Warden.

Major.
Humphry Willyams, 11 July 1844. M.P., D.L., J.P.—*Carnanton.* Deputy-Warden.

CAPTAINS.	Date of Appointment to Present Rank.		Remarks exhibiting Services of Officers, whether L.L., D.L., M.P., or J.P.—Country Seats, &c.
George P. Smith......	5 June	15	
J. M. K. Chadwick...	15 July	35	
Charles B. G. Sawle	12 July	44	D.L., J.P.—*Restormel.*
Sir Colman Rashleigh	12 July	44	D.L., J.P.—*Prideaux.*
LIEUTENANTS.			
Robert J. Moore ...	14 Aug.	13	
George Pearce.........	21 March	14	
Carteret C. Price ...	16 June	15	
J. N. V. Willyams ...	12 July	44	J.P.
ENSIGNS.			
Francis Howell	10 June	45	J.P.—*Ethy.*
Henry H. Vivian ...	10 June	45	
Philip Sandy Tom ...	6 Jan.	46	*Rosedale.*
Robert Edyvean......	26 Feb.	46	
ADJUTANT.			
Capt. William Ward	30 May	46	Ensign (unattached) 18th July, 1826; do., 61st Regiment, 25th Oct., 1827; Lieut., 4th Dec., 1832; Adjutant 26th Sept., 1834; Captain 9th May, 1843.
SURGEON.			
W. H. Bullmore......	1 March	45	M.D.

SERVICES OF THE REGIMENT.—First raised in the year 1803. Embarked for Ireland on 10th August, 1811: served in Ireland two years and three months; the remainder of the time whilst embodied stationed in England and Wales, having been employed on the public works at Chatham, Dover, and in Wales, for a considerable period. Disembodied on the 28th June, 1814.

Facings, Blue.

119th, or Royal Meath Regiment of Militia.

Head-Quarters, Kells.

Colonel.
The Most Noble the Marquis of Headfort, 7 April 1823. K.P.

Lieut.-Colonel.—Thomas E. Taylor, 12 Dec. 1846. M.P.

Major—Stephen Moore, 2 Feb. 1838.

	Date of Appointment to Present Rank.	Remarks exhibiting Services of Officers, whether L.L., D.L., M.P., or J.P.—Country Seats, &c.
CAPTAINS.		
Charles Woodward...	11 Jan. 06	
Hon. E. Preston......	17 Nov. 21	
Matthew E. Corbally	2 Feb. 35	M.P.
Gustavus Dalton......	2 Feb. 35	
Hon. R. Plunket......	2 Feb. 35	
Arthur Henry Dillon	30 Dec. 46	
Gustavus Lambart...	12 Nov. 46	
Anthony O'Reilly ...	Feb. 48	
LIEUTENANTS.		
Peter Cruise	11 May 11	
John Goodman	20 July 12	
Hamilton George ...	2 Feb. 35	
William E. Grainger	11 Feb. 42	
W. O'Ferral Caddell	11 Feb. 42	
Earl of Bective	18 March 43	
Charles Battersby ...	12 Nov. 46	
Hon. S. Netterville...	12 Nov. 46	
ENSIGNS.		
Edward Lewis	8 Aug. 13	
Samuel Barry.........	9 July 14	
John Charleton	11 Feb. 42	
John Farrell	12 Dec. 46	
Russell Stanhope ...	12 Dec. 46	
Archdall C. Myrvyn .	Oct. 49	
ADJUTANT.		
Joshua Clare	29 July 29	
PAYMASTER.		
Richard Pepper	28 April 24	
QUARTERMASTER.		
Walter Keating	12 Dec. 46	
SURGEON.		
John O'Reilly.........	12 Dec. 46	
ASSIST.-SURGEON.		
James Wm. Young...	12 Dec. 46	

Facings, Blue.   *Agents*, Messrs. Cane and Co., Dublin.

120th, or North Mayo Regiment of Militia.

Head-Quarters, Ballina.

Colonel.
Charles Knox, 23 June 1839. D.L., J.P.—*Ballinrobe, Mayo.*

Major.
John Gardiner, 22 July 1824. D.L., J.P.—*Farmhill, Mayo.*

CAPTAINS.	Date of Appointment to Present Rank.	Remarks exhibiting Services of Officers, whether L.L., D.L., M.P., or J.P.—Country Seats, &c.
John Knox	23 June 15	D.L., J.P.—*Greenwood, Mayo.*
Henry Wm. Knox	8 July 30	L.L., J.P.—*Netly, Mayo.*
Thomas Palmer	8 May 31	J.P.—*Summerhill, Mayo.*
Thomas Paget	20 Dec. 41	J.P.—*Knuckglass, Mayo.*
Dennis Bingham	21 Dec. 46	J.P.—*Bingham Castle, Mayo.*
LIEUTENANTS.		
James Rennick	17 April 09	*Moville, Donegal.*
William Lundy	9 Sept. 12	*Rossbeg Lodge, Westport, Mayo.*
Francis Knox	15 Nov. 30	*Ballina, Mayo.*
Anthony Gildea	21 April 36	*Beechgrove, Mayo.*
Henry O'Malley	30 April 36	*Castlebar, Mayo.*
Sir Robert B. Lynch	7 May 38	D.L., J.P.—*Moat House, Mayo.*
G. Vignoles	30 April 36	
ENSIGNS.		
Thomas Goodwin	4 July 14	*Springhill, Mayo.*
Robert Jones	13 Jan. 15	*Ballina, Mayo.*
Robert Ovenden	19 March 34	
Francis Little	16 May 42	*Ballycastle, Mayo.*
Francis Knox Orme	24 Sept. 46	*Glenmore, Mayo.*

SERVICES OF THE REGIMENT.—From 1793 to March, 1800.

EFFECTIVE STRENGTH.—1 Colonel, 1 Lieutenant-Colonel, 1 Major, 7 Captains, 8 Lieutenants, 6 Ensigns, 1 Paymaster, 1 Adjutant, 1 Surgeon, 1 Assistant-Surgeon, 1 Quartermaster, 7 Companies.

Facings, Yellow.

Agents, Sir Edward Borough, Armit, and Co., Dublin.

Head-Quarters, Monaghan. **121st, or *Monaghan Regiment of Militia*.**

Colonel.
Right Hon. Lord Rossmore, 28 Nov. 1846.

Lieut.-Colonel.
Arthur Gamble Lewis, 26 Jan. 1846.

Major.
John Cronin, 21 Feb. 1846.

	Date of Appointment to Present Rank.	Remarks exhibiting Services of Officers, whether L.L., D.L., M.P., or J.P.—Country Seats, &c.
CAPTAINS.		
Robert Atkinson	24 Nov. 12	
Thomas Coote	1 Feb. 34	
R. W. Anketell	23 Dec. 44	
Joseph Whitesitt	1 May 46	
Charles Boyle	2 May 46	
E. W. Bond	4 May 46	
Henry Lloyd	29 Feb. 48	
Robert C. Trench	1 March 48	
LIEUTENANTS.		
Alexander Moutray	3 June 00	
James Seaton	26 Feb. 06	
James R. Anketell	5 Feb. 08	
Charles M'Vittie	12 Nov. 08	
Charles Crowe	30 March 09	
Samuel Moorhead	1 Feb. 34	
Matthew Blakeley	12 May 46	
Michael E. Lewis	29 Feb. 48	
— Tennison	49	
ENSIGNS.		
Robert M. Rose	1 Feb. 34	
Thomas Snowe	14 Nov. 42	
Walter Corry	12 May 46	
James Fiddis	2 May 46	
ADJUTANT.		
Capt. John Ross	5 Sept. 10	

Facings, White.

Agents, Sir E. R. Borough, Bart., and Co., Dublin.

122d Regiment of Militia.

Disembodied.

123d, or Royal Limerick County Regiment of Militia.
Head-Quarters, St. Francis-Abbey.

Colonel.—The Hon. R. Fitzgibbon, 4 July 1818.
Lieut.-Colonel.—The Knight of Glin, 10 Jan. 1848.
Major.—Kingsmill Pennefather, 20 Feb. 1816.

	Date of Appointment to Present Rank.	Remarks exhibiting Services of Officers, whether L.L., D.L., M.P., or J.P.—Country Seats, &c.
CAPTAINS.		
Lord Clarina	12 July 19	
John Lowe	9 March 33	
Gerald Blennerhasset	20 April 33	
Richd. Quin Sleeman	20 June 46	
Gibbon T. Fitzgibbon	10 Jan. 48	
Wm. H. Barrington	10 Jan. 48	
J. B. Blennerhasset	14 Feb. 49	
LIEUTENANTS.		
John Hilliard	19 Oct. 99	
Henry S. Browne	8 Sept. 00	
Gilbert S. O'Grady	1 April 06	
Pascal Field	24 Feb. 14	
George Dowdall	8 April 14	
Thomas R. Kane	3 June 14	
Hon. C. W. S. Rice	26 March 42	
Brudenell Plummer	10 Jan. 48	
Standish Holland	27 Nov. 48	
Henry Watson	14 Feb. 49	
ENSIGNS.		
Peter Hely	8 Dec. 10	
Bartholomew Purdon	10 Oct. 12	
William Hilliard	20 June 33	
Pierce K. Mahony	14 Feb. 36	
Henry F. Westropp	8 June 37	
Richard Fosberry	20 June 46	
ADJUTANT.		
Capt. R. B. Low	6 Aug. 48	
QUARTERMASTER.		
Thomas R. Kane	24 March 17	
SURGEON.		
Edward Lloyd	25 March 20	
ASSIST.-SURGEON.		
John Hunt	6 Oct. 15	

Facings, Blue. *Agents*, Messrs. Cane and Co., Dublin.

124th, or Sligo Regiment of Militia.

Head-Quarters, Sligo.

Colonel.
Arthur Knox Gore, 27 Jan. 1847.

Lieut.-Colonel.
Alexander Perceval, 12 April 1809.

Major.
Charles K. O'Hara, 23 July 1807.

CAPTAINS.	Date of Appointment to Present Rank.	Remarks exhibiting Services of Officers, whether L.L., D.L., M.P., or J.P.—Country Seats, &c.
Robert Jones	10 June 39	
John Ffolliott	1 May 46	M.P.
Nicholson Ormsby	19 May 46	
LIEUTENANTS.		
Booth Jones	25 Oct. 03	
James Burrowes	20 Feb. 06	
Richard Fitzgerald	29 March 12	
Samuel Barret	10 June 39	
Richard Wood	11 June 39	
Lewis G. Jones	6 June 45	
ENSIGNS.		
William Ormsby	18 June 39	
Roger Palmer	29 June 39	
Ormsby Jones	30 June 39	
Charles T. Gillmor	1 July 39	
Roger D. Robinson	9 July 45	
ADJUTANT.		
Capt. Thos. Ormsby	23 April 46	
PAYMASTER.		
Robert Ormsby	10 May 26	
QUARTERMASTER.		
Lieut. J. Burrowes	22 Aug. 03	
SURGEON.		
T. E. Lindsay	3 June 46	
ASSIST.-SURGEON.		
James M'Nair	20 Dec. 19	

Facings, Green.   *Agents,* Messrs. Cane and Co., Dublin.

125th, or Third Royal Lancashire Regiment of Militia.

Head-Quarters, Preston.

Colonel.
John Wilson Patten, 15 Nov. 1842. D.L., M.P.—*Bank Hall, Warrington.*

Lieut.-Colonel.
Sir John Gerrard, Bart., 15 Nov. 1842. D.L., J.P.—*New Hall, Wigan.*

Major.—Daniel Hornby, 4 Feb. 1843. *Raikes Hall, Blackpool.*

	Date of Appointment to Present Rank.	Remarks exhibiting Services of Officers, whether L.L., D.L., M.P., or J.P.—Country Seats, &c.
CAPTAINS.		
Wm. Ford Hulton...	10 April 35	D.L., J.P.—*New Brook House, Bolton.*
Montagu J. Fielden	19 Feb. 38	J.P.—*Fleasington Hall, Blackburn.*
Thos. Townley Parker	3 Feb. 43	D.L., J.P.
Fitzjames Watt	4 Feb. 43	*Chester.*
Michael Hughes	4 Feb. 43	*Shadley Hall, Prescot.*
C. H. L. W. Standish	23 March 46	D.L.—*Standish Hall, Wigan.*
Wm. James Garnett	24 March 46	J.P.—*Bleasdale, Garstang.*
Chas. C. De Trafford	25 March 46	*Trafford Park, Manchester.*
Wm. Juxon Hesketh	27 March 46	
Walter C. Strickland	16 March 47	*Sizergh Hall, Kendal.*
LIEUTENANTS.		
Edward Greenall ...	3 Feb. 43	*Wilderspool, Warrington.*
William Nicholson ...	4 Feb. 43	*Warrington.*
Edward Lister	18 March 46	*Everton, Liverpool.*
Ed. Cornelius Moore	19 March 46	*Kirkham.*
Henry Rose Clarke...	20 March 46	*Etwall, Uttoxeter.*
John Worthington...	21 March 46	*Parr Hall, St. Helens.*
James German	22 March 46	*Preston.*
ENSIGNS.		
John Edw. Orrall ...	21 March 46	*Openshaw, Manchester.*
Nicholson Gardener..	22 March 46	*Ballytrasna, Boyle, Ireland.*
J. Mages Clementi ...	12 March 47	
William Ayrton	13 March 47	*Colne.*
ADJUTANT.		
Capt. John Rooper...	27 Feb. 46	Served in the Rifle Brigade, from 1826 to 1845.
QUARTERMASTER.		
Hallows Thomas......	28 Dec. 21	
SURGEON.		
— Norris...............		*Preston.*

SERVICES OF THE REGIMENT.—In Ireland.

Facings, Blue.

126th, or Edinburgh Regiment of Militia.

Head-Quarters, Dalkeith.

Colonel.
His Grace the Duke of Buccleuch, 6 Jan. 1842.—*Dalkeith Palace.*

Lieut.-Colonel.
William M'Donald, 10 May 1831.—*Powder Hall, Edinburgh.*

Major.
Archibald Hope, 2 June 1831.—*Pinkie House.*

	Date of Appointment to Present Rank.	Remarks exhibiting Services of Officers, whether L.L., D.L., M.P., or J.P.—Country Seats, &c.
CAPTAINS.		
James Ritchie	27 Sept. 28	
John Orr	20 June 31	Served in the 42d Royal Highlanders during the Peninsular War. Was present at Salamanca, Siege of Burgos, Storming of San Michael, and several of the Actions in the Pyrenees; was present at the Battles of Quatre Bras and Waterloo, and severely wounded at the last-named Action.
John Mackay	25 June 31	
Archibald Mitchelson	25 June 31	
William Sandilands	4 March 46	
Hector M'Neil	5 March 46	
George Thompson	25 April 46	
John Fletcher	27 June 46	
LIEUTENANTS.		
Andrew Baird	1 July 03	
William Brown	4 March 11	
John Watson	4 Oct. 21	
Peter Lang	7 June 31	
Alexander Stewart	12 Sept. 33	
Alexander M'Gregor	8 Nov. 43	
J. Hay Hardyman	8 Nov. 43	
Thomas S. M'Call	25 April 46	
Charles Wright	25 April 46	
Henry S. Paterson	10 April 47	
ENSIGNS.		
George Bird	4 Oct. 21	
Richard Cannon	25 June 31	
George M'Lachlan	6 March 46	
John Orr	5 April 46	
Francis Kennedy	25 April 46	
Charles Lyon	10 April 47	
ADJUTANT.		
Patk. M'Leod Petley	16 Jan. 46	
PAYMASTER.		
Henry S. Paterson	4 July 27	
QUARTERMASTER.		
Allan Grant	5 Aug. 05	
SURGEON.		
Charles Graham	7 June 31	
ASSIST.-SURGEON.		
Thomas S. M'Call	17 Oct. 42	

SERVICES OF THE REGIMENT.—First embodied in 1798. Served in Scotland until embarked at Leith for England, landing at Harwich July, 1811. Embarked at Plymouth for Ireland, landing at Cork June, 1813. Returned to Scotland, landing at Port Patrick, marched to Dalkeith, March, 1815. Disembodied, April, 1816. Embodied for training (25 days) during the years 1820, 1821, 1825, and 1831.

Facings, Yellow.

Head-Quarters, Kilkenny.] **127th, or Kilkenny Regiment of Militia.**

Colonel.
The Marquis of Ormonde, 14 Nov. 1848.

Lieut.-Colonel.
Henry Wemyss, 20 Sept. 1846.

Major.
Arthur Helsham, 1846.

	Date of Appointment to Present Rank.	Remarks exhibiting Services of Officers, whether L.L., D.L., M.P., or J.P.—Country Seats, &c.
CAPTAINS.		
John Waring	9 Nov. 08	
T. J. O'Flaherty	29 March 16	
Geo. Paul Helsham	31 May 24	
Richard Sause	9 April 27	
Hon. J. Ponsonby	25 March 31	
Pierce S. Butler	6 Nov. 38	M.P.
Frederick Goddard	6 Nov. 38	
Walter Butler	4 Feb. 46	
William H. Candler	4 Feb. 46	
H. M. Dillon		
William Helsham	4 Feb. 46	
LIEUTENANTS.		
Paris Anderson	24 April 09	
William Bell	23 Jan. 11	
John Payne	22 Feb. 11	
B. A. Chambers	6 Nov. 12	
John Power	27 Sept. 13	
Alexander Bell	10 Sept. 14	
John Hewitson	8 March 22	
Viscount Clifden		
Richard Wheeler	4 Feb. 46	
ENSIGNS.		
Samuel Waring	19 March 14	
Edward Briscoe	2 Aug. 20	
John Lentiague	3 July 40	
Michael Val. Aylmer	21 Dec. 40	
M. O'M. Brennan	8 May 43	
ADJUTANT.		
Capt. James M'Intyre	21 Jan. 46	

Facings, Yellow.

Agents, Messrs. Cane and Co., Dublin.

Head-Quarters, Waterford. **128th, or *Waterford Regiment of Militia.***

Colonel.
Lord Stuart De Decies, 1839. Lieut. and Custos Rotulorum.—*County and City of Waterford.*

Lieut.-Colonel.
Sir Richard Keane, Bart., 30 July 1809. D.L., J.P.—*Cappoquin House.*

Major.— — Alcock, 7 Feb. 1810.—*Richmond House.*

	Date of Appointment to Present Rank.	Remarks exhibiting Services of Officers, whether L.L., D.L., M.P., or J.P.—Country Seats, &c.
CAPTAINS.		
Peter T. Anthony	29 April 09	
Cornelius Bolton	31 March 19	
Ed. O'Neil Power	25 May 32	*Newtown House.*
Marquis of Waterford	3 June 32	J.P.—*Curraghmore.*
John Pallisir	20 Sept. 39	J.P.—*Commengh Lodge.*
John Keene	19 Jan. 46	*The Glen Lodge.*
Peter S. Fitzgerald	21 Jan. 46	*Ballysax.*
Robt. P. Ronagar		*D'Leughtane.*
LIEUTENANTS.		
William Poole	21 Aug. 11	
James Farrill	43	
Thomas Welsh, jun.	7 Oct. 45	*Woodstock.*
Richard Power	12 Jan. 46	
Nicholas Ffolliott	12 Jan. 46	
Ed. Wm. Briscoe	24 Jan. 46	
Edward Lymberry	24 Jan. 46	
Richard Musgrave	22 Aug. 49	J.P. Ensign.
ENSIGNS.		
Anthony Lamphier	24 Aug. 10	
Bernard Hayes	12 Jan. 46	
Gabriel Fitzgerald	6 Feb. 46	
Wm. H. Graves	6 Feb. 46	
John Russell Mulcah	6 April 49	
SURGEON.		
Doctor Carroll		
ASSISTANT-SURGEON.		
Doctor Currey		

SERVICES OF THE REGIMENT.—The Regiment served in Ireland during the Rebellion, and volunteered many men to the Line.

Facings, Yellow.

Agents.—Messrs. Cane and Co.

Head-Quarters, Paisley.] **129th, or Renfrew Regiment of Militia.**

Colonel.—William Mure.
Lieut.-Colonel.—Archibald Campbell.
Major.—Robert Morris.

	Date of Appointment to Present Rank.	Remarks exhibiting Services of Officers, whether L.L., D.L., M.P., or J.P.—Country Seats, &c.
CAPTAINS. William Howie ...... Donald Cameron...... Wm. Douglas Dick... Archibald Smith...... Peter Maitland ...... Allan Pollock		
LIEUTENANTS. Wm. Cunningham ... John Caldwell......... James Love............ Thomas Crawford ... John Love		
ENSIGNS. John Morris .... C. B. S. Ryburn......		

Facings, Yellow.

Head-Quarters, Monmouth.] **31st, or Monmouthshire Regiment of Militia.**

Colonel.—H. M. Clifford, 23 July 1847.
Major.—J. F. Vaughan, 23 July 1847.

	Date of Appointment to Present Rank.	Remarks exhibiting Services of Officers, whether L.L., D.L., M.P., or J.P.—Country Seats, &c.
CAPTAINS. J. C. Roberts .... A. Rolls .... E. P. Herbert.........	18 Sept. 21 15 Dec. 48 15 Dec. 48	
LIEUTENANTS. B. Hogsflesh .... R. A. Laurence	1 May 31 15 Dec. 48	
ENSIGNS. T. Walbeoffe .... L. Ellis	8 Sept. 20 1 Jan. 36	
ADJUTANT. Capt. J. M. Carter ...	17 March 46	

Facings, Blue.

INDEX.

ALPHABETICAL LIST OF OFFICERS IN THE YEOMANRY CAVALRY.

Name	Page	Name	Page	Name	Page
Abbott, E. J.	27	Barington, Hon.	38	Boucherett, H.	22
Aberdour, Lord	21	Barff, T.	42	Bouverie, P. P.	32
Ackers, G. H.	33	Barnard, R.	36	Bowden, H.	16
Acland, T. C.	7	Barnes, N.	7	Boyle, P.	1
Adams, H. C.	32	Bartlett, F.	2	Boyle, Hon. G. F.	1
Adderley, C. B.	36	Barton, N.	38	Brackley, Viscount	18
Addison, G.	44	Bass, M.	33	Bradshaw, J. E.	9
Adey, N. M.	11	Bateman, J.	40	Bradford, G. T.	3
Agar, Hon.	27	Bathurst, Sir F.	38	Brinckley, T.	16
Ailsa, Marquis of	1	Bayley, J. J.	11	Bridges, Sir Brook	15
Akroyd, H.	44	Bean, H. J.	31	Bridgeman, F. O.	33
Albert, G.	16	Bearcroft, E.	39	Bridgeman, O. J. C.	30
Alcock, W.	41	Beauclerk, H.	20	Bridge, J. E.	9
Alderson, J.	26	Beaufort, Duke of	11	Bischoff, J.	41
Allen, S. P.	28	Beaumont, Sir G.	19	Bridges, G.	19
Ames, H. M.	11	Beckett, W.	41	Briscoe, R.	37
Anderson, J.	24	Belbin, R.	13	Broadbent	4
Anderton, N. J.	18	Bell, M.	24	Broderip, J. S.	32
Andover, Viscount	38	Bennet, P.	34	Bromley, R.	25
Andrews, R. B.	10	Bennett, D.	38	Bromley, W. D.	33
Anson, Viscount	33	Bennett, J.	31	Brook, C. B.	44
Antrobus	4	Bennitt, W.	39	Brooke, Lord	36
Antrobus, Sir Edmund	38	Bere, M.	7	Brooks, W.	19
Arkwright, R. W.	19	Berens, B. R.	16	Brown, A.	20
Armitage, J. T.	44	Berens, W. J.	16	Brown, G. B.	17
Armstrong, N.	25	Berkeley, R.	39	Brown, J.	42
Amyot, T. G.	35	Bernard, T. T.	2	Brown, J. T.	17
Ashburton, Lord	12	Bernard, W. H.	32	Browne, A. P.	32
Athorpe, J. C.	42	Bewicke, R. C.	24	Browne, B. C.	11
Atkinson, G. C.	24	Biggs, G. H.	39	Browne, J. W.	32
Atkinson, J. R. W.	41	Binford, N.	8	Brown, S. J.	41
Atty, R. J.	36	Bishop, N. R.	7	Browne, T. D.	29
Austen, W. H.	29	Biram, B.	42	Bruce, Earl	38
		Briggs, S.	40	Bruce, Lord	38
Badger, T. J.	30	Blaithwaite, G. W.	11	Bruce, W.	17
Barker	4	Blagrave, J. H.	31	Bryant, J. R.	28
Baillie, W.	21	Bland, T. D.	41	Brydges, T.	8
Bailey, J.	2	Blandford, Marquis of	27	Buck, G. S.	8
Baird, D.	17	Blayds, E.	41	Buckland, J. L.	9
Baird, G.	17	Bloxsome, E.	11	Buckingham, Duke	2
Baird, Sir J. G.	21	Booth, J.	24	Buller, M. E.	33
Baker, T. B.	21	Bonsey, N. H.	2	Buller	7
Baldwyn, J. L.	11	Borbe, St. G.	12	Buller, J. B.	7
Balfour, C.	20	Borthwick, J.	21	Burgh, De, H	22
Balfour, J. R.	20	Borough, J. C. B.	30	Burley, W.	19
Bamforth, W.	42	Boscawen, G.	16	Burlinson, W.	23
Barnardiston, N. C.	35	Bosville, G. W.	41	Burn, R.	37
Barnett, G. H.	27	Boswell, Sir J.	1	Burnaby, C. S.	19
Baring, T.	12	Botfield, B.	30	Burne, J.	7

INDEX.—YEOMANRY CAVALRY.

Name	Page	Name	Page	Name	Page
Burn, R.	37	Corbet, A.	29	Fairlee, J.	1
Burnaby, C. S.	19	Corbet, V.	29	Fairman, H. C.	15
Burnett, J. J.	1	Corbet, Sir A.	29	Farnham, E. B.	19
Burrell, B.	24	Corbett, V.	41	Farquharson, N. J.	9
Burt, J. G.	21	Corbett, G. S.	22	Farrar, H. F.	2
Burton, R.	30	Courtenay, Lord	7	Fenton, —	4
Bushby, W.	37	Coventry, Hon. W. J.	39	Fenton, R.	41
Butler, J.	24	Cox, F. W.	22	Fenwick, H. W.	24
Byers, J. B.	28	Craig, F.	31	Field, C.	36
		Crawford, J. L.	1	Field, S.	27
Caddy, E. H.	8	Crawford, D.	30	Fielding, Viscount	36
Cadogan, B. H.	24	Crawford, J. H.	1	Findly, M.	17
Calvert, A. B.	1	Creswell, O. B.	24	Firth, J.	9
Campden, Viscount	19	Creyke, B.	41	Fisher, C. J.	16
Campbell, Sir A.	17	Crowe, W.	30	Fitzroy, F. H.	27
Campbell, G. J.	1	Croxon, J.	29	Fleming, H.	12
Campbell, G. J.	1	Cruso, J.	33	Fletcher, J.	18
Canterbury, Viscount	11	Cuningham, A.	1	Floyer, J.	9
Capel, A.	32	Cuningham, G. M.	1	Forester, Lord	30
Cartledge, B.	43	Cuninghame, T. S.	1	Foster, J.	42
Cathcart, Sir J.	1	Curling, W.	13	Foulie, J. O.	1
Cathcart, A.	1	Curtler, J.	39	Fowler, H.	42
Cavan, Earl of	13	Curwen, E. S.	37	Frampton, H.	9
Cavendish, W. W.	41	Curzon, Hon. H.	19	Francklin, W.	25
Cecil, Lord R.	14	Curzon, G. R.	25	Franklin, W.	37
Challinor, W.	33	Curzon, Hon. W.	19	Freer, C. T.	19
Chandos, Marquis of	2	Cusack, H. T.	8	Frentz, Baron	28
Channon, J.	32	Cuthbert, W.	24	Fulford, B.	7
Chapman, J.	16				
Charlton, T. B.	25	D'Arcy, J. P.	44	Gairdner, R.	1
Chawner, T.	33	Daniel, T.	7	Galton, D.	36
Chetwynd, G.	36	Darnley, Earl of	16	Galton, J. H.	39
Christie, J.	14	Deane, W. A.	8	Galton, T. H.	39
Churchill, G.	9	Deane, —.	4	Gardner, J.	38
Churchill, Lord	27	Denne, J.	2	Garrad, J.	2
Clarke, C.	44	Dent, J. D.	41	Garratt, J.	7
Clarke, F.	32	Digby, E.	9	Gaussen, F.	14
Clarkson, E. T.	38	Dixie, Sir W. W.	19	Gaussen, R. W.	14
Clayton, M.	24	Dixon, E.	39	George, W. H.	32
Clements, W.	19	Dixon, T.	40	Gerard, A.	17
Clinton, Lord	8	Dobson, J. S.	10	Gerard, F. S.	18
Clinton, Lord W. P.	26	Dodsworth, B.	41	Gerard, R. T.	18
Clive, R.	39	Douglas, Marquis of	17	Gillon, A.	21
Clive, Hon. R. H.	39	Douglas, J. L.	19	Gisborne, T. G.	33
Clode, J.	2	Downe, Viscount	41	Gist, W.	39
Clydesdale, Marquis of	17	Drake, J.	35	Gladdish, W.	16
Coafe, W. C.	2	Drake, C. C.	8	Glascow, R. M.	1
Cochrane, A.	21	Duckworth, Sir J. T.	7	Glubb, P.	8
Codrington, Sir W.	11	Dungannon, Viscount	29	Glyn, G. G.	9
Colisle, E. R.	6	Dungarvon, Viscount	31	Goddard, A. S.	38
Colston, W. W.	31			Goderich, Viscount	41
Colthorpe, J. G.	11	Eastmore, Lord	39	Goldsmid, T.	35
Compton, J. G.	6	Ebrington, Viscount	8	Goodden, J.	9
Connelly, J.	38	Edgeworth, T.	5	Gore, J. R.	30
Cooke, S. A.	42	Edwards, W.	44	Gore, M.	31
Cooke, T. A.	18	Edwards, J.	29	Gough, M.	19
Cooke, E. S.	42	Egerton, Sir P.	4	Grace, H. M.	11
Cooke, R.	42	Egerton, W. T.	4	Graham, F. J.	37
Cookes, J. H.	39	Egerton, Hon. A.	18	Granville, Earl of	33
Cookson, J.	24	Ellesmere, Earl of	18	Græme, W. T.	12
Cookson, I. T.	24	Elmsall, J. E.	42	Gray, S.	17
Cookson, C. E.	24	Evetts, W.	27	Gray, W.	18
Copeland, W. F.	33	Exton, T. C.	30	Gregg, —	4

z

INDEX.—YEOMANRY CAVALRY.

Name	Page	Name	Page	Name	Page
Grey, Earl De	41	Holford, R. S.	11	Lamb, Sir C.	1
Grey, Hon. W. G.	24	Holmes, T. R.	2	Langshaw, J.	18
Griffith, J. W.	33	Hooks, W.	9	Langton, W. H.	31
Grosvenor, Earl of	4	Hope, A.	21	Lawley, H. S.	29
Ground, D. B.	3	Hope, J.	21	Lawley, Hon. B. R.	41
Ground, G.	3	Hornden, W. D.	8	Lawly, Hon. F.	41
Guernsey, Lord	36	Horsfall, J. H.	44	Lawson, B. J.	24
Guppy, J.	7	Hoskyns, C. W.	34	Leach, J.	28
Gurnett, R.	33	Howe, Earl	19	Leach, H.	28
		Howitt, T.	18	Leach, E.	28
Hadden, J.	25	Huddlestone, P.	34	Lee, R.	41
Haigh, G.	44	Hughes, —	18	Lefevre, Hon. S.	12
Hale, R. B.	11	Humphries, T.	5	Legh, C. R.	4
Hales, J. M.	29	Hunt, R.	30	Leigh, —	4
Haliburton, A. F.	18	Hunt, W. Y.	39	Leigh, Hon. W. H.	36
Halford, H.	19	Hunter, J. W.	20	Levi, W.	2
Hall, J.	33	Hunter, R.	1	Lewis, R. E.	23
Halsey, T. P.	14	Hunter, H. L.	12	Ley, J. H.	7
Hamer, D.	23	Hurt, F.	6	Ley, J. P.	8
Hamer, J.	23	Hussey, J.	9	Ley, H.	8
Hamilton, A. E.	7	Hyde, F. C.	15	Leycester, —	4
Hamilton, J.	1			Lichfield, Earl of	33
Hamilton, W. F.	39	Ilchester, Earl of	9	Liddell, H. G.	24
Hamilton, W. F.	1	Innes, T. S.	20	Lishman, R. W.	33
Hammersley, H.	22	Innes, A. M.	20	Lloyd, C. S.	30
Hare, S.	21	Innes, G. M.	21	Lloyd, H. B.	30
Hardcastle, J.	26	Irving, G. V.	17	Lloyd, Sir H.	5
Harding, —	31			Lloyd, R.	5
Hardinge, Hon. C. S.	16	Jackson, F.	19	Lockhart, H.	17
Harper, G.	29	Jackson, J.	18	Lockhart, A. M.	17
Harris, Lord	15	Jacob, G. T.	9	Lockhart, R.	17
Harrison, A. R.	19	James, T.	24	Long, H.	38
Harrison, M. B.	37	Jamieson, J. C.	1	Long, R.	38
Harrison, W.	37	Jebb, C. N.	11	Loscombe, F. R.	12
Harrison, W. H.	41	Jeffcock, H.	41	Lowther, H.	37
Hartop, J.	42	Jeffcock, J.	42	Lowther, A.	37
Hartopp, E. B.	19	Jeffcock, E.	42	Lucas, S.	32
Harwood, J.	39	Jenkins, R. C.	11	Lumly, R. G.	42
Hasell, E. H.	37	Jessop, J.	10	Lye, B. L.	31
Harvey, R. B.	2	Johnson, R.	5	Lyon, —	4
Hawkins, C. S.	11	Johnson, J.	38		
Hawley, N. H.	12	Johnson, H. E.	40	M'Adam, W.	31
Hayward, W. C.	16	Jones, N.	5	Macartney, J. N.	8
Heartley, A.	15	Jubb, A.	44	Macauley, T.	19
Heath, H.	24			Macauley, C. C.	19
Heathcote, S. H.	13	Keck, G. A.	19	M'Call, —	17
Hemming, W. C.	39	Keene, P. K.	38	Machin, J. V.	26
Herbert, Hon. S.	38	Kekewich, T.	7	Mackinnon, W. A.	13
Heysett, L. R.	8	Kellie, J.	20	Maclaine, W. O.	11
Hickman, R.	39	Kemble, T.	14	M'Lean, J.	17
Highmore, W.	9	Kennedy, Lord F.	1	Madocks, J. E.	5
Hildyard, R.	25	Kennedy, Lord H.	1	Maher, M. C.	32
Hildyard, T. B.	25	Kenyon, Hon. T.	29	Maher, M. V.	32
Hill, Hon. Viscount	29	Kerrison, Sir E.	35	Maher, M. C.	32
Hill, Sir R.	29	Kerrison, E. C.	35	Maitland, Sir A.	21
Hill, G. S.	29	Kinchant, R.	29	Manley, A. E.	33
Hill, R. S.	12	Knatchbull, H. F.	31	Mansel, J. C.	9
Hillman, J.	40	Knight, F.	39	Mansel, G. P.	9
Hobson, E.	11	Kynaston, Sir J.	29	Marill, H.	31
Hodgson, J. S.	29			Marlborough, Duke of	27
Holden, R.	25	Lascelles, Viscount	41	Mansell, T.	28
Hole, A. R.	8	Lascelles, Hon. G. E.	41	Marshall, W. J.	34
Hole, J.	32	Lacy, J. P.	26	Marshall, H.	19

INDEX.—YEOMANRY CAVALRY.

Name	Page	Name	Page	Name	Page
Marshall, B. M.	8	Northey, N. F.	2	Ridgway, J.	18
Marsland, —	4	Nott, J.	8	Ridley, Sir M.	24
Martin, J. J.	39			Rivers, Lord	9
Martin, —	19	Oates, J. P.	33	Robarts, A. G.	2
Martin, J. H.	29	Ord, J. T.	35	Roberts, J.	5
Masefield, R.	29	Orkney, Earl of	3	Robertson, W.	33
Matcham, W. E.	38	Owen, B. H. B.	29	Robinson, W.	33
Maunsell, T. P.	24			Rocke, J.	30
Maunsell, H. T.	24	Packe, C. N.	19	Rode, De, W. H.	42
Maurice, R. M.	23	Paget, A.	31	Rogers, J. J.	7
Maycock, D.	8	Palin, —	4	Rollings, G.	30
Mellish, W. L.	26	Palmer, G.	10	Rose, J.	40
Merriman, W. C.	38	Palmer, G.	19	Rosser, T.	7
Merriman, A. C.	10	Papillon, P. O.	15	Rowland, N.	5
Merry, J.	17	Parker, Viscount	27	Royds, A. H.	18
Messiter, H.	31	Parker, J. S.	36	Royds, W. E.	18
Meux, Sir H.	14	Parker, R. J.	42	Rudge, E. C.	40
Meyer, J.	14	Parkes, N.	40	Rufford, F.	39
Michaelson, T. Y. P.	18	Parkyns, T. G.	25	Rufford, F. T.	39
Middleton, J.	17	Parry, G.	28	Russell, Hon. E. S.	19
Mildmay, Sir J.	12	Paul, N. M.	11		
Mildmay, E. S.	12	Paynter, J. N.	28	Salmond, J.	36
Mildmay, P. H. S.	31	Peel, R.	40	Sanders, E. A.	7
Miles, J. W.	31	Peel, E.	33	Sandford, T. H.	29
Miles, P. J.	31	Peel, F.	33	Sandilands, W.	20
Miles, W.	31	Peel, F. A.	33	Sanford, E. A.	32
Miles, P. W.	31	Peyton, N.	27	Sclater, G.	12
Milner, W. M. E.	41	Phelps, N. J.	11	Sanford, W. A.	32
Milner, B. W.	42	Phillips, J. S.	27	Scott, Sir F.	33
Milton, J.	40	Pierrepoint, Hon. S.	26	Scott, E. D.	33
Milton, Viscount	42	Pigott, F.	12	Seaham, Viscount	23
Milward, R.	25	Pinney, W.	32	Seymer, H. K.	9
Mogg, J. G.	31	Pirault, N. St. G.	8	Seymore, H. D.	38
Mogg, J. R.	31	Pole, E. S.	6	Shafto, J. A.	24
Moore, F. C.	32	Portal, M.	12	Shape, J.	43
Monckton, Hon. E.	42	Pollard, G.	44	Shelburne, Earl of	38
Monteith, R.	17	Pollard, G. T.	44	Sheldon, H. J.	36
Montgomery, Sir G.	21	Popham, A. N.	2	Sherbrook, H.	25
Montgomery, H.	27	Portal, N.	12	Sherwin, J. S.	25
Morley, J.	25	Potts, —	4	Shirley, J.	29
Morris, E.	2	Powis, Earl of	30	Short, F. B.	7
Morrison, A.	38	Pownall, —	4	Short, W.	41
Morritt, W. S.	41	Powys, Hon. H.	30	Sicard, A.	15
Moubray, J.	21	Preedy, R.	40	Skey, A.	39
Mulcaster, F. M.	15	Preston, T. H.	41	Skey, J.	40
Musgrave, Sir G.	37	Preston, C.	42	Slade, F. W.	32
Mynors, R.	40	Pudsey, J.	33	Slade, W.	32
Mytton, J. F.	29			Sleddale, W.	36
		Ramsay, W. R.	21	Sleigh, B. W. A.	22
Naish, N. B.	31	Ramsay, P.	21	Smith, A.	42
Nash, H. F.	2	Ramsay, R.	21	Smith, B.	31
Napier, E. B.	31	Randolph, J.	32	Smith, C.	3
Naylor, W. B.	42	Rawson, G.	26	Smith, F.	39
Nelson, N. E.	38	Rees, S.	28	Smith, H.	2
Nevill, C. G.	19	Rees, G. R.	37	Smith, J.	39
Neville, Viscount	16	Rees, B. E.	37	Smith, J. B.	7
Neville, R.	32	Renton, J. C.	20	Smith, R.	40
Newbould, H. J.	42	Reynard, E. H.	41	Smith, T. A.	12
Newdegate, C. N.	22	Reynard, C.	41	Smith, T. R.	16
Nicholl, —	4	Reynolds, J.	32	Smith, W. S.	41
Nicholson, —	4	Richards, T.	24	Smyth, J. G.	41
Nicolls, R.	29	Richmond, —	4	Smythies, C.	35
Northcote, S. H.	7	Ricketts, W. H.	40	Sneyd, J. W.	33

INDEX.—YEOMANRY CAVALRY.

Name	Page	Name	Page	Name	Page
Snow, T.	7	Taylor, T.	42	Weatherhead, S.	6
Snow, T. M.	7	Taylor, W. F.	39	Webster, C. F.	31
Snow, W. M.	7	Temple, R.	39	Webster, B.	33
Soden, J.	31	Tennant, C.	17	Wellfitt, W. S.	26
Spencer, Hon. H.	27	Thexton, J. Y.	36	Wells, T.	2
Spencer, H.	36	Thomas, W. L.	14	Welman, C. N.	32
Spettegue, J.	7	Thornton, G. S.	14	Wheler, Sir T.	8
Square, H. B.	43	Thring, T.	32	White, Sir T.	26
Standish, L. C.	18	Tindal, A.	2	Whitmore, T. C.	30
Stanhope, W. T.	42	Tomlinson, F.	33	Whitmore, W.	30
Stanley, C.	42	Townshend, —.	4	Wickham, J. C.	11
Stanton, G.	29	Tredway, R. C.	31	Wickham, —.	37
Sterling, W.	17	Trevor, W.	32	Willes, G.	2
Stevens, J. C.	8	Trotter, R.	21	Williams, J.	12
Stevenson, J. W.	7	Trower, H. S.	2	Williams, R. L.	5
Stone, E. G.	39	Turk, C.	40	Williams, T. P.	2
Stone, W. W.	2	Turner, C. C.	8	Williams, W.	9
Story, J. B.	19	Tynte, C. K.	32	Willoughby, H.	41
Story, W.	6			Wilmot, F. S.	6
Stratford, J.	16	Upton, T. E.	41	Wilmot, W.	36
Stratton, J.	27			Wilson, F. M.	34
Studholme, J.	36	Vandeleur, G.	6	Wilson, G. E.	37
Surtees, R. L.	24	Vaughan, H.	11	Wilson, H. J.	36
Sutton, C.	25	Vernon, G. G.	26	Wise, M.	36
Sutton, J. H.	26	Verulam, Earl	14	Wise, W. C.	36
Sutton, R.	25	Vickerman, C. R.	10	Withers, H.	11
Swete, H. B.	7	Villiers, Viscount	27	Wolcott, J. M.	7
Sydney, Viscount	16			Wood, F.	41
		Wade, G. D.	13	Woodhouse, M.	25
Tabley, Lord de	4	Walford, R. C.	2	Worthington, —	4
Tailby, W. W.	19	Walker, W. S.	21	Wright, E.	27
Talbot, Hon. G.	33	Walsh, W. E.	40	Wright, J. F.	42
Tamberlain, C. L.	23	Ward, T.	38	Wrightson, R. H.	42
Tardrew, W.	8	Warner, P.	1	Wyndham, W.	38
Tatton,—.	4	Warrington, Earl	4	Wynn, Sir W.	23
Tawmy, A. R.	27	Waterhouse, S.	44	Wynn, C. W.	23
Taylor, E.	43	Watson, W. C.	39		
Taylor, E. C.	41	Watts, W.	7	Yeatman, H. F.	9
Taylor, J.	39	Watts, W.	25		
Taylor, J. A.	39	Wauchope, A.	21	Zoomes, E.	3
Taylor, J. W.	38	Wauchope, J.	21		

INDEX.

OFFICERS OF THE MILITIA.

Name	Page	Name	Page	Name	Page
Abbott, W.	135	Arkenstall, W.	94	Barker, W. F.	118
Abbott, T.	90	Arkman, H. R.	111	Barker, W.	88
Ablott, C. A.	79	Armstrong, W. H.	120	Barle, J. V.	125
Acton, W.	129	Armstrong, J. H.	85	Barlow, R.	153
Acton, E. F.	94	Arnold, H.	78	Barnes, M.	54
Acton, E.	92	Arter, W.	57	Barnett, J.	45
Adams, R.	155	Aspinal, R. A. A.	152	Barnewall, T.	122
Adams, S.	103	Astell, J. H.	60	Barret, S.	162
Adcock, W. R.	89	Astle, E.	103	Barrett, S.	123
Adney, H.	58	Atherly, J.	57	Barrington, W.	161
Ainsworth, B.	48	Atkins, R.	155	Barry, R.	130
Alavoine, C.	97	Atkinson, C.	63	Barry, S.	158
Alcock, —	166	Atkinson, A.	69	Barter, W.	149
Alcock, J. St. Leger	102	Atkinson, R.	160	Barter, T.	149
Alderman, A.	103	Atkinson, W. G.	122	Barth, J.	98
Alderson, R.	63	Atkinson, B.	147	Bartlett, J.	80
Aldwell, T. B.	121	Atkinson, D.	147	Barton, E.	108
Aldworth, R.	155	Austen, H. E.	52	Barston, J.	63
Alexander, N.	116	Austen, W.	85	Bass, E.	149
Alexander, J.	132	Austin, H.	65	Bass, J.	149
Alford, Viscount	51	Austin, T. W.	97	Bateman, J.	146
Allen, G.	47	Austin, H.	97	Bateman, N.	100
Allen, J.	48	Austin, G.	106	Bateman, —	81
Allen, C.	64	Austin, W. F.	124	Bates, G.	53
Allen, W.	79	Aylmer, Sir G. G.	125	Bates, R. M.	76
Allen, T.	145	Aylmer, M.	165	Bates, N. W.	93
Allen, J. H.	145	Ayre, G.	64	Bates, C. C.	93
Alston, F. B.	72	Ayrton, W.	152	Bateson, S.	132
Amy, J. R. J.	143			Batten, H. B.	58
Anders, J.	98	Bagot, E. R.	95	Battersby, C.	158
Anderson, P.	165	Bagot, T. C.	125	Bayce, N.	94
Anderson, A.	156	Baillie, A. H.	110	Bayle, B.	120
Anderson, W.	93	Baillie, J.	151	Bayly, C. O.	95
Andrew, H. P.	80	Baily, J. A.	134	Bayly, L.	121
Andrews, A.	71	Bailz, C. C.	105	Bayly, G. A.	129
Anketell, R. W.	160	Bainbridge, J.	45	Bayne, J.	113
Anketell, J.	160	Baines, C. A.	48	Beach, Sir M. H.	106
Anketell, R. C.	117	Baird, A.	164	Beachamp, T. T.	80
Annesly, R.	155	Baird, T. E.	123	Beadon, J. H.	58
Annesly, R. J.	130	Baird, V. C.	115	Beare, R.	149
Annesly, J.	148	Baker, T. H.	135	Beath, J.	115
Annesly, M. J.	151	Baker, T. E.	81	Beatty, D.	136
Ansley, A. F. G.	149	Balfour, J.	115	Beatty, J. T.	136
Anstruther, Sir W.	111	Balgrave, J.	50	Beatty, W.	125
Anstruther, W. C. J.	111	Bannister, N.	78	Beauchamp, C.	105
Anthony, P.	166	Barington, Hon. B.	52	Beauman, E.	125
Anwyl, W.	99	Barker, E.	99	Beaumont, F.	47
Arden, W.	78	Barker, J. P.	112	Beaumont, J.	52

	Page		Page		Page
Beaumont, M. T.	64	Blagrave, E.	50	Brinly, J.	101
Beavan, J. G.	92	Blair, D.	109	Briscoe, E.	165
Beckford, W.	62	Blair, D.	123	Briscoe, E.	166
Beckham, H.	75	Blair, P.	154	Brock, A.	122
Bective, Earl of	158	Blake, J.	135	Brock, T. C.	104
Bedingfield, C.	81	Blake, S.	128	Brockman, J.	80
Beer, J.	67	Blakely, M.	160	Brogdon, N.	121
Belfast, Earl of	116	Bland, J.	126	Bromby, F.	48
Belhaven, Lord	111	Bland, F. W.	63	Bromehead, W. B.	102
Bell, A.	165	Blatch, J.	54	Brook, T.	52
Bell, W.	165	Blayney, R.	104	Brook, F. W.	52
Bell, J. S.	55	Blennerhasset, G.	161	Brooke, M.	100
Bell, J.	55	Blennerhasset, J.	161	Brooke, M.	61
Bell, J.	56	Bliss, H.	97	Brookes, N. P.	65
Bell, J.	59	Blois, C.	75	Broune, W. K.	59
Bell, J.	59	Blundell, N.	152	Brown, W.	91
Bellew, Lord	147	Boardman, E.	81	Brown, A.	114
Bellew, Hon. E.	147	Bodhill, J.	98	Brown, B.	128
Belram, J.	154	Bolton, C.	166	Brown, D.	119
Bence, N. B.	75	Bonar, W. G.	115	Brown, J. W.	122
Benison, T.	139	Bond, —.	110	Brown, N.	135
Bennet, L.	111	Booky, J.	97	Brown, R.	136
Bennet, W.	100	Booth, R. B.	64	Brown, T.	143
Bennett, R. G.	80	Booth, W.	103	Brown, J.	143
Bennett, J.	84	Borlase, S.	80	Brown, J.	156
Bennett, W.	92	Borough, Sir E.	137	Brown, V.	146
Benson, W.	139	Borrer, J. H.	93	Brown, C.	96
Bentinck, G. A.	59	Boulby, J. R.	47	Brown, W.	164
Berford, R.	134	Boultbee, J. M.	78	Brown, J.	51
Berham, R.	81	Bourke, G. W.	125	Brown, H.	71
Berkley, J.	145	Bourne, J.	152	Brown, J.	76
Bernard, Hon. H.	155	Bourne, J. T.	152	Browne, H.	161
Bernard, Lord	149	Bourne, R. E.	137	Browne, Hon. T.	146
Bernard, R. W.	135	Bourrien, J.	117	Browne, T. C.	46
Bernerd, C.	104	Bouthron, W.	115	Browne, B. P.	81
Berrington, J.	92	Bouverie, Hon. E.	50	Brownlow, Earl of	71
Berry, J. R.	153	Bower, J.	63	Bruce, C. L.	113
Bethel, W. F.	55	Bowes, J.	47	Bruce, G. R.	124
Bethune, A.	115	Bowles, G.	124	Bruce, S.	132
Beverly, Earl of	69	Bowles, W.	124	Bruen, —	107
Biddle, W. A.	83	Bowles, C. O.	91	Brune, C. G.	80
Biddulph, R.	49	Bowman, F.	71	Bryan, J. W.	67
Biddulph, T. W.	78	Boyce, T.	94	Buccleuch, Duke of	164
Biddulph, R. M.	87	Boyle, J.	138	Buchanan, W. B.	135
Bignell, J.	57	Brabazon, W. P.	147	Buckle, J. T.	55
Bigsby, R.	98	Brabazon, Viscount	148	Budd, R.	57
Bigsby, R. H.	98	Bradfield, H.	97	Budgen, T.	62
Bingham, D.	159	Bradley, H.	139	Bulkely, Sir R.	99
Birch, C.	151	Bradley, O.	59	Bull, W. N.	103
Bird, G.	164	Brady, J. C.	107	Buller, Sir J.	67
Bird, N.	61	Brailford, S.	71	Buller, J. B.	67
Bird, J.	85	Brailsford, R.	95	Bullmore, W. H.	157
Bisdee, R. B.	88	Brander, N. A.	56	Bullock, H.	61
Bishop, N.	107	Brandling, C. T.	63	Bulteel, J.	67
Bishop, J. D.	58	Brash, J.	120	Bulwer, W. E. J.	81
Bisset, D. W.	123	Bray, E.	62	Bunbury, B.	121
Black, A.	127	Brennan, M.	165	Bunbury, J. H.	147
Black, R. H.	53	Brett, C.	84	Bunbury, T.	107
Blacker, W.	112	Brew, C.	97	Bund, T. H.	104
Blacker, W. J.	136	Brew, W.	97	Bunny, J.	103
Blackford, W.	129	Brewster, D.	144	Burchell, F.	97
Blackwood, P.	114	Brewster, C.	56	Burdon, C.	63
Blackwall, S. W.	122	Bridger, J.	76	Burgess, J.	120

	Page		Page		Page
Burgh, De F.	135	Carington, Lord	76	Christie, J.	115
Burgh, De J.	97	Carleton, H.	114	Churchill, H.	82
Burghley, Lord	89	Carlton, G.	139	Chute, F.	146
Burkett, A. W.	106	Carnaby, G.	102	Chute, R.	146
Burnett, M.	148	Carne, J.	67	Clare, J.	158
Burrowes, J.	162	Carpenter, A.	125	Claridge, R.	95
Burnet, G.	109	Carr, G.	93	Clarina, Lord	161
Burton, G.	107	Carrick, T. M.	102	Clark, W. S.	71
Burton, S. S.	104	Carroll, R.	63	Clark, R.	89
Burton, T.	131	Carroll, —	166	Clark, J.	76
Butcher, J.	61	Carrothers, C.	116	Clark, J.	127
Butler, A.	131	Carson, R.	118	Clarke, H. C.	57
Butler, Hon. St. J.	137	Carter, D.	53	Clarke, I.	81
Butler, Hon. J.	148	Carter, J.	64	Clarke, E.	82
Butler, Hon. D.	95	Carthew, E.	80	Clarke, W.	107
Butler, J. A.	121	Carthy, R.	122	Clarke, H.	133
Butler, J.	107	Castlereagh, Viscount	114	Clarke, J.	139
Butler, P.	165	Caulfield, J.	130	Clarke, W.	142
Butler, R.	120	Caulfield, H.	112	Clarke, C.	45
Butler, W.	165	Caulfield, J.	117	Clancarty, Earl of	128
Butler, W. P.	107	Cavendish, W.	76	Clanricarde, Marquis	128
Butler, W.	70	Chadwick, W. B.	54	Clifton, G.	104
Butter, J.	67	Chadwick, R. W.	54	Clayton, E.	86
Button, T.	61	Chadwick, J. M.	94	Clayton, W.	97
Byers, J.	117	Chadwick, J.	157	Clayton, R. B.	152
Byng, Hon. G.	97	Chaigneau, A.	153	Clementi, J.	163
Byrne, R.	107	Chamberlain, W.	106	Clementi, J.	152
Bythesea, H. F.	74	Chamberlaine, C.	92	Clements, Hon. C.	139
		Chamberlayne, E.	79	Clements, Lord	150
Caddell, B.	158	Chalmers, M.	55	Clements, Hon. T.	150
Cairey, J.	129	Chalmers, W.	45	Clendining, G.	119
Caldwell, J.	167	Chalmers, T.	120	Cleveland, Duke	47
Caledon, Earl of	117	Chambers, F.	103	Clifden, Viscount	165
Calmady, V.	67	Chambers, S.	53	Cliffe, A.	136
Calmeley, H.	49	Chambers, B.	165	Clifton, J.	50
Calthorpe, G.	81	Chambers, D.	139	Close, J.	52
Calvert, C.	98	Chambers, J.	139	Clowes, T.	104
Call, W.	80	Chambers, N.	45	Clutton, T.	49
Callanan, E.	88	Chapman, G.	85	Clydesdale, Marquis	111
Callander, J.	127	Chapman, W.	76	Coats, C.	129
Calley, T.	56	Charleton, R.	69	Cobbold, B.	75
Camel, F.	66	Charleton, C.	69	Cochraine, W.	138
Cameron, D.	167	Charleville, Earl of	135	Cochrane, W.	111
Cameron, G.	126	Charleton, J.	158	Cock, T.	62
Cameron, J.	113	Charms, D. de	88	Cocking, J.	102
Campbell, A.	167	Charteris, C.	118	Coe, E.	97
Campbell, W.	105	Chayton, J.	121	Coggin, P.	124
Campbell, C.	156	Chelsea, Viscount	95	Coghlan, J.	155
Campbell, Sir A.	156	Chelwood, J.	49	Coke, T.	100
Campbell, C.	156	Chennell, T.	51	Cole, G.	105
Campbell, M.	156	Cheslyn, R.	68	Cole, H.	93
Campbell, D.	156	Childs, G.	145	Cole, E.	102
Campbell, J.	156	Cholmey, G.	45	Cole, Hon. H.	108
Campbell, J.	127	Cholmondeley, Hon. H.	49	Coles, W.	50
Campbell, J.	154	Chichester, Hon. F.	93	Coleman, J.	145
Candler, W.	165	Child, J. M.	70	Collet, A.	75
Cantelupe, Viscount	97	Child, R.	70	Colling, R.	64
Cannon, R.	164	Chiver, G.	48	Collins, J.	98
Carew, Hon. R.	136	Chivers, C.	58	Collis, W.	146
Carew, W.	80	Chivers, W.	88	Collis, M.	146
Carey, C. H.	86	Chorley, W.	58	Collis, W.	128
Carey, O.	107	Christie, W.	89	Colthurst, C.	143
Carington, W.	76	Christie, J.	127	Connellan, E.	58

INDEX.—MILITIA.

Name	Page	Name	Page	Name	Page
Conyers, H. H.	56	Crowe, C.	160	Dayly, P.	128
Conyngham, Marquis	131	Crozier, F.	95	Deane, A.	50
Conyngham, W. F.	132	Crozier, A.	114	Deans, J.	145
Cook, W.	58	Cruikshank, W.	144	Decies, Lord De	166
Cooke, G. E.	95	Cruise, P.	158	Delaes, J.	62
Cooke, C. M.	68	Cuddy, S.	149	Dennis, J.	93
Cooke, W.	142	Cuffley, J. R.	53	Dennis, P.	69
Cookman, C.	136	Cumberlege, N.	102	Denniston, J.	109
Coone, J.	124	Cuming, G.	91	Dent, J.	104
Coone, J. N.	124	Cumming, F.	90	Denton, H.	52
Cooper, W.	139	Cumming, A.	90	Dering, C.	90
Cooper, H.	107	Cumming, G.	130	Despard, W.	142
Cooper, W.	60	Cunningham, W.	167	Dewes, E.	102
Cooper, G. G.	98	Cunningham, Sir J.	154	Dick, J.	125
Cooper, J.	113	Cunningham, R.	129	Dick, J.	139
Coote, Sir C.	142	Cunningham, R.	110	Dick, Q.	61
Coote, T.	160	Curl, G.	118	Dick, W.	167
Cope, E.	103	Currey, —	166	Dickenson, C.	78
Corbally, M.	158	Curtis, H. C.	120	Dickenson, J.	120
Corbett, H.	95			Dickinson, D.	73
Corker, F.	149	Dacie, G.	82	Dickson, A.	144
Cornewall, Sir V.	92	Daintree, J.	105	Dillon, A.	158
Cornish, R.	82	Dakins, H.	75	Dillon, H.	165
Correy, J.	130	Dale, E.	69	Dillon, T.	119
Corrigan, W.	55	Dalhousie, Marquis	134	Dinorben, Lord	99
Corry, W.	160	Dalison, M.	79	Diven, E.	96
Corry, W.	108	Daly, S.	107	Dixon, F.	100
Corry, J.	114	Daly, Hon. S.	131	Dixon, R.	111
Cosby, E.	138	Dallinger, R.	145	Dixon, T. S.	105
Coulson, E.	55	Dampier, S.	58	Dodds, J.	110
Coulson, J.	69	Daniell, H.	121	Dodds, P.	118
Coulston, R.	116	Daniell, J.	62	Dolton, T.	47
Coupland, E.	55	Daniell, J.	65	Donaldson, J.	127
Coupland, E.	55	Dansey, G.	79	Donaldson, R.	109
Couly, W.	142	D'Arcy, Duke of Leeds	64	Donegal, Marquis	116
Courteney, F. F.	134			Donelan, S.	45
Courtney, E. H.	104	Darley, H. F.	137	Doneraile, Viscount	124
Coveny, J.	79	Darley, W.	135	Dopping, J.	122
Cowell, L.	120	Darnell, R.	48	Dormer, E.	93
Cox, T.	135	Darrien, C.	93	Dorset, T.	94
Cox, J.	110	Dartmouth, Earl of	103	Douglas, W.	127
Cox, S.	83	Daunt, A.	121	Drought, J.	135
Cox, T.	100	Davenport, E.	70	Drought, J. A.	135
Coyney, C.	103	Davidson, F.	110	Dowdall, G.	161
Cracroft, N.	51	Davidson, W.	125	Dowling, W.!	135
Craig, J.	114	Davies, D.	66	Downshire, Marquis	151
Cranly, Viscount	54	Davies, G.	73	Doyne, B.	107
Crawford, T.	167	Davies, J.	128	Drax, J. S.	90
Crawford, S.	122	Davies, W. C.	152	Draycott, G.	105
Crean, F.	119	Davies, J.	72	Duckworth, Sir J.	67
Creaser, T.	102	Davinson, W.	89	Duckworth, W.	130
Creed, G.	53	Davis, G.	72	Dudgeon, W.	130
Cressall, G.	145	Davis, S.	103	Duff, S.	148
Crichton, Hon. H.	108	Davis, J.	83	Duff, W.	113
Crichton, J.	154	Davis, T.	71	Duguid, W.	125
Crichton, R.	154	Davis, W.	91	Duke, W. A.	148
Cripps, R.	93	Dawbin, W.	87	Duke, J.	150
Croker, S.	146	Daws, J.	54	Dumayne, T.	70
Crompton, J.	63	Dawson, C. E.	55	Dunbar, Hon. R.	133
Cronin, J.	150	Dawson, W.	112	Duncan, A.	115
Cross, W.	86	Day, E.	58	Duncombe, P.	89
Crosse, R. F.	104	Day, E.	97	Dundas, C.	73
Croughton, W.	79	Daykin, W.	96	Dunne, F.	142

INDEX.—MILITIA. 177

Name	Page	Name	Page	Name	Page
Dunne, R.	114	Farrant, F.	82	Fotheringham, A.	111
Dunscomb, J.	149	Farrell, J.	158	Foulks, A.	79
Durham, J.	116	Farrer, W.	141	Fowke, F.	68
Durham, P. F.	48	Farrill, J.	166	Fowler, H. M.	133
Durrell, F.	54	Faucett, T.	79	Fox, F.	102
Dyson, J.	63	Faulkner, G.	137	Foy, H. G.	58
Dyson, J.	48	Faussett, R.	108	Frampton, J.	69
		Feally, J.	67	Franklin, J.	98
Eames, M.	119	Fearns, J.	122	Fraser, C.	133
Earle, T.	65	Feddis, J.	160	Fraser, C.	94
Eaton, G.	105	Feilden, H.	86	Fraser, C.	126
Eaton, J.	58	Ferguson, G.	116	Fraser, J.	127
Eaton, R.	105	Ferguson, H. B.	116	Frazer, Sir W.	129
Ebowern, J.	115	Ferguson, J.	126	Frederick, Sir R.	54
Echlin, G.	151	Ferguson, J.	132	Fredericks, F.	85
Ede, D.	56	Ferguson, Sir R.	132	Freeman, J.	124
Eden, Sir W.	47	Ferrers, M. E.	78	Freeman, T.	155
Edgyear, R.	157	Fetherstone, Sir G.	122	French, C.	130
Edinborough, H.	61	Ffolliott, J.	162	French, G.	130
Edward, E.	99	Ffoulkes, J.	87	French, S.	124
Edwardes, H. D.	138	Ffrance, R.	86	French, W.	130
Edwardes, J.	67	Field, P.	161	French, W.	155
Egan, J.	128	Fielden, M.	163	Friend, C.	62
Eley, J.	79	Finucane, M.	131	Friend, J.	62
Ellison, R.	51	Fisk, W.	67	Frith, B. G.	108
Ellicombe, C. R.	82	Fitkin, R.	106	Frizell, C.	129
Elliott, C.	121	Fitzgerald, G.	58	Fry, H.	130
Elliott, H.	78	Fitzgerald, G.	166	Fullarton, G.	109
Elliott, J. F.	138	Fitzgerald, P.	166	Fullarton, W.	154
Ellis, F.	138	Fitzgerald, R.	131	Fuller, C.	88
Elly, J.	142	Fitzgerald, R.	162	Fulton, T.	112
Elton, Sir E.	82	Fitzgerald, P.	146	Fursdon, G.	82
Elton, R.	58	Fitzgerald, T.	85	Fyfe, W.	143
Elton, R.	65	Fitzgibbon, G.	161		
Emery, J.	100	Fitzgibbon, Hon. R.	161	Gaisford, T.	74
Emery, C.	83	Fitzhardinge, Earl	65	Galindo, P.	104
Emery, G.	83	Fitzherbert, J.	103	Galindo, S.	104
Enfield, Viscount	97	Fitzhugh, T.	87	Gall, J.	49
Enniskillen, Earl	108	Fitzmarice, J.	146	Gamber, C. M.	92
Errington, J. E.	49	Fitzroy, G.	76	Gambier, M.	102
Erskine, H.	68	Fitzwilliams, J.	54	Gandon, J.	148
Erskine, H.	126	Flanagan, J.	130	Gant, J.	134
Erskine, Sir T.	87	Flemming, J.	126	Garden, A.	54
Eustace, H.	56	Flemming, T.	84	Gardener, N.	163
Eustace, H. F.	81	Fletcher, D.	123	Gardiner, J.	123
Evans, C.	79	Fletcher, J.	164	Gardiner, S.	91
Evans, D.	92	Foaker, L.	61	Garmston, J.	104
Evans, H.	96	Forbes, J.	126	Garnett, N.	163
Evans, J.	128	Ford, W.	151	Garrett, C. H.	96
Evans, L.	66	Ford, J. H.	152	Gascoyne, H.	128
Evans, P.	101	Forde, F.	114	Gason, R.	121
Evelegh, J.	97	Forde, M.	114	Gatehouse, J.	58
Eveleigh, E.	80	Forster, E.	78	Gates, G.	89
Evered, J. G.	88	Forster, J.	97	Gath, T.	149
Eyre, J.	128	Forster, J.	147	Gatune, E.	94
		Fortescue, Earl	82	Gayfer, W.	105
Fair, J.	118	Fortescue, Hon. J.	82	Gazely, E.	61
Fairfield, G.	146	Fortescue, G.	57	Gemmell, W.	154
Fairless, E.	47	Fortescue, J.	67	Gemmell, W. C.	154
Fairman, S.	72	Forth, F.	93	German, J.	163
Falls, R.	117	Fosberry, R.	161	Gem, J.	78
Fane, J.	91	Foster, G.	146	Gerrard, Sir J.	163
Faris, G.	150	Foster, J.	75	Gibbons, Sir J.	97

A A

INDEX.—MILITIA.

Name	Page	Name	Page	Name	Page
Gibbons, J.	123	Green, J.	46	Handcock, Hon. —	153
Giffard, T.	103	Green, J.	103	Handcock, Hon. G.	116
Gilchrist, D.	133	Green, T.	47	Hannah, G.	115
Giles, H.	104	Greenall, E.	163	Hannah, D.	109
Gilfillan, J.	118	Greene, P.	153	Hannay, R.	109
Gillanders, J.	133	Greenhead, C.	50	Hansler, R.	56
Gillard, N.	67	Greenway, C.	78	Hardwick, T.	94
Gillett, J.	134	Greenway, H.	50	Hardy, J.	63
Gillmor, C.	162	Greer, J.	117	Hardyman, J.	164
Gilpin, R.	60	Greer, T.	117	Harford, H.	65
Glengall, Earl	121	Gregg, J.	124	Harland, J.	76
Glentworth, Viscount	120	Gregg, T.	151	Harland, W.	64
Glin, Knight of	161	Gregory, W.	128	Harman, Hon. L.	130
Glossop, J.	95	Greig, J.	126	Harper, W.	81
Goddard, H.	74	Grenfell, C.	97	Harraden, E.	52
Godolphin, Lord	105	Grey, G.	50	Harris, W.	85
Godsell, S.	124	Grey, T.	47	Harris, H.	112
Goldfinch, H.	85	Grierson, W.	118	Harris, J.	102
Goldie, R.	113	Grieve, J.	118	Harris, J.	82
Goldney, A.	65	Griffin, E.	89	Harrison, E.	150
Goldsmid, A.	62	Griffith, T.	73	Harrison, E. S.	49
Gollop, J.	83	Griffiths, W.	97	Harrison, J.	68
Golly, W.	111	Grillett, R.	64	Harrison, J.	45
Goodall, N.	129	Grimston, C.	55	Harrison, S. S.	128
Gorden, R.	114	Grimston, M. J.	55	Harrison, T.	57
Gordon, A.	143	Grogan, E.	129	Hart, J.	122
Gordon, G.	126	Grogan, W.	129	Hart, R.	57
Gordon, J.	126	Groome, F.	128	Hartnoll, H.	82
Gordon, T.	113	Groton, C.	75	Harwood, E.	68
Gordon, T.	126	Grove, C.	77	Hassard, F.	108
Gore, A.	162	Grove, H. T.	74	Haselfoot, C.	61
Gore, C.	131	Grove, J.	76	Hatch, J.	54
Gore, M.	74	Grove, W. C.	74	Hatchard, F.	76
Gore, Hon. W.	102	Grunley, J.	138	Hatton, H.	136
Gort, Lord	141	Gunthorp, J.	47	Haverkam, W.	49
Gosford, Earl of	112	Gwynne, J. B.	66	Hawes, H. S.	71
Gosselin, R.	138	Gwynne, S.	66	Hawker, H.	68
Gould, G.	74	Gwynne, T. G.	66	Hawker, P.	56
Gould, T.	83			Hawkes, J.	136
Gower, J.	50	Haggard, J.	95	Hawkins, B.	50
Graham, C.	115	Haig, N.	103	Hawkins, C. S.	104
Graham, C.	164	Hall, W. T.	145	Hawkins, J.	92
Graham, J.	115	Hall, L.	130	Hay, G. J.	109
Graham, R.	123	Hall, T. D.	98	Hay, W.	110
Granby, Marquis of	68	Halfpenny, J.	150	Hay, J.	143
Grant, A.	113	Hallen, J.	48	Hayes, B.	166
Grant, A.	164	Halpin, C.	138	Haythorne, J.	106
Grant, Hon. J.	113	Halsall, R. J.	152	Hazlewood, H.	122
Grant, J.	152	Hames, W.	106	Headfort, Marquis	158
Grant, J.	135	Hamilton, Lord	117	Healey, G.	64
Grant, W.	113	Hamilton, C.	153	Heath, T.	145
Grantham, —	71	Hamilton, Sir G.	110	Heathcote, J.	94
Graves, A.	63	Hamilton, H. C.	111	Heard, R.	124
Graves, A.	148	Hamilton, D.	111	Heard, F.	124
Graves, J.	136	Hamilton, F.	103	Helsham, A.	165
Graves, S.	132	Hamlon, J.	147	Helsham, G.	165
Graves, W.	132	Hamlyn, S.	82	Helsham, W.	165
Graves, W.	166	Hammond, H.	78	Heron, A.	148
Gray, J.	136	Hammond, J.	49	Hesketh, W.	163
Gray, T.	99	Hammond, W.	105	Hesketh, Sir F.	152
Gray, N.	129	Hamner, A.	51	Hey, P.	161
Graydon, A.	51	Hamson, E.	72	Hemming, W.	83
Green, E. H.	105	Hancock, W.	73	Hemsworth, C.	141

Name	Page	Name	Page	Name	Page
Henderson, J.	132	Homer, C.	88	Irvine, H.	108
Hendrick, H.	114	Hood, G.	110	Irvine, J.	117
Henery, W.	114	Hood, J.	154	Irvine, J. G.	108
Herbert, J.	48	Hooper, T.	74	Irvine, H. C.	86
Hetherington, H.	108	Hooper, W.	78	Irving, G. A.	111
Hett, W. W.	71	Hope, A.	164	Irwin, A.	61
Hevie, W.	167	Hopkins, E.	106	Irwin, H. K.	130
Hewett, L.	130	Hopkinson, F.	71	Irwin, R.	125
Hewitson, D. B.	151	Hopton, J.	106	Irwin, W.	117
Hewitson, J.	165	Horan, W.	137	Isaacs, R. T.	151
Hewitt, C.	97	Hornby, D.	163	Isaacson, W.	46
Hewitt, T.	131	Horne, C.	102	Isdale, J.	123
Hewitt, J.	85	Horne, W.	110		
Hewitt, T.	149	Horne, J.	145	Jack, J.	144
Hewitt, J. G.	98	Hornidge, G.	129	Jackson, J.	103
Hewitt, R. T.	98	Hornsby, A. F.	106	Jackson, J.	52
Hewson, C.	136	Horton, G.	66	Jackson, R.	64
Hickland, W.	114	Horton, J.	99	Jackson, R. W.	47
Hickman, P.	149	Houlton, C.	45	Jacob, G.	83
Hicks, R.	145	Howard, Sir R.	129	Jacobs, R.	100
Hicks, G.	80	Howard, T.	55	James, E.	72
Higginbotham, R.	125	Howe, G. H.	114	James, G.	70
Higgins, F.	119	Howe, W.	114	James, T.	101
Higgins, C. F.	119	Howell, T.	157	Jameson, R.	52
Higgins, O.	119	Howett, W.	86	Jeffries, H.	104
Higgins, A. B.	143	Hovenden, T.	142	Jenkins, J.	75
Higgins, W.	60	Huband, A.	155	Jenkins, J.	103
Higgon, J.	70	Hubbard, J.	120	Jenner, M.	79
Hilcoat, A.	103	Hudson, J.	120	Jenner, R.	65
Hill, Lord	151	Hueston, J. S.	112	Jermyn, Earl of	53
Hilliard	161	Hughes, J.	87	Jervis, T.	141
Hilliard, W.	161	Hughes, M.	163	Jervis, W.	62
Hilliard, B.	146	Hugo, C.	58	Jesse, R.	58
Hinde, E.	79	Hull, R.	143	Johns, R.	80
Hinde, J.	102	Hulse, E.	84	Johns, R. P.	80
Hinton, Viscount	58	Hulton, W.	163	Johnson, H.	79
Hetherington, R.	88	Humble, G.	61	Johnson, M.	71
Hoare, E.	155	Hume, J.	110	Johnson, R.	152
Hobhouse, E.	65	Humphries, H. G.	52	Johnson, S.	125
Hobhouse, Sir J.	74	Humphries, I.	148	Johnson, W.	56
Hodder, W.	155	Hunt, J.	161	Johnston, H. J.	114
Hodges, T.	102	Hunter, Sir C.	145	Johnston, J.	114
Hodges, G.	131	Hunter, C.	145	Johnstone, Hon. H.	118
Hodges, E.	102	Hunter, H.	100	Johnstone, G.	97
Hodges, T.	79	Huntley, Marquis of	126	Johnstone, J. W.	88
Hodgson, C.	54	Hurst, G.	68	Johnstone, W.	57
Hodgson, F.	79	Hurst, R.	93	Joliffe, J.	58
Hodgson, L.	151	Huson, R.	125	Jones, A.	106
Hocy, R.	129	Hutton, C.	52	Jones, B.	162
Hogg, G.	130	Hyde, W.	117	Jones, C.	152
Hoggan, G.	118	Hyde, C.	102	Jones, C. S.	99
Hoile, H.	144	Hyde, J.	108	Jones, E.	86
Holbrow, W.	106	Hyne, C.	60	Jones, E.	87
Hole, T.	57			Jones, F.	124
Hole, W.	57	Ibbetson, L. L.	71	Jones, H.	99
Holland, J.	70	Impey, M.	91	Jones, H.	56
Holland, S.	161	Ince, H.	50	Jones, J.	56
Holloway, P.	91	Ingle, J.	89	Jones, J.	132
Holman, —	82	Inglis, J.	115	Jones, J.	139
Holmes, G.	55	Inman, E.	55	Jones, J. J.	149
Holmes, J.	72	Innes, G.	102	Jones, L.	162
Holt, J.	77	Irby, Hon. G.	77	Jones, M.	159
Holt, W.	65	Ireland, J.	91	Jones, O.	162

Name	Page	Name	Page	Name	Page
Jones, P.	73	Ladd, J. P.	90	Lewes, M.	66
Jones, R.	99	Lafarque, A.	68	Lewes, W.	69
Jones, R.	162	Lafarque, W.	68	Lewis, A.	160
Jones, T.	137	Laird, D.	143	Lewis, H.	85
Jones, T.	87	Lamb, C.	154	Lewis, W.	85
Jones, W.	132	Lamb, R. H.	78	Lewis, W. H.	70
Judd, S.	50	Lambert, J.	100	Lewisham, Viscount	103
Judd, W.	60	Lambert, W.	121	Light, M.	56
		Lampeer, J.	67	Lindley, A.	111
Kane, T.	161	Lamphier, A.	166	Lindsay, T.	162
Kay, W.	112	Lander, T. J.	80	Lindsay, R.	139
Kean, H.	116	Landon, A.	56	Lindsay, J.	115
Keane, Sir R.	166	Landor, W.	103	Lindsell, C.	60
Kearney, J.	149	Lane, E.	155	Linkskill, W.	63
Keating, J.	121	Lane, T.	136	Linton, —	92
Keating, W.	158	Lane, T.	152	Lipyeatt, P.	82
Keene, J.	166	Lang, P.	164	Lister, E.	163
Kellet, W.	148	Lang, G.	142	Little, F.	159
Kelly, J.	130	Langley, J.	85	Little, R.	139
Kelly, J.	130	Lardner, P.	82	Lloyd, E.	161
Kemble, H.	148	Lassan, T.	78	Lloyd, H.	160
Kendall, N.	80	Laughton, F.	45	Lloyd, O.	130
Kenmare, Earl of	146	Laurie, W.	109	Lloyd, T.	130
Kennedy, F.	164	Lavens, J.	139	Lloyd, W.	130
Kennedy, H.	116	Lavie, E.	104	Lloyd, D.	73
Kennedy, H.	143	Law, J. H.	78	Lloyd, J. E.	95
Kennedy, R.	154	Lawrence, H.	66	Lloyde, H.	129
Kerr, Hon. A.	116	Lawrence, A.	73	Lobban, J.	113
Kerr, R.	114	Lawrie, A.	109	Lodge, R.	142
Kerr, M.	122	Lawson, W.	115	Loftus, Lord A.	136
Kerstman, J.	56	Layton, T.	83	Loftus, Lord H.	136
Kidd, J.	111	Leacroft, R.	100	Loftus, G.	83
Kidd, W.	112	Leader, W.	155	Lomax, J.	72
Kildare, Marquis of	125	Leader, J.	67	Long, W.	74
Kinder, T.	104	Leaf, J.	45	Long, L.	62
King, A.	131	Ledger, G.	90	Long, F.	62
King, R.	107	Ledwith, W.	122	Long, C. E.	62
Kingsbury, W.	89	Lee, J.	84	Longe, J.	81
Kingscote, T.	106	Lee, W.	84	Longford, C. S.	54
Kingscote, R. A.	106	Leeder, C.	105	Lorton, Viscount	130
Kingsmill, W.	84	Lees, J.	137	Lovaine, Lord	69
Kinlake, C.	88	Lefroy, G.	130	Love, J.	167
Kinnoull, Earl of	123	Legge, W.	103	Love, J.	167
Kipping, W.	93	Leigh, H.	152	Lovell, R. H.	61
Kirby, S.	56	Leigh, A.	90	Loveridge, C. W.	58
Kirwan, E.	128	Leigh, G. C.	49	Lovett, W.	94
Kirwan, H.	128	Leigh, R.	49	Low, R.	161
Kirwan, M.	119	Leith, J.	113	Lowden, J.	60
Knight, A. T.	152	Leith, W.	90	Lowe, J.	161
Knight, J.	68	Leitrim, Earl of	139	Lowe, A.	98
Knox, A.	132	Leman, W.	65	Lowe, P.	86
Knox, J.	139	Lennard, T. S.	152	Lowe, H. P.	98
Knox, C.	159	Lenthal, W. J.	55	Lowth, G. T.	102
Knox, F.	119	Lentrague, J.	165	Lowther, Sir H.	48
Knox, F.	159	Leslie, P.	146	Lowther, Hon. H.	52
Knox, H.	159	Leslie, J.	113	Loyde, S.	124
Knox, J.	159	L'Estrange, W.	135	Lucas, F.	151
Knox, T.	114	L'Estrange, F.	88	Lucas, J.	124
Kyrke, R.	87	Lethbridge, A.	88	Lucas, A.	124
Kyrle, M.	92	Lethbridge, J.	88	Lucas, H.	85
		Levinge, R.	153	Lucas, H.	71
Lacon, Sir E.	81	Levinge, Sir R.	153	Lucas, W. J.	61
Lacy, S. W.	52	Levinge, W.	153	Lunder, W.	117

INDEX.—MILITIA. 181

Name	Page	Name	Page	Name	Page
Lundy, W.	159	M'Mill, H.	116	Massy, H.	131
Luttrell, F.	88	Macnab, J.	127	Matthews, T.	98
Lynch, P.	119	M'Nair, J.	162	Matthews, T.	94
Lynch, J.	56	Macnamara, M.	76	Matthews, A.	91
Lyon, C.	164	M'Neel, N.	154	Maude, T. M.	47
Lyons, C.	153	Macneil, A.	144	Maund, C.	104
Lysaght, Hon. J.	67	M'Neil, G.	156	Maunder, W.	145
Lysaght, Hon. S.	80	M'Neil, H.	164	Maunsell, E.	112
Lyster, C.	155	Macneill, T.	147	Maunsell, R.	116
Lyster, C.	148	MacNicol, J.	156	Maunsell, J. B.	89
Lyster, J.	62	M'O. Boy	121	Maunsell, T.	89
Lyster, J.	62	Macpherson, A.	113	Mawbey, J.	59
Lyster, C.	62	Macpherson, C.	113	Maxwell, Sir D.	109
		Macpherson, E.	113	Maxwell, E.	109
M'Adam, J.	45	M'Pherson, E.	126	Maxwell, Hon. R.	138
M'Adam, Q.	154	M'Vittie, C.	160	Maxwell, R.	155
M'Allister, C.	154	Magenis, F.	106	Maxwell, Sir W.	109
MacArthur, A.	156	Magrath, W. C.	116	Maxwell, J.	69
M'Call, T.	164	Maher, M.	102	Maxwell, H.	90
M'Call, T.	164	Mahon, A.	115	May, J.	57
M'Carthy, J.	146	Mahon, C.	119	May, S.	102
Macartney, E. A.	116	Mahon, C.	131	Maybey, W.	56
Macauley, Z.	133	Mahon, R.	131	Mayhew, E.	102
M'Clelland, J.	151	Mahon, T.	128	Meade, H.	149
M'Clintock, G. F.	132	Mahoned, D.	146	Meadows, W.	103
M'Clintock, J.	132	Mahony, P.	161	Meek, W. P.	52
M'Clintock, J.	132	Maingay, R.	86	Menzies, F.	123
M'Clintock, J.	147	Mainwaring, E.	103	Menzies, G.	126
M'Kay, M.	148	Maitland, P.	167	Menzies, R.	123
Mackay, L.	164	Malone, J.	153	Mercer, H.	114
M'Cririe, W.	111	Mangan, T.	148	Meredith, T.	90
M'Dakin, S.	50	Mangles, C.	54	Messenger, J. B.	80
Macdonald, A.	156	Mann, R.	45	Messenger, W. H.	80
M'Donald, —	164	Manners, Lord J.	68	Methuen, Lord	74
M'Donald, R. C.	111	Manners, Lord	121	Methuen, Hon. St. J.	74
M'Donald, A.	62	Manning, C.	54	Meyer, P. H.	61
M'Donnell, L.	116	Mansell, J.	89	Michell, C.	120
M'Gill, W.	130	Mansfield, Earl of	127	Middlemiss, W.	102
M'Gregor, A.	102	Mansfield, G.	125	Milbank	121
M'Gregor, J.	102	Mansfield, J.	139	Miles, T.	78
M'Gregor, J. D.	123	Mansfield, R.	139	Miles, G.	97
M'Gregor, R. S.	127	Mansergh, —	117	Miller, A.	117
M'Gregor, A.	164	Markham, A.	116	Miller, C.	102
M'Gregor, J.	79	Markham, W.	63	Miller, C.	132
M'Intyre, D.	154	Markie, T.	118	Miller, G.	100
M'Intyre, J.	165	Markland, B.	48	Miller, J.	154
M'Kay, R.	154	Marriott, H.	97	Miller, R.	132
M'Kay, W.	137	Marriott, E. B.	104	Mills, O.	78
M'Kenzie, J.	126	Marsh, H. G.	58	Milner, C.	47
Mackenzie, C. F.	145	Marsh, E.	82	Milward, J.	124
Mackenzie, G.	123	Marsh, H.	82	Minchin, J.	129
Mackenzie, J.	133	Marshall, S.	152	Mitchell, W.	111
Mackenzie, R.	113	Martin, J.	98	Mitchell, J.	48
Mackenzie, R.	133	Martin, J.	110	Mitchell, J. A.	78
Mackenzie, T.	133	Martin, R.	129	Mitchell, H.	104
M'Kinley, J.	74	Martin, S.	138	Mitchelson, A.	164
Maclachlan, C.	156	Martin, J.	104	Molyneux, T. B.	152
M'K. Ross, S.	133	Mason, W.	81	Monck, C.	69
M'Lachlan, —	164	Massareene, Lord	147	Moncreiffe, Sir T.	123
M'Laine, A.	156	Massey, Sir H.	141	Monerris, W.	52
M'Laren, B.	110	Massey, G.	141	Moneypenny, R. T.	79
Macleod, J.	113	Massey, H.	121	Moneypenny, T. G.	79
M'Mahon, Sir B.	137	Massy, G.	131	Monro, Sir G.	133

	Page		Page		Page
Montague, Lord	46	Mure, W.	167	Ogle, G.	136
Montague, G.	88	Murray, Hon. C.	111	Ogle, S. C.	63
Montgomery, A.	151	Murray, Hon. D.	118	O'Grady, G.	161
Montgomery, H.	150	Murray, E.	143	O'Hara, C.	162
Montgomery, J.	137	Murray, J.	110	Oliver, T.	67
Montmorency, De, H.	138	Murray, R.	137	O'Malley, H.	159
Montrose, Duke of	127	Murray, W.	122	O'Neil, H.	80
Moor, F.	93	Murry, W.	116	Onslow, A.	54
Moore, A.	135	Musgrave, R.	166	Onslow, Hon. T.	54
Moore, E.	163	Myers, W.	97	Orde, Sir J.	156
Moore, H.	121	Mynors, R. B.	92	O'Reilly, A.	158
Moore, R.	117	Myrvyn, A.	158	O'Reilly, J.	158
Moore, R.	125			Orme, F.	159
Moore, R.	138	Naas, Lord	125	Ormonde, Marquis of	165
Moore, R.	157	Naismith, J.	111	Ormsby, N.	162
Moore, R. L.	125	Nalbon, W.	73	Ormsby, R.	162
Moore, S.	138	Nanney, O. J.	95	Ormsby, W.	162
Moore, S.	158	Nash, W.	93	Orpwood, J.	120
Moore, W.	117	Nash, W.	149	Orr, J.	164
Moore, W.	121	Nagle, J.	124	Orrall, J.	163
Moore, E.	57	Neale, J.	48	Ottley, C.	149
Morgan, E.	76	Necrassoff, C.	96	Overend, J.	98
Moore, J.	76	Need, T.	98	Ovenden, R.	159
Moorhead, S.	160	Neill, W.	154	Owen, H.	70
Moreton, J.	150	Nelson, G.	47		
Morgan, A.	149	Nelthorpe, G.	81	Page, T.	155
Morgan, J.	149	Nesbit, J.	138	Paget, C.	64
Morgan, J. F.	152	Nesbitt, F.	139	Paget, T.	159
Morgan, Sir C.	85	Netterville, Hon. S.	158	Palk, J.	67
Moriarty, J.	102	Newbury, W.	88	Palliser, M.	136
Morice, J.	118	Newcombe, J.	63	Pallisir, J.	166
Morley, Earl of	64	Newenham, T.	155	Palmer, J.	104
Morley, W.	100	Newland, R.	93	Palmer, T.	84
Morley, F.	64	Newman, H.	65	Palmer, T.	92
Morony, E.	141	Newman, S.	90	Palmer, T.	159
Morony, E.	141	Newton, W.	53	Pardy, J. E.	94
Morrice, F.	79	Nicholl, T.	123	Parke, G.	110
Morrill, W.	81	Nicholls, P.	53	Parker, C.	71
Morris, L.	167	Nicholls, J. F.	88	Parker, J.	50
Morris, R.	167	Nicholson, W.	163	Parker, M.	57
Morris, C.	68	Nind, J.	65	Parker, M.	92
Morris, J.	92	Nixon, A.	108	Parker, M.	149
Morris, G.	87	Nixon, T.	108	Parker, N.	149
Mortimer, E. H.	74	Nixon, E.	47	Parker, T.	163
Morton, Hon. A.	106	Noake, C.	118	Parker, T. C.	97
Moses, J.	59	Noble, A.	102	Parker, W.	97
Mosley, J.	106	Noel, Hon. W.	48	Parker, W. H.	119
Mostyn, Hon. E.	99	Noel, R. R.	68	Parkinson, J.	106
Mostyn, H.	101	Noland, A.	151	Parkinson, —	92
Motte, De la, G.	102	Norcott, H.	124	Parrott, H.	54
Moulin, Du, C.	78	Norman, H.	58	Parry, T.	99
Mount, C.	90	Norris, J.	51	Parry, W.	101
Mount, W.	90	Norris	163	Parsons, G.	102
Mountcharles, Earl of	139	North, J. S.	120	Parsons, P.	90
Mowbray, R.	115	Northland, Lord	117	Parsons, Hon. L.	135
Mudd, F.	49	Norton, J.	84	Paton, J.	126
Mulcah, J.	166	Nugent, Sir P.	153	Paterson, M.	131
Mulcahy, E.	121	Nugent, J.	114	Paterson, W.	131
Mulcahy, E.	121	Nunn, E.	136	Paterson, H.	164
Mulcahy, J.	121	Nunn, A.	136	Patten, J.	163
Mulgrave, Earl of	64	Nuttall, —	103	Patterson, W.	112
Munn, W.	90			Patton, D.	139
Munro, F.	133	Ogle, J.	134	Pattulo, A.	123

INDEX.—MILITIA. 183

Name	Page	Name	Page	Name	Page
Paulett, Sir W.	56	Pochen, T.	68	Rait, J.	143
Payne, J.	165	Poe, C.	135	Ralfs, W.	95
Pearce, W. L.	82	Pokard, W.	153	Ralph, J.	67
Pearse, E.	149	Poke, Sir J.	57	Ramsay, W.	116
Pearse, G.	157	Pole, H.	50	Ramsay, Sir A.	143
Pearson, F.	74	Pole, P.	84	Ramsden, C.	97
Peel, E. H.	71	Poley, J.	53	Ramsey, S.	55
Peel, T.	104	Poltimore, Lord	57	Rashleigh, Sir C.	157
Peers, H. D.	116	Pollen, Sir W.	84	Rattenbury, R.	80
Pell, P. M.	71	Pollock, A.	167	Rawlins, W.	51
Pellett, J. T.	125	Pollock, D.	48	Rawson, T.	107
Pendarves, E.	157	Pollock, T.	48	Rawson, W.	45
Pendleton, H. L.	147	Ponsonby, Hon. J.	165	Rawstone, G.	86
Pennefather, M.	121	Poole, D.	49	Rawstorne, L.	86
Pennefather, R.	161	Poole, T.	124	Rayer, W.	57
Pennington, R.	52	Poole, W.	166	Rayworth, T.	51
Penrose, C.	155	Porter, H.	64	Reade, J.	136
Pentland, R.	147	Possin, B.	105	Reed, —	69
Penton, H.	95	Postle, H.	81	Reed, W.	114
Pepper, R.	158	Potts, J.	69	Reed, W.	102
Perceval, A.	162	Powell, —.	52	Reilly, J.	114
Perceval, H.	108	Powell, G. E.	131	Reilly, J.	151
Perham, W.	88	Powell, R. O.	101	Redmond, J.	136
Peridess, P.	123	Powell, W.	78	Rennie, R.	115
Perkins, G.	79	Powell, W. E.	101	Renton, J.	110
Perkins, R.	88	Powell, W. H.	58	Reynard, R.	55
Perriman, J.	74	Power, E.	166	Reynell, S.	153
Perrott, E.	90	Power, J.	165	Reynolds, R.	139
Perrott, R. E.	88	Power, R.	166	Riall, G.	121
Perry, J.	75	Powles, J. P.	64	Rice, H.	102
Perry, T.	139	Powley, J.	81	Rice, W.	66
Peter, T.	80	Pratt, J.	138	Rice, H.	125
Petley, P.	164	Preedy, C.	91	Rice, Hon. C.	161
Peyton, J. H.	150	Prentice, J.	123	Rice, S.	116
Peyton, G.	150	Preston, Hon. E.	158	Richards, R.	99
Phibbs, R.	152	Price, C.	157	Richardson, J.	59
Philips, J. C.	72	Price, D.	74	Richardson, J.	55
Phillips, F.	97	Price, H.	95	Richardson, H.	60
Phillips, G.	154	Price, R. A.	87	Richardson, W. E.	63
Phillips, J.	101	Price, R. J.	99	Richardson, H.	108
Phillips, J.	103	Price, T.	155	Richardson, P.	115
Phillips, L.	142	Price, W.	98	Richardson, A.	117
Phillips, M.	138	Priest, W.	126	Richardson, G.	120
Phillips, S.	136	Prince, C.	94	Richmond, Duke of	93
Phillipson, R.	99	Prince, J.	102	Ricketts, H.	90
Phipoe, T.	147	Pringle, J.	110	Riddell, R.	69
Picknell, W.	148	Pritchard, C. A.	101	Ridgeway, H.	125
Piere, S.	135	Probart, T.	51	Ridgway, A.	97
Pierpoint, M.	104	Proby, C.	97	Ridgway, J.	57
Pigott, G.	76	Proby, J.	129	Riddleston, R.	103
Pigott, G.	136	Prosser, J.	106	Ridley, C.	69
Pigott, H.	142	Puleston, R.	73	Rigge, H.	152
Pigott, W.	136	Puleston, Sir R.	73	Rimmer, R.	118
Pilkington, A.	132	Poulet, Earl	58	Risly, D.	155
Pilkington, C.	153	Purdon, B.	161	Rix, F.	60
Pilkington, J.	128	Purdon, S.	131	Roberts, P.	155
Pingean, J.	102	Purvis, J.	115	Roberts, H.	155
Pinny, W.	88	Pyncr, F.	54	Roberts, R.	91
Piper, R.	95	Pyrke, D.	65	Roberts, T.	95
Pitman, R.	102	Pytches, T.	75	Roberts, T.	87
Place, T.	85			Robertson, W.	156
Platt, G.	145	Quarles, W.	53	Robertson, S.	106
Plunket, Hon. B.	158			Robertson, W.	111

INDEX.—MILITIA.

Name	Page	Name	Page	Name	Page
Robertson, A.	113	Sanderson, S.	104	Sherlock, W	128
Robertson, D.	143	Sandes, G.	146	Sherlock, J.	107
Robinson, A.	54	Sandford, W.	56	Sherrard, C.	63
Robinson, H.	153	Sandilands, W.	110	Sherwin, S.	98
Robinson, J.	51	Sandilands, W.	164	Short, F.	82
Robinson, G.	91	Sankey, W.	79	Shrapnell, H.	79
Robinson, R.	149	Sankey, J.	137	Shuckburg, W.	74
Robinson, R.	162	Sanse, R.	165	Shum, A.	91
Robinson, F.	95	Sargint, H.	121	Sibthorp, C. D.	71
Robinson, J. J.	64	Saunderson, A.	138	Sibthorp, J.	51
Roche, P.	135	Sawbridge, S.	90	Simon, J.	73
Roche, C.	153	Sawers, J.	110	Simpson, T.	117
Rodd, J.	80	Sawle, C.	157	Simpson, T.	112
Rodgers, J.	132	Sawry, J.	49	Sims, A.	116
Roe, J.	155	Sawyer, J.	106	Sinclair, C.	133
Roe, R.	67	Sayer, A.	120	Sinclair, Hon. L.	133
Roe, J.	155	Scott, J.	108	Sinclair, J.	132
Rolleston, J.	98	Scott, J.	93	Sinclair, T.	133
Rollo, Hon. J.	123	Scott, J.	118	Singleton, J.	68
Rooke, A. B.	106	Scott, J. R.	69	Sirr, C.	95
Roper, E.	130	Scott, P.	100	Sirr, W. H.	119
Rose, R.	160	Scott, P.	115	Skelton, J.	127
Rose, T.	89	Scott, W.	91	Skimner, C.	47
Rose, W.	150	Scott, T.	143	Skipton, C.	132
Rosengrave, W.	128	Scott, W.	143	Sleeman, R.	161
Ross, A.	156	Scott, W.	115	Sligo, Marquis of	119
Ross, J.	160	Scott, W.	118	Slegg, J.	86
Ross, S.	133	Scott, J.	131	Small, W.	83
Ross, T.	53	Scott, B.	129	Smart, W.	144
Rosse, Earl of	135	Scudamore, J.	92	Smartt, J.	120
Rossmore, Lord	160	Seafield, Earl of	113	Smith, B.	86
Roulston, S.	139	Seale, Sir H.	67	Smith, C. H.	60
Rowe, T.	85	Searle, S.	139	Smith, E.	59
Rowe, W.	50	Seaton, J.	160	Smith, R.	148
Rowland, F.	149	Sebright, C.	126	Smith, G.	157
Roy, J.	126	Segrave, O.	53	Smith, J.	141
Royse, T.	141	Semple, M.	80	Smith, J.	143
Rugby	86	Severy, J.	90	Smith, W.	138
Rumly, C.	82	Seward, L.	92	Smith, E.	59
Rush, C.	56	Seymour, F.	116	Smith, J.	93
Russel, C.	60	Seymour, T.	128	Smith, J.	83
Russell, F.	97	Seymour, E.	128	Smith, N.	60
Russell, S.	137	Seymour, H.	85	Smith, R.	76
Rutherford, A.	150	Shafto, C.	69	Smith, T.	60
Rutland, Duke	68	Shairp, T.	110	Smith, W.	103
Rutledge, F.	86	Shannon, Earl of	124	Smith, W.	96
Ryder, W.	124	Shrapnell, H. R.	88	Smyth, C.	141
Ryder, W.	125	Shaw, J. R.	86	Smyth, D.	141
Ryffe, J.	115	Shaw, Sir J.	79	Snell, J.	56
		Shaw, R.	117	Snell, W.	102
Sadler, G.	61	Shaw, D.	127	Snowe, T.	160
Sadler, T.	68	Shaw, R.	137	Snyth, B.	141
Salisbury, Marquis	72	Shaw, H.	137	Somers, Earl	92
Salmons, T.	88	Shaw, R.	137	Somerset, F.	56
Salton, J.	110	Shawe, R.	93	Somerville, P.	124
Sampson, S.	57	Shawe, E.	135	Souvin, S.	120
Sampson, T.	57	Shegogg, G.	108	Spaight, J.	141
Samuel, G.	95	Sheil, A.	148	Spaight, W.	131
Sanctuary, J.	93	Shelly, Sir P.	93	Sparks, T.	62
Sandback, H.	87	Sheppard, H.	121	Sparrow, J.	136
Sander, G.	68	Sheppard, J.	75	Sparrow, J.	136
Sanders, E. H.	68	Sheppard, R. H.	75	Spear, J.	117
Sanders, F.	90	Shepard, W.	51	Spedding, J.	59

INDEX.—MILITIA.

Name	Page	Name	Page	Name	Page
Spencer, Hon. H.	91	Supersrutt, J.	49	Thompson, G.	55
Spicer, H.	102	Surman, J.	65	Thomson, C.	109
Spitty, T. J.	56	Sutherland, W.	126	Thomson, J.	143
Spoor, N.	47	Sutherland, W.	102	Thomson, J.	111
Squire, A.	120	Sutter, R.	115	Tomline, J.	51
Stable, D.	134	Sutton, B.	68	Thornton, F.	65
Standert, F.	58	Sutton, J.	63	Thorold, H.	51
Standish, C.	163	Sutcliffe, G.	125	Tibeando, J.	135
Stainforth, W.	45	Swan, T.	84	Tighe, T.	151
Stanhope, R.	158	Swanton, J.	51	Tobin, —	106
Stanhope, H.	92	Swettenham, T.	93	Toll, J.	67
Stanley, E. J.	152	Swiney, S.	137	Todd, J.	55
Stanley, E.	49	Sykes, J.	49	Todd, H. W.	55
Stanly, Hon. F.	152	Sykes, W.	49	Tom, P.	157
Stanners, T.	116	Symes, J.	151	Tomline, W.	51
Stanton, H.	134	Symonds, G.	83	Tomlinson, J.	56
Starkey, R.	155	Symonds, —	92	Tonge, A.	74
Starkey, W.	155	Symonds, H.	92	Torkington, W.	71
Steele, E.	81			Tottenham, H.	136
Steele, G.	85	Talbot, Hon. W.	103	Tottenham, C.	136
Steele, J.	145	Tate, J.	65	Touche, Le, D.	137
Steele, W.	58	Tattwell, G.	71	Touche, La, R.	107
Stenart, R.	123	Taylor, R.	62	Townsend, C.	124
Stephenson, J.	52	Taylor, F.	55	Trafford, De, C.	163
Stephenson, W.	55	Taylor, H.	94	Trant, J.	121
Stewart, A.	164	Taylor, J.	103	Tranter, W.	78
Stewart, J.	151	Taylor, J.	98	Treby, P.	82
Stewart, A.	132	Taylor, W.	98	Trelawney, J.	80
Stewart, Sir J.	139	Taylor, J.	71	Trench, C.	128
Stewart, J.	139	Taylor, J.	132	Trench, R.	160
Stewart, W.	139	Taylor, J.	118	Trevor, Hon. G.	66
Stewart, W.	109	Taylor, R.	141	Trick, T.	80
St. George, C.	141	Taylor, T.	158	Trick, F.	80
St. John, J.	53	Temperly, W.	152	Trigge, S.	61
Stone, E.	56	Tempest, J.	86	Trigge, J. D.	61
Stone, G.	102	Templemore, Lord	93	Tucker, J.	67
Stone, J.	120	Tench, F.	58	Tucker, C.	88
Stonor, Hon. T.	91	Tennant, W.	148	Tucker, W.	74
Stopford, Lord	136	Tennant, H.	71	Tufnell, H.	97
Storer, A.	91	Tennant, A.	111	Tufnell, W.	61
Story, J.	138	Tennent, Sir J.	116	Turnbull, M.	110
Story, T.	91	Tennison, M.	160	Turner, E.	112
Snowe, T.	160	Terry, H.	89	Turnskie, J.	144
Stowell, W.	124	Thackeray, T.	88	Twiss, F.	146
Stoyle, T.	130	Thackery, D.	80	Tyler, C. H.	90
Strang, J.	111	Theobald, T.	74	Tyndell, W.	84
Strangeways, H.	88	Thetford, J.	136	Tynte, C. J.	85
Stretton, W.	78	Thomas, H.	163	Tyrrell, Sir J.	61
Strickland, W.	163	Thomas, A.	120		
Strode, C. H.	72	Thomas, C.	78	Unett, —	92
Strode, J.	72	Thomas, T.	66	Upton, J.	147
Stuart, J.	127	Thomas, D.	66	Upton, A.	153
Stuart, B.	117	Thompson, T.	64	Urmston, H. M.	127
Stuart, J.	102	Thompson, R.	123	Ussher, J.	137
Stuart, W.	60	Thompson, W.	118		
Stubbs, T.	153	Thompson, B.	146	Vandeleur, C.	131
Stubbs, W.	98	Thompson, E.	108	Vankeythusen, H.	120
Studdert, R. W.	131	Thompson, G.	164	Vatchell, T.	105
Studdert, R. A.	131	Thompson, J.	138	Vaughan, F.	106
Suirdale, Lord	121	Thompson, J.	145	Vaughan, R. W.	106
Summers, W.	64	Thompson, W.	139	Vaughan, E. W.	106
Sumner, W.	62	Thompson, F.	79	Vaughan, T.	46

B B

INDEX.—MILITIA.

Name	Page	Name	Page	Name	Page
Vaughan, E.	66	Watson, S.	55	Wilde, W.	53
Vavasour, Sir H.	55	Watson, T.	63	Wilkinson, R.	60
Vereker, Hon. C.	141	Watson, T.	107	Wilkinson, G.	108
Vereker, Hon. S.	141	Watson, W.	93	Wilkinson, —	141
Verner, T.	116	Watson, W.	106	Will, J.	126
Vernon, F.	89	Watson, H.	141	Willard, N.	134
Vernon, G. C.	104	Watson, G.	107	Williams, R.	132
Vesey, G. W.	117	Watson, H.	161	Williams, A.	61
Vignoles, S.	153	Watt, F.	63	Williams, C.	86
Vincent, T.	45	Watt, F.	163	Williams, H.	106
Vincent, H.	50	Webb, G.	57	Williams, —	92
Vivian, T.	89	Webb, J.	68	Williams, Sir J.	82
Vivian, H.	157	Webb, V.	101	Williams, J.	95
		Webb, J.	138	Williams, M.	66
Wade, G.	136	Webber, O.	57	Williams, R.	73
Wadley, T.	74	Webster, W.	63	Williams, T. P.	99
Wagner, R.	101	Weeks, G.	93	Williams, F.	102
Waite, W.	45	Weeks, G.	93	Williamson, R.	86
Wake, R.	82	Weight, E.	65	Willis, J.	93
Wakefield, E.	98	Weir, F.	66	Willock, J.	52
Wakeford, J.	79	Weir, A.	113	Willoughby, A.	95
Wakeman, H.	68	Weir, J.	152	Wills, C.	82
Walker, G.	98	Welby, G.	71	Willyams, H.	157
Walker, J.	75	Welch, J.	106	Willyams, J.	157
Walker, T.	63	Weld, J.	152	Wilmhurst, —	78
Walker, T.	93	Weller, T.	127	Wilmot, P.	52
Walker, W.	63	Welsh, T.	166	Wilshere, C.	72
Walker, W.	93	Wemyss, J.	115	Wilson, J.	151
Walker, W.	122	Wemyss, H.	165	Wilson, H.	78
Walker, A.	115	Wentworth, V.	89	Wilson, J.	52
Walker, W.	145	West, C.	83	Wilson, Sir T.	79
Wall, G.	137	Western, T.	53	Wilson, P.	113
Wallis, J.	61	Westmeath, Marq. of	153	Wilson, G.	110
Wallis, H.	124	Westropp, R.	141	Wilson, J.	138
Walmer, R.	63	Westropp, H.	161	Wilson, J.	136
Walroad, J.	67	Wetherelt, J.	135	Wilson, H.	148
Walsh, —	134	Wetherelt, G.	135	Wilson, J.	63
Walsham, Sir J.	92	Wharncliffe, Lord	48	Wilton, Earl of	120
Walton, J.	124	Whatman, J.	79	Winchester, Marquis.	56
Warburton, B.	105	Wheatley, T.	85	Winter, C.	90
Warburton, R.	135	Wheatley, W.	97	Winterton, Earl of	93
Ward, J.	80	Wheble, E.	50	Winton, Earl of	154
Ward, E.	87	Wheble, J.	50	Wisdom, J.	129
Ward, T.	151	Wheeley, S.	104	Withers, J.	152
Ward, V.	151	Whichcote, Sir F.	71	Wodehouse, Hon. B.	81
Ward, W.	151	White, A.	64	Wood, T.	102
Ward, W.	157	White, E.	63	Wood, H.	102
Wardle, H.	63	White, Sir T.	98	Wood, R.	162
Waring, G.	138	White, W.	56	Wodd, W.	100
Waring, J.	165	White, F.	121	Woodgate, D.	79
Waring, S.	165	White, H.	122	Woodhouse, G.	112
Warner, P.	154	White, S.	148	Woods, T.	128
Warren, C.	137	White, Hon. W.	149	Woodward, W.	104
Warren, Sir A.	149	White, R.	142	Woodward, C.	158
Waterford, Marq. of	166	White, T.	142	Workman, H.	119
Waterpark, Lord	100	Whitehead, J.	79	Worsey, W.	103
Waters, J.	135	Whitesitt, J.	160	Worsley, F.	100
Watkins, W.	101	Whitmore, J.	94	Worth, J.	57
Watson, B.	91	Whittaker, H.	45	Worthington, G.	65
Watson, C.	55	Whittaker, J.	90	Worthington, —	163
Watson, J.	164	Wigfield, J.	120	Wragg, H.	100
Watson, J.	61	Wight, W.	54	Wray, J.	131

	Page		Page		Page
Wright, C.	67	Wright, G.	123	Wynne, R.	87
Wright, H.	58	Wright, D.	129	Wynne, W.	99
Wright, J.	61	Wrightson, T.	45	Wynne, R. W.	87
Wright, C.	164	Wrottesley, Hon. W.	103		
Wright, J.	58	Wyatt, St. G.	83	Yorke, S.	87
Wright, T. B.	88	Wyche, R.	71		

MACINTOSH, PRINTER,
GREAT NEW-STREET, LONDON.

ADDENDA.

YEOMANRY CAVALRY.

ALTERATIONS AND ADDITIONS SINCE GOING TO PRESS.

BERKS.—*Hungerford Troop of Yeomanry Cavalry.*—Henry Coe Coape, Gent., to be First-Lieutenant, vice Alexander Hugh Leyborne Popham, resigned; Capel Coape, Gent., to be Cornet, vice Edward Morris, resigned.—March 29th.

DORSET.—*Queen's Own Regiment of Dorsetshire Yeomanry Cavalry.*—Lewis George St. Lo, Gent., to be Cornet, vice Bridge, promoted.—February 22d.

LANARK.—*Lanark Upper Ward Regiment of Yeomanry Cavalry.*—Lieutenant Stephen Gray to be Captain; Cornet Robert Lockhart to be Lieutenant; D. C. R. C. Buchanan, Gent., to be Cornet, vice Lockhart, promoted.

MONTGOMERYSHIRE.—*Montgomeryshire Yeomanry Cavalry.*—Edward Salisbury Rose Trevor to be Lieutenant.—April 12th.

OXFORD.—*Queen's Own Regiment of Oxfordshire Yeomanry Cavalry.*—Lieutenant Philip Thomas Herbert Wykeham to be Captain, vice Viscount Parker, resigned.—April 1st.

SALOP.—*South Salopian Regiment of Yeomanry Cavalry.*—Cornet John Rocke to be Lieutenant, vice C. S. Lloyd, promoted; Ralph Augustus Benson, Gent., to be Cornet, vice Rocke, promoted.—Jan. 11th.

SOMERSET.—Captain Maher has received the Gold Medal for War Services.

SUFFOLK.—*Suffolk Yeomanry Cavalry, Melford Troop.*—Nathaniel Clarke Barnadiston, Esq., to be Captain, vice Thomas Hallifax, the younger, Esq., deceased.—April 1st.

WILTSHIRE.—*Royal Wiltshire Yeomanry Cavalry.*—Captain William Wyndham to be Major, vice Long, resigned; Captain Henry Earl of Shelburne to be Supernumerary Major, without pay; Charles Henry Wyndham, Esq., to be Captain, vice Wyndham, promoted; John Alexander Marquis of Bath to be Captain, vice the Earl of Shelburne, promoted.—March 22d.

WORCESTERSHIRE.—*The Queen's Own Worcestershire Regiment of Yeomanry Cavalry.*—George Francis Dowdeswell, Gent., to be Lieutenant, vice Stone, promoted.—Jan. 4th.

YORKSHIRE.—*Yorkshire Hussar Regiment of West Riding Yeomanry Cavalry.*—The Honourable William Ernest Duncombe to be Cornet, vice Fenton, resigned.—Jan. 11th.

MILITIA.

MILITIA.

ALTERATIONS AND ADDITIONS SINCE GOING TO PRESS.

9th, or Cumberland Regiment of Militia.—Thomas Mitchell to be Surgeon.—April 12th.

24th, or Royal Carmarthenshire Fusiliers.—George Watkin Rice, Esq., to be Major; First-Lieutenant Rice Price Benyon to be Captain; First-Lieutenant Morgan Pryse Lloyd to be Captain; Second-Lieutenant Frederick Ross Cowell to be First-Lieutenant; Second-Lieutenant James Dewis Thomas to be First-Lieutenant; William George, Gent., to be Second-Lieutenant; Frank Alexander Stackpoole, Gent., to be Second-Lieutenant.—April 1st.

39th, or 1st or West Norfolk Regiment of Militia.—Henry Drummond Wolff, Gent., to be Lieutenant, vice Bean, deceased.—April 1st.

47th, or 2d Somerset Regiment of Militia.—William Pinney, Esq., M.P., to be Colonel, vice Sir Thomas Buckler Lethbridge, Bart., deceased.—Jan. 18th.

58th, or Royal West Middlesex Regiment of Militia.—St. Leger Glyn, Gent., to be Lieutenant.—March 15th.—Captain James Godfrey de Burgh joined the Head Quarters of H. M. 17th Regiment, in New South Wales, the beginning of 1836, and proceeded the same year to Bombay, East Indies, with the second detachment of the Regiment.

59th, or Royal Sherwood Foresters, or Nottinghamshire Regiment of Militia.—Frederick Byron, Esq., commonly called the Honourable Frederick Byron, to be Lieutenant.—April 12th.

76th, or Inverness, Banff, Elgin, and Nairn Regiment of Militia.—George Cumming, Gentleman, to be Captain, vice Alexander Macpherson, deceased.—12th May, 1841. Commission signed 24th April, 1841.

113th, or Second Duke of Lancaster's Own Regiment of Militia.—Lieutenant Williams Crouch Davies served in the late Hungarian Campaign, as Lieutenant in the 1st Regiment of Austrian Hussars, and as Aide-de-Camp successively to Lieut.-Generals Wohlgemuth and Prince Franz Leichtenstein, and took part under the former in the Battle of *Pered*, 21st of June, and that of *Raab*, on the 28th of June; and under the latter in the successive Battles of *Segedin*, the 4th, *Sëreg*, the 5th, and *Temeswar*, the 9th of August, 1849; besides several intermediate minor affairs.

www.ingramcontent.com/pod-product-compliance
Lightning Source LLC
LaVergne TN
LVHW011346080426
835511LV00005B/160